THE SECRET LIFE OF COPYRIGHT

In *The Secret Life of Copyright*, copyright law meets Black Lives Matter and #MeToo in a provocative examination of how our legal regime governing creative production unexpectedly perpetuates inequalities along racial, gender, and socioeconomic lines in a manner that also impoverishes the arts. Drawing on numerous case studies – Harvard's slave daguerreotypes, celebrity sex tapes, famous Wall Street statues, beloved musicals, and dictator copyrights – the book argues that, despite their purported neutrality, key rules governing copyrights – from the authorship, derivative rights, and fair use doctrines to copyright's First Amendment immunity – systematically disadvantage individuals from traditionally marginalized communities. Since laws regulating the use of creative content increasingly mediate participation and privilege in the digital world, *The Secret Life of Copyright* provides a template for a more robust copyright system that better addresses egalitarian concerns and serves the interests of creativity.

John Tehranian is an academic, attorney, and author. He is the Paul W. Wildman Chair and Professor of Law at Southwestern Law School, and he has previously served as a Professor of Law at the University of Utah, S.J. Quinney College of Law, and as Visiting Professor of Law at University of California, Los Angeles, School of Law and Loyola Law School.

A graduate of Harvard University and Yale Law School, John has authored of dozens of scholarly articles and two other books: *Whitewashed* (New York University Press, 2009) and *Infringement Nation* (Oxford University Press, 2011). His work has also appeared in such publications as the *Yale Law Journal, Harvard Journal of Law & Gender, Northwestern University Law Review, Southern California Law Review, University of Pennsylvania Journal of Constitutional Law, Iowa Law Review, William & Mary Law Review*, and the *Chronicle of Higher Education*. John's work has been widely cited, from testimony before the United States Congress and decisions of American and foreign courts to briefs before the United States Supreme Court in such landmark intellectual property cases as *Warhol* v. *Goldsmith* (2023), *Google* v. *Oracle* (2021), *Kirtsaeng* v. *John Wiley & Sons* (2013), *Golan* v. *Holder* (2012), and *MGM* v. *Grokster* (2005).

John is also a founding partner of One LLP, where his practice focuses on litigation and crisis management, and he has handled high-profile disputes and transactions involving numerous legends from the worlds of music (Madonna, B. B. King, Don Henley, and Bootsy Collins), film (Harold Lloyd and Luis Buñuel), fashion (Jeremy Scott), photography (Annie Leibovitz and David LaChapelle), literature (Frank Hebert and John Fante), and athletics (Oscar de la Hoya, Tony Parker, and Dean Potter). He has served as counsel in numerous published appellate decisions on copyright matters, including *Mavrix* v. *LiveJournal*, 873 F.3d 1045 (9th Cir. 2017), *Direct Technologies, LLC* v. *Electronic Arts, Inc.*, 836 F.3d 1059 (9th Cir. 2016), and

Mavrix Photo, Inc. v. *Brand Technologies, Inc.*, 647 F.3d 1218 (9th Cir. 2011). He led the trial team in *Hargis* v. *Pacifica* (C.D. Cal. 2023) to earning a $6.3 million jury verdict, the largest maximum statutory damages award for photography infringement in the history of the United States. *Variety*'s Legal Impact Report has recognized John as one of the world's top fifty entertainment lawyers, *Billboard Magazine* has identified him as one of the top music lawyers in the business, and he has been repeatedly honored as a Southern California *Super Lawyer*.

The Secret Life of Copyright

INTELLECTUAL PROPERTY AND INEQUALITY IN THE AGE OF AI

JOHN TEHRANIAN
Southwestern Law School

CAMBRIDGE
UNIVERSITY PRESS

CAMBRIDGE
UNIVERSITY PRESS

Shaftesbury Road, Cambridge CB2 8EA, United Kingdom

One Liberty Plaza, 20th Floor, New York, NY 10006, USA

477 Williamstown Road, Port Melbourne, VIC 3207, Australia

314–321, 3rd Floor, Plot 3, Splendor Forum, Jasola District Centre, New Delhi – 110025, India

103 Penang Road, #05–06/07, Visioncrest Commercial, Singapore 238467

Cambridge University Press is part of Cambridge University Press & Assessment, a department of the University of Cambridge.

We share the University's mission to contribute to society through the pursuit of education, learning and research at the highest international levels of excellence.

www.cambridge.org
Information on this title: www.cambridge.org/9781009346993

DOI: 10.1017/9781009347044

When citing this work, please include a reference to the DOI 10.1017/9781009347044

First published 2025

A catalogue record for this publication is available from the British Library

Library of Congress Cataloging-in-Publication Data
NAMES: Tehranian, John, author.
TITLE: The secret life of copyright : intellectual property and inequality in the age of AI / John Tehranian, Southwestern Law School.
DESCRIPTION: Cambridge, United Kingdom ; New York, NY : Cambridge University Press, 2025. | Includes bibliographical references.
IDENTIFIERS: LCCN 2024055344 | ISBN 9781009346993 (hardback) | ISBN 9781009347044 (ebook)
SUBJECTS: LCSH: Copyright. | Intellectual property. | Artificial intelligence – Law and legislation. | Equality before the law
CLASSIFICATION: LCC K1420.5 .T43 2025 | DDC 346.04/82–dc23/eng/20241119
LC record available at https://lccn.loc.gov/2024055344

ISBN 978-1-009-34699-3 Hardback
ISBN 978-1-009-34701-3 Paperback

Contents

Figures

Acknowledgments

I would like to give special thanks to my editor, Matt Gallaway, whose unflagging enthusiasm and backing from the outset made this book possible; my family and friends for their love and encouragement; Southwestern Law School, its administration, my colleagues, and the Kenneth and Harle Montgomery Foundation for their support and funding for this project; my partners, associates and staff at One LLP for their inspiration and collaboration; and Zach F. Dawson, Levon Devoian, Lindsey Hay, Jeffrey Laufer, Rana Shalhoub, Kimia Shariat, Sarah Swanson, and Michael Worth for their outstanding research assistance and thoughtful notes and suggestions. At the risk of appearing antiquated, I used no artificial intelligence in the researching and drafting of this book.

Portions of this book were previously published in part, or inspired by, my prior articles, including: Attributive Use: Toward a New Fair Use Standard and the Closing of Copyright's Crediting Gap, 96 SOUTHERN CALIFORNIA LAW REVIEW 1 (2022); The Subject Strikes Back: Intellectual Property Law, Visual Pleasure and Resistance in the Arts, 71 AMERICAN UNIVERSITY LAW REVIEW 1367 (2022); Copyright's Male Gaze: Authorship and Inequality in a Panoptic World, 41 HARVARD JOURNAL OF LAW & GENDER 343 (2018); Sex, Drones & Videotape: Rethinking Copyright's Authorship-Fixation Conflation in the Age of Performance, 68 HASTINGS LAW JOURNAL 1319 (2017); The New ©ensorship, 101 IOWA LAW REVIEW 245 (2015); Derivative Works 2.0: Reconsidering Transformative Use in the Age of Crowdsourced Creation, 109 NORTHWESTERN UNIVERSITY LAW REVIEW 383 (2015) (co-authored with Jacqueline Lipton); Towards a Critical IP Theory: Copyright, Consecration & Control, 2012 B. Y. U. LAW REVIEW 1237 (2012); Parchment, Pixels and Personhood: Users Rights and the IP (Identity Politics) of IP (Intellectual Property), 82 UNIVERSITY OF COLORADO LAW REVIEW 1 (2011); and The Emperor Has No Copyright: Registration, Cultural Hierarchy, and the Myth of American Copyright Militancy, 24 BERKELEY TECHNOLOGY LAW JOURNAL 1397 (2009).

Acknowledgments

Introduction

DON'T BORE US, GET TO THE CHORUS

If I've learned anything from living and working in proximity to Hollywood over the past two decades, it's this: every project must have an elevator pitch. As an academic, I'd like to pretend I'm immune to the forces of the marketplace. I'd prefer to think that I don't have to sacrifice my prolix ways to the modern competition for reader attention and the realities of declining attention spans. But that ignores the wisdom of Berry Gordy, Jr., the founder of Motown Records. As he famously exhorted, "Don't bore us, get to the chorus."[1]

This book examines what happens when copyright law meets BLM and #MeToo. Its chorus is simple: Our copyright regime has a social justice problem. Despite their purported neutrality, key doctrines governing the vesting and scope of copyrights – authorship, derivative rights, fair use, and First-Amendment immunity – have systematically disadvantaged individuals from traditionally marginalized communities by exacerbating inequalities along racial, gender, and socioeconomic lines. By itself, this is troublesome. But, at the same time, these very doctrines have also prevented our copyright regime from best promoting progress in the arts. A re-evaluation of copyright canon would therefore advance both egalitarian and artistic interests, an especially important step in a world where laws regulating the use of creative content increasingly govern our cultural, political, and economic lives.

Through the course of the ensuing pages, I'll develop this argument further – albeit in a manner that's far less succinct but, hopefully, far more convincing. While it may not have the capacity to touch your heart or entertain you as much as a Motown hit or a Hollywood blockbuster (though the author will try), this book speaks to critical issues involving the design and operation of a legal regime that mediates our daily lives in the digital era. By lifting the shroud off the secret life of copyright, the book seeks to contribute to two important, ongoing conversations: how the law can promote equality and how the law can better serve the interests of creativity and creatives.

COPYRIGHT AND SOCIAL JUSTICE

In recent years, the Black Lives Matter and #MeToo movements have rattled our country's collective conscience and provoked a long-delayed national reckoning over our enduring legacy of racism and sexism. In response to this pivotal moment in history, there has been no shortage of important works that have critiqued, among other things, our electoral system, racial and gendered capitalism, our tax regime, the history of white governmental welfare, our educational system, explicit and implicit biases, and structural economic issues for their role in ossifying existing disparities and preventing reform. But the sources of inequality and the contributing factors to systemic racism and gender discrimination – which we must address to achieve a truly just society – can find themselves in even the most unexpected places. This book focuses on one such area: copyright law.

At first blush, our nation's intellectual property laws, which never mention race, gender, sexual orientation, or socioeconomic status and appear completely neutral on their face, would seem far removed from the debate over social justice and equality. For example, as the language of the Copyright Clause in Article I, section 8, clause 8 of the United States Constitution tells us, Congress has the power to grant authors, for a limited time, copyrights to their creative output for one specific reason alone: "to promote the progress of … useful Arts."[2] But, as a robust bundle of exclusionary powers vested by grace of the state, copyright protection provides rights holders with a potent government-sanctioned monopoly over creative content that lines their pockets and gives them significant control over cultural and political discourse. This is particularly true in an information economy, where the wielding of intellectual property rights constitutes an inextricable part of the exercise of wealth and power.

The significance of our intellectual property laws on daily life in the twenty-first century is worth pondering and was the subject of my prior book on copyright law, *Infringement Nation: Copyright 2.0 and You*. Intellectual property laws regulate our ability to participate in the body politic and social media; they set out the metes and bounds of our expressive choices; they provide ownership of and control over the representation of the human body and form; they patrol the line between speech and property; they define the range of permissible public narratives of resistance and subversion; and they privilege certain types of creative production and activity over others. As a result, the government's role in doling out intellectual property monopolies – to whom and under what circumstances – warrants special scrutiny.

With its analysis, this book advances two central assertions. First, by employing the methodology of critical theory and applying it to the doctrinal development of our copyright regime, the book contends that the ways in which courts have adjudicated the vesting, scope, and enforcement of copyright interests, particularly in the wake of technological changes over recent decades, have played a vital role in propping up, and even exacerbating, inequality and disadvantaging already marginalized communities. This study therefore provides a systematic analysis of how our copyright regime has effectively negotiated privilege and participation in the digital age, intensifying disparities along racial, gender, and socioeconomic lines. Second, the book demonstrates how such doctrinal turns have frequently flouted the purported goals of our copyright regime, thereby impoverishing its role in promoting progress in the arts. I ultimately contend that remedying these shortcomings in the law will not only address issues of equality but also make for a more robust copyright system that better serves the interests of creativity.

To build this case, the following pages will examine a wide range of case studies involving high-profile controversies that run the full gamut of copyrightable subject matter, including photography (the earliest known images of slaves), literature (a classic American novel), nonfiction (the infamous autobiography of a dictator), motion pictures (a notorious case of revenge porn), art (two famous statues on Wall Street), theater (a beloved Broadway musical), and broadcasting (a popular radio talk show). In the process, we will explore why:

- When Tamara Lanier discovered that Harvard University was commercially exploiting naked daguerreotypes of her enslaved ancestors, copyright's wholesale rejection of subject rights in photographic works largely rebuffed her legal efforts to stop the institution's conduct. As a consequence, the law of authorship directly inhibited her ability to seek a small measure of justice for herself, her relatives, and the descendants of all enslaved people.
- When sportscaster Erin Andrews found out that an intimate recording had leaked online, copyright law's fixation and authorship doctrines told her that the felon who illicitly captured the footage owned the copyright, not her. As a result, like many victims of digital trespass and revenge porn, Andrews found herself powerless to scrub the video online without striking a deal with her tormentor.
- When Lynn Thomson's creative partner, Jonathan Larson, died just hours after the final rehearsal for the musical *Rent*, copyright law's mutual-intent requirement told her that she had no copyright interest in the Broadway hit. So while *Rent* continues to capture the world's imagination and the Larson estate has made millions, Thomson, like so many collaborators lacking contractual leverage (especially persons of color and women), received no economic participation in the musical's runaway success, and her contributions remain a forgotten footnote.
- When the *Fearless Girl* statue took on Wall Street's famous *Charging Bull* and challenged its unabashedly masculine celebration of American capitalism by calling attention to the underrepresentation of women in the world of finance, copyright law said that her placement within the bovine's gaze might render her an unauthorized derivative work, both without copyright protection and subject to destruction. As a result, legal objections raised by *Charging Bull*

sculptor Alberto Di Modica enabled him to force the removal of *Fearless Girl*, thereby silencing a powerful message of resistance to patriarchal narratives that had touched and inspired millions.

- When, in the 1930s, a young journalist (and future Senator and presidential candidate) learned that the official English translation of the autobiography of Germany's new leader had been carefully sanitized to appeal to an American audience, copyright's derivative rights doctrine stymied his attempt to publish an unexpurgated and annotated edition to warn the American public about the leader's insidious plans. Adolf Hitler, through his publisher, successfully sued the journalist and convinced a federal court to permanently enjoin the journalist's translation, thereby frustrating early opposition to the Nazi movement and leaving the American public to learn the full extent of his iniquity only after it was too late.
- When Alice Randall recast the story of *Gone with the Wind* to tell the story from an African-American, rather than White, point of view and criticize the myopic romanticism of the original novel, copyright's fair use doctrine initially determined that she could not publish her work. Although Randall ultimately received vindication of her rights on appeal, her attempt to give a voice to the silenced narratives of those who faced discrimination and disenfranchisement in Mitchell's idealized setting came with significant struggle and cost, and, for a time, Randall's book was literally banned in the United States; and
- When an anti-discrimination group sought to expose the hateful views of radio show host Michael Savage, who had launched into a nakedly bigoted rant on his nationally syndicated program, the organization found its speech effectively silenced by Savage's cynical invocation of copyright law. In the process, Savage joined an ignominious list of dictators, billionaires, human rights abusers, and supremacists who have exploited copyright's exemption from First Amendment scrutiny to censor those who dare criticize them and to squelch political and cultural debate in a manner that is antithetical to the freedom of speech.

In advancing its argument, this book draws from a theoretical framework that helped animate the modern social justice movements of our era, including Black Lives Matter and #MeToo. After all, intellectual property regimes increasingly inform the way in which social order is maintained. By regulating cultural production and patrolling the dissemination of knowledge, copyright law mediates the exercise of important social, political, and economic rights, thereby playing a critical role in the construction of our information society. In theory, ostensibly neutral ground rules guide the vesting, scope, and enforcement of rights pertaining to creative works in a way that best advances the constitutionally mandated purpose of the copyright regime: progress in the arts. But, in reality, copyright law's procedural and substantive doctrines do more than just advance progress in the arts and can serve as powerful tools for the regulation, control, and manipulation of meaning. This book identifies and builds on an emerging literature to introduce a framework for studying just how copyright transcends its small corner of the legal universe and plays a fundamental role in shaping society and regulating individual behavior as part of a larger hegemonic project.

As John Fiske writes, "Popular culture always is part of power relations; it always bears traces of constant struggle between domination and subordination, between power and various forms of resistance to it or evasions of it...."[3] Thus, it is not surprising that intellectual property laws that control access to and use of popular culture are a function of power relations. In the early 1970s, cultural theorist Pierre Bourdieu introduced the concept of cultural reproduction to explain the processes through which the dominant class retained its power.[4] Drawing on the example of schooling in modern society and likening a diploma to a "juridically sanctioned validation of the results of inculcation," he argued that educational institutions function largely to preserve entrenched interests by perpetuating the reproduction of the cultural and social values of the dominant class.[5]

Bourdieu's work on cultural reproduction has inspired waves of scholarship in the social sciences,[6] but has not generated as much interest in the field of intellectual property. Yet the notion of cultural reproduction is instrumental to understanding the consequences of intellectual property laws on societal hierarchies. Bourdieu's work and the scholarship it has inspired suggest that the inviolate recitation of the cultural production of dominant social forces is a profound vehicle for the inculcation of a set of values and symbols that consolidate existing power structures.[7] If that is the case, the act of imperfect reproduction, or of customization, of cultural production can translate into an act of subversion or reproduction of the existing social order in a particular form. These acts of differentiation and similitude, or the acts of imperfect reproduction and customization, are carefully regulated by intellectual property laws. And, the selective protection granted to cultural production under the guise of copyright reveals the role of intellectual property law in shaping social relations, molding identities, enforcing dominant values, and controlling expressive rights.

In short, user and creator rights, as determined by intellectual property laws, can both help maintain and perpetuate existing social structures.[8] Copyright's procedural and substantive rules therefore serve as a key vehicle for the discursive exertion of control on individual conduct. Building on these insights, this book constructs a theoretical model for assessing the broader impact of intellectual property protections on hegemonic practices by examining two primary areas of analytical interest: whom the law empowers to wield copyright's monopolist powers and the scope of these powers. As I argue, decision-making in both of these theaters of operation reveals the intricate way in which ostensibly neutral laws have combined to create hierarchies of informational and cultural rights that patrol relations between the center and periphery and mediate participation and privilege.

INTELLECTUAL PROPERTY AS CULTURAL BATTLEGROUND

Copyright law represents a hegemonic battleground, especially in the twenty-first century, as various societal actors struggle for the rights to control, regulate, or manipulate cultural content. For example, mature industries use intellectual property enforcement to resist competition from start-ups and consecrate their cultural content[9] while innovators often flout, or design around, existing protections. An examination of historical conflicts between intellectual property maximalists and minimalists illustrates this point. As Larry Lessig has argued, many of the same industries that now lobby heavily for strong intellectual property rights established themselves precisely because of their flagrant, unauthorized exploitation of the intellectual property of others.[10]

From publishers and cable networks to movie studios and record labels, the very players now advocating copyright maximalism benefitted from brazen infringement during their formative years. For more than a century, American publishers reaped handsome economic rewards from their unbridled ability to reproduce the works of foreign authors – especially those from the United Kingdom – without paying a penny in royalties.[11] In fact, for a significant portion of US history (until 1891), we denied foreign authors any copyright protection within our borders, making us the world's largest pirate nation (and not as in eye patches, planks, and parrots), a particularly inconvenient fact when we now try to skewer countries for allowing violations of American intellectual property. Cable television blossomed because of the retransmission of the signals (i.e., the copyrighted content) of the major networks without authorization.[12]

Meanwhile, Hollywood became the center of the motion picture universe when Louis Mayer famously travelled to the West Coast to seek better weather and light and to reduce production costs.[13] But, less famously, Mayer and his cronies were seeking to evade the watchful eye of Thomas Edison and his attorneys.[14] Edison, it turned out, owned numerous patents for technology used by the burgeoning film industry and, in combination with other patentees, had formed the Motion Picture Patents Company to pool intellectual property rights and effectively control nearly all motion picture technology by bringing infringement claims against any producer not using properly licensed equipment. Filmmakers, eager to reduce their production costs by not having to license these patent rights, fled West.[15]

Of course, Hollywood did not just free-ride on technological innovation; it has also made unabashed use of cultural patrimony. As Lessig notes, major studios such as Walt Disney have long profited by freely exploiting the rich tradition of folklore in such works as *Snow White* (1937), *Fantasia* (1940), *Pinocchio* (1940), *Dumbo* (1941), *Bambi* (1942), *Song of the South* (1946), *Cinderella* (1950), *Robin Hood* (1952), *Peter Pan* (1953), *Lady and the Tramp* (1955), *The Jungle Book* (1967), and *Mulan* (1998), among others.[16] And, the modern music industry saw much of its early success from the unauthorized exploitation of old blues riffs, many stolen directly from unacknowledged African-American folk artists.[17] In short, the publishing, motion picture, television, and music industries were all born of infringement.

We continue to see the clash between prior creators and emerging innovators in action today. For example, leading Internet sites are pushing the line on copyright law as they challenge the dominion of established interests. Consider showdowns in recent decades between content creators and Silicon Valley. Hollywood and the major record labels have fought with YouTube, which thrives on the exploitation of "user-generated content" – much of which consists of either the copyrighted works of third parties or works by users that, without authorization, make use of their copyrighted movies, television shows, and sound recordings. Major news organizations have fought with Google and Facebook over their uncompensated exploitation of news stories shared on their networks, a struggle that has led some countries to pass legislation that overrides exemptions in the law that have immunized these technology companies from infringement liability. Music publishers have fought with online platforms such as Roblox over the use of their compositions in video games. And just about every type of creator (from photographers and novelists to comedians and journalists) has challenged nascent generative artificial intelligence (AI) platforms such as OpenAI, Stability AI, and Midjourney for training their models on scraped copyrighted content and for spitting out responses to prompts that arguably constitute unlawful derivatives of that content.

The resolution of these intellectual property struggles does not simply impact the distribution of the private wealth of individuals and companies. Just as significantly, it also determines the future control of informational and cultural content. In this way, the contours of intellectual property law shape important social structures. Of course, such battles may have nothing to do with race, class, gender, or sexual orientation. But, as we shall see, jolts to the regime regularly do produce fissures along such fault lines, despite the seeming neutrality of copyright law and its various doctrines, which, on their face, say nothing whatsoever about these identity markers.

CRITICAL STUDIES, CRITICAL RACE THEORY, AND CRITICAL COPYRIGHT THEORY

In assessing the broader impact of copyright law on social structures and issues of race, class, gender, and sexual orientation, this book draws inspiration from a body of literature in critical legal studies and critical race theory. Building on the work of such social theorists as Antonio Gramsci,[18] Max Weber,[19] and Michel Foucault,[20] the critical legal studies movement has explored the link between power relationships in society and the development of legal doctrine and the structure of legal practice.[21] In particular, critical legal theory has questioned claims over the naturalness, objectivity, and neutrality of certain legal discourses, including formalism, essentialism, and law and economics.[22] In so doing, critical legal theorists have deconstructed the politics of law and "the role that the myth of 'neutral law' plays in legitimating legal discourse" by examining the way in which appeals to so-called natural principles such as welfare maximization can allow political actors to wield legal doctrine as a tool to convert "power into authority" by masking the advancement of ideological agendas.[23]

Critical race theory, which began as a subset of,[24] and even a reaction to,[25] the critical legal studies movement, has focused on the particular role that law and its institutions have played in both maintaining and perpetuating racial subordination.[26] In particular, critical race theorists have explored the ways in which the trope of colorblindness and ostensibly neutral ordering rules have "not only allowed law to ignore the social and institutional structures of oppression created historically and recreated presently in law and practice" but have also "blunted efforts to dismantle the racial caste system."[27] Take the debate over the regulation of hate speech, for example. As Derrick Bell notes, some critical race theorists have provocatively argued that

> being committed to 'free speech' may seem like a neutral principle, but it is not. Thus, proclaiming that 'I am committed equally to allowing free speech for the KKK and 2LiveCrew' is a non-neutral value judgment, one that asserts that the freedom to say hateful things is more important than the freedom to be free from the victimization, stigma, and humiliation that hate speech entails.[28]

While one may not agree with all of the positions taken by such scholars, these perspectives have played an important role in identifying and critiquing systemic features of our legal system that may contribute to the disenfranchisement of communities of color.[29]

Of course, in recent years, critical race theory has become something of a boogeyman in certain political circles for allegedly justifying the politics of wokeness and purportedly teaching that America is an inherently racist society, that race is central to understanding every aspect of both past and present American life, and that White people are to blame for the ongoing inequities of our society. As a result, populist demagogues keen on exploiting social anxieties and insecurities about the changing demographics and power relations in our society have placed this previously obscure legal theory and its so-called Ivory Tower adherents under fire. Unaware of the irony, the enemies of so-called Cancel Culture have tried to cancel critical race theory. And, now, even my friends in industries as far afield as the arts, real estate, hospitality, and finance are talking about it.

Although I have strong feelings about this particularly remarkable turn of events, I will refrain from veering too far off topic except to say that critical race theory has been egregiously mischaracterized and, while it should certainly be open to criticism, its opponents have regularly failed to recognize the invaluable tools the movement has provided for analyzing the devastatingly effective work purportedly neutral legal regimes have done in perpetuating and even exacerbating racial inequalities. So, for example, works inspired by critical race theory have informed some of our most vital policy debates in recent years. Richard Rothstein's *The Color of Law: A Forgotten History of How Our Government Segregated America* (2017) and Ira Katznelson's *When Affirmative Action Was White: An Untold History of Racial Inequality in Twentieth-Century America* (2005) have documented how practices such as red-lining and key provisions of the New Deal and Fair Deal inured to the benefit of White Americans, often at the expense of non-Whites. Meanwhile, Dorothy Brown's *The Whiteness of Wealth: How the Tax System Impoverishes Black Americans – and How We Can Fix It* (2021) has poignantly unveiled the ways in which our tax laws have systematically privileged the accumulation and intergenerational transfer of white wealth and financially disadvantaged Black economic activity. These studies have established that the vast disparities in wealth between Whites and non-Whites are not merely the product of slavery or overt manifestations of Jim Crow, but, rather, seemingly neutral legal practices that reached well into the twentieth century and even continue today. All told then, whatever else one may want to say about critical race theory, it has played a crucial role in advancing public discourse about the vexing inequalities that continue to plague our society.

Meanwhile, a new body of intellectual property literature has emerged in recent years, imbued with the spirit of critical legal studies and critical race theory. Just a generation ago, intellectual property law was the province of a group of scholars who, no matter how thoughtful and erudite, were homogenous along racial and gender lines. In the course of a few decades, however, the composition of academics devoting their research activities to intellectual property has changed dramatically and the increasing diversity in the field has brought different perspectives and given rise to a critical intellectual property scholarship that assesses how copyright, patent, and trademark laws have worked to both maintain and perpetuate based on race, gender, sexual orientation, and class. Scholars have therefore begun to explore the relationship between gender and intellectual property by examining the gendered aspects of copyright's fair use doctrine,[30] the alarming divergence between "attribution and presence" in crediting practices for female patent attorneys in Office Actions before the United States Patent and Trademark Office,[31] and the role of copyright law in dissuading "non-hierarchical, associative webs" critical to feminist discourse.[32] Similarly, scholars have assessed the complex interface between intellectual property laws and race in assessing, for example, the role of copyright rules in legitimating the unacknowledged and uncompensated usurpation of traditional African-American folk and blues in the development of the modern music industry.[33] More broadly, research within the field has addressed the relationship between intellectual property and sexual orientation[34] and the impact of intellectual property regimes on global inequalities and class-related issues.[35]

This book draws direct inspiration from this body of scholarship and, at the risk of missing some important names, I want to acknowledge the debt I owe, and gratitude I have for, the important, influential, and inspiring work done by my intellectual property colleagues in this particular area, including (but not limited to!) such scholars as Keith Aoki, Fumni Areya, Ann Bartow, Bob Brauneis, Dan Burk, Irene Calboli, Anupam Chander, Maggie Chon, Julie Cohen, Rosemary Coombe, Debbie Halbert, Llewellyn Gibbons, Shubha Ghosh, K. J. Greene, Steven Jamar, Peter Jaszi, Sonya Katyal, Deidré Keller, Bobbi Kwall, David Lange, Jessica Littman, Lateef Mmtima, Malla Pollack, Betsy Rosenblatt, Madhavi Sunder, Rebecca Tushnet, Anjali Vats and Siva Vaidhyanathan, among others (whom I have neglectfully failed to name).

While this particular corpus has not acquired a collective appellation, it shares a common methodology and inquisitive approach. For lack of a better term and in recognition of its philosophical roots, I refer to it as "critical IP theory," which I loosely define as the deconstruction of trademark, copyright, and patent laws and norms in light of existing power relationships to better understand the role of intellectual property in both maintaining and perpetuating hierarchy and inequality. This book locates itself within this emerging critical literature and builds upon Kimberlé Crenshaw's influential theory of intersectionality, which cautions that a proper understanding and assessment of the ways in which a legal regime impacts inequality can only occur when one considers the linkages amongst issues of race, gender, sexual orientation, and class.[36]

To paraphrase George Orwell, while the law may tell us that all copyrighted works are created equal, it turns out that some are more equal than others, and while the law may tell us that all creators are treated equally, it turns out that some are treated more equally than others. Under our copyright regime, some works receive beatification as sacred texts while others remain subject to unadulterated manipulation and reinterpretation; and some creators reap the rewards of powerful government-backed protection while others do not. Troublingly, these disparities in treatment fall on traditional racial, gender, and socioeconomic fault lines and they diminish the efficacy of our regime and its promotion of creative production. My argument proceeds in four parts to investigate the egalitarian and utilitarian implications of copyright's rules governing authorship (Chapter 1), collaboration and crediting (Chapter 2), derivative works and fair use (Chapter 3), and free speech (Chapter 4).

CHAPTER AND VERSE

Captured: How Copyright's Authorship Doctrine Empowers the White Male Gaze

The book begins by examining how copyright's vesting doctrines have privileged those with the economic might to control the tools of production, much to the bane of those operating in front of the camera. In the process, Chapter 1 argues that copyright's authorship doctrine has all too often deprived traditionally subordinated groups of agency over their creative output by propertizing what film theorist Laura

Mulvey has called the male gaze, giving legal bite to a system of rights that imbues copyright holders with the problematic and largely unbridled power to control representations of female (and non-white) bodies.

The chapter builds this argument by initially drawing on two events that took place roughly a century and a half apart: the infamous Zealy daguerreotypes taken in 1850 (which featured two enslaved individuals, Renty and Delia Taylor, photographed at the behest of famed Harvard biologist Louis Agassiz) and the intimate video of sportscaster Erin Andrews leaked online in 2009. In the former case, when one of the Taylors' descendants, Tamara Lanier, attempted to recapture the rights to her ancestors' naked images, which had been taken without legal consent, she ran up against the authorship-as-fixation doctrine, which vested the rights and title to the images in Harvard University, which had long supported Agassiz's work promoting white supremacy. By denying rights to subjects, the doctrine enabled Harvard to control the daguerreotypes and to profit from them (and, in effect, from the institution of slavery). In the latter case, the authorship-as-fixation doctrine bizarrely vested the copyright to the intimate footage in the felon who had stalked and recorded Andrews, leaving Andrews without sufficient legal tools to fight the video's widespread dissemination online. Thus, the operation of copyright law took an already devastating situation with troubling gender dynamics and compounded the harm suffered by Andrews immeasurably.

Copyright's law of authorship controlled the outcomes of both the Taylor and Andrews cases. Under established law, absent a contract to the contrary, a copyright is generally earned by the individual who fixed the work in a tangible medium. Thus, the exclusive right to distribute, reproduce, publicly display, publicly perform, or make derivatives of a creative work vests in the individual who owns the equipment and presses the shutter or record button, not the performer in front of the camera or anyone else behind the scenes who contributes creative elements to the final work. On the surface, such a rule seems neutral enough while promoting efficiency by making identification of a rights holder more facile. But, when one considers the disproportionately male and white identity of fixers, who have often captured women and people of color with their lens, the control that copyright law provides over the representations of subjects takes on troubling gendered and racial valence.

Moreover, the authorship-as-fixation rule is neither dictated by statute nor consistent with the notion of rewarding creativity. Although the conflation of authorship and fixation may have some sound bases, this doctrinal development has impeded efforts by those in front of the camera and other nonfixers working behind the scenes to earn copyright recognition for their significant creative efforts. The resulting rules surrounding the vesting of copyright interests have not only disproportionately immiserated women and communities of colors but also failed to reward an entire class of individuals who provide invaluable creative contributions to works of authorship.

To understand how we arrived at such a situation, Chapter 1 examines the origins of copyright's authorship-as-fixation rule, tracing its theoretical roots to *Burrow-Giles Lithographic Co.* v. *Sarony* (1884), a dispute (involving an image of Oscar Wilde) that became the very first American case to address the copyrightability of photography. For more than two centuries, the Copyright Act has largely eschewed the task of defining authorship. However, with the decoupling of the act of creation from the act of fixation and the dramatic advance of technology in recent years, the issue of authorship has gained renewed relevance, as questions of authorship have permeated numerous high-profile legal controversies in the past decade. To cite a few examples, the metaphysics of authorship has laid at the heart of legal squabbles involving Naruto (the crested macaque who famously took a selfie), photographer Arne Svenson's voyeuristic art project *The Neighbors*, Cindy Lee Garcia's judicial gambit to fight death threats for her appearance in the controversial movie *The Innocence of Muslims*, and Hulk Hogan's battle against Gawker Media to suppress unflattering surveillance footage of him caught *in flagrante delicto*.

Following a close reading of the resulting case law involving Oscar Wilde, Cindy Lee Garcia, Arne Svenson, and Hulk Hogan and an analysis of authorial inquiries raised by interviews, drone and surveillance footage, bootlegs, early recordings of African-American artists working in the oral tradition, paparazzi photographs, classroom note-taking, revenge porn, and celebrity sex tapes, this chapter identifies and critiques the problematic juridical conflation of copyright's authorship and fixation requirements. As it argues, copyright's authorship-as-fixation regime rests on a faulty premise, betrays copyright law's role in recognizing and rewarding creativity, and denies copyright interests to the very individuals who have provided significant, if not the most important, original contributions to works within copyright's traditional subject matter. Just as significantly, given the dramatic racial and gender disparities in capital accumulation and control over the tools of creative production, the distinctive dynamics of revenge porn, and continuing inequalities in the representation of women and persons of color behind the camera, the authorship-as-fixation doctrine exacerbates inequality by reifying the male gaze and transforming it into a property right rationalized along traditional binaries of activity and passivity, object and subject, male and female. In the process, this chapter begins to trace the profound inegalitarian impact of copyright's ostensibly neutral principles on issues of gender and race.

Tick Tick … Boom! *How Copyright's Law of Collaboration and Crediting Privileges Might Over Right*

Chapter 2 turns its attention to how copyright's treatment of collaboration and crediting has come to elevate power dynamics over creative production. The resulting rules on joint authorship and attribution have therefore systematically disadvantaged already marginalized groups. They have also undermined the efficiency of the copyright regime by failing to reward, and stymieing the allocation of capital resources toward, the very individuals with the capacity to best advance progress in the arts.

This chapter begins with the tragic tale of Lynn Thomson. In 1995, the New York Theatre Workshop (NYTW), recognizing the promise in a script for a new musical from a composer named Jonathan Larson, encouraged Larson and set him up to work with a dramatist to prepare the work for a hopeful Broadway stint. Larson and the dramatist collaborated extensively and the show was ultimately set for an off-Broadway premiere. But tragedy struck just hours after the final dress rehearsal, as Larson suffered an aortic dissection and died shortly thereafter. The show proceeded, however, and it immediately received universal acclaim and enjoyed a quick move to Broadway. The musical was called *Rent* and it went on to become one of the longest-running shows in theatrical history and a bona fide global sensation.

The success of *Rent* and Larson's heartbreaking story are well known and dramatized in the Netflix movie *Tick, Tick … Boom*! Less appreciated, however, is the story of the dramatist, Lynn Thomson, whose instrumental role in *Rent*'s success finds little to no place in the motion picture or most accounts about the musical. Although Thomson was paid by the NYTW for her work and received an official billing credit as "Dramaturg," the relevant contracts relating to her collaboration were notably silent on the issue of authorship and copyright ownership and, in the end, Thomson was denied any authorship credit to the musical and, as such, lacked any control over the exploitation of the work or any participation in the author's royalty share enjoyed from the success of the work. When she took her case to court, her claim to joint authorship was resoundingly rejected, both before a trial court and on appeal.[37] The Second Circuit ultimately found that, even if Thomson had made "major" contributions to *Rent*, including verbatim drafting of "significant language" in the work, these facts would be irrelevant since Larson did not share in Thomson's desire to be co-authors. Citing the vesting of ultimate decision-making authority in Larson, Larson's formal billing as the sole "author," and his reference to himself as a sole author in third-party agreements, the court found Larson lacking such mutual intent. Since Larson did not regard himself as a co-author, the court concluded he could not have been one and, instead, deemed him the sole legal author.

By examining how it could be possible for someone like Thomson to suffer such a fate – where she received no authorial credit and lost out on its attendant economic and moral rights despite indisputably providing significant creative contributions to *Rent* – Thomson's story frames a critique of the way in which our copyright's joint authorship jurisprudence, with its mutual intent requirement, has rebuked the rights of those lacking or unwilling to enforce bargaining power and those operating under different modalities of creative production. The result is the systematic and disproportionate thwarting of authorial claims from traditionally marginalized groups within the creative classes, including women, indigenous communities, and performers.

After locating the origins of the mutual intent requirement in the romantic conception of authorship that has pervaded copyright law and has long sought to attribute creative enterprise to a single "master mind" and detailing how the Supreme Court problematically imported this trope from a late nineteenth-century English case, the chapter assesses how American courts ultimately deployed these biases in the joint authorship case law by imposing a requirement that all collaborators must mutually intend their creative contributions to be indistinguishably merged into a joint work. To determine intent, courts frequently rely upon crediting practices. As I argue, the mutual-intent requirement, with its reliance on crediting practices, have served to further consolidate the power of those already with superior leverage, access to capital, and control over the tools of production. In the process, therefore, the contributions of real creators – often those at societal margins – go unrecognized and unrewarded.

With its problematic reliance on formal crediting and power relations, the mutual-intent requirement has transformed joint-authorship queries into a referendum on the relative leverage of the competing parties and their willingness to use it. Not only does such a vision of joint authorship disincentivize and fail to recognize modalities of creation that are more collaborative in nature, it also disproportionately burdens groups of people who may be more likely to engage in such collaborative activities. Indeed, viewed through the prisms of gender, race, and class, crediting practices have a remarkably troubling track record of privileging existing power relations over actual creative contributions and simultaneously exacerbating existing societal inequalities.

The privileging of power over creative contribution does not merely infect copyright's joint authorship doctrine. As a direct result of our copyright regime's surprising indifference to attribution rights, it also reigns supreme in crediting practices. After detailing the importance of attribution to authorial and public policy interests and charting our legal regime's startling crediting gap, this chapter assesses the impact of this choice on the operation of the crediting marketplace and draws on notable cases from academia (a contentious suit stemming from a professor-graduate student collaboration), motion pictures (the Director Guild's infamous use of the "Adam Smithee" pseudonym), and music (the real origins of Little Richard's *Tutti Frutti*, Duke Ellington's *Sophisticated Lady*, and Beyoncé's *Hold Up*) to illustrate the infirmities of the current crediting regime. By writing creative crediting out of our intellectual property law and leaving the matter solely to negotiating leverage, we ensure that people who should receive credit often do not. The resulting state of the law has a particularly grave impact on creators from traditionally marginalized communities who lack bargaining power, thereby depriving them of the dignitary and the economic opportunities that come with attribution. But the harm is felt even more widely, as a lack of a proper crediting regime also diminishes the efficacy of resource allocation in creative enterprises, which ultimately impoverishes progress in the arts.

Controlling the Narrative: How Copyright's Derivative Rights Doctrine Creates Sacred Texts

The next section of the book focuses on the way in which legal doctrine has evolved to define the scope of protection provided under the copyright monopoly. Chapter 3 examines how the derivative rights doctrine, with its ever-expansive breadth, has played a powerful role in privileging dominant narratives over resistive ones, reducing the latter to acts of infringement. By outlawing such acts of "semiotic disobedience,"[38] copyright renders important cultural symbols inviolable and plays a vital, but unappreciated, role in protecting and preserving prevailing ideologies by suppressing challenges to them. In short, the derivative rights doctrine creates sacred texts in two senses: works that are sacrosanct and epistemologies that are incontestable.

The chapter begins by exploring two long-forgotten, copyright-related events during the lead-up to World War II: the translation, from German to English, of *Bambi* and Hitler's autobiography, *Mein Kampf*. Though one could scarcely name two more different works, they shared a remarkable commonality: their authorized translations for the American market were not entirely true to the originals. But because of the operation of the derivative works doctrine, copyright law proscribed the distribution of any alternative (and more accurate) rendition, with significant consequences on the American views of the war in Europe and the march of history. In the case of *Bambi*, the authorized translation overlooked (perhaps deliberately or perhaps out of the sheer hubris of first-time translator Whittaker Chambers, a writer who was later outed as a Soviet spy) one of the story's most haunting and unappreciated themes: the persecution of Germany's Jewish population. In fact, this theme would not come to fore until this century, when the work finally fell into the public domain in 2022 and a scholarly translation seeking greater fidelity to author Felix Salten's original German text became available.

In the case of *Mein Kampf*, the deception was entirely intentional as the Nazi Party's propaganda wing sought to make Hitler's message more palatable to American audiences (where the Nazi leader had a shockingly large base of support during the 1930s) by selective removal of some (but certainly not all) of the incendiary sections. When a future United States Senator, Alan Cranston, assembled an unexpurgated edition of the book to alert the public to this pernicious act of subterfuge and to Hitler's real agenda, his efforts came to a grinding halt when Hitler, through his publisher, Houghton Mifflin, enjoined Cranston's version in a successful infringement suit. In both cases, neutral application of the law of copyright enabled entrenched powers to control narratives that stifled – even if marginally – resistance to Nazi Germany, fascism, and antisemitism. As a result, copyright law had a surprisingly problematic impact on American public discourse in the midst of deliberations over whether, and how, to respond to the troubling events in Europe in the 1930s and early 1940s.

The battles over *Bambi* and *Mein Kampf* reflect a critical problem with copyright's broad derivative rights doctrine. Curiously, for the first century of American copyright law, there was no such thing as a derivative rights doctrine. Copyright holders merely had the right to prevent others from reproducing, publishing, or selling their works. But, over time, we began to embrace the concept of a limited derivative right. In 1870, Congress amended the Copyright Act to grant authors the exclusive rights to translate and dramatize their works. The 1909 Copyright Act went even further, extending the scope of protection to novelization and musicalization. Finally, the 1976 Copyright Act explicitly gave authors the exclusive right to prepare all "derivatives" of their copyrighted works and provided an expansive definition that included all creations "based upon" a work, including any form in which a work "may be recast, transformed, or adapted."[39]

While this change has served as a boon to rights holders, it has come at a significant cost to the rights of consumers by placing significant limitations on their abilities to interact with and respond to creative works. As Chapter 3 posits, such a state of affairs has impoverished the creative marketplace, preventing the authorship and distribution of countless works of ingenuity simply because they may owe their existence to a pre-existing work. If the goal of copyright law is to ultimately promote the production of new works, the derivative rights doctrine actively impedes this ambition. But, just as significantly, the expansive derivative rights doctrine also severely restricts the ability to make critical uses of pre-existing works, thereby constraining the range of expressive activities enjoyed by the public and limiting challenges to prevailing cultural and social narratives. Copyright protection therefore lies at the heart of the discursive struggle to police hierarchy, to beatify sacred texts, and to proscribe their unwanted embellishment, abridgement, transformation, manipulation, and alteration.

With the tools of copyright law put to use, sacred works can remain relatively inviolable, subject only to reinterpretation when the powers-that-be deem a project worthy (artistically, monetarily, or otherwise). In other words, the sacred work is shielded from the open marketplace through the derivative rights doctrine, which forbids alterations in all forms, thereby proscribing challenges to both public and private power by reconceptualizing such actions as infringements. With respect to public power, the analysis assesses how use of the derivative rights doctrine can suppress acts of semiotic resistance, including classic anti-government protest activity such as flag burning, draft card destruction, and license plate tampering. With respect to private power, the chapter examines the infamous artistic stand-off on Wall Street between Artura Di Modica's *Charging Bull* – the long-time icon of the financial markets that has stood at the northern corner of Bowling Green since 1989 – and Kristan Visbal's *Fearless Girl*, a statue of a young Latin female standing proud and confident, her ponytail and dress swishing in the wind and arms against her hips, a look of calm on her face as she gazes assuredly and defiantly ahead … at the Bull. When *Fearless Girl* took her place before the Bull in 2017, the resulting tableau garnered global interest. But it also provoked a firestorm of controversy when Di Modica argued that *Fearless Girl*'s positioning in the immediate eye-line of his growling, menacing beast fundamentally altered his work and subverted his artistic vision. While the Bull was once a "symbol of prosperity and for strength" and an awakener of the "animal spirits" of the market, in front of *Fearless Girl*, it became a pusillanimous oppressor, threatening a diminutive girl. In short, the Bull had become a *bully*. Di Modica therefore claimed *The Fearless Girl* constituted an unauthorized derivative work, violating his right to preserve *Charging Bull*'s artistic integrity. To Di Modica, *Fearless Girl* was nothing more than an infringing work, both without copyright protection and subject to destruction. Though novel, Di Modica's claims were not wholly unprecedented or without support in the extant law of copyright. So, in the end, the City of New York relented to Di Modica's demands and relocated *The Fearless Girl* to the front of the New York Stock Exchange – far from the *Bull*'s gaze. This ultimate resolution illustrates the power of copyright's derivative rights doctrine to quell resistance to dominant narratives about capitalism, power, and cultural meaning.

Meanwhile, even the biggest check on the copyright monopoly – the fair use defense – has often failed to provide adequate breathing room for semiotic disobedience and other actions challenging prevailing social and political narratives. With alarming frequency, aesthetic judgments have permeated applications of the doctrine, allowing juridical conceptions of history, hierarchy, and value to operate selectively to immunize certain epistemologies from interrogation or inversion. Two significant fair use rulings illustrate this dynamic in action. In the first case, the Margaret Mitchell Estate brought an infringement suit seeking to enjoin publication of *The Wind Done Gone*, Alice Randall's subversive send-up of the bucolic and whitewashed vision of the antebellum South portrayed in *Gone with the Wind*. Randall's novel recast the story from the point of view of Cynara, a recently freed slave who happens to be Scarlett's half-sister, featured a gay Ashley Wilkes and numerous interracial relationships, and emphasized the quotidian travails of the victims of the South's rigid and racist social hierarchy. In the second case, the modern art world's *enfant terrible*, Richard Prince, found himself in legal hot water after making unauthorized use of the images of ethnographer photographer Patrick Cariou for his *Canal* series that exhibited at New York's swanky Gagosian Gallery. A close reading of the decisions in both cases illustrates how aesthetic judgments drove the courts' fair-use analysis, thereby revealing how embedded cultural assumptions and biased notions of value can impact infringement holdings on issues related to the depiction of race, class, and sexual orientation in history and the representation of indigenous bodies.

In the end, therefore, Chapter 3 highlights the powerful role of the derivative rights doctrine, and the weaknesses of fair use, in limiting resistance to prevailing ideologies and the symbols that prop them up. A derivative rights doctrine lacking sufficient checks not only betrays the core purpose of the copyright regime – progress in the arts – but also undermines the ability of marginalized groups to resist dominant orthodoxies and entrenched powers.

©ensored: How Copyright's First Amendment Exemption Enables the Powerful to Silence the Powerless

Chapter 4 identifies one of the most troubling developments in copyright law over the past generation: the surprising story of how copyright law's exemption from First Amendment scrutiny has enabled powerful interests to cynically weaponize intellectual property as a forceful, state-backed vehicle of censorship to silence critics and suppress dissent. As I argue, copyright has a growing free speech problem – one that threatens to undermine both the vitality of our regime governing the use of creative works and our most basic free speech rights.

The chapter begins with the story of political talk show host Michael Savage and the Council on American–Islamic Relations (CAIR). During a 2007 radio broadcast, Savage launched into an unrepentantly Islamophobic polemic that declared the Koran to be "a book of hate" and deemed Muslims "throwbacks" who should be deported "without due process." He punctuated his outburst by telling Muslims to take their "religion and shove it up your behind. I'm sick of you." In response to Savage's bigoted rant, CAIR posted an online critique of his vitriol and encouraged "radio listeners of all faiths to contact companies that advertise on Michael Savage's nationally syndicated radio program to express their concerns about the host's recent anti-Muslim tirade." In this denunciation, CAIR excerpted (without permission) approximately four minutes from Savage's two-hour broadcast. The use of the broadcast appeared to be a quintessential form of commentary and criticism, seemingly immunized from liability both under the strictures of copyright law's fair-use doctrine and the First Amendment. Savage, however, felt that CAIR had illicitly impinged on his exclusive dominion over his intellectual property, so he sued for copyright infringement. In the process, CAIR and its allies effectively had their speech silenced and Savage joined an ignominious list of dictators, billionaires, human rights abusers, and racists who have exploited copyright's exemption from First Amendment scrutiny as a powerful mechanism to censor those who dare criticize them and to squelch political and cultural debate in a manner that is antithetical to our commitment to the freedom of speech.

At first blush, copyright law seems far afield from matters of journalistic freedom and censorship. And therein lies its power, as claims of infringement have become the weapon *par excellence* of the twenty-first-century censor. Fueled by a desire to prevent their perceived foes from engaging in criticism or dissent, well-heeled individuals and entities have no better friend. Copyright violations are ubiquitous – with smartphones in our pockets and networked computers at our desks, we all infringe copyright law multiple times a day and leave digital fingerprints to document our infringing activities if a putative rights holder bothers to investigate.

Liability can be massive – up to $150,000 per willful act of copyright infringement. Copyright suits are difficult to fend off – the average suit costs hundreds of thousands of dollars to defend. And, perhaps most saliently to the sophisticated censor, the federal courts have almost systematically immunized infringement suits from meaningful First Amendment checks. As the Supreme Court blithely asserted in *Eldred* v. *Ashcroft* (2003), "[C]opyright's built-in free speech safeguards are generally adequate to address" any conflict with the First Amendment.[40] As a result, the privileged (and legally represented) have increasingly seized upon this key blind spot in constitutional jurisprudence by recharacterizing unfavorable acts of speech as copyright infringements. In the process, they have harnessed a formidable mechanism to circumvent the First Amendment and suppress speech that is hostile to their interests. Played out in the federal court system, this gambit has effectively transformed our intellectual property laws into a potent tool of censorship.

The cynical use of copyright law as a means of empowering censorship has grown alarmingly commonplace in recent years as powerful, monied interests have drawn upon this device to silence their opponents. Military personnel ginned up copyright claims to suppress photographs documenting human rights abuses at Abu Ghraib (*Four Navy SEALs* v. *Associated Press* [2005]). The billionaire owner of a notable sports franchise seized upon copyright law to destroy the life of a blogger who reported on allegations of corruption and financial impropriety against him (*Katz* v. *Chevaldina* [2012]). In a custody proceeding over his ability to provide a suitable environment for his children, a husband even cynically exploited copyright law as a means to prevent his ex-wife's introduction of an unpublished manuscript in which he confessed to murdering his father (*Bond* v. *Blum* [2003]). And, as ridiculous as it may sound, in the years since the brutal murder of George Floyd at the hands of a Minneapolis police officer, wily law enforcement officials who wish to suppress video recordings of them engaging in potential wrongdoing have effectively taken to playing copyrighted pop music in the background to prevent the videos of them from being uploaded on social media, since they know the uploading of such videos would constitute acts of copyright infringement. As a result, the cynical invocation of copyright law has repressed important political dialogue and impoverished public discourse.

After surveying the growing use of copyright law for the purposes of censorship, Chapter 4 examines just how this trend has undermined the vitality of our copyright regime and stifled the free exchange of ideas, opinions, and information by enabling powerful rights holders to wield copyright law as a means to silence their critics, especially those from the political, cultural, racial, and socioeconomic margins. In the process, we explore how our regime got to this point; how some courts have attempted to deal with this problem through the use of procedural machinations, including early adjudication of cases through motions to dismiss; and how the law might better respond as a whole to ensure that copyright law is used to vindicate the appropriate economic interests of rights holders, rather than to serve as a transparent proxy for censorship. In an era of increasing media conglomeration, individuals at the margins already feel their voices are diminished. The use of copyright law to further silence these voices stymies progress and undermines efforts to establish a more egalitarian society.

An Unhurried View of Copyright in the Age of AI

As the various chapters to the book illustrate, the secret life of copyright is riddled with seemingly innocuous public policy decisions that have metastasized, in the long term, into persistent sources of inequality and marginalization along racial, gender, and socioeconomic lines. So, for example, a decision to vest copyrights in the individuals who fix works in a tangible medium has not only failed to recognize the creative contributions of those in front of the camera but also resulted in the propertization of the white male gaze. A desire to avert the fracturing of rights by imposing a mutual-intent requirement for joint authorship has disproportionally deprived female, non-white, and poorer creatives of full participation in the creative economy. A well-intentioned ruling to prevent holders of expired copyrights from extending their monopolies through the cynical invocation of trademark law has all but assured that crediting practices reward clout over creativity, thereby damaging the efficacy of the creative marketplace and disadvantaging those with the least negotiating leverage. An extension of copyright protection to incorporate the universe of spin-offs from an original work has ended up suppressing acts of semiotic disruption, propping up entrenched powers, and limiting resistance to prevailing ideological narratives on issues of race, gender, religion, geopolitics, identity, colonialism, capitalism, and corporatism. The immunization of copyright law from First Amendment scrutiny, which was meant to facilitate the recognition of property rights in one's creative speech, has resulted in the disingenuous weaponization of copyright law as a tool of censorship, helping the powerful to silence their critics with alarming force.

The consistent theme of these cautionary developments is simple: we ignore the social-justice implications of copyright law at our peril. In this spirit, the book closes with an examination of the challenges that generative AI poses to copyright law and issues of social justice. Specifically, the conclusion considers the ways in which generative AI will force reconsideration of copyright's authorship, attribution, fair-use, and derivative-works doctrines. For example, questions over the creative input necessary to earn rights over AI creations will call into question copyright's authorship doctrine as courts begin to wrestle with whether copyrights for AI output can exist at all and, if so, in whom. And, as authorship questions grow more complicated with the use of pre-existing content to develop new works, norms of attribution will have to evolve, potentially creating pressure for new legal protections related to crediting. Meanwhile, the wave of infringement litigation over generative AI will force Congress and the courts to determine the extent to which, and how, pre-existing copyright content can be used for the training of AI. In the process of applying the fair-use and derivative rights doctrines to this new technology, the law will determine which (and whose) works will become fodder of remix and which (and whose) works will remain sacrosanct in the age of AI.

The outcomes of these debates will have significant creative and egalitarian implications. As we witnessed only two decades ago with the advent of digital sampling – a major technological development that enabled new forms of creativity and gave birth to a novel genre of music, hip hop – pre-existing inequalities in the distribution of resources and societal prejudices can combine with facially neutral rules to craft a legal regime for a new technology that exacerbates racial divides. Meanwhile, ostensibly innocuous procedural requirements in copyright law – such as the timely registration requirement – not only determine the substantive protection given to different types of copyright works but also split the effective scope of rights authors enjoy on sharp racial, gender, and socioeconomic lines. So, how copyright doctrine evolves in the age of AI will impact the vitality of our creative economy while also having the potential to either soften or exacerbate racial, gender, and socioeconomic disparities. Which direction the impact flows will stem from the sum of our collective choices, and the age of AI presents an opportunity to recalibrate copyright law in a way that promotes both progress in the arts and economic inclusion.

COPYRIGHT'S SECRET LIFE AND ME

As the impact of intellectual property law on the development of the forthcoming age of AI will make clear, copyright has had a far more colorful life than most imagine. I've been fortunate enough to spend more than two decades as both an academic and attorney, teaching, writing, representing, and advising all manner of clients in the creative industries – including novelists, musicians, songwriters, record labels, movie studios, directors, producers, actors, screenwriters, photographers, artists, fashion designers, jewelers, video game developers, coders, and architects – on virtually every aspect of intellectual property law. My experiences directly inform the perspectives presented in this book.

I started my legal career as a patent litigator, handling disputes over the ownership and infringement of new technologies. After a time, however, I started receiving queries from clients in the neighboring area of copyright law and, before long, I found myself thoroughly seduced by the work. To underline the point, it's been more than two decades since I handled any patent matter. Operating at the intersection of law, creativity, and technology and implicating public policy at the cutting edge of new developments in artistic expression and dissemination, copyright has always proven a dynamic and provocative area of law. But beyond satisfying my intellectual interests, the counseling of artists has fulfilled me on a personal level. And if I'm going to engage in a bit of armchair psychoanalysis, the driving force for this emotional satisfaction has come from an unusual place: my complete lack of artistic aptitude.

I'm the first to admit that such an assertion could lead to confusion without some proper context. But if you will indulge me, I can provide a critical personal detail – one which I am loathe to recognize but which honesty compels me to admit – that helps explain things. The art gene in my family skipped a generation: mine. My mom was a professional artist, an exhibited painter with a talent for both remarkable figurative work and abstract expressionism. But, alas, I cannot so much as draw a stick figure. In fact, my greatest success within the arts is a meager ability to bang out sloppy power chords to my favorite indie rock songs. As a result, I'm in thrall to those who can create and I'm filled with admiration for their gift. My lack of artistic talent drives me to better understand and serve those in the arts. After all, if I can't make any art myself, the least I can do is summon everything in my power to enable and assist those who can.

So, unbeknownst to my clients and students, practicing and teaching copyright law has helped me work out my personal issues. But, in the process, it has also led to something else: a growing awareness about the limits of our copyright regime and the way in which it serves the creative community. Years of litigation work, classroom discussions, client counseling, and scholarly research have revealed the troubling ways in which the operation of certain copyright doctrines has not only systematically disadvantaged individuals from marginalized communities but how, in the process, these same doctrines betray copyright's constitutionally mandated goal of progress.

The inspiration for this book comes from myriad moments during that time. I began to scrutinize the egalitarian implications of copyright's authorship-as-fixation doctrine when an actress client found herself unable to fight the distribution of intimate footage that an ex-boyfriend had leaked online because she had not shot the videos and, therefore, had no copyright interest in them. I questioned the state of copyright's law of crediting when I had to advise a veteran session musician who had made invaluable contributions to a Grammy-nominated artist's work that he was largely powerless to receive any credit, let alone a co-authorship interest, due to his lack of negotiating leverage. I probed the inequities of copyright's music-royalties regime in working with a prominent hip-hop artist and erstwhile pop diva who had recorded dozens of hits but never received full profit participation in their creative output because they were "merely" performers (and not songwriters). I interrogated the surprising lack of rights enjoyed by the subjects featured in copyrighted content when I represented the family of the deceased extreme sports legend who could not bring an infringement claim despite the fact that a major conglomerate had impermissibly featured him in a national advertising campaign for a product that represented everything he stood against in his life. I investigated copyright's two-tiered system of protection when I had to break the news to an artist that she was unable to pursue a meaningful claim against a major retailer despite its clear commercial infringement of her work because of the operation of the timely registration requirement. I began to challenge copyright's vesting rules as I consoled the crestfallen musician in a Grammy-winning band whose manager accidentally sent him one of his bandmate's royalty checks – which was several orders of magnitude greater than his – leading him to the terrible realization that he had been cut off from the most valuable interests in his band's work by virtue of copyright's vesting rules. And, I witnessed the censorial power of copyright law when I counseled a scholar who, because of the potential threat of infringement litigation, feared citing the unpublished letters of powerful lobbyists to expose a concerted effort to suppress on-campus discussion of a major civil rights issue.

In all these matters, I tried to bend the law as best as I could to level the playing field for my clients. But there is only so much that strategic and creative lawyering can accomplish. So, to make up for what I was not able to accomplish, I've written this book in the hope of provoking a reconceptualization and reconsideration of copyright doctrine in light of its broader social impact. In the pages to follow, I'll tell the story of copyright based on these experiences, with the goal of identifying key areas where copyright can do a better job of advancing both creative and egalitarian interests.

1

Captured

How Copyright's Authorship Doctrine Empowers the White Male Gaze

In which we discuss: Renty and Delia Taylor's daguerreotypes, Erin Andrew's leaked peephole video, Oscar Wilde's infamous publicity shot, Naruto the Macaque's selfie, Arne Svenson's voyeuristic photography, Richard Prince's appropriationist *New Portraits* series, Emily Ratajkowski's act of meta-resistance, Hulk Hogan's moment *in flagrante delicto*, and Cindy Lee Garcia's unwittingly incurred *fatwa*.

COPYRIGHT AND CONSENT

In the midst of the Black Lives Matter movement, our country's most elite academic institutions have started to address some of the more unsavory aspects of their legacies, including their complicity in the slave trade and their promotion of white supremacy. In a wave of symbolic efforts undertaken in recent years, universities have changed the appellations of buildings, residential colleges, and even entire schools whose names celebrated individuals who had played instrumental roles in resisting the fight for civil rights. Yale dropped the honorifics for Vice President, Senator, and ardent anti-abolitionist John C. Calhoun from its residential college; Princeton removed former President Woodrow Wilson's name from its School of Public Policy because of his active support for segregation and white supremacy; and University of California, Hastings, rebranded itself as University of California College of Law, San Francisco, after the involvement of founder Serranus Clinton Hastings in the genocide of the Yuki people of Mendocino County became widely known. Some schools have gone even further, making strides that extend beyond the ceremonial and titular. For example, Georgetown University has apologized for its profiteering from slavery, including its infamous auctioning of 272 men, women, and children in 1838 in order to help finance the school, and the Jesuits have taken steps toward making amends by, among other things, creating a fund to support descendants of those individuals.

But many institutions are only willing to go so far – particularly when concrete steps come at a real, rather than nominal, cost – and skirmishes over accountability and remediation continue to flare. In one such instance, Harvard University found itself in the crosshairs of a lawsuit that garnered significant public attention for its compelling and sympathetic facts. In 2019, after years of failed efforts to appeal to the moral conscience of administrators at the school, Tamara Lanier reluctantly sought legal relief instead, filing claims against Harvard for its continuing exploitation and profiteering from one of the vestiges of slavery: a series of notable daguerreotypes. In 1850, as part of his work to support the (supremacist and long-debunked) theory of polygenism, which claimed that the different races of humanity had divergent ancestors, celebrated Harvard biologist Louis Agassiz commissioned a series of images on a South Carolina cotton plantation. The resulting shots featured two of Lanier's ancestors: Renty Taylor, an African from the Congo Basin whom slave traders had captured and brought on a Spanish slave ship to the United States around 1800, and his daughter, Delia. The clinical and voyeuristic daguerreotypes depict the Taylors disrobed from a variety of angles, and they are also deeply poignant for the cruelty they depict. In one image, reproduced here but cropped to show its subject only from the neck up (Figure 1.1), Mr. Taylor stares directly into the camera with his "eyes blazing," as one observer has heartbreakingly noted.[1] The daguerreotypes are among the earliest and best-known images of slaves, and Harvard University has exploited this scarcity by licensing them over the ensuing years for hefty fees, even making use of them as cover shots on its own publications and conference materials.

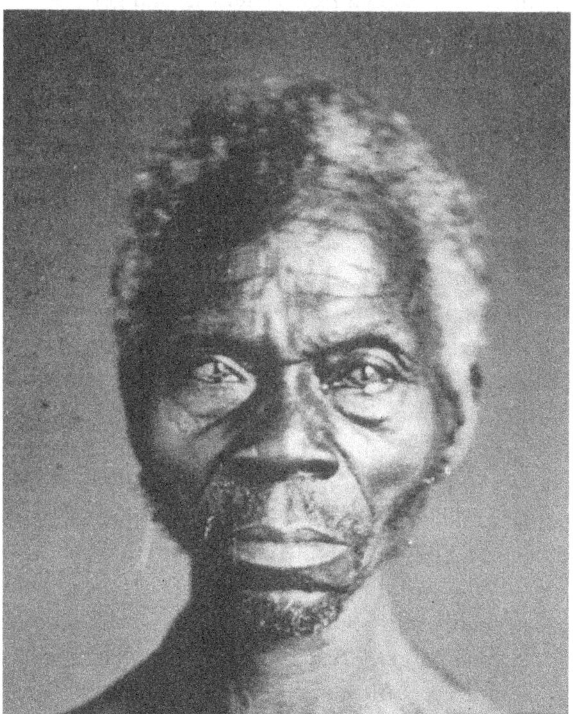

FIGURE 1.1 Portrait of Renty Taylor (1850), cropped

Lanier's suit sought damages and injunctive relief from Harvard, claiming that the school had, among other things, unlawfully converted the daguerreotypes and illicitly traded on the image of her ancestors for profit. In short, Lanier attempted to obtain custody of the images – taken without the lawful consent of Renty and Delia – so that she could put an end to the unsanctioned and ongoing exploitation of her ancestors' bodies that began with their enslavement and continued to this day.

While Lanier's suit generated headlines, it made little judicial headway. A Massachusetts trial court promptly granted Harvard's motion to dismiss the suit in toto on the grounds that, even assuming all the facts were true, they did not provide Lanier a basis upon which she could seek legal or equitable relief. Lanier appealed to the Massachusetts Supreme Court, and the results, issued in 2022, were little better. Although it notably revived a single claim for intentional infliction of emotional distress (for which Lanier faces significant challenges, including arguments that her claim for intentional infliction is preempted by the Copyright Act since it stems from the exploitation of rights governed thereunder), the Court otherwise affirmed the trial court's rejection of Lanier's claims, leaving Lanier without a basis, at least legally speaking, to reclaim title to the daguerreotypes or potentially limit their further exploitation. In a concurring opinion, Justice Elspeth Cypher expressed her sympathy with the plight of litigants such as Lanier, noting, quite correctly, "the plaintiff now faces a legal system several generations later devoid of a sufficient remedy for the injuries and injustices she has faced as a descendant of enslaved Africans and African-Americans."[2]

As it turns out, intellectual property law lies at the heart of the decision, as the case grappled with basic legal principles that have long propertized images of (frequently non-white and female) bodies and given control over their reproduction and dissemination to corporate interests. Remarkably, Harvard can make a claim of copyright ownership to the Taylor images through a rather Byzantine factual scenario, even though just about every other work created before the late 1920s has fallen into the public domain.[3] Although neither the Superior Court nor the Supreme Court decision in *Lanier* squarely raised the issue of copyright (or, whether, in fact, the work was still under copyright protection or had fallen into the public domain), the trial court noted that, "Fully acknowledging the continuing impact slavery has had in the United States, the law, as it currently stands, does not confer a property interest to the subject of a photograph regardless of how objectionable the photograph's origins may be."[4] Such a result is, of course, problematic. From the point of view of human dignity, it is disquieting that the law would allow those who supported the institution of slavery and its rationalizing ideologies to continue to control bodily representations of those slaves and commercially benefit from them more than a century and a half after emancipation. However, the outcome of the lawsuit was little surprise to legal observers because it was dead on arrival based on existing precedent. Its holding was dictated by a foundational aspect of copyright doctrine: the law of authorship.

Authorship, of course, is a core concept in copyright law. Quite importantly, it determines the most immediate question when grappling with the rules surrounding the exploitation of any creative work: Who owns the rights to it? As a default matter, the author does. And the modern law of authorship typically vests copyrights in the person behind the camera, not those in front of it. In other words, the law fetishizes the act of fixation, and, through the annals of copyright jurisprudence, the federal courts have generally presumed that, absent work-made-for-hire status, the author/rights holder of a work is the individual controlling the equipment that fixes a creative work in a tangible medium – that is, the producer/engineer on a sound recording, the director behind the camera, or the photographer taking the snapshot. Thus, Renty, Delia, and their heirs had no rights, title, or interest in the photographs.

But the seemingly neutral principle of authorship as fixation, developed without express consideration of slavery, race, gender, or even socioeconomic status, has had an enduring and underappreciated impact on social inequality by disproportionally vesting (valuable) intangible properties rights to creative works in the privileged, often granting them full control over representations of the underclass – people of color, women, and the socioeconomically disadvantaged. And, to make matters worse, the authorship-as-fixation rule often works at odds with, and actively undermines, the goal of the copyright regime to promote progress in the arts by rewarding those who create. So while the controversy involving the images of Renty and Delia is particularly disturbing, it has had analogues – albeit in less horrific circumstances – in myriad other situations through the decades.

About 158 years later and a few hundred miles northwest from the Columbia plantation upon which Renty and Delia toiled, a woman checked into a Nashville Marriott in late 2008, unaware that her life was about to change forever due to a stalker's actions and the bizarre operation of copyright law's authorship doctrine. While the result of this encounter was nothing akin to slavery or the continued exploitation of its vestiges, it involved its own unique terror and a deep and painful injustice.

Erin Andrews was a well-known sports reporter working for ESPN traveling to Tennessee to cover a football game. Michael David Barrett, an insurance salesman, had grown increasingly obsessed with Andrews and, after determining her travel plans, stalked her to the Nashville Marriott where, after learning her room number, managed to cajole the front desk into giving him the room next door to her. Once in the adjacent room, he sawed through the door between her room and his to create a peephole and proceeded to record her naked in a video that he then shared with the world a few months later. Barrett ultimately served over two years in prison for his crime and, in 2016, Andrews famously won a $55 million civil judgment against both Barrett and the owners and operators of the Marriot for the invasion of privacy she suffered as a result of the incident.[5]

Curiously, however, despite Andrews' legal victory, she continues to suffer injury from the incident to this very day. In particular, her invasion of privacy claims against Barrett and the Nashville Marriot only partially vindicated her interests, as they did little to address or account for the irreparable and accruing harm that came from internet users around the world continuing to view the video.[6] As Andrews poignantly testified at the trial, "It's on the Internet now.... It's going to be on the Internet until I die."[7] Indeed, the video remains widely available online to anyone who puts even a modicum of effort into seeking it out.[8] Among other things, long-established First Amendment principles[9] and the liability immunization granted by section 230 of the Communications Decency Act of 1996[10] make invasion of privacy claims against internet entities who simply further the recording's distribution far more difficult to sustain than those against the individual who made the recording and his abettors.

But if Andrews could possess a copyright interest in the work by virtue of the fact she alone appeared in it, all of that could change. She could have arguably wielded a much more formidable weapon with which to seek relief, as copyright is largely immunized from express First Amendment checks,[11] liability is easier to establish,[12] and damages can add up quickly.[13] Moreover, copyright law provides a series of potent extrajudicial means for enforcement. Specifically, the Digital Millennium Copyright Act (DMCA) conditions its grant of a safe harbor from infringement liability to internet services hosting user-generated content on the condition that, among other things, internet services responding expeditiously to remove any allegedly infringing materials from their network upon receipt of a proper takedown notice from a copyright holder.[14] As a result, without even relying on litigation, a rights holder can frequently have speech that makes unauthorized use of their copyrighted materials (even if it likely constitutes fair use) effectively removed from the online world – something without comparison in the world of privacy torts.

Instead, perversely, Andrews had to *acquire* the putative copyright to the video from the very individual who perpetrated the invasion of her privacy[15]: Michael David Barrett. Records with the Copyright Office indicate that Andrews received the copyright to the video by written assignment (presumably from its listed author, Michael David Barrett) and registered it with the Copyright Office in mid 2011 – some two years after it hit the internet.[16] In other words, she had to cut a deal with Barrett. Until then, for a period of two years, Andrews was legally powerless to enforce copyrights to the video due in large part to the authorship-as-fixation regime, since it was her tormenter, rather than she, who owned the exclusive rights to control reproduction, distribution, and public display of the recording.

Such a strange circumstance is the direct product of the authorship-as-fixation trope that, without compunction, automatically vests copyright wholly in the peeping tom who took the illegal recording without Andrews' consent or knowledge.[17] In this way, copyright law has weaponized what theorist Susan Sontag once called the "camera as phallus,"[18] a mordant reference to the linguistics of photography, which are steeped in the terminology of hunting, as photographers *load*, *aim*, and *shoot* as they attempt to *capture* their subjects/prey. As Sontag argued,

> [t]o photograph people is to violate them, by seeing them as they never see themselves, by having knowledge of them that they can never have; it turns people into objects that can be symbolically possessed. Just as a camera is a sublimation of the gun, to photograph someone is a subliminal murder – a soft murder, appropriate to a sad, frightened time.[19]

For years, the subjects of works, caught by the gaze of the camera's eye, have remained relatively powerless. Once their images are *captured* – to be reproduced, distributed, and publicly displayed in perpetuity – subjects recede from the legal equation. As the government-sanctioned monopoly that superintends the exploitation of creative works, copyright usually vests in the person behind the camera. Thus, it is the depicter, not the depicted, who typically controls further use of the image with the full backing of the state – an uncomfortable result with which Andrews had to contend.

If, however, Andrews had possessed a more plausible argument for copyright ownership at the moment the video leaked online (e.g., she possessed a copyright interest based on her "performance"),[20] she would have had a far greater chance to limit the recording's dissemination.

Ownership of a copyright is no panacea to the problem of online infringement, but it certainly helps. Although it would not wipe the internet completely clean of the video, a broad DMCA takedown campaign, combined with targeted infringement actions, could have reduced the video's reach appreciably. But, for two years after the video's leak, Andrews remained unable to bring a copyright claim to enjoin its further distribution and public display, meaning the video found its way to all corners of the internet universe. So even though Andrews ultimately acquired the copyright by virtue of a transfer, her interest in the video came too late. To this day, despite Andrews' best efforts, the footage remains accessible to anyone in the world with an internet connection.[21]

VISUAL PLEASURE AND THE WHITE MALE GAZE

As illustrated by the plights of Renty and Delia Taylor and Erin Andrews, the authorship-as-fixation doctrine raises significant concerns about the trafficking of visual pleasure because of its propertization of the white male gaze. This latter term, of course, draws from the work of Laura Mulvey, whose celebrated psychoanalysis of film, *Visual Pleasure and Narrative Cinema*, critiqued the way that popular culture – through the visual arts – has depicted the world, and women in particular, through a male gaze. "In a world ordered by sexual imbalance," Mulvey famously argued, "pleasure in looking has been split between active/male and passive/female. The determining male gaze projects its phantasy on to the female figure which is styled accordingly."[22] The male gaze, or masculine point of view, replicates the patriarchal hierarchy of traditional society, thereby normalizing a world of subordination where women are deprived of agency.[23] In the shadow of the male gaze, a woman in front of the camera has no independent existence or value of her own outside of the impact she has on the male either in front of or behind the camera. She exists for visual pleasure – a passive erotic object only significant for how she "plays to and signifies male desire" and how she serves as a spectacle to the male role as "the active one [] forwarding the story, making things happen."[24]

Mulvey's concept of the male gaze has generated widespread discussion in academic discourse, including in the literature on gender-based subordination practices in the law[25] and in neighboring work on racial discrimination.[26] However, the relationship between copyright law and the white male gaze has remained altogether unexplored. While critics have debated the issue of subject/performer copyright in the context of the copyright regime and its specific goals, they have seldom explored the role of our reigning authorship doctrine in exacerbating traditional subordination practices, particularly those along racial and gender lines. As we shall explore, the authorship-as-fixation doctrine propertizes the male gaze by extinguishing the agency of the subject at the moment of fixation and imbuing the (typically male and white) gazer/fixer, through copyright ownership, with the unilateral authority to control representations of (typically female and, often, non-white) bodies. Thus, copyright law, through its authorship rules, gives legal bite to the white male gaze by constructing intangible property rights that facilitate and even augment its authority. In cases ranging from revenge porn and celebrity sex tapes to voyeuristic art and modern photography, this chapter highlights just how the authorship-as-fixation regime has reified the male gaze in the performance arts and translated it into a property right rationalized along traditional binaries of activity and passivity, object and subject, male and female, and white and black.

DEFINING AUTHORSHIP

To understand the problematic relationship of copyright's authorial-vesting rules to the white male gaze, it is first helpful to examine just how the law defines authorship and how we arrived at a position where courts presume, if not dictate, that the authorship of a particular creative work should vest in the individual who fixed it in the tangible medium. The Copyright Act is replete with definitions – after all, section 101 of the Copyright Act provides an exhaustive list, elucidating the specific meaning of all manner of terminology – from such general and fundamental concepts as "derivative work[s]," "public display," and "publication" to such occasionally relevant terms as "gross square feet," "children," and "establishment."[27] But despite the litany of copyright-related terms for which the Copyright Act provides definition, there is a striking omission: the words "author" or "authorship."[28]

Authorship, of course, forms the very basis of our copyright regime. The Constitution's Copyright Clause, which empowers Congress to provide intellectual property protection for creative work, dictates that such rights will vest in "Authors."[29] Not surprisingly, therefore, authorship is repeatedly referred to throughout the course of the Copyright Act. Section 102, for example, provides an illustrative list of various types of works of "authorship."[30] Section 201, to take another example, mandates that, by default, copyright ownership vests in the "author."[31] But neither section gives us a better sense of exactly what constitutes authorship and, just as importantly, who the author might be. And therein lies the rub. For all of copyright's statutory and regulatory authority and its enormous body of interpreting jurisprudence, there is a surprising dearth of analysis on one of its most basic concepts.[32] As David Nimmer has deadpanned, "the constitutional reference to 'authors' went wholly unconstrued for over a century. When the moment came, the [Supreme] Court simply recited from the dictionary."[33] Specifically, the Court elided the task of defining authorship by merely citing to *Worcester's Dictionary* and tautologically positing that an author is "he to whom anything owes its origin; originator; maker; one who completes a work of science or literature."[34]

In the end, while subjects undoubtedly provide innumerable creative contributions to finished works of art in which they feature, courts have traditionally rejected efforts to grant them any kind of authorial recognition, which they typically reserve for the individual fixing the work in a tangible medium. This view is best captured in the Supreme Court's most recent (albeit decades old) language on the subject. In *Community for Creative Non-Violence* v. *Reid* (CCNV), the Court noted that, "as a general rule, the author is the party who actually creates the work, that is, the person who translates an idea into a fixed, tangible expression entitled to copyright protection."[35] This statement, however, begs two rejoinders. First, whence does the Supreme Court derive the doctrine of authorship-as-fixation? And, second, if authorship-as-fixation is "a general rule," what are the exceptions that the Court implicitly acknowledges with its circumscribed language?

On the first question, the Court points us to a single citation to support its view: section 102 of the Copyright Act. However, this reference sheds little light on, or support for, the Court's contention. Section 102 makes no statement about authorship-as-fixation. Instead, it simply states that "[c]opyright protection subsists … in original works of authorship fixed in a tangible medium."[36] If anything, section 102 goes out of its way to avoid saying *in whom* copyright subsists. And it certainly does not imply that copyright vests in the person who actually fixes a work in a tangible medium. Authorship-as-fixation might be one way to read the Copyright Act's vesting of rights, but it is certainly not the only way.

And this leads to the second question: If there are exceptions to the general rule of authorship-as-fixation, one can and should fairly ask why authorship cannot vest in someone else, such as those in front of the camera or those behind the scenes who contributed the creative elements expressed in the fixation. Yet the Court has never provided satisfactory guidance on what circumstances and conditions would warrant the vesting of authorship in such individuals. Indeed, the idea of authorship-as-fixation, although regularly presumed by courts when treating issues of ownership and dictated by the Supreme Court as a general rule, has surprisingly thin legal support. In short, the Copyright Act itself does not appear to dictate a result where only individuals behind the camera can obtain copyright interests.

Although the lack of jurisprudence on such a fundamental matter in copyright law might be surprising, the issue has not received much play until very recently for a number of reasons. First, since the earliest days of copyright law, such ontological questions of authorship have not arisen in litigation because of what we will call the *creation-fixation convergence*. In the past, the very person providing the creative fuel for a copyrightable work was typically the same person who fixed it in a tangible medium. Recall that, at the time of the framing, copyright protection only extended to books, charts, and maps.[37] For these types of subject matter, there was no distinction between those in front of the proverbial camera and those who were behind it. They were one and the same. The writer who came up with the creative storylines and characters, and then gave them life with unique selections of word strings, was the very same person who fixed the word in a tangible medium by way of quill, pen, or typewriter.

However, that began to change with the expansion of copyright law into visual and audio arts. Such subject matter only began to receive federal copyright protection in the past century or so (the latter half of the nineteenth century, in the case of paintings and photographs,[38] and the latter half of the twentieth century, in the case of sound recordings[39]). And, such subject matter often decoupled the act of creation and fixation. Specifically, in these forms of artistic expression, real human subjects often perform in the work, and, other than in the case of "selfies," someone else captures their performances. In paintings and photographs featuring individuals, the subjects contribute to the final product with their positioning, expressions, and other creative choices. In movies, actors contribute to the final product with their delivery, intonation, body language, and myriad other creative nuances. In sound recordings, the people making the actual noise contribute with their syncopations, rhythm, and style. Thus, in the performing and visual arts, not all of the creativity involved in the project lies in the hands of the person behind the camera who is hitting the record button. In fact, much of the creative input comes from individuals appearing in front of the camera. In addition, there is also significant creative contribution from those who may be behind the camera – the make-up artist, the costume designer, the lighting operator, and maybe even the long-suffering assistant key grip.

Second, the advance of digital technology has further highlighted the problem of the creation-fixation gap. In the past, the act of producing commercially viable creative works was largely the province of professionals – the Hollywood studios, the major labels, the big publishers, and other corporate media entities. Such parties use contractual measures to legally preclude any question regarding authorship. As a result, all individuals who worked on a movie, wrote an article, or had a song recorded would have assigned any conceivable copyright interest they might have had in the work to the relevant corporate entity financing the production. Actors would sign contracts that transferred any rights they might have in a motion picture to the studio; sound engineers, record producers, and performers would contract away any rights they might have to the record label; and subjects would sign releases waiving certain rights they might have that would encumber the unfettered use of photographs of them by the photographer.[40]

But, with every member of modern society now armed with a smartphone (featuring a camera) in their pockets and a networked computer at their desks, the tools for the creation, publication, and distribution of copyrighted works to the four corners of the earth are at everyone's fingertips. Consequently, the sophisticated corporation, with its ability to mold the notion of authorship via contract, no longer automatically mediates the terms under which creative works reach the public. The explosion of amateur social media has given us all the ability to record videos or capture images and share them instantly through the world on Facebook, TikTok, Snapchat, X, and Instagram. As a result, the question of authorship has come to the forefront of copyright in previously unappreciated ways.

It should therefore come as no surprise that questions of authorship have permeated numerous recent high-profile legal controversies, from the cases of Naruto, the crested macaque who famously took a selfie,[41] and Cindy Lee Garcia, the performer who received death threats for her appearance in the controversial movie *The Innocence of Muslims*,[42] to the lawsuit involving Terry Bollea, the wrestler professionally known as Hulk Hogan, who famously bankrupted Gawker Media for posting intimate footage of him shot on a hidden surveillance camera.[43] But before examining the way in which authorship issues have played out in contemporary jurisprudence, it is worth examining how the Supreme Court first addressed the issue more than a century ago in a case involving an Oscar Wilde photograph.

THE PROBLEMATIC ARRIVAL AT AUTHORSHIP-AS-FIXATION

The historical exclusion of subjects from the copyright conversation begins with the starting point of American authorship jurisprudence: *Burrow-Giles Lithographic Co. v. Sarony*.[44] As we shall see, courts have read copyright's authorship doctrine in a manner that fetishizes singularity and the control of fixation, resulting in a doctrine of authorship-as-fixation. This doctrine has served us well by promoting the alienability of (intellectual) property rights and market efficiency. But it has come at an expense – both in fealty to copyright's utilitarian goals and to equitable concerns regarding the consumption of visual pleasure and the right to control representations of the human form, with significant resulting implications for equality along racial and gender lines.

In 1865, Congress extended the subject matter of copyright to include the output of a recent invention: the photographic camera.[45] But it was unclear whether Congress had the authority to do so, as the Constitution only authorizes grants of copyright protection to "authors" for their "writings."[46] In 1884, the Supreme Court finally confronted the question of photographic copyrights by considering whether a posed shot of Oscar Wilde taken by Napoleon Sarony involved sufficient human originality to constitute a work of authorship (Figure 1.2). In short, the Court had to ascertain whether photography was more science or art – that is, whether it merely represented an act of mechanical reproduction facilitated by a scientific process involving the transmission of light or it constituted the product of a series of deliberate creative decisions made by a human being.[47] In the pivotal *Sarony* decision,[48] the Court concluded the latter, thereby affirming the extension of copyright protection to the then-new technology of photography.

But besides deciding the issue of whether photography constituted a work of authorship, *Sarony* seemingly did something else altogether: it vested the copyright to the particular image in question to the photographer – the individual *behind* the camera. In 1884, such a conclusion was by no means foregone and the Court could have identified significant creative contributions from a variety of sources. For example, authorship could just as well have vested in the person *in front of* the camera. After all, "self-proclaimed aesthete" Oscar Wilde added key expressive elements to the photograph at issue with his carefully constructed persona, expression, and "trademark look with his head resting on his hand."[49] In addition, there were other individuals behind the scenes who possessed viable claims to authorship of the photograph in question. Benjamin Richard, Sarony's long-time cameraman and collaborator, actually clicked the shutter and, in the process, contributed "creative choices in the precise timing to click the shutter, the angle of the shot, the frame, the focus, the distance from the subject, [and] the centering of the subject."[50] But the Court seems to overlook this fact through an implicit application of the work-made-for-hire doctrine (which had not been fully expressed at the time) by vesting the copyright to labor's output in the hiring party (in this case, Sarony). And it is entirely possible that an unknown make-up artist and costumer helped set out the distinctive compositional elements of the scene, which featured tapestries, fur, and a carefully mounded rug on which Wilde rested his foot.

Yet the Court did not consider these alternative sources of authorship at all. As Christine Haight Farley points out, it is "reasonable to question why the Court had chosen not to locate authorship in other practices" besides the directorial activities of the photographer.[51] The answer, at least in part, may come from a key fact established at the outset of the opinion: Wilde and Sarony had expressly contracted away the issue (at least vis-à-vis each other) and entered into an agreement that specifically deemed Sarony, and not Wilde, the "author, inventor, designer, and proprietor of the photograph."[52] The existence of this contract – long overlooked by readers of the case – is critical for at least two reasons.

First, the contract precluded consideration of Wilde's authorial role. Thus, while subsequent observers and courts have frequently read *Sarony* as vesting authorship in the person behind the camera, it says nothing of the sort. Instead, the court merely considered whether photographs were works of authorship coming within the scope of the Constitution's Copyright Clause.

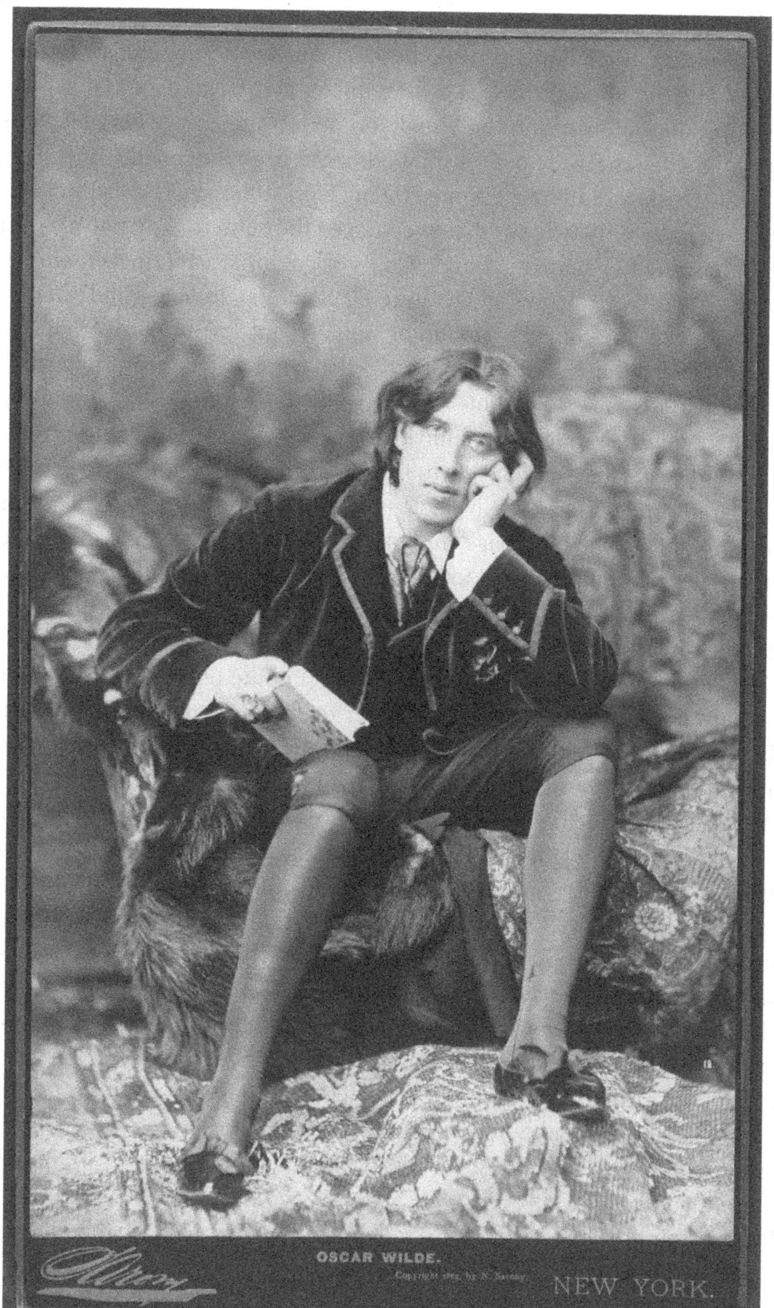

FIGURE 1.2 Portrait of Oscar Wilde (1882) by Napoleon Sarony

Second, Sarony and Wilde's contract, which settled the matter of authorship *ex ante*, suggests the uncertainty surrounding that question otherwise, as various parties, including the photographer and the subject, may have made viable claims to authorship. After all, works in the visual and performing arts, where creation and fixation might diverge, were entirely new additions to copyrightable subject matter.

That said, *Sarony* did provide some guidance on authorship by shaping the concept in manifestly unitary terms that encouraged the conferring of rights in a single master mind: "***he*** to whom anything owes its origin; originator; maker; ***one*** to who completes a work of science or literature."[53] *Sarony*'s "master mind" heuristic,[54] which epitomizes the romantic notion of "solitary authors" birthing original works "ex nihilo through their intellectual labors"[55] that pervades our jurisprudence,[56] has, in turn, led courts to bestow rights automatically in the one who fixes the work in a tangible medium. While many individuals can appear in front of the camera or assist in wardrobe, scene-setting, and make-up behind the scenes, the fixer is usually singular – only one person literally clicks the button on the camera. The fixer is also readily knowable, since the image (in both the development processes of yore and the instant production process of today) usually remains with him or her – thereby rendering identification of authorship more facile. Crediting norms also favor the fixer as his or her identity is usually memorialized. So although a contract precluded the Court in *Sarony* from considering the subject of the photograph as the author, it is perhaps not surprising that we have (over)read *Sarony* as announcing a default standard vesting copyright in the person behind the camera – a move that triggered a century-long move toward the conflation of authorship and fixation.

A century later, the High Court obliquely touched upon the vesting of authorship once again, but again served up little real guidance. In CCNV, the Court offhandedly noted that, "[a]s a general rule, the author is the party who actually creates the work, that is, the person who translates an idea into a fixed, tangible expression entitled to copyright protection."[57] But while this language seemed to indicate that authorship usually vests in the person who fixes a creative work in a tangible medium, it came with little discussion or authority for the proposition.[58] Just as importantly, the equivocating statement left open the door for instances where copyright would not vest in the fixer. The circumstances that would support such a tantalizing possibility remain shrouded in mystery, however, as the Court gave us no understanding whatsoever as to what conditions might call for a deviation from the general rule.

The 2014 controversy involving Cindy Lee Garcia's role in the movie *The Innocence of Muslims* provided a high-profile opportunity to apply CCNV's guidance and resulted in a holding that is the apotheosis of the authorship-as-fixation doctrine. In the suit, actress Cindy Lee Garcia sought to enjoin Google from continuing to make the movie *Innocence of Muslims* available on YouTube.[59] Garcia had a small role in the movie, which producers had spun to her as a breezy Arabian adventure (under the obfuscating working title *Desert Warrior*) when, in fact,

Innocence of Muslims was an unabashed polemic indicting Islam.[60] To make matters worse, the movie's director took Garcia's performance – solicited under false pretenses – and overdubbed it so that she appeared to be asking such things as "Is your Mohammed a child molester?"[61] Understandably concerned about the grave threats to her life she began to receive when the movie's thirteen-minute trailer was distributed on YouTube and a *fatwa* issued against her, Garcia turned to copyright law to make her condemnation of the movie known and to limit its distribution.[62]

For a time, Garcia's gambit succeeded. Sympathetic to Garcia's troubling plight, the initial 2014 Ninth Circuit opinion by Judge Alex Kozinski recognized Garcia's authorial interests in her performance,[63] which, as a creative work of authorship fixed in a tangible medium, met threshold copyright requirements.[64] Furthermore, Garcia had not granted the filmmakers license to use her performance in the manner embodied in the final cut. As a result, to Kozinski, *Innocence of Muslims* infringed Garcia's copyright interests, and she had the right to enjoin further distribution of the versions featuring her.[65]

It would be difficult to overstate the unadulterated disgust that this decision provoked on seemingly all sides of the copyright spectrum. The opinion was roundly condemned as "truly awful,"[66] "butcher[ing] copyright law," "wrong on the law, terrible for Hollywood, even worse for the Internet, and doesn't even make things right for the poor actress,"[67] and "incredibly troubling."[68] In short, critics suggested that, if it were left standing, the decision would doom our copyright system.

All of these criticisms precipitated the unthinkable: an unholy alliance of two of the Ninth Circuit's most powerful lieges, Hollywood and Silicon Valley. Though at diametric odds over copyright law for much of the past two decades, members of the former (major broadcasters, news organizations, and other media companies) and the latter (Adobe, Kickstarter, Tumblr, Twitter [now X], and Pinterest) joined forces to overturn the decision. No less than twenty-three amicus briefs were ultimately filed.[69] Motion picture studios abhorred the decision because it opened up the ability of everyone involved in a production to make a claim to a copyright interest in it. Internet companies detested the opinion because of how it fractured rights, thereby threatening to increase, by an order of magnitude, claims of infringement against them. And in the end, an *en banc* panel resoundingly reversed the initial Ninth Circuit decision, with a near-unanimous opinion that contained only a single dissenting vote: Kozinski's. In its decision, the panel rightfully expressed reservations about a potential future dominated by "'copyright cherry picking,' which would enable any contributor from a costume designer down to an extra or best boy to claim copyright in random bits and pieces of a unitary motion picture."[70] As even Kozinski admitted, recognition of Garcia's independent copyright interest in (parts of) the final cut raised the specter that rights to any creative enterprise with multiple contributors could "quickly become entangled in an impenetrable thicket of copyright."[71]

That said, despite its flaws, the original *Garcia* decision was not without its merits. Specifically, it raised fundamental questions about copyright's buggy treatment of authorship – serious queries entirely ignored by the *en banc* panel and long absent from the copyright discourse. Indeed, despite its troubling aspects, Kozinski's opinion had a great deal of value – something lost in the shuffle to condemn it wholesale.

As Kozinski argued, the *en banc* panel's conception of authorship and its derogation of subject copyrights "artificially shrinks authorial rights by holding that a performer must personally record his creative expression in order to retain any copyright interest in it."[72] Long hinted at in claims brought by performers, including actors, interviewees, porn stars, photographic subjects, and musicians, the idea of authorship-as-fixation had now become the official law of a circuit for the first time, making it an express requirement that an author must fix her own creative output (or, at the very least, play a substantial role in the act of fixing) to obtain a copyright interest in it.[73] But such a position conflates copyright's fixation requirement[74] with copyright's authorship requirement and creates an entirely new requirement – absent from the Copyright Act – that mandates the author do the fixing.[75] If our copyright system serves utilitarian interests and rewards creative activity – as the Constitution states[76] – then it makes no sense to preclude the rewarding of creativity from anyone (including the subject) other than the fixer. Meanwhile, demanding that the author of a work and its recorder necessarily be one and the same also elevates form over function and threatens to allow minute and seemingly irrelevant procedural differences to trigger wildly different outcomes. For example, if Garcia had incidentally recorded herself on a smartphone while practicing for her shoot, she would have fixed her performance in a tangible medium and likely earned a copyright therein. She could then use that copyrighted work to argue that the makers of *Innocence of Muslims* infringed the recorded performance when they created an unauthorized derivative version in their final cut.

Yet the concept of authorship-as-fixation is not at all dictated by the Copyright Act, which is silent as to whether creative input from performers in front of the camera or even nonfixers behind the camera can give rise to authorial interests.[77] Similarly, the Supreme Court has only generally embraced the concept of authorship-as-fixation.[78] Nevertheless, by virtue of the *en banc* holding in *Garcia*, it is now a general rule in the "Hollywood Circuit."[79] While not every circuit has adopted such a hardline view and there are still pockets of authority to support claims that nonfixers should also enjoy copyright interests for their creative contributions,[80] vindication of subject rights through the prism of copyright remains an uphill battle, at best. After all, in modern copyright jurisprudence, the federal courts have usually vested authorship in the person controlling the equipment that fixes a creative work in a tangible medium – the producer/engineer on a musical recording, the director behind the camera, and the photographer taking the snapshot.[81] And the widespread conception of authorship as fixation raises significant concerns about how we vest rights to creative works. Along with its absence in the text of the Copyright, it promotes troubling results. By betraying the utilitarian logic of our copyright regime, the conflation of authorship with fixation harms efficiency. And, while the doctrine appears neutral on its face, its racial and gender-based valence in practice raises vital egalitarian concerns.

EVERY BREAKING WAVE: CREATIVE EFFORTS IN FRONT OF AND BEHIND THE CAMERA

The authorship-as-fixation doctrine makes for problematic public policy in light of the goal of promoting progress in the arts. Indeed, it is not uncommon for the person in front of the camera to contribute far more, creatively speaking, to the ultimate expressive work captured in a tangible medium than the person behind the camera. In these instances, the intellectual coherence of the default rule of authorship-as-fixation can begin to unravel.

Consider an example from the world of musical performance. On August 22, 2010, at a concert in Helsinki, U2 performed a previously unrecorded song, *Every Breaking Wave*, before a packed house at Olympic Stadium.[82] A random fan made an audiovisual recording of this first-time performance on his iPhone and later uploaded it to YouTube, where it was viewed almost a half million times.[83] The authorship-as-fixation doctrine would dictate that all copyright interests in the work would vest in the fan. Of course, one could question just what constitutes "the work." It could simply be the fan's particular visual selection of angles from which to view the band. But the recording also captures a song that had never been fixated before and, without a doubt, the fan captured that ephemeral combination of sounds in a tangible medium. And although the fan exercised precious little creativity in so doing, he arguably met the minimal "modicum of creativity" threshold required under the law[84] by choosing the equipment, audiovisual settings, beginning and end point, capture angles, and location to make the recording. Thus, one might argue that the fan is no different than the studio owner who uses her recording equipment to capture the performance of a band and earns the copyright thereto as a default rule.

If copyright in the recording does, in fact, vest in the fan, copyright's default rules begin to raise some significant concerns. After all, the fan's copyright could potentially have far reach.[85] Absent any contractual obligations to the contrary, the fan might enforce his copyright interest in the work against any third party – perhaps even against the band itself as punishment for its ill-fated *Songs of Innocence* album, which forcibly populated itself on the world's iPhones on December 9, 2014.[86]

It is the absence of the normal creation-fixation convergence that gives rise to the problems in this scenario. Under ordinary circumstances, the fan's fixation of the musical performance at a concert would constitute an infringing "bootleg" recording – an unauthorized reproduction/derivative version of the copyrighted musical composition[87] – and would enjoy no copyright protection.[88] But in this instance, there is no musical composition with copyright protection because it has (presumably) never been fixed in a tangible medium. As a result, there is presumably nothing illicit about the "bootleg,"[89] and it will enjoy its own independent copyright protection. In fact, one might reasonably wonder if, so long as the recording is captured with sufficiently good technology (something eminently possible these days), the fan can now exploit the recording with unfettered rights to reproduce, distribute, and license it for global use.[90]

If we take a step back from the facts and return to basic principles, we quickly see that the relative balance of the creative contributions by the various parties to this "work" make such a result almost absurd. The random fan's minimal contributions to creative aspects of the recording pale by comparison to those of Bono and the Edge, whose singing and guitar playing form the ingenuity captured in "the work." In short, the fan appears to be nothing more than a mechanical scrivener of Bono and Edge's "creative spark." It therefore seems strange (at best) to vest the copyright interest in the fan rather than the band. Of course, as Rebecca Tushnet has argued, "manageability rather than creativity is generally the basis for the rights allocations and distinctions copyright law makes,"[91] and perhaps things are that way for good reason. But with the U2 example, we begin to see the manageability arguments break down, thereby suggesting that such default rules for copyright vesting could have perverse consequences in certain situations.

Such concerns have not gone unnoticed. In fact, they led to the passage of a federal anti-bootlegging scheme in § 1101 of the Copyright Act, which codified the Uruguay Round Agreements Act § 512 in 1994. § 1101 provides a limited, albeit significant, exception to the default rule of authorship-as-fixation. Specifically, it provides musical performers the equivalent of a copyright interest in their unfixed acts and enables them to bring an infringement claim, with copyright remedies, against anyone who, without their authorization, fixes their act in a tangible medium and seeks to publicly distribute that recording.[92] Thus, under § 1101, the fan recording in the U2 example would constitute an infringing work and, therefore, would not enjoy its own copyright protection.[93]

§ 1101 represents a sharp and fundamental departure from the authorship-as-fixation assumptions that seem to permeate the rest of copyright law. But the provisions of section 1101 are carefully circumscribed, applying only to musical performances.[94] As a result, they do not cover the myriad endeavors of so many others who find themselves in front of the camera contributing creatively to works of authorship. Such individuals might include innovative skateboarders whose daring rides or epic wipeouts (captured by third parties) could end up as profitable viral videos on YouTube; professional lecturers, such as academics, whose presentations are potentially subject to unauthorized exploitation by for-profit companies; amateur sexual performers whose bedroom fireworks, as recorded by others, can generate significant audiences and revenues for "NSFW" websites; interviewees whose colorful and thoughtful musings attract eyeballs for newspapers, magazines, and other media outlets in which they are featured; and numerous other forms of creative output (much of which has economic value) where there may not be a creation-fixation convergence. Section 1101's narrow reach necessarily begs the question as to whether anything – besides Congress's solicitude to targeted lobbying efforts by powerful interest groups – can justify the fact that only musical performers, and not other such creatives operating in front of the camera, enjoy an exception to the authorship-as-fixation rule.

Indeed, there are numerous instances where the creative efforts of those in front of the camera clearly exceed the creative efforts of those behind it. For example, with each passing year, surveillance technologies monitor and record a greater percentage of our daily existence. Besides the human rights and privacy issues that such practices raise, the emergence of the surveillance society has also produced some intriguing copyright issues. These issues have further challenged the propriety of a strict authorship-as-fixation rule.

In 2012, with the quiet help of his Silicon Valley benefactor, Peter Thiel,[95] Hulk Hogan launched a multi-pronged legal attack against Gawker Media when the entity published excerpts of a leaked video of Hogan having sex with the wife of his best friend, Bubba the Love Sponge, who had recorded the footage via a surveillance camera he had set up in his home. While the main focus of Hogan's claims rested on the invasion of privacy, as part of a strategy to obtain a preliminary injunction against Gawker,[96] Hogan's legal team added a copyright infringement claim to the federal portion of his lawsuit.[97] Of course, to bring such a claim, a plaintiff needs standing and, in the copyright context, that means demonstrating either ownership of or beneficial interest in the protected work.[98] Formalities-wise, the quickest way to claim copyright ownership is to prove that the plaintiff is the author. Hogan could have made such an argument, though existing precedent and the authorship-as-fixation doctrine would make such a position an uphill battle. So, instead, he obtained the copyright from Bubba the Love Sponge through a transfer of interests via written agreement.[99] And, although the court ultimately rejected Hogan's request for a preliminary injunction (and Hogan subsequently dropped his infringement claim), the court never addressed the threshold issue of whether Bubba the Love Sponge was, in fact, the author of the work and whether he had any rights at all to grant to Hogan.[100] Indeed, under the authorship-as-fixation regime, it was simply assumed that he did since he superintended the fixation of the work in a tangible medium.

But further analysis raises serious questions about Bubba's ability to claim authorship and an initial vesting of the copyright interest to the videotape. First, one might argue that there was no copyright interest in the tape at all. After all, the tape was effectively no more than surveillance footage taken by a pre-positioned indiscriminate recording device with little, if any, human intervention involved in the actual reduction of the "work" to a tangible medium.[101] Although copyright's originality requirement is hardly demanding, it does require some level of human creativity, and there appears to be a distinct lack of it in the production of the video – at least behind the camera. Specifically, Bubba the Love Sponge did little, if anything, to contribute to the creative qualities of the film. He simply owned the camera, which recorded whatever came within the view of its lens, as it pointed in a stationary position from the corner of the room. Since the film was simply the product of a passive, fixed surveillance camera, Bubba made no real creative, authorial choices – certainly none of the "disposition, arrangement or representation" flowing from "arranging the subject so as to present graceful outlines, arranging and disposing the light and shade, [or] suggesting and evoking the desired expression"[102] that the *Sarony* court deemed to be the *sine qua non* of photographic authorship.

This leads to a second issue. While it might be difficult to argue that Bubba contributed in any meaningful creative way to the video, both Hulk and Bubba's (now former) wife, Heather Clem, certainly seem to have done so with their vital role in all of the video's proverbial thrills, spills, and (quite literally) bellyaches.[103] Without delving too deeply into the particular artistry involved all around, Hogan and Clem contributed original (though admittedly banal) dialogue and performed coital hijinks of the most mundane order. While Fellini's 8½ it was not, their creative efforts at least appeared to exceed the meager legal threshold and those of the putative author, Bubba the Love Sponge.

In the end, the Hulk Hogan sex tape illustrates the ways in which the authorship-as-fixation can break down. At a minimum, it calls into question whether fixation of copyrightable subject matter should always generate a copyright interest and, if so, why it should not vest in the performer, whose creative efforts sometimes exceed that of the person superintending the fixation. Indeed, such a result was bemoaned by Pamela Anderson when her leaked 1990s sex tape with Tommy Lee became the foundation of *Pam & Tommy*, a limited-edition series that aired on Hulu in 2022. The show enjoyed great commercial success and received numerous Emmy nominations. But, it triggered a debate about profiteering on trauma when Anderson revealed that the incident remained "very painful" to her and that the series had proceeded without her consent (but, notably, with the blessing of Tommy Lee).[104]

AIN'T NO MONKEY BUSINESS: NARUTO THE MACAQUE ON ART, ARTIFICE, AND AUTHORITY

Strict application of the authorship-as-fixation rule does not merely elevate form over function in copyright's authorship doctrine and ignore the significant creative contributions of subjects to artistic imagery; it can also lead to strange, if not absurd, results, including in the arts. Consider the case of wildlife photographer David John Slater and Naruto, the Celebes crested macaque living on the Indonesian island of Sulawesi. In 2014, Slater was responsible for capturing a series of evocative 'selfie' shots of Naruto playfully vamping for the camera (Figure 1.3). When images of Naruto went viral, Slater and his representatives sought to enforce copyrights to the works. But, to Slater's surprise, Naruto struck back.

FIGURE 1.3 Portrait of Naruto the Crested Macaque (2014) by Naruto the Crested Macaque

Through his Next Friends – nonprofit People for the Ethical Treatment of Animals and primatologist Dr. Antje Engelhardt[105] – Naruto sued Slater, claiming that he, and not Slater, authored the selfies and owned the copyrights to the images and that Slater's unauthorized commercial exploitation of the images constituted copyright infringement. After all, Naruto had fulfilled all the criteria needed for a human being to earn copyright protection in the selfies and had literally fixed the work by clicking the camera.[106]

Ultimately, deferring to the view of the Copyright Office, which had expressly rejected the possibility of nonhuman authorship in its official Compendium,[107] a federal district court dismissed the case[108] and the Ninth Circuit affirmed.[109] But the incident garnered widespread media coverage by triggering a conversation that lay at the intersection of animal and property rights and raising important questions about subject rights. After all, in these remarkable images, Naruto seemed profoundly aware of his audience.

Meanwhile, if one put aside Naruto's place in the animal kingdom, the authorship-as-fixation regime would have vested the image copyright in Naruto for snapping the shot himself. But such a result seems to betray the creative contributions of Slater to the final work, which was a product of Slater's own design and fulfilled his vision to communicate the agency, acuity, and sentience of macaques in a striking visual.[110] Slater therefore had no compunction about claiming ownership of the image copyrights because, in his view, he was the "master mind" of the work. Drawing on his applied knowledge from long periods working with the macaques, he had engineered the shot[111] and made numerous critical artistic choices, including those pertaining to "camera lens width, positions and settings (e.g., predictive autofocus, motorwind, and flashgun)."[112] These elements – from luring the subject to controlling the lighting, shading and positioning – seem to echo the very creative contributions upon which the *Sarony* decision rested authorship.[113]

Even if he had not depressed the shutter button, Slater provided critical creative contributions to the final work. But, absent reconsideration of the authorship-as-fixation doctrine, we are left with the unusual result that the selfies – creative works fixed in a tangible medium – may have ***no copyright at all***. Naruto apparently cannot enjoy any copyright interest since he does not belong to the correct species, and Slater cannot enjoy any copyright interest since he did not click the magic button. This is an unusual result for a series of photographs that were among the most captivating and creative images taken in recent years.

INFRINGING ONESELF: THE RISK IN MAKING USE OF ONE'S OWN IMAGE

The authorship-as-fixation doctrine has also led to troubling results in cases where individuals face suit for infringing photographs of themselves. In recent years, federal courts have been inundated with lawsuits brought by the paparazzi against various celebrities, including Justin Bieber, Ariana Grande, Gigi Hadid, Khloe Kardashian, Nicki Minaj, Emily Ratajkowski, and Jessica Simpson, for posting photos of themselves on social media.[114] Emily Ratajkowski's experience illustrates the typical dynamics at play. In 2019, after she published an Instagram post containing a photograph of her taken on the New York streets, the paparazzo who captured the image sued her for copyright infringement.[115] These suits take advantage of the availability of statutory damages to savvy rights holders who systematically register their copyrights. But despite facing up to $150,000 in liability,[116] Ratajkowski fought the allegations for a time, though the case ultimately settled.[117]

While there is no doubt that celebrity postings of these images constitute technical infringements under existing law – they are, after all, unauthorized reproductions, distributions, and public displays of a copyrighted work without permission from the rights holder – they do raise the question of whether such uses should constitute fair use or whether pursuit of such claims is ultimately in the interest of rights holders themselves. After all, vindicating such claims in the federal courts could turn into a myopic move that may generate some short-term profits at the risk of issuing case law that ultimately enervates the scope of photographer rights by putting sympathetic instances of unauthorized use before judges. For example, Ratajkowski used the paparazzo shot – which was captured on a public sidewalk as she placed a large vase of flowers to cover her face from an unwanted intrusion by the paparazzo himself – since, with the "bouquet as shield[,] … I liked what it said about my relationship with the paparazzo."[118] By giving rise to potentially unfair results, cases such as Ratajkowski's raise equitable concerns about the unilateral vesting, in the fixer, of copyrights to works featuring human figures, particularly when there is no inkling of subject consent. At the very least, such situations suggest more capacious readings of the fair-use or implied-license doctrines. More broadly, they threaten to bring authorship-as-fixation to the breaking point. As Ratajkowski reluctantly concluded in the midst of this problematic state of affairs, "I have learned that my image, my reflection, is not my own."[119]

That said, some litigants have found potential ways around such liability – authorship-as-fixation doctrine be damned. But the results of these cases raise only further doctrinal questions. When a paparazzi agency sued noted Italian fashion house Moschino, its creative director (Jeremy Scott), and singer Cardi B for publishing a photo on their respective social media sites of Cardi B wearing a Moschino/Scott dress on the streets of New York,[120] the defendants, through their counsel of record (which included the author of this book), fought back. Even though she was the subject matter of the image, Cardi B could not claim a copyright interest in the photograph. But someone else – or, rather, something else – could: Moschino/Scott's dress.

The particular frock in question was no ordinary vestment; entitled *When Spring Is in Bloom*, it was an original Jeremy Scott design that featured a whimsical arrangement of stylized flowers affixed to the outer garment and, as such, its sculptural elements enjoyed copyright protection as a work of applied art and pursuant to the Supreme Court's decision in *Star Athletica, LLC v. Varsity Brands, Inc.*,[121] which widened the ability of creators to create copyrights for clothing designs. So Moschino and Scott registered the copyright to the work with the Copyright Office and then promptly filed a counterclaim against the agency and the photographer, claiming that the image constituted an unauthorized derivative work that reproduced the garment without permission of the copyright holder.[122] Since unauthorized derivative works enjoy no copyright protection, no matter how much additional creativity they may contain,[123] such a finding would both doom the agency's lawsuit and preclude its ability to make infringement claims against the rest of the world. Additionally, the agency and photographer would also face potential liability for copyright infringement themselves. Not surprisingly, the claims against Moschino, Scott, and Cardi B were dismissed with prejudice shortly thereafter.[124]

If anything, the machinations in the Moschino/Scott lawsuit revealed some uncomfortable, if not bizarre, results dictated by authorship-as-fixation. To wit, if you photograph individuals without permission, you can sue them if they post that image on their social media. However, if you photograph an inanimate object (that may have some copyrightable portions) without permission, you might lose your copyright and also face claims of infringement for exploiting the work. Subjects, it would seem, may have fewer rights to control their representation than some inanimate objects.

THE BLURRED LINES OF SUBJECT RIGHTS: RICHARD PRINCE'S *NEW PORTRAITS*

The loss of agency triggered by the authorship-as-fixation doctrine is widely felt. Consider the most recent legal controversy involving Richard Prince, the copyright bête noire of the art world. In 2013, Richard Prince won a seismic victory in federal court by prevailing against infringement claims brought by photographer Patrick Cariou, whose Rastafarian images Prince had taken, altered (including by painting "lozenges" over the faces of the subjects), and combined with other appropriated art to form pastiche compositions.[125] In the case, *Cariou* v. *Prince*, the United States Court of Appeals for the Second Circuit deemed Prince's works largely transformative and, as such, fair uses immunized from infringement liability.[126]

Emboldened by *Cariou*, Richard Prince doubled down on the unauthorized use of copyrighted materials with the release of his *New Portraits* series, which turned Prince's attention to social media and self-representation in digital frontiers. For each work in the series, Prince usurped a provocative (and often sexual) image posted on Instagram and, without permission from the original authors, blew the photographs up to "absurd proportions,"[127] adding only a footer with his own cryptic reactions – which one litigant characterized as "gobbledygook nonsensical comments"[128] – posted through his Instagram account, richardprince4. *New Portraits* enjoyed a successful exhibition at the Gagosian Gallery and the works sold for as much as $100,000 each.[129]

Not surprisingly, Prince faced a storm of protests and new allegations of liability. He naturally drew the ire of photographers for his misappropriation of their copyrighted images, and some of them even pursued formal infringement claims, despite his victory in *Cariou* v. *Prince*.[130] After all, Prince had reproduced their images – in whole, without authorization, and with only minimal 'transformative' elements – and had garnered significant financial rewards therefrom. Not surprisingly, litigation followed, with the photographers of the images at issue bringing legal action against Prince. But, just as significantly, Prince's project also raised concerns related to the subjects featured in art: the rights of the objectified, who were seemingly left without legacy remedy and, as a result, had to seek extralegal relief through public pressure.

For example, intrigued by a snapshot that Zoe Ligon, a sex educator and boutique owner, had posted on Instagram of herself donning a red bra, Prince made the image the focus of one of his *New Portraits* – a turn of events that horrified Ligon.[131] In response, Ligon publicly objected, sharing her own personal story as a sex-abuse survivor in an attempt to lobby museums and galleries against the exhibition of Prince's series. As Ligon explained, she had long used sexualized photographs of herself to reclaim control over (the representation of) her body.[132] But Prince's unauthorized seizure and exhibition of Ligon's image (at the Museum of Contemporary Art in Detroit, where she resides) made Ligon feel the trauma of the sexual abuse she had previously suffered all over again. "My being harmed only contributes to the 'art' of it all, and this resembles revenge porn and harassment more than anything else,"[133] she explained.

Although the Museum ultimately offered to remove her portrait from the show, Ligon refused the gesture, demanding instead the cancellation of the entire exhibit, which Ligon decried as "expropriation – the seizure of property for an intended public benefit, except it is the wealthy one-percenter art world which benefits in this case, not the public."[134] Museum Director Elysia Borowy-Reeder declined, arguing that the exhibition encouraged discourse around provocative questions about ownership at the heart of Ligon's concerns.[135]

Another subject featured in Prince's *New Portraits* series offered capitalistic resistance instead. In 2020, Emily Ratajkowski penned a poignant essay, *Buying Myself Back: When Does a Model Own Her Own Image?*,[136] that detailed the sense of powerlessness she had felt helplessly watching men exploit and profit from her image through the years. In the piece, she recounted the sexual assault she had suffered at the hands of an abusive photographer, Jonathan Leder, during an unpaid 2012 photoshoot. Adding to the pain Ratajkowski had endured, Leder proceeded to publish the naked Polaroids he had shot of Ratajkowski that day in three different books. While neither Susan Sontag's theories nor the metaphor of predation was specifically cited by Ratajkowski, those concepts permeated her narrative as she vowed to resist future attempts to exploit her representation. She pledged that she would "own[] the high-art Emily" and "carve out control where she can find it."[137] Just months later, she made good on her promise.

In a shrewd riposte, Ratajkowski got the last laugh against Prince when she auctioned off a digital-only nonfungible token (NFT) version of a photo of her posing in front of the very *New Portrait* in which Prince had featured a Ratajkowski bikini shot (Figure 1.4). In the process, Ratajkowski provided a resourceful meta-response to Prince's unwanted misappropriation of her likeness: she profiteered from an image of herself posed before an image of Prince's work in which she had unwittingly starred. She dubbed her work (and, for that matter, her resistive act of performance art) *Buying Myself Back: A Model of Redistribution*. Her NFT sold through Christie's auction house for a whopping $140,000 – almost twice the cost of Prince's *New Portrait* featuring her, which sold for $81,000 … to none other than Ratajkowski herself.[138]

Unfortunately, not everyone can use the power of the marketplace to resist unauthorized exploitation of their likeness.[139] Without such resources, however, others cannot level the playing field as Ratajkowski has. Moreover, if greater recognition of subject rights were desirable, leaving the preservation of such dignitary interests to the marketplace's invisible hand hardly seems ideal or equitable.

Of course, Ligon, Ratajkowski, and the other subjects of the *New Portraits* are not alone in finding themselves unwittingly objectified by the art world. Frank Benson has come under fire for *Juliana*, a nude sculpture he created from a 3D scanning of artist Juliana Huxtable's body and featured at the 2015 Whitney Biennial. While

FIGURE 1.4 Publicity image to promote the sale of an NFT featuring Emily Ratajkowski posing in front of Richard Prince's artwork impermissibly featuring her

critics praised the work for its celebration of trans bodies,[140] Huxtable notably objected, publicly decrying the sculpture as "A LITERAL EMBODIMENT OF EXPLOITATION I HAVE COME TO HATE IT."[141]

AUTHORSHIP-AS-FIXATION AND THE SURVEILLANCE SOCIETY: TO THE GAZER BELONG THE SPOILS?

In a world where the tools of surveillance lie at everyone's fingertips, the authorship-as-fixation doctrine has powerful and troubling consequences, particularly along gender lines. When individuals become unknowing subjects in works of authorship fixed in a tangible medium, powerful exclusive rights vest in the voyeur. As a result, the ubiquity of panoptic technologies and our reigning vesting rules on authorship have combined to empower the male gaze, giving it the force of property over all those who "are watched." While there is nothing inherently gendered about such surveillance technologies and their use, the implications of a regime that vests rights in *the watcher* rather than in *the watched* are inextricably gendered when such technologies are employed in a society where men are disproportionately behind the camera and female representations constitute the objects of their gaze – a posture celebrated not just throughout cinematic history, as Mulvey explains,[142] but in Western art more generally.[143] As a result, the debate over whether *the watcher* or *the watched* should enjoy authorial rights in captured images becomes an important consideration when evaluating the broader, egalitarian ramifications of the authorship-as-fixation trope. To illustrate this point, consider the legal controversy relating to the work of photographer Arne Svenson.

The Neighbors: Surveillance Art and Copyright in the Panopticon

In 2012, Arne Svenson, a fine art photographer living in New York, embarked on an ambitious new project called *The Neighbors*. From his TriBeCa loft, he surreptitiously took photographs of his well-heeled neighbors – who were visible from Svenson's perch with the assistance of high-powered telephoto lenses intended for bird watching – as they napped, cleaned, and engaged in other mundane activities in their luxury apartments.[144] The provocative results formed the basis of a noted exhibition, commanded significant prices on the art market, and – on artistic, rather than moral, merits – received acclaim.[145] When they learned of their roles in his work, some of the subjects, including Matthew and Martha Foster, sued Svenson, who remained unapologetic about his actions and rebuffed allegations that he had done anything wrong.[146] Since the individuals were visible to the outside world through the transparent glass of their homes, Svenson contended that "[f]or my subjects, there is no question of privacy,"[147] adding, "I am not unlike the birder, quietly waiting for hours, watching for the flutter of a hand or a movement of a curtain as an indication that there is life within."[148]

The exquisite artistry in Svenson's work is unmistakable. There is a naked and unfiltered poignancy to the works precisely because the subjects are completely unaware that they are being watched. In Svenson's defense, he also took some preemptive measures to limit exposure of his subjects' identifying features.[149] "I was stringent about not revealing the identities of the subjects because I was not photographing these people as specific, identifiable personages, but more as representations of humankind, of us," he explained.[150] "I only reveal the turn of the head, the back against a window, the legs under a table. These tiny scenarios and actions reveal a humanness that is unconsciously truthful and tender."[151]

That said, Svenson's anonymizing techniques were not entirely effective.[152] In fact, the face of the Fosters' daughter was visible in at least one photograph and information about her address was made public in information about the project.[153] Furthermore, regardless of the downplaying of personal identity in the photographs, one cannot help but sympathize with the subjects who now unwittingly find an image of themselves captured in an unguarded moment in the privacy of their own home being strewn about in promotional materials for Svenson's exhibits, hanging in a gallery, or on permanent display at some museum or wealthy collector's home. After all, as a society, we regularly send people to prison for being "peeping toms," and the perpetrators of such crimes have not typically captured the fruits of their voyeurism and shared them with the world.[154] Yet, the suit against Svenson was dismissed at the trial court level,[155] a decision affirmed by a New York appeals court.[156] As both rulings reflected, Svenson's reasoned and poignant artistic purpose behind the creation and worldwide distribution of his work gave him a legitimate First Amendment defense that a peeping tom would ordinarily lack.[157]

The Fosters did not raise a copyright claim, however. The state of authorship jurisprudence, which fetishizes the work of the fixer at the expense of those in front of the camera, would make such a claim difficult. But if the authorship-as-fixation doctrine were not as rigidly applied, the Fosters might have had a legitimate claim to a copyright interest in their "performance" as it was captured by Svenson. After all, the initial Ninth Circuit holding in *Garcia* achieved nothing less for the actress who brought the suit. Although the Fosters were not duped like Cindy Lee Garcia, they did find themselves unwittingly (and from the ostensible "privacy" of their own home, no less) captured in works that were commercially exploited and distributed worldwide in a manner that caused them great embarrassment and, potentially, danger. Admittedly, Garcia knew she was giving a performance, while Svenson's subjects were simply leading their ordinary lives. But such a distinction is subverted by Svenson's own characterization of his subjects as "performing behind a transparent scrim on a stage of their own creation with the curtain raised high."[158]

If Garcia had a plausible argument for a copyright interest, then so do Svenson's subjects. And, with such an interest, they would have likely rebuffed any claim that they had given Svenson an implied license or that their creative contributions were made for hire. Specifically, they could have pursued an infringement claim against Svenson and, assuming recognition of their copyright, enjoyed a strong likelihood of success given the general immunization of copyright claims from independent First Amendment scrutiny[159] and the heavy (if not outcome-determinative) presumption against unauthorized use of unpublished works[160] in any fair use defense that Svenson might proffer.[161] In short, performer copyrights would empower the subjects of Svenson's work to have a say in his use of their performances and to enjoin Svenson's work, if they were so inclined – something they could not achieve through privacy law.

While those sympathetic to the Fosters might applaud, such an outcome may not be entirely unproblematic. Giving subjects veto rights over expressive activities raises legitimate concerns about the suppression of basic artistic freedoms. As a result, we must carefully balance the possibility of granting performance copyrights with appropriate respect for First Amendment protections. Moreover, given Svenson's own unquestionable creative input and artistry, he is certainly owed an authorial interest in the photographs – be it full or partial – too.

Of course, a default regime of granting authorship rights solely to the voyeur becomes far more troublesome in scenarios where our voyeur is not exercising credible artistic liberties and makes little in the way of artistic contributions to the ultimate work. The high-profile Erin Andrews case provides just such a situation and speaks to the potentially dangerous consequences of an authorship-as-fixation regime in a surveillance society. By invoking common gender dynamics involving the male gaze and copyright ownership, the case highlights the problems that emerge when our authorship regime automatically rewards voyeurs with a powerful monopoly over the fruits of their criminal stalking activities. It is a dynamic all too common in the production and distribution of sex-related content.

Revenge Porn and the Male Gaze

When one considers the legal controversies involving sex tapes in a broader context, the gender-based consequences of a copyright-vesting regime dominated by the notion of authorship as fixation become clear. Celebrity sex tapes have always garnered attention. But with the ubiquity of smartphones equipped with cameras, the problems surrounding the unauthorized distribution of personal recordings have transcended fame and become a serious concern for private citizens and celebrities alike. For example, several websites have gained notoriety, large audiences, and financial success by serving as repositories for individuals to upload personal sexual recordings and share them with the world.[162] While some amateur sexual content is shot and distributed with the enthusiastic consent of all participants, not all of it is. In particular, jilted lovers and other malefactors bent on vengeance have leaked explicit recordings of their former sexual partners on these sites, often to humiliate and embarrass them.[163]

There is an unmistakable gender-based dynamic to this phenomenon of revenge porn, where victim-subjects (usually women) have found themselves legally impotent to stop public distribution of intimate photographs or videos featuring them (either entirely without consent or in blatant violation of a specific request to keep the materials private) because the copyrights to the leaked materials have vested in their former partners (usually men) who "created" them. Indeed, the Cyber Civil Rights Initiative, the leading advocacy group for victims of revenge porn, estimates that approximately 90 percent of revenge porn victims are female.[164] The internet is forever, and such actions can cause profound personal and professional harm and quite literally destroy the lives of their victims. The historical double standard on sexual promiscuity and the prevalence of practices such as slut-shaming mean that the impact on a young woman who finds her naked body trending on X may be quite different than that on a similarly situated young man.[165]

There are few viable legal remedies afforded to victims of revenge porn,[166] and recent pieces of legislation seem to face significant First Amendment challenges.[167] Thus far, the most meaningful potential relief, meager as it might be in many instances, appears to have come from copyright law.[168] With the DMCA's takedown regime, internet service providers hosting infringing content are strongly incentivized to expeditiously remove or disable access to infringing materials – but only upon specific demand from a rights holder.[169] Thus, such relief is only available to those with ownership of a copyright or an exclusive license thereto.[170] And that is where the victims of revenge porn often hit a brick wall: copyright's authorship-as-fixation doctrine, with its reification of the male gaze, makes reliance on copyright law a nonstarter under many revenge-porn scenarios, where the woman-victim is not in control of the camera that fixed the sexual performance in a tangible medium. Without a colorable claim to being the "master mind" who fixed the sexual performance in a tangible medium, the possibility of pursuing the DMCA's takedown remedies or litigation for copyright infringement falls by the wayside.

By contrast, in celebrity sex-tape controversies, D-listers with colorable copyright claims (i.e., they controlled the camera and actually shot the video) have generally enjoyed relative success in suppressing distribution of racy recordings by making infringement claims. Bret Michaels, for instance, famously enjoined online dissemination of a sex tape featuring him and Pamela Anderson after Internet Entertainment Group claimed it had obtained rights to the recording and would begin making the recording available to members of its "Club Love" subscription service.[171] Michaels had little trouble establishing the requisite copyright ownership over the tape – an instrumental element in his success – because as the maker of the tape, he was deemed the copyright holder.[172] Similarly, Fred Durst recorded his sexual escapades on equipment that he owned and "set up the camera angle and position, turned on the camera, and held the camera throughout the recording of the [v]ideo,"[173] making him the copyright holder by conventional standards conflating fixation and authorship. As a result, Durst filed suit and successfully settled infringement claims against entities distributing the recording shortly after a copy of it leaked online.[174]

Compare the success of men such as Michaels and Durst to the struggles of revenge porn and peeping tom victims, who are often women. Both Michaels and Durst were celebrities who made their sexual conquests a matter of public interest, and they clearly consented to the making of the recordings in question. But because they happened to be in control of the cameras that captured their sexual performances, they presumptively enjoyed copyright ownership and the rights to enjoin unauthorized use of the explicit recordings.

By sharp contrast, stalking and revenge porn victims are typically private citizens who have not even consented to the making of the explicit recordings, let alone their worldwide distribution. In addition, they are often not the ones in control of the camera. Erin Andrews and other victims of peeping toms, for example, are not even aware that they are on film. Revenge porn victims who are aware that they are being recorded have certainly not consented to the works' publication and distribution. Nevertheless, it is the person behind the camera – often the peeping tom or the vengeful ex-boyfriend bent on humiliating his former girlfriend – that owns the copyright under the authorship-as-fixation regime. Erin Andrews had to obtain the copyright by written transfer agreement after presumably striking a deal with her tormentor, Michael David Barrett, who presumptively enjoyed copyright to the recording he made while invading Andrews' privacy. Many revenge porn victims, however, are not able to acquire a copyright to the work, stymieing their best shot at legal relief. In the new-fangled world of intimate videos and privacy invasions, copyright's authorship-as-fixation doctrine appears to disproportionately work to the disadvantage of women over men.

SUBJECTED: GENDER, PERFORMER RIGHTS, AND THE CAMERA

The authorship-as-fixation regime and its failure to recognize performer copyrights have an impact beyond issues related to revenge porn and sex tapes, however. The rights regime also accentuates existing inequalities within professional industries that exploit performative art. For example, consider the gender implications of the authorship-as-fixation doctrine in Hollywood. Ongoing disparities in motion-picture production help contextualize the gender dynamics behind an authorship regime that privileges activities behind the camera over those in front. While women are frequently represented in front of the camera (though still not equally with men),[175] they continue to be shockingly underrepresented behind the camera. As of 2023, women still accounted for just 14 percent of all directors in the top 100 Hollywood productions.[176] The numbers were not much better for all major behind-the-scenes jobs (director, writer, producer, executive producer, editor, and cinematographer), as women occupied just 21 percent of all such positions.[177] And these numbers are, generally, a large improvement from historical norms, where they lay in the single digits.

FIGURE 1.5 1989 *Guerilla Girls* billboard

The Guerilla Girls, a feminist art group, once famously created a poster that wondered, "Do women have to be naked to get into the Met Museum?"[178] (Figure 1.5). Their query, unfortunately, was no whimsical exaggeration. At the time, while 85 percent of the humans depicted nude at the Metropolitan Museum in New York were female, less than 5 percent of the modern artists exhibited at the Museum were women.[179] The pattern repeats itself in a variety of artistic milieus and fields: women continue to find themselves disproportionately in front of the artistic lens rather than behind it, at least in the works most celebrated by the cognoscenti.

The first large-scale study of the demographics of copyright registrations also confirms just how widely claims of ownership skew along gender lines, even among a broader set of works. Robert Brauneis and Dotan Oliar, the study's authors, found that men represented about 80 percent of the listed authors of motion pictures registered with the United States Copyright Office between 1978 and 2012.[180] And, in other areas of copyrightable subject matter, the numbers are not much better, as women are the listed authors of only about one-third of the works registered each year.[181]

By failing to recognize copyright interests arising from creative contributions in the act of performance, we are not merely reducing the economic leverage of performers: we are, in effect, diminishing the economic leverage of women in the industry. By vesting rights exclusively in the fixer, we are not merely empowering those behind the camera: we are, effectively, granting greater agency to men under the aegis of the law.

COPYRIGHT AND THE WHITE GAZE

The conflation of authorship with fixation does not merely have implications along gender lines; it also cuts along other societal schisms. Since the fixer obtains the spoils of creative industry, it is the owner of the equipment or the tools of production, rather than other creative contributors to a work of authorship, who typically enjoy the benefits of authorial designation. Thus, copyright vests in the studio that controls the expensive recording equipment, the photographer who owns the fancy camera, or the director who has access to the set, costly lighting, and filming technology – a series of results that grant intangible property interests to the owners of tangible production equipment rather than creative labor. Admittedly, the recent boom in relatively inexpensive recording and reproduction technologies of all types has softened the socioeconomic inequities of such a regime. But its historical consequences can be seen in a variety of contexts, including along racial lines.

In his seminal work on colonialism, Frantz Fanon introduced the concept of the white gaze, whereby the black body is problematized as something less than fully human, characterized as anomalous and the other, and viewed with trepidation and foreboding. As he poignantly wrote in his classic inquiry on the psychology of racism, *Black Skin, White Masks*,

> [w]e were given the occasion to observe the white gaze. An unusual weight descended on us. The real world robbed us of our share. In the white world, the man of color encounters difficulties in elaborating his body schema. The image of one's body is solely negating. It's an image in the third person. All around the body reigns an atmosphere of certain uncertainty.[182]

By granting an author the right to control depictions of the body[183] captured as part of a creative work, copyright law grants remarkable power to rights holders to both economically exploit the creative products of the body and to determine the presentation of the body. When the vesting of copyright interests cuts along racial lines, it risks propertizing reproductions of non-white bodies and placing them under white control, thereby facilitating a white gaze.

A powerful example comes from the history of the modern recording industry. What K. J. Greene has characterized as "the oral predicate of Black culture"[184] has, in the past, left many African-American artists without copyright law to protect their creative musical endeavors. Driven by rock 'n' roll, the modern music industry saw much of its early success from the unauthorized exploitation of old blues riffs, many stolen directly from unacknowledged and uncompensated African-American folk artists.[185] And it was the authorship-as-fixation doctrine in copyright that gave legal blessing to this wholesale misappropriation.[186] The oral tradition in African-American folk and blues music and the improvisational nature of jazz ensured that a sizeable portion of the historical African-American musical legacy was not fixed in a tangible medium and, therefore, did not enjoy copyright protection.[187] Thus, these works only earned copyright protection when they were fixed by the (usually white) owners of recording equipment who captured the works on early recording devices or re-recorded the works (or versions of them) with white artists.[188] And, with authorship-as-fixation to support them, these appropriators effectively seized the copyright interests to these musical works and reaped the benefits denied to the works' original creators. In short, copyright vested in the author who was defined as the fixer and fixation was not possible without access to vital capital resources, such as the recording and publishing equipment, which remained in the hands of almost exclusively white businessmen. Thus, just as sharecropping resulted in the "pervasive exploitation of agrarian Blacks, despite [its] theoretical race-neutrality,"[189] copyright law did the same with the creator class in the African-American community by rewarding ownership of capital resources and record-keeping over artistry and creative activity. The emphasis on fixation also faces broader criticism for its North-South implications. Emily Behzadi, for example, has called for reformation of copyright's fixation requirement, arguing that it has systematically privileged the rights of imperialists over indigenous populations by providing protection only to fixed works – thereby giving preference to those with the technology to fixate (which, of course, required capital) and disadvantaging traditional cultures.[190]

Thus, despite its ostensible neutrality, the technicalities of our copyright regime exist in a "concrete social milieu"[191] where "not all creators of intellectual property are similarly situated."[192] The privileging of certain modalities of creativity (those fixed in a tangible medium over those that are not) has broader consequences, including vesting powerful rights to control and exploit the body to an authorial class that is all too often not just male, but also white and privileged. In the process, the authorship-as-fixation regime has systematically devalued the creative contributions of individuals from minority racial groups and those from socioeconomically disadvantaged circumstances and has given the white gaze the power (through intellectual property law) to control and exploit non-white bodies.

BLACK LIVES MATTER, #METOO, AND COPYRIGHT'S AUTHORSHIP DOCTRINE

Despite this analysis and the powerful strides of the Black Lives Matter and #MeToo movements in raising public awareness about issues related to the devaluation of Black and female bodies in our legal system, the rights of subjects continue to remain largely absent from juridical discourse. The Supreme Court's splashiest copyright case in years – *Goldsmith* v. *Warhol* (2023) – vividly illustrates this point even though it was decided in the wake of these social justice movements. Shortly after Prince's death, photographer Lynn Goldsmith's attorneys fired off a cease-and-desist letter to the Estate of Andy Warhol and claimed that Warhol's famous 1984 silkscreen prints and pencil illustrations of the singer constituted an infringing, derivative version of Goldsmith's 1981 photograph of Prince, upon which they were indisputably based. After discussions failed to resolve the issue, the Estate sued Goldsmith in 2017 for declaratory relief of non-infringement, claiming Warhol's transformative portraits were protected under the fair use doctrine and that Goldsmith, in waiting more than three decades, had taken too long to raise her claims.[193] Although the district court found Warhol's actions protected under the fair use doctrine,[194] the Second Circuit stunned the art and legal worlds by finding that Warhol's portraits were not entitled to a fair use defense and did, in fact, infringe Goldsmith's photograph[195] – a decision that the Supreme Court ultimately affirmed.[196]

The holding in *Warhol* v. *Goldsmith* has resulted in much consternation, as critics have charged the decision with threatening vital freedoms of expression in the art world and backtracking on, if not outright defying, several decades of jurisprudence that had seemingly embraced a broader reading of fair use that protected the ability of appropriationist artists to engage in transformative use of pre-existing work.[197] Now, creative-rights advocates rue that artists (and, just as importantly, their galleries and other exhibitors and distributors) will fear even getting close to the line, lest they face multi-million dollar infringement liability.

But, perhaps just as importantly, the *Goldsmith* holding raises another threshold issue: if the underlying rights holder to the photograph can come after Warhol some three decades after the creation of allegedly infringing work, what about Prince's Estate? Of course, the *Goldsmith* decision does not address this question, but the equitable argument for the exercise of rights by Prince is seemingly just as plausible as Goldsmith's.[198] Putting the extant law aside, from a creativity perspective, Prince's carefully cultivated look – deliberate, studied, and the result of numerous stylistic decisions by the man himself – interplayed synergistically with his music, inextricably weaving together the image and sound. Goldsmith's artistry was no doubt essential to capturing the indelible expression in the underlying photograph, but so was Prince's. From an economic and cultural perspective, the commercial magnetism and semiotic value of Warhol's work owe as much, if not more, to Prince than Goldsmith.

That said, in the seminal case establishing the transformative-use test used in California to balance First Amendment rights with that state's right of publicity, the California Supreme Court took pains to note, in *dicta*, "we emphasize that transformative elements or creative contributions that require First Amendment protection are not confined to parody and can take many forms, [including] subtle social criticism."[199] It then directly cited Warhol's celebrity portraits as a quintessential example of the type of works that should not give rise to publicity-rights liability.[200] But if the use of Prince's likeness in Warhol's painting is transformative and protected under the First Amendment, it is only fair to ask why the use of Goldsmith's image (which stylistically captures Prince's visage at a moment in time) should not also be deemed so. More to the point, why should the Warhol Estate be immune from litigation from Prince's Estate but face liability from Goldsmith? In a sense, such a state of affairs prioritizes the rights of a second-order creative party (Goldsmith) over both a first-order creative party (Prince) and a third-order creative party (Warhol).

So, while Prince will have no control over the use of his image by either Goldsmith or Warhol, Goldsmith enjoys a panoply of rights over the use of her photograph, which is almost entirely based on Prince's image, regardless of Prince's say; and she has the ability to control Warhol's dynamic reinterpretation of her work as well. Goldsmith is a deeply talented artist deserving of intellectual property protection in her work, but so are both Andy Warhol and Prince Rogers

Nelson. For the former, the creative freedom to grapple with and comment on the world of popular culture remains at stake. For the latter, it is the ability to maintain some say "over the circulation, commodification and meaning of their visual likeness."[201] Yet the issue of Prince's potential rights was wholly absent from any discussion in *Goldsmith* v. *Warhol*. To put it in bluntly reductionist terms, while a White woman may have prevailed over a dead White man in the case, the entire controversy strikingly lacked any discussion about the rights of the dead Black man without whom none of the art at issue would have been possible. That discussion must happen. And when it does, it will require a wholesale reassessment of the way in which our intellectual property regime balances expressive freedoms with the rights of creators, the rights of users, and – although long treated as tertiary – the rights of subjects.

Until then, however, the authorship-as-fixation doctrine will reign supreme, with troubling consequences both for the utilitarian goals of the copyright regime and distributive justice. As we have detailed, the authorship-as-fixation standard reifies the male gaze with vested property rights in the form of copyrights that, with the imprimatur of the state, carry considerable power. The moment of fixation usurps the agency of the subject and all but extinguishes it by granting the (typically male) gazer/fixer copyright ownership. This ownership, in turn, enables the gazer/fixer to wield unilateral authority in exploiting the resulting image of the subject in any way he sees fit and to prevent others from presenting countervailing narratives.[202] The authorship-as-fixation regime therefore vests property rights in the interloper, the penetrator, and the watcher/voyeur. It echoes gender-ridden binaries of passivity and activity as proxies for traditional visions of femininity and masculinity, casting the woman in front of the camera in the role of the subject, the gazed, the spectacle, and the captured (image), and conceptualizing the man behind the trigger as the doer, the "master mind," the author, and, above all, the rights holder. Meanwhile, as the story of the Renty and Delia Taylor daguerreotypes illustrates, the legacy of slavery and long-standing racial disparities in access to the capital and technology needed for content creation have combined with the authorship-as-fixation doctrine to exacerbate imperialist dynamics, allowing non-white bodies to be disproportionally exploited by corporate interests for both entertainment and profit.

While copyright's authorship doctrine may have seemed, at first glance, far afield from the Black Lives Matter and #MeToo movements, a close analysis of the way in which our copyright regime vests exclusive rights over the exploitation of creative content has demonstrated otherwise. The authorship-as-fixation regime has enabled the abstract white male gaze to metastasize into a tangible series of intellectual property rights in a process that empowers masculine and white social control and replicates dominant patriarchal and colonial narratives. As a result, copyright's authorship doctrine has subtly but insidiously caused the disproportionate propertization, commodification, and devaluation of indigenous, colonized, enslaved, and female bodies and their representations, thereby revealing copyright's understated, but profound, role in exacerbating inequality along racial and gender lines. The social justice movements of our time are now grappling with their next steps, seeking to determine where to focus their ongoing efforts for change. Copyright law may represent a surprising candidate for consideration. But it is an important one, as true agency does exist without the ability to exercise control over one's own body and its representations, and true equality cannot exist without legal and social recognition of bodily autonomy, integrity, and dignity.

2

Tick Tick … Boom!

How Copyright's Law of Collaboration and Crediting Privileges Might Over Right

In which we discuss: the origins of pasta and tomatoes, the provenance of a prayer, Virginia Woolf's Anon, General Eisenhower's World War II campaigns, the dirty underbelly of the piratical dark web, the Matilda Effect, Alan Smithee's consistent history of bad moviemaking, and this book's vain author.

LA VIE BOHÈME

In the mid-1990s, the New York Theatre Workshop (NYTW) saw promise in a young composer named Jonathan Larsen. But Larsen's new work, which riffed on an idea by playwright Billy Aronson to take the themes of Puccini's opera *La Bohème* and set it in modern-day New York, needed significant rewriting. So at NYTW's behest, in the spring of 1995, Larson agreed to work with dramatist Lynn Thomson to work on the musical's storyline and to prepare the project for a potential stint on Broadway. They worked "extremely intensively together on the show" through the course of the summer and fall of 1995, in anticipation of an early 1996 opening.[1] By October, they had a new draft of the entire script – one characterized by experts as a "radical transformation of the show."[2] And, in February of 1996, the show opened to rave reviews. Larsen and Thomson succeeded beyond anyone's wildest imagination and the result of those efforts – *Rent* – is one of the most beloved and successful musicals of all time.

But this success story was marred by tragedy. As the movie *Tick Tick … Boom!* famously depicted, Larson died suddenly and unexpectedly of an aortic dissection, just hours after the final dress rehearsal for the musical and right before its premiere to universal acclaim (Figure 2.1).[3] As a result, he never had the opportunity to enjoy his success and appreciate the extent to which his work resonated with millions of people around the world. But the tragedy to Larson and his friends and family was not the only misfortune to come from the show. Less famously, Lynn Thomson also suffered a devastating loss: being written out of history. Thomson, it turns out, never received authorship credit for her work, and, as a result, her contributions to the success of *Rent* are largely invisible to the public, and her efforts are relegated to a mere footnote in the story of the making of the musical.

FIGURE 2.1 Publicity poster for the movie *Tick, Tick … Boom!*; *Netflix*

To be fair, Thomson did not go wholly unrewarded for her work. NYTM paid for her services and she did receive an official billing credit as "Dramaturg." But the relevant contracts relating to her collaboration with Larson were notably silent on the issue of authorship or ownership of copyright interests[4] in the musical and, based on her indisputably significant contributions to the final product, she believed she was entitled to authorial crediting and some of the remuneration that comes with it. So she approached the Larson heirs to reach a deal regarding profit participation and final crediting. But when those efforts failed, she felt that she had no choice but to bring suit claiming co-authorship status and seeking 16 percent of the author's share of the royalties to the work.[5]

Unfortunately for Thomson, her claim to joint authorship was resoundingly rejected, both before a trial court and on appeal. The latter ultimately conceded that, even if Thomson may have made "major" contributions to *Rent*, including verbatim drafting of "significant language" in the work, such contributions would not impact the legal question of joint authorship since Larson did not share in Thomson's desire to be co-authors.[6] Citing the vesting of ultimate decision-making authority in Larson, Larson's formal billing as the sole "author," and his reference to himself as a sole author in third-party agreements, the court found Larson lacking such mutual intent.[7] Since Larson did not regard her as a co-author, the court concluded she could not have been one.[8]

To the uninitiated, this holding may seem unusual. After all, while it acknowledged "major" authorial-like contributions by Thomson, the decision denied her authorship not because of the extent of her creative efforts as part of the final work but, rather, because of how she was (likely) viewed by her (now deceased) co-author. In other words, the outcome of this joint authorship lawsuit came down to intent rather than action and to the relative bargaining power of the parties rather than their relative creative contributions. As a result, a woman whose indispensable efforts secured *Rent*'s success will never have her name associated with it – except as a litigious interlocutor. Legally speaking, therefore, *Rent* is the sole work of Jonathan Larson. This chapter will examine how a court came to that determination and will locate the *Thomson* suit in the broader development of our legal regime's rules on joint authorship and attribution. In the process, we shall reveal the way in which copyright's law of collaboration and crediting has systematically privileged clout over contribution, thereby harming both distributive justice and efficiency in the operation of the creative marketplace.

COPYRIGHT'S QUIXOTIC SEARCH FOR AUTHORIAL SINGULARITY

As a default rule, copyright vests in authors, endowing them with powerful rights of exclusion vis-à-vis the rest of the world – monopoly-like control over certain forms of expression as a reward for their originality and intellectual efforts. However, authorship is not always easy to determine. The process of creation is irretrievably iterative.[9] Additionally, many works are the result of numerous creative efforts by a multiplicity of individuals. But this reality – that creators build on the efforts of predecessors and that creation is often a collaborative process – has long existed in tension with copyright law's romantic conception of authorship, which often attributes creation to the genius of a single person acting *ex nihilo* to bring great art to life.[10] Reflecting this viewpoint, from the earliest days of Anglo-American copyright law, courts have sought to locate authorship in a "master mind," a concept that reflects a Platonic ideal and suggests singularity. But the quixotic search for a "master mind" betrays the conditions of creativity and potentially renders efforts to grant exclusive rights to such a person inequitable.

To understand juridical constructions of the rules of joint authorship and their resulting implications, it is instructive to first consider how courts have grounded the definition of authorship in the search for a "master mind." The term "master mind" entered the copyright lexicon with *Nottage* v. *Jackson*,[11] an English case decided just months before the United States Supreme Court's seminal decision in the *Sarony* case discussed in Chapter 1. In *Nottage*, the Court of Queen's Bench had its first major foray into the world of photographic copyrights, and the *Sarony* court would rely extensively on its holding in the matter.[12] In fact, *Nottage* was the only case law cited in the *Sarony* opinion. As such, its impact on American copyright jurisprudence, and the conception of authorship in particular, is worth further examination.

Nottage was an infringement action brought by George Swan Nottage and Howard John Kennard, the owners of the London Stereoscopic and Photographic Company.[13] Nottage and Kennard claimed that the defendants had unlawfully misappropriated their photograph of the Australian cricket team.[14] The defendants demurred, arguing that Nottage and Kennard could not maintain the action since they were not the authors of the photograph in question.[15] Unlike *Sarony*, *Nottage* did not ascertain the validity of a statute that had extended copyright protection to photography.[16] Instead, it determined who, as between two competing parties, would be the author of the cricket photograph: Nottage and Kennard, on one hand, or their employee-photographer (a certain Mr. Reynolds, whom Nottage and Kennard had sent at their behest to the Oval cricket grounds in Kennington to take a portrait of the Australian national team), on the other.[17] The court chose the latter option.[18] And, in the process, all three members of the panel – Lord Justice Cotton, Lord Justice Bowen, and Justice Brett, the Master of the Rolls – undertook a similar approach to authorship by assigning the role to the individual who, among several choices, ultimately superintended the work's realization. Cotton formulated authorship as vesting in the "master mind" behind the work[19]; Bowen said the author is "the man, in fact, who … is most nearly the effective cause of the representation when completed"[20]; and Brett proclaimed that the author is the person who "effectively is, as near as he can be, the cause of the picture which is produced."[21] By locating authorship in the "master mind," or the person who most plausibly served as the but-for cause of the final work, all three justices seem to take an identical step in their reasoning: that authorship is usually, if not always, singular and the rights associated with authorship generally vest in a sole individual.[22] Bowen even expressly espoused this position, rationalizing that, since the statute used the singular term "author" and the term of protection was deemed to be the natural life of said author, the statute did not envision "the case of an author being more than one person."[23] In short, *Nottage* embraced a romantic vision of authorship that vests copyright in a lone creator.

Only months later, the United States Supreme Court adopted the single "master mind" notion wholesale. As such, *Sarony* formulates authorship in strictly unitary terms as "*he* to whom anything owes its origin; originator; maker; *one* who completes a work of science or literature."[24] Epitomizing the romantic notion of the "solitary author[]" birthing original works "ex nihilo through their intellectual labors,"[25] *Sarony*'s foundational concept of the "master mind" pervades our jurisprudence and "lies at the normative heart of our vision of copyright."[26]

CONSIDER THE TOMATO

At a minimum, the romantic quest to identify the "master mind" behind each work exists in tension with many modalities of creation. A brief digression into the history of cuisine highlights the peril in such a reductionist errand to seek purity in provenance. For example, tomato sauce and pasta are inextricably associated with Italian cuisine, and we typically view both products as integral to any "authentic" old-fashioned Italian meal. But that view is largely misguided. The tomato is indigenous to the New World and did not make its way to Europe until it was brought back by the Spanish in the sixteenth century.[27] In the United States and in many parts of Europe, the fruit was grown only for ornamental purposes. For many centuries, tomatoes were actually considered poisonous.[28] This popular view persisted until the late eighteenth century, when fears receded after such prominent individuals as Thomas Jefferson vouched for the fruit's safety.[29] Meanwhile, pasta was not even known to the city-states that later became Italy until the Renaissance.[30] According to legend, Marco Polo brought noodles to Europe from China.[31] In short, a truly traditional Italian meal would feature neither pasta nor tomato sauce.

The same observation extends to other purportedly "authentic" ethnic cuisines. While noodles come from China, the chili peppers often associated with spicy Szechuan cuisine are not indigenous to East Asia. In fact, it was not until European expansion into the New World that chili peppers made their way from their native lands in Central and South America across the Pacific.[32] Meanwhile, the plantains that now form a staple of Central and Latin American cuisine actually came from South Asia.[33] Potatoes, a quintessential feature of Germanic cuisine, are, of course, a New World discovery and did not make their way across the Atlantic until the 1500s.[34] The same is true of corn, a typical product in "traditional" African cuisines.[35] In short, many of the quintessential ingredients of national cuisines are relatively modern additions.

By the same token, the creation myths we assign to the origins of copyrighted works can be similarly suspect. Indeed, the idea of purity and the notion that one can trace any innovation to a single source are concepts fraught with oversimplification. Just as tomato sauce and pasta are not "authentic" to Italian cuisine, we oversimplify matters when we assign authorship of certain expressions to a single individual. In his seminal work, *The Death of the Author*, published in 1968, Roland Barthes challenged the notion of authorship, positing that the "text is a tissue of quotations drawn from the innumerable centres of culture."[36] Origins are a far more complicated concept than we typically admit. In the words of Christian Stallberg, "It is a common occurrence that intellectual works never originate exclusively from the person that authorship is attributed to. Instead, every author is integrated into the manifold social and cultural contexts from which he steadily borrows. Thus, creating intellectual works always means the appropriation of preceding ideas."[37] A generation after Barthes, digitization of the world's texts is allowing us to quantify just how far astray the mythology of authorial creation may have led us.

SERENITY NOW

To illustrate this point, consider the extent to which the availability of Google Books has radically undermined some of the creation myths that we have long told to guide our attribution practices. After digitizing a huge swath of the published books in human history, Google has made them text searchable, an invaluable boon to researchers for a variety of reasons.[38] But, for our purposes, the most notable consequence of making humanity's literary output text-searchable is how it has begun to undermine the creation myths of copyrighted works. Librarians, historians, and bibliophiles have already used the feature to make some surprising findings about the origins of numerous works.

While using Google Books and some other digital archives, Yale Law School librarian Fred Shapiro recently discovered that the most famous piece of liturgy in the twentieth century, *The Serenity Prayer*,[39] may not have been authored by theologian Reinhold Neibuhr – the man who has historically received credit for the text.[40] Shapiro uncovered various versions of *The Serenity Prayer*'s text published and in use as early as 1936 – at least five years before Niebuhr had apparently claimed its creation.[41] As Shapiro speculates, Niebuhr may have subconsciously adopted the prayer as his own after having come into contact with prior incarnations.[42] Indeed, Shapiro's work led to the unearthing of a number of prior versions of the *Prayer* that existed before the date of Niebuhr's ostensible creation, when the prayer took "final" and "official" form. Like different versions of an edited page on Wikipedia, these iterations of the *Prayer* gradually evolved into the precise verbiage and format of the final product that we know today: "God grant me the serenity to accept/the things I cannot change,/courage to change the things I can,/and wisdom to know the difference."[43] As such, Shapiro's new evidence suggests that the work was collective in nature and that it was crowdsourced in voluntary, educational, and religious circles for a number of years before being popularly attributed to Niebuhr.[44]

The consequences of this finding are not merely trivial; they can have important real-world consequences. If Neibuhr had been inclined to protect his putative authorship and enforce his potential intellectual property rights to the maximum extent possible under the law, the consequences of this creation myth would have been widespread. Neibuhr, as the ostensible author of the *Prayer*, would have been granted a copyright in it, and that copyright could still be in effect.[45] While performance (but not reproduction) of the prayer in the course of religious services might be protected from liability per a limited exemption codified in section 110(3) of the Copyright Act,[46] Neibuhr and his heirs could potentially control use of the *Prayer*, deciding which favored groups might be allowed to use it and which ones might not be. For example, Alcoholics Anonymous – which has adopted the *Prayer* for its twelve-step program[47] – would be beholden to the rights holders for permission to use the *Prayer* at its meetings under all but the most generous readings of section 110(3). Millions who have found solace in the comforting words of the *Prayer* may have been denied its use (or would have had to pay a licensing fee). In short, both formative and expressive identity interests would be impacted. The palliative use of the *Prayer*, and the internal comfort it has given to millions, could be significantly tempered. Meanwhile, its expressive use – its power as a collective benediction that forms a unifying bond, sense of community, and shared purpose among the friends of Bill W. – would be compromised.

The control of religious works through copyright law can allow a third party to dictate aspects of a fundamental and intimate area of personal development – both in the formation of spiritual identity and its expression.[48] In the case of *The Serenity Prayer*, what is likely to have been a work of many individuals – rather than one – has become reified as a work of one individual who, under copyright law, is then given the ability to control use by the many. Concepts of authorship and labor-desert are then elevated above user interests, with potentially profound consequences on the way in which individuals can form and conduct their spiritual lives, celebrate their religious convictions, and develop their theological identities. This scenario is not merely relegated to the realm of the theoretical. In a panoply of cases, religious organizations have (often successfully) sought to enjoin the unauthorized use of their scriptures through claims of copyright infringement.[49] As a result, religious groups have silenced criticism of their doctrines and also effectively quashed the worship activities of splinter groups. With the assistance of the modern copyright regime, religious texts have become truly sacred, with the beatifying power of the law leading the way.

The Serenity Prayer is not unique in its multiplicity of origins. In the parlance of documentarian Kirby Ferguson, who wrote and directed the poignant *Everything Is a Remix* series, creative evolution is – like physical evolution – a process of copying, transforming, and combining.[50] But, instead of the genes of physical evolution, the raw materials for creative evolution are memes.[51]

THE "MASTER MIND" CONCEPT AND JOINT AUTHORSHIP'S MUTUAL-INTENT REQUIREMENT

Despite these realities, however, the search to identify a "master mind" has remained at the heart of our copyright jurisprudence ever since *Sarony*'s indiscriminate embrace of the romantic conception of authorship. Not surprisingly, therefore, the "master mind" trope has played a central role in developing the reigning joint-authorship standard, which makes the possibility of co-authorship exceedingly difficult to achieve. As the case law has evolved, federal courts have generally held that mutual intent is a necessary requirement for recognition of joint authorship (i.e., the possibility that a work may have more than one legal author). Thus, joint authorship cannot occur unless there is express intent on the part of *both* parties to perceive themselves as co-authors and to enter into a co-authorship relationship.[52]

Interestingly, while this position has effectively become the law of the land, the relevant precedent and statutory authority hardly make such a reading of the requirements for joint authorship a foregone conclusion. Ironically, the very jurisprudence upon which we have based our quest for a "master mind" has long abandoned the fetishization of unitary authorship.[53] Among other things, copyright law in the United Kingdom does not require the mutual intent of both co-authors to support a finding of joint authorship,[54] making courts there far more receptive to claims of joint authorship than American courts.[55] Moreover, although the text of our own Copyright Act embraces some sort of intent requirement, it is not necessarily a mutual intent *to co-author*. Specifically, the definition of "joint work" in Title 17 of the United States Code requires that such a work be prepared "with the intention that their contributions be merged into inseparable or interdependent parts of a unitary whole."[56] But this statutory reference to intent could be read in a variety of different ways.[57] Most obviously, it could be interpreted as merely requiring an intent by both parties *to merge* individual contributions together – a process-based conception that would appear, at first blush, consistent with the relevant language's "plain meaning," the universal standard of legislative interpretation. Alternatively, it could constitute an ends-based perception, achieved through the desire to conceive of oneself as a co-author. Or, it could even constitute a legal understanding, achieved through a design to enter into a co-authorship relationship.[58] But, for reasons that seem – at least unconsciously – influenced by traditional notions of what and/or who an author is, the federal courts have arrived on a construction of the "mutual intent" requirement that strongly disfavors joint authorship and effectively vests authorship in the party who, amongst collaborators, possesses the greatest negotiating leverage, regardless of the weight of that party's actual creative contribution.

As a powerful barrier to otherwise viable joint-authorship claims, the intent requirement flows directly from ideations of the author-as-mastermind.[59] With its uncritical embrace of a mastermind-driven, rather than collaborative, narrative about the creative process, "the Romantic view of authorship seems to pervade the operation of copyright's joint authorship doctrine."[60] For example, the Ninth Circuit has expressly manifested its discomfort with the possibility of multiple authorship. In its leading case on joint authorship, *Aalmuhammed* v. *Lee*, the court invokes the romantic conception of the individual author creating ex nihilo by informing us, without any support, that "[t]he word 'author' is taken from the traditional activity of one person sitting at a desk with a pen and writing something for publication."[61] The court then summarily concludes that, while it is

> relatively easy to apply the word 'author' to a novel [or even to the work of] two people who work together in a fairly traditional pen-and-ink way, like, perhaps, Gilbert and Sullivan ... [,] as the number of contributors grows and the work itself becomes less the product of one or two individuals who create it without much help, the word is harder to apply.[62]

The Second Circuit fares no better in succumbing to romantic conceptions of the mastermind. In fact, it has explicitly justified its reading of the intent requirement as necessary to protect "master minds" from hangers-on or lesser talents swooping in and receiving authorship credit. In *Childress* v. *Taylor* – its leading case on the joint authorship doctrine – the Second Circuit held that the requirement of intent is particularly important when "one person … is indisputably the dominant author of the work and the only issue is whether that person is the sole author or she and another … are joint authors."[63] Therefore, we are told, "care must be taken … to guard against the risk that a sole author is denied exclusive authorship status simply because another person render[s] some form of assistance."[64] Notably, the Second Circuit's invocation of the concept of a "dominant author" is entirely novel. As Mary LaFrance points out, the idea of a dominant author "does not appear anywhere in the 1976 [Copyright] Act or its legislative history" and is even "inconsistent with both,"[65] though it certainly reflects the mastermind/romantic view of authorship. Moreover, the court provides us no real reason why sophisticated dominant authors – those who are more visible and credited – would need such a munificent and protective intervention from the state when they are already blessed with superior bargaining power.[66] However, the mastermind rubric of authorial jurisprudence tilts courts toward rejecting claims that fracture copyright ownership.[67] In the process, instead of rewarding originality and artistic innovation by vesting rights in the creative forces behind a work, courts have chosen to vest rights in those with the greatest bargaining power.

POWER AND PRIVILEGE IN THE DEPLOYMENT OF THE MUTUAL-INTENT REQUIREMENT

The reluctance to recognize co-authorship contradicts the realities of the artistic process and the multiplicity of creative contributions to works protected under the Copyright Act. By fetishizing the search for a "master mind" through the adoption of the intent requirement, courts have mutated authorship from a concept serving creative utilitarianism to one subservient to existing power relations. Such a move deserves particular scrutiny. Peter Jaszi, for one, has criticized the "tendency to mythologize 'authorship,'" and the resulting failure "to recognize the foundational concept for what it is – a culturally, politically, economically, and socially constructed category rather than a real or natural one."[68] He therefore calls for a more fulsome inquiry into how the concept of authorship is "deployed."[69] Jaszi implicates the concept's service of broader interests through his pregnant use of the word "deploy" to reference the problematization of authorship in our jurisprudence.[70] In the process of defining joint authorship, courts have imputed an intent requirement that threatens to give dominant collaborators "the power to unilaterally 'will away' joint work status by forming the subjective intent to deny joint authorship to other collaborators."[71] Entities and individuals with superior bargaining power will typically preempt the possibility of such co-authorship claims via contractual means, by having weaker parties sign work-made-for-hire agreements or assignments.[72] But, even when "dominant" authors (often negligently) fail to take such steps, courts have protected them from a loss of full control over collaborative works with the narrow reading of the joint authorship doctrine, which allows them to deny the possibility of joint authorship by relying on their intent to take full credit for the work. In short, the intent standard adopted by courts has assured that joint authorship is an unlikely outcome in authorship disputes.

The elevation of bargaining power over creative contributions in the authorial calculus also dramatically disadvantages traditionally disenfranchised communities and individuals. Creators from underprivileged backgrounds are therefore caught in joint authorship's double-bind. In the first instance, they have limited bargaining power, and as a result, through the contracting practices of their more sophisticated collaborators/partners, they often waive and/or assign their rights away for limited consideration. But even if they should somehow avoid such a fate, their joint authorship claims can be swept aside – despite the scope of their creative contributions – based on the very fact that they do not enjoy bargaining power in the first place.[73] For example, low bargaining power will often result in an artist receiving no crediting as an author, despite her substantial creative contributions to a project. The absence of crediting will then, in turn, be read by a court as an "objective manifestation" preventing the recognition of joint authorship.[74]

To illustrate the grave problems inherent to the courts' approach to mutual intent, consider their inquiry into crediting practices, which they have deemed a "significant" part of the mutual-intent determination.[75] As we shall discuss in greater detail in the second half of this chapter, crediting practices are notoriously disconnected from the realities of creative production,[76] and the risks of placing significant weight on such practices should be obvious to any student of history. For instance, when viewed through the prism of gender, crediting has a particularly undistinguished track record. As the problematic reliance on formal crediting reveals, the mutual-intent requirement has transformed joint-authorship queries into a referendum on the relative leverage of the competing parties and their willingness to use it. As Bobbi Kwall has argued, "By virtue of its inevitable operation, this standard will always result in privileging the narrative of the dominant author over the non-dominant author. Indeed, under a subjective standard focusing on what the parties said and thought, the dominant author or his representatives (as was the case in *Thomson*), will always dispute the intent of co-authorship."[77] Not only does such a vision of joint authorship disincentivize and fail to recognize modalities of creation that are more collaborative in nature, it also disproportionately burdens groups of people who may be more likely to engage in such collaborative activities.[78]

ANONYMOUS WAS A WOMAN: JOINT AUTHORSHIP, GENDER, AND THE DISPUTE OVER *RENT*

Returning to the dispute that began this chapter – Lynn Thomson's claims of joint authorship over the musical *Rent* – we see this dynamic in action. In sweeping aside the relevance of Thomson's creative contributions and almost exclusively emphasizing the relative bargaining power of the parties, the *Thomson* court concocts a vision of joint authorship that "privileges the narrative of the dominant author by effectively ignoring the narrative of collaborative creation."[79] In her thoughtful commentary about her experience litigating her claims to joint authorship of *Rent*, Thomson writes how removed such a vision is from the reality of creative activity. "The primary experience of the lawsuit, especially in the Second Circuit and with the strangeness of the *Childress* decision," she tells us, "was that the law – or perhaps, the interpretation and application of the law – was remote from the truth of what happened to me, remote from the truth of how, in fact, art is actually made at the end of the century. What happens 'in the room' and what is protected in the law are so unconnected."[80] The potential gender-related implications of such a turn are troubling. As Ann Bartow notes, "Male writers, male singers, male visual artists, male actors, male directors, male producers, male composers, male architects, and male authors of almost any form of copyrightable work dominate the cultural terrain and thereby acquire and control a substantial majority of the financial resources that creative works accrue."[81] To confirm this point, she suggests looking at any list featuring the most recognized or highest-paid individuals in various creative fields: Invariably, they are disproportionately male.[82] With that in mind, given long-extant disparities in artistic recognition, any legal test that rests on bargaining power within the authorial class is, in the aggregate, inevitably going to favor males over females.

All the while, social imposition of behavioral norms may diminish the opportunity for women to receive authorial credit under the intent standard. For example, Bartow argues that women may feel pressure to avoid being labeled greedy or selfish if "they violate perceived gender-linked social norms of sharing, caring, and selfless collaboration because they seek to procure … authorship rights and attributive credit."[83] As Virginia Woolf once posited, "I would venture to guess that Anon, who wrote so many poems without signing them, is often a woman." (Figure 2.2).[84] In addition, there may also exist gender differences in typical modalities of creative production.[85] Recent neuroscience and psychology literature has suggested the possibility. As Anna Abraham has noted, "gender differences in cognition and behavior may not necessarily be instantiated in actual behavioral outcomes, but may instead be observed in terms of employed strategy differences when performing a task."[86] Thus, there is "intriguing evidence that men and women enact their creativity in potentially disparate ways,"[87] including collaborative processes that may reflect the greater role of social relationships in female, rather than male, creativity.[88] In fact, studies on the role of gender in team performance have revealed the increased adoption of collaborative activities with the presence of women.[89]

Lynn Thomson seems to capture these phenomena – the existence of potential gender differences in the norms surrounding creative production and in approaches to creative production – in describing her work with Larson:

FIGURE 2.2 Portrait of Virginia Woolf (1902) by George Charles Beresford

> I am often asked why I had no contract. The short answer is that I didn't know Jonathan Larson was going to die. I trusted his decency and I still do. We discussed our relationship and his obligations and beyond that I made no efforts to draw attention to my contributions. I knew that was what I was supposed to do, focus on our work and give over to the larger good.[90]

Her words reflect her conscientious adherence (whether gender-based or not) to the "gender-linked social norms of sharing, caring, and selfless collaboration"[91] described by Bartow. Moreover, Thomson contextualizes her act of creation in communal, rather than individualistic, terms – a viewpoint reflected in the themes of her work itself. "I believed in the precepts of collaboration and community, and had faith that my community would stand by me as I stood by it. Out of that faith came many of my contributions to Rent – a play which is about community,"[92] she writes. There is, of course, deep irony in this reference to community. After all, *Rent* is a play about individuals in marginalized and disempowered communities. Whether or not she belonged to such a community before her work on *Rent*, the end result of Thomson's quest for joint authorship was her legal disenfranchisement from control of, and economic participation in, the intellectual property of the musical.[93]

MUTUAL INTENT AND MARGINALIZED COMMUNITIES

The impact of the mutual-intent regime also extends beyond gender lines. Other marginalized communities, including indigenous and non-Western peoples, may be similarly disadvantaged under the standard. For example, as Nzingha Hooker has argued, the mutual-intent requirement for joint authorship has enabled the law to "remain blind to collaborative authors commonly found in indigenous societies."[94] By viewing "the community or society as the possessors of ideas, information, and knowledge," non-Western modalities of creation often eschew notions of a dominant author, or even an author at all.[95] Since they often constitute the product of an entire cultural or ethnic group, communal enterprises such as folklore lack a clear author or set of authors. As such, many works of cultural patrimony struggle to gain protection under Western copyright regimes beholden to the mastermind conception of authorship.[96]

In addition, the inherently collaborative work of performers also receives little legal respect under the mutual-intent doctrine. Since performers are rarely the "dominant" creator or the "master mind," they will typically be precluded from making viable claims of joint authorship (even in the absence of an authorship-as-fixation roadblock). After all, without ownership and control over the tools of production, they almost certainly lack the bargaining power to generate the requisite intent to co-author with those who do hold ownership and wield control. Just as the conflation of authorship with fixation has frequently foreclosed actors from asserting copyright interests in their performances, the mutual-intent requirement has additionally prevented the possibility of joint authorship claims. The result is a powerful one-two punch against performer rights.

Thus, in the examples discussed in Chapter 1, litigants such as Cindy Lee Garcia, Erin Andrews, the Fosters, and victims of revenge porn would be unlikely to enjoy colorable joint-authorship claims based on the contribution of their performances to copyrighted works fixed in a tangible medium.[97] As a result, not only does the authorship-as-fixation doctrine occlude their ability to receive a separate copyright interest in their performances, they also have trouble earning co-author status that would at least enable them to participate economically in the exploitation of works featuring their performances.[98] By depriving performers of the possibility of co-authorship, the mutual-intent requirement further ossifies the power of those in front of the camera to control and profit from copyrighted works that employ the male gaze and scrutinize female and non-white bodies.

All told, driven by a romantic conception of authorship that attributes creative enterprise to a single "master mind," judicial adoption of a mutual-intent requirement for joint-authorship claims has, all too often, deprived significant contributors to copyrighted content of authorship credit. Just as with the conflation of authorship and fixation we explored in Chapter 1, the mutual-intent requirement has served to further consolidate the power of those who already enjoy superior leverage, access to capital, and control over the tools of production. In the process, our extant joint-authorship regime has served the interests of certain types of authors employing certain modes of creation – much to the systemic disadvantage of women and indigenous and non-Western communities whose creative contributions have long gone underappreciated and under-recognized by the law.

* * * * * * * * *

CREDIT AND DEBT

The privileging of power over creative contribution does not merely infect copyright's joint authorship doctrine. As a direct result of our copyright regime's surprising indifference to attribution rights, it also reigns supreme in crediting practices. By generally declining to recognize claims for crediting, our intellectual property laws leave the matter of attribution to private parties to determine, thereby elevating the primacy of negotiating leverage. In the process, individuals who should receive credit often do not, and vice versa. The resulting system has a particularly grave impact on creators from traditionally marginalized communities who lack bargaining power, thereby depriving them of the dignitary and the economic opportunities that come with attribution. But the harm is felt even more widely, as a lack of a proper crediting regime also diminishes the efficacy of resource allocation in creative enterprises, which ultimately impoverishes progress in the arts.

In the visual arts, meaning is communicated not only by what occupies the positive space but also by the metes and bounds of the negative space. Similarly, copyright law can sometimes be best understood not just for what it protects but for what it expressly declines to protect. Attribution falls into this latter category. At first blush, our legal regime's lack of crediting rights appears peculiar. After all, from the earliest age, we are all taught to give credit where credit is due, and our social norms strongly support proper crediting. "Both authors and audiences," explains Rebecca Tushnet, "generally accept that attribution is important to authors, and that false attribution, especially plagiarism, is a moral wrong."[99] But as with many of the things we learned in kindergarten, adherence to the precept is far from perfect. Moreover, while the exhortation remains a universal aspiration, it enjoys little legal bite. Indeed, the lack of development in the law of crediting is nothing short of surprising. As Jane Ginsburg has argued, "Of all the many counter-intuitive features of US copyright law – and they abound – the lack of an attribution right may present the greatest gap between perceived justice and reality."[100]

If the Copyright Act and our broader intellectual property regime seek to serve their constitutionally mandated purpose – to promote progress in the arts – by incentivizing the creation of works of authorship, they should ideally respond to what truly motivates creators. To be sure, the exclusive rights of reproduction, distribution, public performance, public display, and derivatization secured for authors under section 106 of the Copyright Act appeal to authorial incentives in at least two ways. First, they serve utilitarian interests by providing monetary rewards to creators by necessitating licenses for the exploitation of their work. Second, they promote natural law and the dignitary interests of authors by enabling them to decide whether (and under what terms) their works are made available to the public at all.[101] But control over reproduction, distribution, public performance, public display, and derivatization are not the only rights that galvanize creators. Specifically, authors gain value – both monetary and otherwise – through other mechanisms. For example, building one's brand and reputation for creative excellence – achieved only through attribution – is a powerful means of earning long-term economic rewards and satisfying the dignitary interests that can also motivate authors. As a result, traditional copyright enforcement is not necessarily profit-maximizing for creators, and there is often a disconnect between how creators feel about the unauthorized exploitation of their work and how distributors/publishers might feel about it. Meanwhile, authors who may value attribution over enforcement of their copyrights are not necessarily immune to the temptations of the marketplace or more noble than the rest of us. To be sure, some authors may create solely to fulfill their own needs or to edify, amuse, or impact others, and they may merely seek recognition rather than profit. But there is also a monetary component to proper attribution. In the long run, attribution promotes one's name and its standing, a phenomenon that drives economic demand in a variety of forms – whether it is for further creative production, appearances, endorsements, or ancillary activities. Indeed, attribution is part and parcel of the economic equation of copyright and its incentive structure.

With all of this in mind, if our intellectual property regime serves to encourage progress in the arts by motivating and incentivizing authors, the absence of attribution rights would appear to leave the regime wanting. Copyright law has surprisingly limited protection for attribution. And, as we shall discuss later in this chapter, although courts provided alternative relief for a time through a broad reading of the term 'designations of origin' under the Lanham Act, that loophole has been closed since the Supreme Court's decision in *Dastar* two decades ago. Thus, current law provides little protection for crediting, leaving it up to the forces of the marketplace. This, in turn, has left crediting practices subject to significant abuses that disproportionately impact marginalized communities and result in a more inefficient allocation of resources to members of the creative class.

ADVENTURES IN CREDITING: YOUR AUTHOR CONFESSES

To illustrate the importance of attribution and its link to motivating creative enterprise, I turn to the perspective of the author I know best: me. Such a focus is admittedly biased and may be completely unrepresentative. But it illustrates how the current law of copyright – where infringement receives stiff punishment but failure to credit receives none – can be inadequate to protect the motivating interests of at least some creatives. Specifically, two recent incidents involving the use of my published work provoked strong, but diametrically opposing, reactions within me. And while I do not claim that my attitude toward these events mimics how typical authors might respond, my contemplations are nonetheless instructive as to how some authors might experience issues related to infringement and crediting.

Not long ago, while doing some research on the dirty underbelly of the piratical dark web, I came across a site that resembled a veritable *Library of Babel*,[102] providing free access to a remarkable collection of digital books to all comers. While publishers would not hesitate to characterize this "celestial jukebox"[103] of books as a cesspool of wanton infringement, I felt compelled, as a good academic, to investigate further before drawing any definitive conclusions. So, in an act of curiosity and thorough vanity, I punched my own name into the site's search box. To my surprise, a beautiful e-book edition of one of my tomes popped up, available freely (and for free) to all who had interest in it. I can neither confirm nor deny whether I immediately downloaded a copy, but some context might help explain why I may have made a decision to do so.

A number of years earlier, I had posed what I thought was an innocent request of the publisher of my forthcoming book: I sought a final PDF copy of the work for my records and personal use. The response was rapid and reproachful. "We don't do that, John." The implication was clear: they had to protect against piracy, even if it meant denying authors copies of their books in digital format. Instead, they offered me a compromise: the first three chapters. Since they made it clear this was not a negotiation, I took what they gave me. Fast forward a decade and it should be easy to understand why I may have been elated when a website offered me what my own publisher had denied me: a final, electronic form of my book without any encryption or digital rights management (DRM) associated with it.

My book's appearance on the website also pleased me for an entirely different and more fundamental reason. As a delusional academic, I dream of my ideas getting attention, impacting the way people might approach or think about an issue, and, ultimately, influencing policy. So I naturally fantasized about individuals (at least one or two!) potentially stumbling on this website, finding my book, and then reading it when they otherwise may have never known about my work or ponied up the cash necessary to buy it. The royalties I see from my writing are trivial and economically irrelevant. Instead, I want my books to reach as many people as possible (that is, more than my mother) and I want to maximize their exposure. Whether that is accomplished through sales or piracy, I care not. After all, as science fiction writer and librarian Eric Flint once put it, "The real enemy of authors – especially midlist writers – is not piracy … It's obscurity."[104]

So far from making me angry, the discovery of my book pirated online for anyone to read resulted in nothing but sheer delight. Yes, this was an infringement of my copyright, pure and simple. But I was all smiles.

Around the same time, I had another experience related to one of my publications – but, this time, what occurred was far less welcome. One day, I received an email from a local law school about an upcoming distinguished lecture. While I might usually give only fleeting attention to such a notification, this one caught my eye because of the topic, which happened to be the exact subject matter of my first book, which I wrote in 2008. I naturally took an interest and thought about attending. But as I read further, my curiosity turned to disappointment. The talk was about a recently released book whose description was, almost word for word, based on the book I had written. And then I saw the name of the author, which was one I recognized.

I had met the author a decade ago when she was a graduate student attending a talk I had given about my own book. I distinctly remember her chatting with me after my lecture and expressing how much she had enjoyed and appreciated my book. It turns out those comments weren't mere puffery. She had proven that by writing her own version. As I read the full description of her lecture and then found her recently released book, I was struck by how the summation literally encapsulated my own book in its entirety.

Imitation is the sincerest form of flattery, I told myself in a failed attempt to downplay the anger I felt. But more than flattery, I wanted acknowledgment. Of course, no one's work is wholly original. But her book came uncomfortably close to mimicry of mine. It was not just drawing on or borrowing ideas to build and expand on my book; it was literally taking my entire work and rehashing it as purportedly original material. Specifically, and most egregiously of all, the use of my work was wholly without proper credit. And, to add insult to injury, as the email before me indicated, she was now giving a distinguished lecture at a local university that had never shown the least bit of interest in my work.

Even if I were inclined to pursue some kind of legal remedy against her, there was none readily forthcoming. Because of the nature of the use, an infringement claim would be difficult to make. Meanwhile, current law provides no general right of crediting or attribution. Admittedly, I did have a form of extralegal relief; if I wanted to pursue the matter, university policies against plagiarism and the failure to properly credit sources offered some remedies. Certainly, I could have notified the author's publisher and her university employer to trigger potential investigations. But, at the end of the day, such an effort would be purely punitive and would not undo the real damage I had already suffered; the book, after all, was already published. So, in the end, I concluded that, instead of going through the pain of a vindictive letter-writing campaign that would only waste my own time, I would work out my issues far more constructively: by writing about it in *this* book.

These two incidents – close in time – provided a remarkable study in contrasts.[105] In the first matter, I encountered the wholesale piracy of my work, and I found myself not merely indifferent but hopeful (please don't tell my publisher). After all, I had received credit for my work, and the work's unauthorized distribution helped disseminate my ideas more broadly. I would take whatever boost I could get. The website in question had undoubtedly infringed my work, but I was perfectly content to let that happen. In the second instance, while it was arguable whether the subsequent author had infringed my work, she had indisputably failed to give me proper credit for my work – upon which she had indisputably and heavily drawn – and had, in my view, violated basic norms of attribution. I was disturbed and troubled by what had happened.

While I found the second incident far more offensive than the first, the law saw things differently. I possessed a colorable claim for infringement if I were inclined to fight the piracy of my book. By contrast, I had little hope of a legal remedy for my fellow academic's abysmal failure to provide me appropriate attribution. In short, our copyright regime provided no shortage of remedies for an injury that I cared little about – infringement. By sharp contrast, it provided no remedy for something that more directly motivates my production of content – crediting and recognition.

As a result of these two incidents, I began to wonder whether I was the kind of author the Copyright Act wanted to encourage in the first place.[106] As a writer, I meet the definition of what the Framers referred to as "authors" in the Intellectual Property Clause of the Constitution, and my work comes under the subject matter of the Copyright Act. But I am also not the kind of author who makes a living (or even seeks to make a living) on the sale of my works. Consequently, my incentives might be quite different from someone whose income solely or largely comes from authoring works – the kind of author who might care substantially more about piracy.

That said, however, the vast majority of authors make little to no money from their work. Some, of course, may still pursue the craft for (in part) future potential riches. But, for many, remuneration is far lower on their list of motivations than other factors, such as attribution and recognition. As Laura Heymann points out,

> [F]or many creators, particularly individual creators, the profit motivation is not paramount. Rather, the creator is motivated most by the public knowledge that she is the creator – by attribution of the work to her. Indeed, as others have noted, such creators value wide dissemination of their work over compensation, and so benefit from the fair use doctrine and, even, the movement of their work to the public domain, both of which ensure that their work reaches as large an audience as possible.[107]

As my reaction to the two incidents indicates, I belonged to this (simultaneously vain and altruistic) class of authors. And, by failing to reflect the importance of attribution and recognition as a motivating factor in the production of creative content, it appeared that the existing copyright regime did not know members of this class very well and did not appear fully responsive to their incentives and needs. For a utilitarian regime dedicated to progress in the arts, this curious result begs further investigation.

THE EMPIRICS OF ATTRIBUTION

There is no doubt that our moral sensibilities strongly support the practice of proper attribution, and common sense tells us that authors value crediting and recognition as well. As Heymann has posited, "[I]t seems safe to conclude that the two things that virtually all creators desire is to receive credit when appropriate and to eliminate the suggestion of association when it is not."[108] But before taking these assumptions to heart based on mere intuition, it is worth scrutinizing them more closely. While the value of attribution has traditionally received scant attention in the academic literature and little empirical testing, all of that has changed in recent years as an emerging body of data and experimental work has provided overwhelming support for the notion that attribution serves a vital role in motivating and incentivizing creatives.[109]

One of the largest innovations (and concomitant behavioral experiment) to ever take place in the creative world occurred with the launch of the Creative Commons some two decades ago. Founded by law professor Larry Lessig, computer scientist Hal Abelson, and literary advocate Eric Eldred, the Creative Commons sought to give creators the ability to opt out of the protection-heavy default rules of copyright, which automatically vest in authors[110] the exclusive right to control reproduction, distribution, public display, public performance, and derivatization of their works[111] for a period of their lifetime plus seventy years after their death.[112] Such rights spring into existence for all original works of authorship fixed in a tangible medium, regardless of formalities. In subverting these default protections and the "permission culture"[113] that they serve and support, Creative Commons allowed authors to make their works available to the public to promote educational access and spur further creativity by increasing the pool of works from which others can freely build without the need for costly licenses. By ceding their works to the Creative Commons, creators opt into a different regime, where all rights are *not* reserved. Thus, under various Creative Commons licenses, they can make work available for use without payment for noncommercial purposes – to create new derivative works or for any purpose whatsoever.

The notable success of the Creative Commons and the particular manner in which it has operated illustrate two important points. First, millions of creators have deeded hundreds of millions of creative works to the Creative Commons.[114] As Eric E. Johnson has put it, this fact illustrates "the contemporary existence of an attitude held by at least a significant number of people that the full panoply of copyright entitlements is not important to them."[115] Second, while many, but not all, authors want to stop infringement of their works, virtually all authors want attribution and the operation of the Creative Commons provides empirical support for this view. As the data collected over the past twenty years show, authors putting their work on the Creative Commons almost always choose to condition any use on one requirement: proper attribution.[116] For at least a certain set of creators, therefore, the right of attribution trumps the right of exploitation and the ability to receive license fees from the use of one's works.

Even aside from the Creative Commons, the widespread sharing, rather than exclusive reservation, of intellectual property rights in many sectors illustrates the strong incentive social validation can play in promoting creative enterprise. Though long underappreciated in the intellectual property literature,[117] this widespread "non-market form of exchange," characterized by sharing, is particularly attractive for an enormous body of works that may not enjoy clear-cut commercial profitability but are also not entirely valueless.[118] In these sharing regimes, such as open-source software licensing pools and microstock photography collections, pecuniary gain is largely forgone, but, quite notably, attribution is retained and reputational satisfaction constitutes a key part of the value proposition for creators, as they derive "a feeling of satisfaction and a sense of social connectedness out of sharing."[119]

The thriving of the "sharing" economy and of the Creative Commons – where millions of creators are eager to opt out of the default protections of the Copyright Act, but only as long as they continue to receive recognition for their creative efforts – should come as no surprise. Indeed, recent experimental work has validated the intuition and experience that suggests that creators place significant weight on crediting and recognition. Notably, researchers Christopher Sprigman, Christopher Buccafusco, and Zachary Burns have conducted a series of empirical tests that mimic conditions of real-world bargaining in order to put a tangible monetary value on attribution rights. In the first experiment, they found that 180 casual photographers were, in the aggregate, willing to receive far less payment for publication of their work when it came with, rather than without, attribution.[120] These findings were even more pronounced in their second experiment, which involved professional and advanced amateur photographers.[121] In short, these tests produced robust results, leading Sprigman, Buccafusco, and Burns to conclude that, on average, creators actually value attribution and the receipt of recognition for their work more than getting paid and that they are "willing to sacrifice financial benefits to obtain [attribution]."[122] While there are many creators who may value getting paid over attribution, Sprigman et al.'s study highlights the underappreciated importance of crediting in the creative world.

Beyond the valuable case study provided by Creative Commons and the experimental evidence that has quantitatively established the worth of crediting to authors, important qualitative ethnographic and observational work has also supported the stock that creators put in attribution. For example, in her comprehensive qualitative study of innovation, in which she conducted dozens of interviews with creatives and intellectual property professionals across a wide variety of industries,[123] Jessica Silbey concluded that attribution serves as a primary motivator for creative enterprise.[124] As she notes, "[T]he interviews are replete with expressions of how attribution and integrity are crucial to the work's optimal promotion and dissemination, whether or not for profit, because they safeguard and manage the development of professional identity and audience."[125]

Thus, the desire to have one's work reach as large an audience as possible may also mean that the value of crediting can sometimes supplant that of payment, even to those authors seeking future potential riches. On this front, the origins of jazz music's *The Real Book* and the role of Steve Swallow in the project are instructive. Although relatively obscure to general audiences, *The Real Book* is a beloved institution in the world of jazz music. First published in the mid 1970s, this underground, amateur compilation of hand-notated lead sheets for hundreds of jazz standards has, for decades, served as a critical resource for musicians seeking to perfect their craft. Created by two students at the renowned Berklee College of Music, the work remains anonymous; since the volume was created without the permission of music publishers, *The Real Book* is a massive act of infringement. Steve Swallow, a professor at Berklee, assisted the students with the selections for the work and he has kept their identities secret over the years. Notably, his own work is also featured (i.e., infringed) in the volume. But he was more than happy to have his compositions (his music publisher's consternation notwithstanding) included in the book, even if it were infringement. The reason was simple: attribution. By having his works cast as standards and included in the corpus of legendary jazz compositions with the likes of Miles Davis, Herbie Hancock, and Charlie Parker, Swallow would achieve a huge boost in credibility and longevity, which would ultimately translate into more royalties.[126] As Swallow explains, "I think that, to this day, my songs are played to the extent that are[] chiefly because they were available in the *Real Book*. It's been a blessing."[127]

Swallow's views are no outlier. In her sweeping survey on the legal and normative standards of attribution across a wide range of industries – including Hollywood, journalism, political speechwriting, software, advertising, graphic design, science, and medicine – Catherine Fisk has also documented the significant value creators place on crediting.[128] As she puts it, "Attribution is foundational to the modern economy" and, as such, "greater legal recognition of attribution rights is desirable."[129]

Finally, recent literature in the field of organizational behavior[130] and psychology[131] has emphasized the crucial role of crediting in nurturing innovation and promoting perceptions of fairness in creative environments. For example, Teresa Amabile, a leading theorist on creativity and innovation, has highlighted how proper credit allocation can motivate employees to work harder and enhance productivity.[132] In short, a burgeoning body of work in the social sciences has strongly supported the intuition that crediting matters – a lot.

ATTRIBUTION, RESOURCE ALLOCATION, AND THE CREATIVITY ECONOMY

But in focusing largely on the impact of attribution on creatives – both in the way that crediting incentivizes innovation and how it serves the dignitary interests of authors – this emerging literature has actually understated the case for attribution rights. Quite critically, attribution does not merely serve authorial interests. Rather, it also benefits other players in the marketplace for creative works and advances broader societal interests.[133]

First, proper attribution practices advance the efficacy of the marketplace, particularly in an information economy dominated by the production of intellectual property. Generally speaking, free and open exchange of relevant information facilitates the optimal functioning of markets by improving the efficiency of allocation decisions. Information about inputs, such as labor, guides the dedication of scarce resources. Crediting provides actionable data about labor involved in the production of intellectual property – data that are often onerous to divine elsewhere or without substantial additional cost. Indeed, "because it is difficult to measure worker knowledge directly in the way that the ability of the typists and machinists of the industrial economy could be tested simply by watching them perform a task,"[134] attribution is particularly valuable in an information economy. A reliable, accurate, and comprehensive crediting regime can therefore dramatically advance interests in the efficient allocation of resources in creative enterprises. Crediting, after all, provides vital information to financiers of those enterprises about the nature and quality of a particular author's work.[135]

Second, a more rigorous attribution regime can also serve the interests of those who consume creative works and other forms of intellectual property. Authorship represents a form of branding akin to trademark, and accurate authorship labeling helps promote many of the basic goals of the trademark regime, which serves consumers (and not just authors) by "reduc[ing] the customer's costs of shopping and making purchasing decisions" and "help[ing] assure a producer that it (and not an imitating competitor) will reap the financial, reputation-related rewards associated with a desirable product."[136] Heymann has highlighted the value that a meaningful crediting regime provides to even nonauthors. Instead of calling for an attribution right that recognizes an inherent moral right that authors might have in proper attribution, she calls for what she dubs "authornymic" attribution, the recognition of crediting for the sake of "organizational integrity" – a "reader-centered" law that ensures that "reader responses [to creative works] will be informed and minimizes the likelihood of confusion a consumer of creative commodities might otherwise experience."[137] In this way, she argues, a law of attribution is vital to supporting "efficient literary consumers" who can have "some confidence that the works that we read – and later draw on for our own creative activity – are situated within a coherent literary structure."[138]

Third, a robust crediting system can also promote public respect for intellectual property law. It does so in at least two different ways. As Stephanie Plamondon Bair argues in her study of the role of fairness in copyright law, when we align copyright law more closely with public perceptions of equity, we heighten the regime's legitimacy in the eyes of society.[139] Given the strong popular support for the norm of attribution, a copyright system that protects crediting rights bolsters respect for the regime itself. Separately, the act of putting a real face (or, at least, name) behind creative works humanizes them and can help buttress support for the intellectual property rights that protect them. As Catherine Fisk explains, such a task is particularly important "[i]n a world of corporate production, and in particular skepticism about corporate production."[140] After all, it is no secret why corporate interest groups bring relatable artists to the forefront when making pitches for greater protection and rights enforcement, especially in the war on piracy – even when those artists are not the real rights holders.[141] When the music industry sought to apply pressure to Google to provide more favorable use fees for the exploitation of music on YouTube, it had the likes of Taylor Swift and others sign off on an open letter that was used to drum up public support for the cause and to lobby Congress for reform.[142] And when the Motion Picture Association sought an alternative to an unpopular litigation campaign against piracy, it put together testimonial advertisements that highlighted the ways in which piracy hurt those people whom we only know as lines at the end of the credit roll.[143] Thus, attribution promotes the very operation of the intellectual property regime by giving it a human face that legitimizes the sometimes impersonal and intangible rules it enforces. In an era where digital technology has made mass piracy on a global scale all too easy, this function is perhaps of greater value now than ever before.

All told, therefore, our common sense tells us that crediting is deeply important to authors, a position backed by the emerging social science literature on the subject. Meanwhile, a proper attribution regime also has critical benefits to the efficient functioning of the marketplace for creative works and thus has strong benefits for consumers and investors as well. Despite all of this, the law provides little protection for crediting rights. The situation has grown particularly dim in the past two decades in the wake of the Supreme Court's decision in *Dastar*, a subject to which we now turn.

COPYRIGHT'S SURPRISING CREDITING GAP

Despite the critical value of attribution – to creators, investors, and the public as a whole – we are left with a strange conundrum: the law of crediting is surprisingly thin and underdeveloped. Indeed, it is counterintuitively so, as the wholesale absence of any broad law of attribution runs counter to the assumptions of many in the creative community. As Jessica Silbey reported in her survey of artists and authors, "Many interviewees were stunned to learn that copyright law does not require attribution or prohibit misattribution."[144] Indeed, the law of copyright only provides protection of crediting under remarkably circumscribed circumstances – through carefully hemmed provisions in the Visual Artists Rights Act (VARA) and the Digital Millennium Copyright Act (DMCA).

On the surface, VARA would appear to provide significant protection for attribution. Codified in section 106A of the Copyright Act, VARA offers creators an independent cause of action "to claim authorship of [their] work," and "to prevent the use of his or her name as the author of any work of visual art which he or she did not create."[145] VARA claims are eligible for recovery of both statutory damages and attorneys' fees and, making matters even better for potential plaintiffs, unlike for infringement claims, an author does not even need to timely register the work in question as a condition for these remedies.[146] But while a cursory examination of VARA might elicit hope for the vindication of crediting rights, a closer look reveals otherwise.

First, as the very name of the legislation makes clear, VARA's attribution rights only encompass works of visual art.[147] As such, the Act fails to apply to large swaths of subject matter otherwise protectible under the Copyright Act, including writings, music, and other important works. But the limits do not end there, as the attribution right does not even attach to all forms of art that might be characterized as visual in nature. Rather, the statute covers only paintings, drawings, prints, sculptures, and photographs created for exhibition purposes only.[148] It therefore excludes the most commercially important of visual art – film.[149] It also does not apply to any "poster, map, globe, chart, technical drawing, diagram, model, applied art, ... book, magazine, newspaper, periodical, data base, electronic information service, electronic publication, or similar publication" or any "merchandising item or advertising, promotional, descriptive, covering, or packaging material or container."[150] In addition, works made for hire unilaterally fall outside of VARA's protections.[151] Finally, for the narrow category of visual art works to which VARA might apply, the attribution right only attaches to original versions of those works or limited editions thereof issued in sets of "200 copies or fewer that are signed and consecutively numbered by the author."[152] At the end of the day, therefore, VARA's attribution right pertains to a limited set of visual art works that are not prepared as works made for hire. In short, VARA provides no crediting protection for the vast majority of authors.

Crediting protection finds a similar dead end under the copyright management information (CMI) provisions of the DMCA. Introduced into law in 1998 and codified in 17 U.S.C. § 1202, these amendments to the Copyright Act make it unlawful to falsify, alter, or remove CMI, which includes any authorship and copyright ownership data accompanying a work.[153] These provisions – which apply to all copyrighted works, rather than VARA's narrow subset thereof – would seemingly serve as a powerful vehicle to vindicate attribution rights, but their reach is deliberately constrained in other important ways. Among other things, the structure of the causes of action provided under section 1202 – a claim for falsification of CMI[154] and a claim for removal or alteration of CMI[155] – renders the protections therein subservient to the goal of fighting infringement rather than recognition of the inherent value of crediting. In other words, the guiding principle behind section 1202 is to prevent further infringement, not vindicate an author's very real, but potentially separate, interest in attribution. As such, section 1202 fails to provide a meaningful right to crediting for authors.

Specifically, a claim for falsification of CMI requires that plaintiffs show that defendants "knowingly and with the intent to induce, enable, facilitate, or conceal infringement ... provide[d] copyright management information that is false."[156] Similarly, a claim for removal/alteration of CMI requires that plaintiffs show that defendants "intentionally remove[d] or alter[ed] copyright management information ... knowing, or ... having reasonable grounds to know, that it will induce, enable, facilitate or conceal an infringement."[157] Thus, both falsification and removal/alteration claims have a strict double scienter requirement that necessitates plaintiffs demonstrate that defendants acted with a particular *mens rea* – that is, ***knowingly*** and ***with intent*** to facilitate infringement.

This onerous scienter requirement is significant in at least three ways. First, it contrasts markedly from the complete absence of any scienter requirement in matters of direct copyright infringement.[158] Specifically, infringement has always been a strict liability tort,[159] where a defendant's state of mind is wholly irrelevant to the issue of liability.[160] By sharp distinction, to prevail on an attribution claim through section 1202, a plaintiff must meet not one but two (if not three[161]) showings on the defendant's state of mind.

Second, by conditioning attribution relief on an intent to facilitate infringement, section 1202 firmly grounds its protections in service of the fight against infringement rather than any broad vindication of crediting rights. This position is further buttressed by the fact that section 1202 only protects CMI that is "conveyed in connection with copies or phonorecords of a work or performances or displays of a work."[162] Furthermore, some courts have even read the legislative history and intent behind section 1202 to preclude application of falsification and removal/alteration claims to nondigital works.[163] According to the logic of these courts, section 1202's primary purpose – fighting the scourge of piracy in the online environment because of the unique ease of digital infringement – compels such a limitation on section 1202 claims. Such a position, however, leaves attribution rights outside of the digital environment unaddressed.

Third, and relatedly, the dual scienter requirement makes it extraordinarily difficult to prevail on a section 1202 claim. To state a cognizable removal/alteration claim, for example, a plaintiff must demonstrate that either a work "came into Defendant's possession with CMI attached, and Defendant intentionally and improperly removed it" or a work "came into Defendant's possession without CMI attached, but Defendant knew that CMI had been improperly removed, and Defendant used the [work] anyway."[164] A plaintiff may be unable to show how or in what form a work came into the defendant's possession in the first place[165] and, even if they can, it is rare to additionally have sufficient evidence showing that the removal/alteration was specifically with the intent to facilitate infringement. For example, an erroneous belief about the copyright status of an image can preclude a finding of the knowledge required to state a claim under section 1202.[166] Meanwhile, even intentionally cropping out a copyright notice from an image is insufficient to meet the intent-to-facilitate requirement.[167]

Not surprisingly, therefore, plaintiffs regularly see their CMI claims disposed of as a matter of law based on the failure to adequately make even a threshold showing of knowledge and intent.[168] This typical result is not surprising when one considers the difficulties an author might face in bringing a section 1202 claim even against someone who both knowingly and intentionally crops an image to cut out the authorship information. Even assuming such authorship information qualifies as actionable CMI, there are myriad reasons (that may have nothing to do with the concealing of infringement) to crop out such authorship information. Among other things, the person making use of the image could claim to have cropped the images for aesthetic purposes, because of inherent space limitations for the usage, or without any idea that they were removing CMI.[169] In all these instances, authors may have legitimate, if not strong, interests in seeing uses of their work include attribution. Yet the conduct would be unactionable under section 1202.

THE RISE AND FALL OF ATTRIBUTION RIGHTS

For a time, copyright's shortcomings in the area of attribution rights were not fatal to the cause of proper crediting because rights holders could achieve such protection in a neighboring field of law: trademarks. Specifically, a line of case law had emerged that considered improper crediting of someone else's work as one's own to constitute a "false designation of origin ... or false or misleading representation" actionable under section 43(a) of the federal legislation protecting trademarks, the Lanham Act.[170] In these cases, courts found that, in the words of Thomas McCarthy, the Lanham Act "has progressed far beyond the old concept of fraudulent passing off" – when one tries to pass off one's goods and services as those of someone else – "to encompass any form of competition or selling which contravenes society's current concepts of 'fairness.'"[171] Such a capacious reading of the Lanham Act allowed for recognition of a cause of action for reverse passing off – when someone passes off the goods or services of another as their own – and, therefore, provided a viable claim for their failure to provide credit.

In 1981, this reading of the Lanham Act received the blessing of the Ninth Circuit for the first time, a move that propelled it to widespread acceptance. In *Smith* v. *Montoro*, the Ninth Circuit held that the failure to credit an actor for his role in the movie *Convoy Buddies* (and, in fact, the substitution of his name with that of another actor in both the film credits and advertising material) constituted reverse passing off under section 43(a).[172] The court opined that such conduct was "wrongful" as a matter of public policy, in that "the originator of the misidentified product is involuntarily deprived of the advertising value of its name and of the goodwill that otherwise would stem from public knowledge of the true source of the satisfactory product."[173] The *Montoro* decision proved widely influential, and, within a few short years, federal courts throughout the country were entertaining attribution-related claims under section 43(a) for reverse passing off.[174]

But all of that changed in 2003 when the Supreme Court announced its decision in *Dastar* v. *Twentieth Century Fox*.[175]

In the mid 1990s, to commemorate the fiftieth anniversary of the ending of World War II, Dastar Corporation had decided to put out a new video set titled *World War II Campaigns in Europe*. The collection made extensive, but unauthorized, use of a television series based on President Dwight Eisenhower's book, *Crusade in Europe*.[176] Twentieth Century Fox had owned the copyrights to this program until it had inadvertently forgotten to renew them and the show fell into the public domain.[177] As a result, Fox could not sue Dastar for infringement of its *Crusade in Europe* television series to prevent publication and distribution of *World War II Campaigns in Europe*.[178] So, like many other entities who have lost their erstwhile rights in one of our intellectual property regimes, Fox turned to a neighboring intellectual property regime to rest its claims,[179] and made a Lanham Act claim instead.

The procedural posture of the case was unusual and suggested something significant was afoot by the time it got to the Supreme Court. Both the district court and Ninth Circuit upheld the reverse passing off claim. Indeed, the Ninth Circuit thought so little of the issue's overall significance that the decision was unpublished. The Supreme Court, of course, typically grants certiorari to only a tiny fraction of cases, so it certainly raised eyebrows when it granted certiorari to a seemingly routine and mundane decision that the Ninth Circuit did not even bother to designate for publication.[180] The action presaged the Court's view that the preceding opinions missed something fundamental and salient, about which the Court appeared ready to opine.

In its decision, the Supreme Court unanimously reversed the Ninth Circuit and rejected Fox's attempt to use a Lanham Act claim for false designation of origin as a means of preventing Dastar's reproduction of an audiovisual work (to which Fox had previously owned the copyright) that had fallen into the public domain.[181] In so holding, the Court warned against the risk of creating a "species of mutant" intellectual property protection that would impede the public's right to make unfettered use of creative works that no longer enjoy copyright protection.[182]

As the old saw goes, hard facts make bad law. Fox's gambit to eschew the "limited times" requirement in copyright law by ginning up trademark claims against Dastar struck a nerve with the Court, and the case came before it at a particularly opportune time (as far as Dastar was concerned). As Justin Hughes points out, the close proximity of the *Dastar* decision to the holding in *Eldred* v. *Ashcroft*[183] suggests that the former may have intentionally served as a "2003 Term counterweight" to the latter,[184] which rejected concerns about the public domain in declining to find a twenty-year extension of copyright terms unconstitutional.[185] Indeed, fears that aggrieved former rights holders, like Fox, might use the Lanham Act as a backdoor mechanism to circumvent copyright's carefully calibrated balance between private protection and public access expressly animated the *Dastar* decision. Specifically, the Court sought to thwart future efforts by lapsed copyright holders to make disingenuous use of trademark law to assert monopolistic control over the exploitation of works that had fallen into the public domain, in contravention of the very intent of the copyright regime and its (constitutionally mandated) policy of allowing ownership over creative works to eventually expire so that the public may make free use of them.[186]

Thus, under *Dastar*, the Supreme Court found that reference to "origins of goods" in the Lanham Act could not be read to mean the authorial origins of a work; instead, it referred only to the physical source of the embodiment of that work in tangible products.[187] As the Court reasoned, the reference to "origin of goods" in section 43(a) was "incapable of connoting the person or entity that originated the ideas or communications that 'goods' embody or contain. Such an extension would not only stretch the text, but it would be out of accord with the history and purpose of the Lanham Act and inconsistent with precedent."[188] So, even if Dastar had failed to give proper credit to the intellectual source(s) of the materials contained in its video collection, this did not, and could not, constitute a violation under the Lanham Act. All that mattered for the purposes of section 43(a) was that there was no false designation of the origin of the actual physical video collection. Since Dastar literally published and distributed the video collection, self-attribution was entirely proper as far as the Lanham Act was concerned. As such, Fox had no actionable claim for false designation of origin.

At the same time, however, the Court's holding reached broader than necessary to achieve the laudable goal of protecting the public domain. By grounding its ruling in a reading of the Lanham Act that definitively excluded the intellectual wellspring of a product from the meaning of "origin," the Court precluded attribution claims under section 43(a) for all creative works. Thus, in the past two decades, courts have generally rejected all such claims, whether they apply to public domain works (as in *Dastar*) or works still under copyright protection (unlike *Dastar*).[189] In the process, therefore, *Dastar* eliminated relief for those seeking remediation of a harm quite distinct from unlawful reproduction, distribution, display, or performance of a creative work: the act of not giving credit to its original author. In one fell swoop, "the Court swept away close to twenty-five years of precedent that held that failure to give credit to an entertainment product such as a film or song, or providing misleading credit, was a violation of trademark law."[190]

In all fairness, two concerns can explain and warrant, at least in part, broader application of the holding to all creative works, not just ones in the public domain. First, the Court noted the Catch-22 to manufacturers of products containing creative works posed by attribution-related reverse passing off claims. "On the one hand," notes the Court, "they would face Lanham Act liability for *failing* to credit the creator of a work on which their lawful copies are based; and on the other hand they could face Lanham Act liability for *crediting* the creator if that should be regarded as implying the creator's 'sponsorship or approval' of the copy."[191] In other words, if Dastar had put out its video set and kept the original credits to Fox, Fox could have sued Dastar for violating the Lanham Act for direct passing off by suggesting that Fox sponsored or approved Dastar's product. Meanwhile, because it had removed Fox's name, Dastar now faced a claim for failure to attribute under a theory of reverse passing off. If the Court had affirmed the availability of an attribution-related passing off claims, the resulting quagmire could stifle the use of works – both those in the public domain (for which no licensing is required) and those still under copyright protection (when lawful copyright clearance might leave a licensee subject to exposure for a Lanham Act violation).

Second, the Court raised its concern that an attribution requirement could leave distributors of copyright content with a duty to credit that might grow impossibly burdensome and impractical.[192] To illustrate this point, the Court turned no further than the case at hand, opining that

> [w]hile Fox might have a claim to being in the line of origin, its involvement with the creation of the television series was limited at best. Time, Inc., was the principal, if not the exclusive, creator, albeit under arrangement with Fox. And of course it was neither Fox nor Time, Inc., that shot the film used in the Crusade television series. Rather, that footage came from the United States Army, Navy, and Coast Guard, the British Ministry of Information and War Office, the National Film Board of Canada, and unidentified "Newsreel Pool Cameramen." If anyone has a claim to being the *original* creator of the material used in both the Crusade television series and the Campaigns videotapes, it would be those groups, rather than Fox.[193]

Interestingly, the Court's language on this issue referred only to the context of uncopyrighted works, noting that "[w]ithout a copyrighted work as the basepoint, the word 'origin' has no discernable limits."[194] But unless the reference to uncopyrighted works meant works that had never enjoyed copyright protection in the first place, it is unclear why this problem would be greater with once-copyrighted works that have fallen out of the public domain as opposed to works still under copyright protection.

While these rationales offer substantive justification to eliminate attribution-related reverse passing off claims through the Lanham Act in all instances – not just claims relating to public domain works – the holding in *Dastar* was not without its problems. Importantly, *Dastar* suffered a seemingly significant incongruity with the purpose of the federal trademark regime. If the goal of the Lanham Act is, indeed, consumer protection, the Supreme Court's central holding in *Dastar* – that the Lanham Act's reference to origin means the source of an actual physical product and not the wellspring of the idea or intellectual property embodied in a particular product – fails to reflect the reality of what factors animate consumer behavior, particularly with respect to intellectual property. Crediting is not just important to authors; it is vital to the public's decision-making process when it comes to consuming entertainment content. As Mary LaFrance has pointed out, contrary to the ultimate thrust of *Dastar*, which held that trademark law only protects against misidentification of the maker of the actual product rather than the ideas behind it,

> in the case of literary works or entertainment works, the identity of the actual author, performer, or creative overseer may frequently be more crucial to the consumer's purchasing decision, than the identity of the party that manufactured the physical embodiment [because] the identity of key creative participants is often viewed as a source indicator that is an important predictor of the quality or content of the goods.[195]

Indeed, *Dastar* creates an unusual result for physical products containing intellectual property, as it provides protection to the designation of origin about which consumers arguably care ***the least***. To put a finer point on it, consumers do not concern themselves with whether the movie they are watching was printed on Kodak film or released by Warner Brothers; they care about the fact that it was directed by Martin Scorsese or written by Charlie Kaufman. Readers do not care about whether Random House or Harper Collins was responsible for the paper and ink on which a book appears; they care about whether the book was written by J. K. Rowling or Thomas Pynchon. Music listeners do not care if the album was issued by SubPop or Merge Records; they care about whether it contains performances by Spoon or The Mountain Goats. The disconnect between the law's protections and this reality could not be more stark or problematic.

Most importantly, for a large swath of creatives, *Dastar* all but eliminated hope for securing crediting rights through legal claims.[196] Admittedly, the Supreme Court took pains to caution that its decision had not necessarily eliminated all means to vindicate attribution rights and that *Dastar* did not speak to alternative causes of action to enforce crediting under common, state, and federal law, including other theories (such as false advertising) available under the Lanham Act. But as one practitioner euphemistically noted in the wake of *Dastar*, the remaining options relied on "creative lawyering"[197] – legalese for *highly unlikely to succeed*. Indeed, *Dastar* marked a significant inflection point in the state of attribution rights – pointedly curtailing (if not altogether eliminating) the ability of most creators to secure credit under the law.[198]

THE STATE OF CREDITING RIGHTS POST-*DASTAR*

In the nearly two decades since *Dastar*, the significant size of the credit gap has become manifest as the jurisprudence of the intervening years has made clear how little bite these alternative legal theories provide for the vindication of crediting interests. One potential remaining option for crediting rights stems from the Lanham Act's separate prohibition on false advertising or misrepresentations of facts.[199] But this cause of action – to which the Supreme Court cited as continuing to provide attribution protection post-*Dastar*[200] – has proven feeble with respect to vindicating crediting interest, complicated by issues such as standing and the need to demonstrate reliance on the misrepresentation in consumers' purchasing decision.[201] This consumer reliance requirement makes eminent sense for false advertising claims, but it makes less sense when dealing with issues of attribution, which should be, first and foremost, about vindicating the rights of authors to receive credit for their works rather than rights of the public from being deceived in material consumption decisions. Moreover, while the most famous and acclaimed of authors may survive such a materiality requirement, the vast majority will have a far more difficult time.

Meanwhile, although there was initially some optimism about attribution rights remaining available under state law post-*Dastar*, such hopes have proven misplaced. In many states, such as California, courts have interpreted unfair competition protections as coextensive with the Lanham Act. Thus, if *Dastar* renders attribution claims no longer viable under the Lanham Act, such claims must necessarily also fail under state unfair competition law.[202] Additionally, to the extent that unfair competition claims at state law can capture miscrediting activities no longer actionable under the Lanham Act, courts have deemed such efforts preempted under the Copyright Act.[203]

The absence of clear legal protections for crediting has left the victims of such wrongdoing with little more than a veritable smorgasbord of common law theories to advance for their (often futile) attempts to cobble together some basis for relief. This result is particularly pernicious in all-too-common instances where traditional gender dynamics and power imbalances culminate in the uncredited use of someone's creative efforts.

Consider, for example, the struggles that Cornell graduate student Antonia Demas faced when asserting that a member of her advisory committee (Professor David A. Levitsky of the School of Human Ecology) had improperly taken credit for research she had conducted into the nutritional habits of elementary schoolchildren, used that research to obtain a significant US Department of Agriculture (USDA) grant without her name, and then actively and publicly rebuffed her allegations of wrongdoing.[204] Although an investigation by the university ultimately censured Professor Levitsky for his actions – deeming him "'insensitive and careless' in failing to attribute the idea for the research to" Demas, concluding that he exhibited a "general patter of lack of attribution" and ordering him to acknowledge Demas in all future conversations about the research – Cornell "curiously" (in the euphemistic words of a later court) declined to punish Levitsky for plagiarism or formal misconduct.[205] The other members of the graduate advisory committee vehemently criticized the lack of more meaningful sanctions against Levitsky, asserting that he had stolen Demas's ideas and intellectual property without attribution, and, interestingly, the USDA ultimately cancelled Levitsky's grant for incompetence.[206] Given perceptions that Cornell had taken insufficient action against Levitsky, Demas brought formal legal action against both Levitsky and Cornell, seeking to vindicate her rights in a situation that had, up to that point, played out like a cautionary tale of academic exploitation involving an older, male professor and a talented, but younger, female student. Demas did not bring a claim under the

Lanham Act for misattribution.[207] Instead, she was left reciting the common law's greatest hits in her complaint by claiming liability for misappropriation, fraud, breach of contract, breach of fiduciary duty, negligence, tortious interference with prospective economic advantage, defamation, and intentional infliction of emotional distress – claims that the court mostly dismissed as legally insufficient, even if Levitsky had engaged in plagiarism.[208] While circumstances may make it possible to prevail on one of these theories, victims of crediting abuse face an uphill battle in meeting all of the required elements of such common law claims.[209]

THE PROMISE AND PERILS OF CREDITING BY CONTRACT

With the law providing little relief in such scenarios, creators are left with private contracting to do the work of crediting.[210] In some industries, private contracting and even social norms have gone a long way toward ensuring proper crediting. But significant lacunae remain and, even where private contracting and norms do provide for crediting, it is not always reflective of authorial contributions. As such, reliance on private systems to govern crediting is insufficient to provide for appropriate attribution rights.

There are some fields where private contracting has given rise to crediting requirements. Two paradigmatic examples are higher education and Hollywood.[211] In academia, strong attribution norms and internal disciplinary rules, including faculty codes of conduct and anti-plagiarism standards, mitigate crediting abuse, giving the bite of law through disciplinary proceedings. At the same time, however, not all university norms support best practices; academia has historically embraced some less savory practices that can lead to crediting abuse, including the occasional use of research assistants who prepare substantive content but do not receive authorship as a result of tradition and power dynamics. Meanwhile, although the carrot of norms and the stick of disciplinary proceedings help promote robust crediting practices in theory, the reality is more complicated. Indeed, as the Demas situation illustrates, the extant system has its limits. Consider, for example, what happened when two of Harvard Law School's most celebrated professors – Charles J. Ogletree Jr. and Laurence H. Tribe – faced allegations of plagiarism for the misuse of sources in 2004.[212] Although both professors admitted to wrongdoing, they claimed that their failings were entirely accidental. The University responded with only a slap on the wrist. Some, including the *Harvard Crimson*, criticized the relatively light sanctions Ogletree and Tribe received, particularly in light of how mild they seemed in comparison to punishments meted out to (barely adult) students in similar situations.[213] Ogletree and Tribe would continue to serve as distinguished members of the Harvard Law faculty for the rest of their careers. Once again, power imbalances seem to impact the actual attribution obligations in place.[214]

Meanwhile, in Hollywood, collective bargaining has helped level the playing field between the studios and talent, and the operative guild agreements have insisted on getting even the most minute of credits done correctly.[215] Thus, movie industry crediting requirements can be deeply nuanced and sometimes vigorously patrolled. Though the system is also not without its flaws,[216] it has worked relatively well.[217] And even if it might seem a tad onerous to any member of the public who has sat through the credits of a motion picture, those credits instill industry professionals with a sense of pride over their brief moment of acknowledgment on the silver screen. Just as importantly, by making the contributions of industry professionals publicly legible in databases such as IMDb.com,[218] the regime also ensures that those individuals can reap the reputational and economic benefits of their credits,[219] or, to give a notable example, help avoid the ruin that might come from an unfair attribution. To wit, from 1968 through 2000, the Directors Guild of America allowed aggrieved directors who believed a studio or other producer had butchered their movie in unimaginable ways to petition to have their directorial credit replaced with the fictional "Alan Smithee" pseudonym, lest the final product sully the real director's good name.[220] Alan Smithee has been quite prolific albeit unaccomplished, having directed dozens of motion pictures, most of them flops.

But in other industries without collective bargaining or finely tuned attribution norms, where crediting is just as important and billions of dollars are on the line, there are no such formal crediting regimes. In such endeavors, crediting decisions are often left to general norms and individual negotiations. As a result, crediting often becomes more about power than actual contribution. As Catherine Fisk points out about most fields of entertainment, "[a]part from the guild-controlled screen credit system, the credit system for other creative and technical people in entertainment seems to be more governed by norms, charity, and power than by law."[221] One notable example of this is producer credits, which are not governed by collective bargaining. As a result, producing credits are notoriously corrupt, and a veritable "prestige market" for production credits exists. Meanwhile, even in the guild crediting systems of the Screen Actors Guild-American Federation of Television and Radio Artists, the Writers Guild of America, and the Directors Guild of America, might still frequently trumps right in determining attribution rights. As Fisk notes,

> Because the guild agreements limit the number of people who can be credited in some roles on any one film, power relations among various possible contenders for credit affect who is listed. Individual workers with significant bargaining power (actors, directors, writers, and producers) negotiate for specific treatment on each project, which may or may not reflect the same level of artistic contribution as compared to others who receive a similar type of credit on a different film or who receive the same credit (or no credit) on the same film.[222]

In the end, therefore, leaving crediting protection entirely up to private contracting can deprive creators of rightful attribution (a benefit that often motivates their activities in the first place) and diminish the efficient functioning of the creative marketplace.

CREDITING, COLLABORATION, AND DISTRIBUTIVE JUSTICE

The absence of legal protection for attribution rights outside of private contracting also has profound consequences for distributive justice. When viewed through the prisms of race, gender, or socioeconomic disparities, crediting practices have a particularly troubling history. Simply put, those who are not white, male, or wealthy have far too often struggled to receive credit, even when they indisputably authored work. This is because crediting is as much (if not more) about power dynamics and contractual leverage as it is about origination. As K. J. Greene has pointed out,

> Top directors, such as a Spike Lee or Steven Spielberg, will have no problem obtaining credit [by exercising their bargaining power in negotiations to contract for it], but anyone else dependent on a contract to secure credit will likely lose out.... [W]hile *Dastar*, on its face, seems completely neutral on the subordination issue, it actually promotes greater subordination; despite the Oprah's and Denzel's of the world, Blacks, women, and other minorities still occupy the bottom of the totem pole in entertainment hierarchies, making them the most vulnerable to misattribution abuses.[223]

Greene's concern is not speculative or hypothetical. Unfortunately, it is widely reflected in the history of scientific and creative enterprise.

Consider, for example, the systematic undervaluing and under-recognition of innovations by women. In the sciences, the phenomenon even has its own term – the Matilda effect[224] – and it is no less prevalent in the world of arts and letters. To take a few illustrative examples, Margaret Keane was the actual painter of the "big-eyed waifs" long credited to her husband, Walter;[225] Elizabeth Magie created the game of *Monopoly*, not Charles Darrow;[226] and although attributed to Marcel Duchamp, *The Fountain* – the infamous urinal that rocked the art world at the inaugural exhibition of the Society for Independent Artists in New York – was likely the work of Elsa von Freytag-Loringhoven (Figure 2.3).[227] In short, crediting is often about who has the leverage (and, in the cases of some swindlers, the gall) to claim authorship, not who really created a work.

The dogged persistence of disparities in attribution has far-reaching consequences, exacerbating existing gender gaps in a number of professions, including the law. For example, Jordana Goodman's empirical analysis of crediting practices for patent attorneys, which examined a set of over 200,000 patent applications and office action responses before the United States Patent and Trademark Office from 2016 to 2020, found an alarming divergence between "attribution and presence" for female patent attorneys, even when accounting for nongendered partner-associate power differentials, years of practice, and other relevant experience.[228] In the field of computer software, for instance, Goodman estimates that female attorneys suffered a 31 percent shortfall in crediting.[229] As she concludes, the "lack of equitable attribution perpetually disadvantages women, negatively impacts their

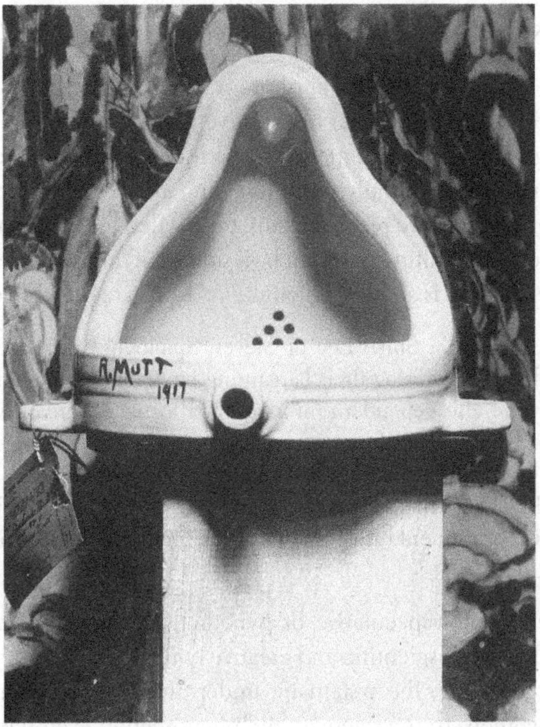

FIGURE 2.3 Marcel Duchamp's *The Fountain* (1917) as photographed by Alfred Stieglitz

career progression, and likely creates an insurmountable chasm between their capabilities and their prestige."[230] Ultimately, such practices "contribute[] to women's systemic underrepresentation at top leadership levels throughout the United States,"[231] a result presided over by private ordering regimes such as the workflow structure of modern law firms.[232]

The problematic dynamics of leaving crediting to private contracting are on full display in the music industry. As Fisk points out, "in music there is a not uncommon practice of people who do not contribute to the writing of a song being 'cut in' on songwriting credit."[233] The practice is not always nefarious, of course. Peter Jackson's Beatles documentary, *The Beatles: Get Back*,[234] provides a notable example. As the film's exhaustive studio footage capturing the crafting of the title song makes crystal clear, the work was the singular product of Paul McCartney's musical ingenuity. But the song's writing credits – "Lennon/McCartney" – tell a very different tale. In this case, a desire to keep an uneasy (though ultimately unsustainable) peace and to honor the duo's (soon-to-be dissolved) songwriting partnership came at the expense of accuracy.

Less innocuously, however, there are myriad instances where crediting practices reflect power more than creative contribution and disturbingly cut along gender or racial fault lines. To take one example, Little Richard co-authored the classic *Tutti Frutti* with Creole songwriter Dorothy LaBostrie.[235] However, as if it were not bad enough that handlers cajoled him into selling his publishing rights to his record company for a proverbial song (a meager fifty dollars), he also provided songwriting credit to a party that likely had nothing whatsoever to do with the authorship of the song[236] – one that may have been the pseudonym for the owner of Richard's record label (who reaped the royalties, which continue to be earned on the song to this day).[237] In another example, one of Duke Ellington's biggest hits, *Sophisticated Lady*, contained a melody created by his African-American bandmates Lawrence Brown and Otto Hardwick. Yet, the official composition credits do not list either man. Instead, Ellington's White manager, Irving Mills, exercised his privilege and superior negotiating leverage to bizarrely secure a credit[238] along with Mitchell Parish, a White lyricist who assisted with the words.[239] For their troubles, Brown and Hardwick were paid a flat fee of $15 each, forgoing millions of dollars and decades of songwriter royalties in the process.[240] The experiences of Richard, Brown, and Hardwick are no outliers; they are par for the course. As Greene observes, "The fact that minority artists received less protection – or in many cases no protection – for their compositions undermines the incentive theory of intellectual property laws. Many Black artists received little to no economic reward for their creations. Others certainly received less than what they should have."[241]

Even beyond issues of race and gender, crediting often reflects relational and power dynamics (including socioeconomic divides) that may have nothing whatsoever to do with real creative contributions, such as the tenured professor receiving sole authorial credit for a work that includes substantial contributions from graduate students, the law firm partner who has no problem enjoying attribution for the work of a junior associate, or the senator whose "words" are actually those of a speechwriter. Indeed, Spenser Clark's deep dive into the crediting practices on *Hold Up*, one of the songs from Beyoncé's acclaimed concept album *Lemonade*, illustrates this point in the world of pop music.[242] As Clark explains, *Hold Up*'s title and some of its lyrics come from a line that Ezra Koenig, the lead singer of Vampire Weekend, had once tweeted (which, itself, was based on lyrics from *Maps*, a song by indie rockers the Yeah Yeah Yeahs) and subsequent lyrics Koenig had developed in the studio with Beyoncé's noted producer, Diplo, while they were working with a loop from an Andy Williams song.[243] Beyoncé ultimately gave Koenig and the Yeah Yeah Yeahs songwriting credit on *Hold Up* and Diplo a producing credit, but, notably, Williams received no credit at all – either as a songwriter or producer.[244] As Clark concludes, "Oftentimes [artist crediting] choices are not based in law, but rather more intangible considerations like the desire to maintain relationships with creators they wish to work with in the future. Andy Williams' song, for example, was released in 1963, and therefore [Beyoncé] Knowles was probably less concerned with that relationship as she was with other, more relevant artists."[245] Notably, in the music industry (just as in some other creative fields), crediting is not only of reputational or ethical significance; it also determines payment of royalties related to the exploitation of sound recordings and musical compositions.

Finally, besides the power dynamics inherent in the private negotiation of credits, the fundamental constraints of contracting also limit how far it can go in ensuring proper attribution. Crediting claims that rest on negotiated obligations require privity for enforcement, and the realities of the marketplace dictate that not all uses of one's work will be by individuals or entities with whom an author could or would contract.[246] Indeed, this is precisely why we do not leave protection against unauthorized reproduction or other unlawful uses of copyrighted works to contracts and, instead, have infringement claims available that require only access and substantial similarity – no privity and, indeed, no knowledge.

All told, while contracting, especially via collective bargaining, has enjoyed some success in certain industries, private law has not proven sufficiently robust to ensure that crediting rights are adequately protected in the many areas of the information economy where they matter vitally to authors, investors, and consumers. As with joint authorship's mutual intent requirement, the absence of any legal entitlement to crediting ultimately leaves those at society's margins – people of color, women, and the underclass – most vulnerable to exploitation and disproportionately susceptible to receiving insufficient credit for, and participation in, the spoils of their creative labors. At their core, the social justice movements of our time, such as Black Lives Matter and #MeToo, represent efforts to ensure that all people enjoy recognition of their inherent dignity and worth. Achieving this goal goes far beyond anything that copyright law can do. But so long as our legal system fails to adequately support something as basic as proper crediting, the attribution structure of creative enterprise not only operates at suboptimal efficiency but also worsens economic and social inequalities by systematically devaluing female and non-white labors of the mind. To better align copyright with its policy goals and to promote social justice, our laws of collaboration and crediting must begin to privilege creativity over clout, and not the other way around.

3

Controlling the Narrative

How Copyright's Derivative Rights Doctrine Creates Sacred Texts

In which we discuss: the Senator and *Mein Kampf*, 3.5-ton gifts, intellectual property in the vernacular landscape, overconfident polyglots, "little ladies" who started "big wars," a legendary stand-off at Wall Street, lost causes and neocolonial romanticism, ownership of the law, the hidden meaning of *Bambi*, the unappreciated legacy of player pianos, and the unexplored consequences of flag burning

WORLD WAR II AND THE RESISTANCE: THE SECRET HISTORY OF *BAMBI*, *MEIN KAMPF*, AND COPYRIGHT'S DERIVATIVE RIGHTS DOCTRINE

Alan Cranston dedicated his life to public service. He was best known as a politician, representing California in Congress for almost a quarter century (1969–1993) and he even ran as a presidential candidate in 1984. But one of Cranston's most meaningful civic engagements occurred, with little to no fanfare, long before his days in the United States Senate. Though largely relegated to the dustbin of history, Cranston's gambit involved his bold attempt to raise public awareness about the growing tide of fascism and antisemitism emanating from Nazi Germany and its leader, Adolf Hitler, in the years before America's entry into World War II. Ultimately, Cranston's efforts met an ignominious end when they were shut down by powerful forces. If Cranston had not faced such resistance, there is no telling how history may have changed. Curiously though, the power that put an end to Cranston's aspirations was not a foreign government, lobbyists with Nazi sympathies, or geopolitical actors. Rather, it was copyright law.

In the summer of 1934, while still an undergraduate at Stanford University, Cranston visited Nazi Germany and, at one point, came face to face with Adolf Hitler. At the time, Hitler had only recently come to power as Chancellor of Germany. Yet he quickly declared the Nazi Party as the sole legal party permitted in the country and appointed himself its Fuhrer and leader for life. What Cranston witnessed shook him to the core: "I saw this man with a glazed look of power in his face," he later recalled.[1] His encounter with Hitler moved him to a career in public affairs. He worked as a journalist for five years and, later, became a politician, explaining, "I was too concerned about events unfolding in the world with Hitler and Mussolini to spend my life just recording such events. I'd rather be involved in the action."[2]

One day in 1939, while browsing works at the bookstore at the New York Macy's (!), Cranston came across a promotion display for a best-seller. The work in question was Hitler's (not quite yet) infamous autobiography, *Mein Kampf*, which Houghton Mifflin had recently published in an English language edition.

Cranston was shocked when he saw the book, but not because two seemingly venerable American institutions – Macy's and Houghton Mifflin – were blithely promoting the execrable views of an antisemite and dictator. Although the passage of time and our subsequent entrée into World War II has obscured the matter substantially, at the time, Hitler and the Nazis had millions of fans in the United States. For example, legions of Americans attended the Nazi rallies that took place at New York's Madison Square from 1934 through 1939 (Figure 3.1), culminating in a convocation of 20,000 individuals on the night of February 20, 1939. So, regrettably, companies such as Macy's and Houghton Mifflin did not even think twice about promoting the book. Rather, Cranston's surprise arose from the fact that the book he held in his hands in New York was not the *Mein Kampf* with which he was familiar and that, as a German speaker, he had read while abroad. Instead, it was a carefully bowdlerized version of it, stripped of some of its most inflammatory portions – language that literally spelled out Hitler's insidious political agenda. Eher Verlag, the central publishing house of the Nazi Party, had approved the English

FIGURE 3.1 Nazi Rally at Madison Square Garden, New York (May 17, 1934); Bettmann Archive/Getty Images

edition – translated by E. T. S. Dugdale – and had exclusively licensed it, with strategic expurgation, to Houghton Mifflin for the American market starting in 1933. The ploy was simple: the Nazis wanted Hitler's work to appeal to the members of the English-speaking world and to rally support for his cause in more abstract terms, but they did not want them to know the full extent of Hitler's real plans.

Cranston and his friend, Amster Spiro, decided to educate the American public about the dangers of Hitler and his brand of fascism in the best way they knew how: by providing the public with the truth. So they created their own derivative version of *Mein Kampf* – a Reader's Digest-style abridgment entitled *Mein Kampf: A New Unexpurgated Translation Condensed with Critical Comments and Explanatory Notes* that took, in Cranston's later words, "what is coherent thought from the midst of Hitler's torrent of 270,000 words" while ensuring that the translation "contain[ed] every important point, every important idea Hitler presented" and also "eliminat[ed] his long-winded digressions and cut[] out much of the endless repetition."[3] In sum, Cranston created a short, annotated version of *Mein Kampf* that was more readable and also made the horror of Hitler's plans clear.

Noram Publishing Company released the dime-store edition and it sold well, amassing half a million sales in just ten days (Figure 3.2). The publication also ensured that Hitler would get no royalties from its sales and, instead, all profits went to help refugees fleeing the Nazis. In releasing the work, Cranston and his publisher were not merely thumbing their nose at any entitlement Hitler might have to royalties because of their strong objection to his political views or out of a brazen disrespect for the law; rather, there was a colorable argument that the work had fallen into the public domain due to the fact that Hitler was a stateless individual at the time of *Mein Kampf*'s publication.[4]

Unfortunately, Hitler's publisher, Houghton Mifflin, took notice of Cranston's English edition and immediately sued to enjoin further distribution of the work. Drawing on a recent ruling from the Second Circuit deeming *Mein Kampf* under copyright protection, the United States District Court for the Southern District of New York quickly issued an injunction that permanently banned Cranston's "bootleg" version from the marketplace after concluding the work infringed Houghton Mifflin's exclusive rights under the Copyright Act.[5] Pointing to the fact that the Cranston abridgment sold for just ten cents while Houghton Mifflin's edition retailed for three dollars, the Court accused Noram of undercutting Houghton Mifflin and "attempt[ing] to take advantage of the public interest in Hitler, and devis[ing] this form of pamphlet or edition [] to profit by the desire of the public to read about Hitler."[6] Meanwhile, the Court ignored the more noble motivations for the publication, which were announced prominently on the cover of each Cranston edition: to reveal to the American public "HITLER'S 10 YEAR PLAN FOR CONQUEST OF EUROPE" and to provide "NOT ONE CENT OF ROYALTY TO HITLER," a claim that Houghton Mifflin certainly could not make. Ultimately, Noram had to destroy some half million copies it had printed

FIGURE 3.2 Cover of unauthorized and annotated English translation and abridgment of *Mein Kampf*; Noram Publishing

but not sold.[7] And, in the end, our own copyright laws quieted Cranston's exposé of Hitler and his perilous agenda, with untold historical consequences.

To be fair, noble motivations operating alone do not ordinarily excuse copyright infringement. But the fair use doctrine – which, in fact, accounts for socially beneficial uses of works such as commentary, criticism, and education – sometimes does. An affirmative defense that allows an unauthorized derivative work to escape liability if the use meets a four-part balancing test now codified in section 107 of the Copyright Act, fair use evaluates: "(1) the purpose and character of the use ...; (2) the nature of the copyrighted work; (3) the amount and substantially of the portion used in relation to the copyrighted work as a whole; and (4) the effect of the use upon the potential market for or value of the copyrighted work."[8] The four fair-use factors are weighed holistically and an accused infringer bears the burden of proving an entitlement to the defense. As such, the doctrine is abstract, vague, and case-by-case. Nevertheless, fair use functions as a safety valve that limits the absolute dominion rights holders might otherwise have over their works in order to serve a host of public policy goals: the protection of free speech rights, the promotion of new production in service of copyright's aim to promote progress in the arts, the redress of market failures where clearances suffer from excessive transactions costs, and the provision of unfettered access to certain works when it serves the public interest. As a result, in myriad circumstances, fair use allows works that make unauthorized use of someone else's creative output to exist without liability. It is therefore especially notable that the court never addressed the issue of whether Cranston's actions might be protected as fair use. Admittedly, copyright law did not codify the fair-use defense until the passage of the 1976 Copyright Act. But fair use had a rich common-law pedigree, dating back to Justice Joseph Story's 1841 opinion in *Folsom* v. *Marsh*. As a result, the defense had gained significant traction by the 1930s and there was ample precedent to warrant its application. But no mention was made of fair use; instead, the court proceeded with the foregone conclusion that, because Cranston's edition was an unauthorized translation and abridgment of *Mein Kampf*, it must necessarily be infringing.

Mechanistically speaking, Cranston was usurping the exclusive right of an author to create a translation and abridgment of his work. And, casting aside the issue of just who the original author was, this would unquestionably constitute an infringement to any modern court. After all, the Copyright Act expressly lists both translations and abridgments as a type of "derivative work" over which authors enjoy absolute control.[9] But, curiously, this was not always the case.

In the first few decades of American copyright law, courts viewed the creation of abridgments and translations as, per se, *not* infringing. Instead of conceptualizing them as impermissible derivatives, courts saw them as new works of authorship that reflected significant originality and creativity by the translator and abridger. For example, in *Stowe* v. *Thomas* (1853), a lawsuit over an unauthorized German translation of Harriet Beecher Stowe's *Uncle Tom's Cabin*,[10] a Pennsylvania federal court did something unthinkable to us today. Even though the court acknowledged that "The sale of [Stowe's] translation ... was impaired [by defendants' work],"[11] the court not only deemed the translation noninfringing but also affirmatively applauded the defendants for creating a better German edition than Stowe, who had released a (poor) translation assisted by her husband. In the case, the defendant argued that any injury to Stowe's authorized translation was the product of competitive forces in the marketplace: "the reason why [her authorized translation] is injured, is that her translation has less genius than ours."[12] The court seized upon this observation when it performed its own utilitarian calculus on the infringement claim, noting that

> To make a good translation of a work often requires more learning, talent and judgment, than was required to write the original. Many can transfer from one language to another, but few can translate. To call the translations of an author's ideas and conceptions into another language, a copy of his book, would be an abuse of terms, and arbitrary judicial legislation.[13]

The court's philosophical framing of the translation issue bears reflection. Stowe's argument for control over derivatives such as translations, that were based on her work, appealed to a natural law vision of intellectual property, where copyrights vindicated an author's rightful exclusive property interests in the product of her labors. As Stowe maintained, "[t]he right is original, inherent; a right founded on nature, acknowledged, we think, at common-law; a right which stands on better ground and is more deeply rooted than the right to any other property whatever.... What a man earns by thought, study, and care, is as much his own, as what he obtains by his hands."[14] Based on Stowe's conception that copyright should grant absolute property rights to its owner, Stowe argued that any value of the defendant's translation to society should be irrelevant to the court's infringement analysis. Instead, she maintained that all that mattered was that the German translation was free-riding on Stowe's intellectual efforts and trampling upon her natural property rights stemming from those efforts: "[t]he translator aims to convey to the mind of his reader the ideas and thoughts of the author; nay, the very shades of his ideas and thoughts; his exact manner and form of expression, and even his words, so far as represented by similarly constructed expressions in the new language."[15] But the court squarely rejected Stowe's claim of a broad natural-law right to use and exploit her creation. Casting the copyright bargain in a light at odds with current law, the court noted that,

> [b]y the publication of Mrs. Stowe's book, the creations of the genius and imagination of the author have become as much public property as those of Homer or Cervantes. (Uncle Tom and Topsy are as much publici juris as Don Quixote and Sancho Panza.) All her conceptions and inventions may be used and abused by imitators, play-rights and poetasters. (They are no longer her own – those who have purchased her book, may clothe them in English doggerel, in German or Chinese prose. Her absolute dominion and property in the creations of her genius and imagination have been voluntarily relinquished.)[16]

With this perspective in mind, it should come as no surprise that the market harm caused to Stowe by Thomas's German edition garnered no sympathy from the court. Instead, the court's calculus involved assessing the value to society that stemmed from the purported infringement. Copyright was not about protection of an authorial monopoly based on a natural-rights theory of property; instead, it was about striking a utilitarian balance that allowed authors to reap economic rewards for publishing and disseminating their creations while also enabling others to make progressive uses of these disseminated works for the public benefit. Thus, the intellectual craft undertaken in the creation of the translation was central to the court's decision. Instead of looking at what was taken from the plaintiff, the court examined what use the defendant made of that work and how it impacted the promotion of the arts. Because the availability of a superior translation advanced progress in the arts, Stowe lost her infringement claim. And, unlike Cranston's warnings about Hitler, Stowe's protest about the horrors of slavery was (owing to the large German-speaking population in the United States at the time) ultimately able to reach a wider audience and have a greater impact on public opinion.

In early American jurisprudence, courts also deemed abridgments noninfringing on similar grounds. Thus, in *Story* v. *Holcombe* (1847), an Ohio federal court rejected a claim that the defendant had infringed Justice Story's 1,856-page *Commentaries on Equity Jurisprudence* by preparing an abridged, 348-page version of the work, noting that "[a] fair abridgment of any book is considered a new work, as to write it requires labor and exercise of judgment."[17] And in *Wheaton* v. *Peters* (1834), the Supreme Court held that Richard Peter's abridgment of the work of Henry Wheaton, his predecessor as Official Reporter at the Supreme Court, from twelve volumes to six, did not constitute infringement. As the Court noted, "An abridgement fairly done, is itself authorship, requires mind; and is not an infringement, no more than another work on the same subject."[18] Thus, as with translations, courts considered abridgment an intellectual exercise, which, when performed with superior competence, only improved an original work. With their focus on what best advanced progress in the arts, these early jurists found abridgments noninfringing.

When determining the availability of derivative rights – which now, of course, include abridgments and translations as part of the copyright monopoly – courts have often considered the respective efforts and investments of the original author and the creator of the "secondary" work. Early courts – in such cases as *Stowe* and *Wheaton* – viewed the act of abridgment and translation (even if unauthorized) as a tremendous authorial labor that should be rewarded, not punished, and left it to market forces to adjudicate the winner among competing versions. By contrast, later courts ultimately viewed abridgment and translation as properly encompassed within the copyright monopoly and therefore granted exclusive rights to such uses to the original author of a work and insulated authorized abridgments and translations from market competition. They did so on the theory that original authors possessed an inherent proprietary interest in the fruits of their efforts, which secondary creators were improperly usurping in preparing unauthorized abridgments or translations – regardless of the ultimate impact on progress in the arts.

Consider the opinion of Justice Story in *Folsom* v. *Marsh* (1841).[19] Although he was a member of the Supreme Court at the time, consistent with the practice of the era, Story was sitting as a circuit court judge and issued his ruling in that capacity. Although the decision is most well-known as the progenitor of the modern fair use doctrine, it also represented a key moment in repudiating the abridgment and translation jurisprudence of the first few generations of American copyright law and laying the foundation for a broader derivative rights doctrine. In the case, plaintiffs argued that the Reverend Charles Upham's 866-page, two-volume *The Life of Washington*, which lifted 255 pages directly from Jared Sparks's former work, infringed Sparks's 6,763-page, twelve-volume *The Writings of George Washington*, a collection of Washington's official and private papers with additional narrative and editorial notes.[20] In prior decades, as illustrated in *Wheaton*, Upham's abridgment would have enjoyed immunity from infringement claims on the grounds that it required immense independent authorial efforts to prepare. But that was not how the case turned out. Instead, Story likened Upham's actions to stealing – a clear violation of property rights. To any potential "free-rider," Story sternly warned, "[n]one are entitled to save themselves trouble and expense, by availing themselves, for their own profit, of other men's works, still entitled to the protection of copyright."[21] With this Blackstonian vision[22] of copyright guiding his opinion and in strong natural-rights language, Story maintained that "[t]he entirety of the copyright is the property of the author; and it is no defense, that another person has appropriated a part, and not the whole, of any property."[23] With a quick stroke of his pen, Justice Story presumed that an act of borrowing, either in whole or in part, constituted an act of infringement. After all, to Story, the borrowing party usurped control of someone else's property. Borrowing could still be excused, but only if it did not amount to conversion – if, in fact, the borrowing was *de minimis* and did not affect the value of the property taken. So, under *Folsom*, a court might *excuse* the act of borrowing if the defendant effectively proffers a defense of fair use (three of the four factors of which focus on what is taken from, rather than what use is made of, the original work). The paramount purpose of an infringement action became the assurance of the rights of an author in the commercial value of her intellectual labors.

Given the widespread influence of *Folsom* and the expansion of the derivative rights doctrine in the jurisprudence of the past century and a half, courts have tended to privilege a natural-law analysis of what was taken from the original author over a utilitarian analysis of what was given to the public. In the process, they have paid insufficient attention to societal "progress" – the express and overall goal of the copyright regime. The decision to forgo such a calculus is particularly problematic when invocation of derivative rights can impact the types of information and works that the public receives. Such considerations appear especially salient when a case deals with public awareness and education over critical issues of the day. In *Stowe*, for example, providing the large German-speaking population in the United States at the time with access to a readable translation of the most influential novel of the nineteenth century had immense value to public education about the evils of slavery. After all, no less than Abraham Lincoln himself praised the novel for solidifying support for the abolitionist movement. When he met Harriet Beecher Stowe in 1862, he reportedly quipped, "So this is the little lady who made this big war." Indeed, one could reasonably argue that – to the extent that *Uncle Tom's Cabin* turned public opinion against slavery (and there is good reason to think that it did) – the holding in *Stowe* swiftened (no matter how marginally) that result.

By contrast, the legal dispute over *Mein Kampf* failed to give any consideration to broader societal interests at stake with the decision to enjoin Cranston's edition. The myopia of this misstep becomes painfully clear when one considers what happened in the world in the years following that 1939 legal decision. Indeed, the impact that the distribution of unexpurgated version of *Mein Kampf* – one that would provide Americans access to Hitler's real plans, in his own words, without euphemism, obfuscation, or editing – may have had is difficult to overstate.

Oddly enough, Cranston's experience with *Mein Kampf* was not the only significant copyright-related matter that impacted American perceptions of Nazi Germany in the lead-up to World War II. One of the most beloved animated films of all time (and the novel upon which it was based) – *Bambi* – had the ability to do so as well. But, because of the operation of copyright law and its derivative rights doctrine, the allegory's more explicit connections to the Jewish experience and the persecution of minorities remained largely unappreciated during that era.

Bambi: A Life in the Woods was written by Austro-Hungarian writer and critic Felix Salten in serial form in 1922 and published as a book, first in Germany in 1923 and then in Austria in 1926. Salten, who was born as Siegmund Salzmann, was the grandson of an orthodox rabbi and had experienced the scourge of antisemitism firsthand in the remnants of the Austro-Hungarian Empire. As such, his book could be viewed as a rather pointed allegory about the mistreatment of the Jewish population. Although Salten never directly addressed the interpretation of his work in such a light, the book was banned in Germany precisely because the Nazi Party read it as a plea for more humane treatment of the persecuted Jewish-German community.[24]

By 1928, Salten's publisher had authorized an English edition, translated by Whittaker Chambers, to hit the American market (Figure 3.3). But with its "textual infidelity" and "softness to the telling," Chambers's translation obscured the persecution theme significantly.[25] However, it is difficult to conclude that the dilution of this message was the product of Chambers's own volition. On one hand, it could have been an innocent outgrowth of Chambers's inexperience as a translator.[26] While Chambers was an autodidactic polyglot who had taught himself

FIGURE 3.3 Cover of *Bambi: A Life in the Woods* (trans. Whittaker Chambers 1928); Simon & Schuster

German, his linguistic skills were perhaps not as refined as he had believed, and the translation was his first such effort for any work. On the other hand, unsavory motivations – whether conscious or not – may have also guided his transliteration. Chambers was, after all, a communist and eventually became a spy for the Soviet Union (Figure 3.4). In light of this fact, it is only fair to ask, as essayist and critic Meghan Cox Gurdon does, "whether Whittaker Chambers, who was soon to join Stalin's payroll [as a Communist spy], might have had an interest in altering Salten's work not just to make a pleasing English-language family story but also to mitigate its searing portrayal of the totalitarian oppression of innocents."[27]

Whatever the reason for the shortcomings in Whittaker's edition, as German language scholar Sabine Strumper-Krobb notes, it ultimately "tones down Salten's anthropomorphism in places and changes its focus in other, thus opening the possibility for the story to be understood less as a human story about persecution, expulsion or assimilation and more as an animal story conveying a strong message about the protection of animals and the necessity of conservation."[28] However, in recent years, a growing body of literature has made the case for reading Salten's original *Bambi* quite differently – as a "dystopic and sobering" tale of

FIGURE 3.4 Portrait of Whittaker Chambers (1948) by Frank Palumbo, wherein Chambers's getup does him no favors in de-emphasizing his history of spying

"the cutthroat manner in which powerless people are hunted and persecuted for sport,"[29] if not as a direct allegory for the Jewish experience.[30] But, because it was the only authorized edition in the English-speaking world, the Chambers translation would dominate the understanding of the work, and, of course, it formed the basis for the 1942 Disney movie, which served as a paean to animal rights and a warning about human callousness and cruelty toward the natural world. The original story could easily be read as a cautionary tale about the treatment of the Jewish population in Europe. But in the hands of Chambers – a Soviet spy – and Walt Disney – a man with a troubling history of cozy relations with notorious antisemitic individuals such as Leni Riefenstahl and antisemitic organizations such as the Motion Picture Alliance for the Preservation of American Ideals – it was cast in a distinctly different light.

In fact, it was not until 2022 that a competing English version would arrive, when Jack Zipes, a professor emeritus of German and comparative literature at the University of Minnesota, finally managed to publish his translation, *The Original Bambi: The Story of a Life in the Forest*. The reason for the absence of a more accurate translation of *Bambi* in the United States was simple: copyright law. Although there were arguments that *Bambi*'s first publication date for the purposes of protection in the United States was its serial publication in 1922 (meaning the copyright would have expired on January 1, 1998) or its book-form German publication in 1923 (meaning the copyright work would have expired on January 1, 2019), *Bambi*'s American publisher maintained that the operative date of protection in the United States was its 1926 publication in Austria. Ultimately, a legal battle resolved the issue, with the Ninth Circuit concurring with the publisher.[31] As a result, *Bambi* did not go into the public domain until January 1, 2022, and it was not until that date that anyone else could publish a version (or translation) of the work. So, for almost a century, the Chambers edition represented the only permissible English rendition of *Bambi*.

When the Zipes edition finally became public, it forced a profound re-examination of the work and its sociohistorical context. In the words of one reviewer, Zipes "sought to restore both the dignity and relevance of Salten's vision; to rescue it, in a manner of speaking, from Disneyfication."[32] As Zipes himself noted,

> Salten's novel is a brilliant and profound story of how minority groups through the world have been brutally treated, even when they try to live peacefully in their own environment. Read in the original language and in its sociohistorical context, Bambi is, if anything, dystopic and sobering, for it reveals the cutthroat manner in which powerless people are hunted and persecuted for sport.[33]

One is only left to speculate how *Bambi* may have shaped public opinion if copyright law had not prevented these themes from achieving greater resonance.

Of course, copyright law did not cause World War II, and we are not beginning to suggest that the operation of a different copyright regime would have prevented the Holocaust either. But, in the cases of both *Mein Kampf* and *Bambi*, neutral application of the law of copyright helped entrenched powers control narratives that stifled – even if marginally – resistance to Nazi Germany, fascism, and antisemitism. As a result, copyright law impacted the public discourse right when the United States was in the midst of contemplating whether, and how, to respond to the troubling events in Europe in the 1930s and early 1940s. The availability of just a single, diluted translation of a cautionary (and extremely popular) work of fiction redolent with themes of human cruelty, totalitarianism, and intolerance dampened (even if just the tiniest bit) the potential impact that *Bambi* may have had on popular perceptions of the dangers facing the world with the rise of the Nazis. And the banning of a critical, rather than laudatory, version of *Mein Kampf* hindered efforts to inform and educate the public about the grave threat emanating from Germany.

Copyright law and its derivative right doctrine unwittingly helped thwart an enormous opportunity to impact popular perceptions about Hitler's irredentist and imperial intentions and the plight of the Jewish population in Europe during the Nazi era. When there is no market competition for the rendering of a work into another language, society can suffer from the availability of only a single, inferior translation, such as the poor German version of *Uncle Tom's Cabin* overseen by Harriet Beecher Stowe's husband. But, just as significantly, limiting public access to a single translation take can additionally obscure an original work's intent and meaning, with potentially significant consequences for political discourse, social commentary and criticism, and, indeed, the tide of public opinion during a crucial moment in history.

THE HISTORY OF DERIVATIVE RIGHTS

When in the throes of a battle over public perceptions and popular opinion, public relations specialists talk about the need to *control the narrative*. The remarkable stories of *Mein Kampf* and *Bambi* illustrate how copyright's expansive derivative rights doctrine does more than merely impact the incentives of authors to create. Rather, it can also serve as a powerful tool to control the narrative better than even the best PR agent.

Long ago, however, copyright was just a law against piracy. Under our Republic's original law of copyright, passed in 1790, authors enjoyed only the exclusive right to prevent copying of books, maps, and charts and nothing more. As a result, the concept of infringement was strictly limited to direct, one-to-one unauthorized reproductions.[34] But times have changed.

The breadth of protections secured for authors under copyright law has swelled markedly over the past two centuries. Most obviously, it has expanded temporally, from an original fourteen-year term to lifetime plus seventy years. The subject matter enjoying protection has also grown; while early copyright laws covered only books, maps, and charts, modern copyright law encompasses any original work of authorship fixed in a tangible medium. Finally, while the regime originally interdicted only the unauthorized copying of works, it now prohibits unauthorized reproduction, distribution, public display, public performance, and derivatization. This last category – derivative rights – gradually crept into law over the course of the past century and a half and profoundly limited the general public's ability to reinterpret, remix, transform, translate, embellish, adapt, abridge, and alter the creative works of others.[35]

Daly v. *Palmer* (1868) represents a key moment in the evolution of copyright from a law protecting an entire corpus from copying to a law protecting kernels of expression, even if used in wholly new works.[36] As such, the case is recognized as a seminal moment in American copyright jurisprudence for its embrace of proto-derivative rights.[37] In the matter, a New York federal court entertained claims that Dion Boucicault's play, *After Dark*, infringed Augustin Daly's play, *Under the Gaslight*. Specifically, Daly claimed a copyright in the now clichéd, but then original, "Railroad Scene," where an evil character ties a victim (often, a "damsel in distress") to a railroad track, only for a hero to leap onto the scene to conduct a valiant rescue only moments before disaster would strike with the appearance of a speeding train.[38] The case's novelty stemmed from the fact that Daly sought to protect not the literal copying of his language (of which there was none) but, rather, the more abstract notion of event sequencing – nonliteral elements of his work. Ultimately, the *Daly* court issued an injunction preventing defendants from publicly performing any version of the Railroad Scene. As the court rationalized, a dramatic work drawing from a portion of a copyrighted play can constitute an infringement "if the appropriated series of events, when represented on the stage, although performed by new and different characters, using different language, is recognized by the spectator, through any of the senses to which the representation is addressed, as conveying substantially the same impressions to, and exciting the same emotions in, the mind, in the same sequence or order."[39] *Daly* consequently accomplished something unprecedented for its time: it conferred copyright in nonliteral, rather than just literal, elements. In the process, the holding represented what Paul Goldstein has characterized as a "great intellectual leap," as it shifted the conception of copyright from merely protecting rights in copies to protecting rights in "an intellectual essence that could appear in a manifold of concrete forms or media."[40] Thus, derivative rights safeguard not just the work itself but other forms into which its "intellectual essence" might be cast.

Only two years after the *Daly* holding, Congress responded to prevailing copyright sentiments with the passage of the Copyright Act of 1870, which, for the first time, extended copyright protection not just to an author's original work (and copies thereof) but also to related works based on the original. Specifically, the Act gave authors of books the exclusive right "to dramatize or to translate their works"[41] – even though neither a dramatization nor a translation constituted a verbatim copy of an original book. With this change, Congress summarily abrogated *Stowe* v. *Thomas*. The 1909 Copyright Act went a step further by granting dramatists the right to convert their works into "a novel or other nondramatic work" and providing authors of musical compositions (which had just received protection) the right to arrange or adapt their works.[42] By 1976, Congress adopted derivative rights in their capacious modern guise. Section 106(2) of the Copyright Act now secures for copyright holders the expansive exclusive right to "prepare derivative works based upon the copyrighted work."[43] The Act then defines a derivative work in remarkably broad terms: as any "work based upon one or more preexisting works, such as a translation, musical arrangement, dramatization, fictionalization, motion picture version, sound recording, art reproduction, abridgment, condensation, or any other form in which a work may be recast, transformed, or adapted."[44]

Today, therefore, the law of copyright does not merely protect an author against the scourge of piracy. It secures the ability of rights holders to control entire derivative franchises that span multiple sectors of the economy and categories of consumption. *Harry Potter* is not merely a book series; it is a movie franchise, a bankable toy line, musical recordings, video and board games, mobile apps, Halloween costumes, branded clothing, jewelry, home décor, fashion accessories, kitchenware, and even a bedding line.[45] And it is a singular feature of modern copyright law, the derivative rights doctrine, that allows *Harry Potter*'s author, J. K. Rowling, and her licensee, Warner Brothers, the exclusive ability to control this universe.

Derivative rights are, no doubt, a boon to rights holders. So it should come as no surprise that lobbyists for content owners have strongly pushed for their extension and maintenance. To be fair, however, derivative rights can serve the public interest by incentivizing the creation of certain types of works that may not otherwise be made. For example, derivative rights enable studios to invest hundreds of millions of dollars in the financing of a movie because, if successful, it will spur the creation of sequels, spin-off television series, and toy and clothing lines.

But there is also a dark side to the derivative rights doctrine. With the dispersal of digital technology and the tools of networked creativity into the hands of ordinary people on an unprecedented scale, we are increasingly forced to confront this conundrum: At a time when individuals have a greater ability to make use of creative works than ever before, the law has sharply curtailed our ability to interact with and respond to them. While this may be warranted in some circumstances, it gives rise to two potential risks.

First, some unauthorized derivatives advance the utilitarian goals of the copyright regime by giving the public new creative works imbued with original insights, meanings, and messages.[46] In the parlance of documentarian Kirby Ferguson, who wrote and directed the powerful *Everything Is a Remix* docu-series, creative evolution is – like physical evolution – a process of copying, transforming, and combining to produce heretofore unknown blends and fusions[47] – except instead of genes, the raw materials for creative evolution are cultural memes.[48] This mixing and remixing of cultural memes from around the globe is a dynamic amalgamating process that spurs innovation by giving rise to new forms of creativity. The derivative rights doctrine can therefore impoverish the creative marketplace by preventing the authorship and distribution of countless new works of ingenuity simply because they may owe their existence to a pre-existing work.

Second, transformative interactions with existing creative works can steer the development of cultural networks, challenge prevailing ideological narratives or social norms, and demarcate or blur social strata.[49] Specifically, our ability to make (or not make) semiotic use of cultural content shapes the way in which individuals express themselves to the world. By limiting transformative use, the derivative rights doctrine can restrict activities such as remixing, sampling, mash-up, appropriationist art, satire, and even parody (if it were not saved by fair use) that can illuminate our values, scrutinize our social institutions, and comment on current events and our culture.

As social theorist Jean Baudrillard posits, the primary function of products, including cultural works, no longer lies in their use, but rather in their communicative status.[50] While one may quibble with this assertion when considering products that provide basic sustenance – to the hungry, the primary function of a loaf of bread is still very much in its use as food – Baudrillard's point is particularly salient in richer societies and in the context of intellectual property. The consumption of intellectual property – both in terms of what we consume and how we consume it – constitutes an act of affiliation and differentiation that is culturally bound.[51] Indeed, the act of conspicuous consumption – to borrow Thornstein Veblen's phrase – can communicate social status, exclusivity, and affiliation,[52] while acts of contestation, rejection, and reinterpretation of cultural texts enable resistance to prevailing ideological narratives. Individuals define their relationship with, and status in, their broader society – be it oppositional or harmonious, insider or outsider – through their consumptive actions. As media scholar John Fiske notes in his landmark analysis of popular culture,

> [c]ulture marking (and culture is always in process, never achieved) is a social process: all meanings of self, of social relations, all the discourses and texts that play such important cultural roles can circulate only in relationship to the social system, in our case that of white, patriarchal capitalism. Any social system needs a cultural system of meanings that serves either to hold it in place or destabilize it, to make it more or less amenable to change. Culture (and its meanings and pleasures) is a constant succession of social practices; it is therefore inherently political, it is centrally involved in the distribution and possible redistribution of various forms of social power.[53]

Intellectual property therefore mediates the way in which the social practice of culture can or cannot occur. By regulating the unwanted embellishment, abridgment, transformation, manipulation, and alteration of creative works, copyright law protects against, or selectively allows, acts of "semiotic disobedience,"[54] Sonya Katyal's potent shibboleth for artistic practices that "interrupt[], appropriate[e], and then replac[e] the passage of information from creator to consumer."[55] Semiotic disobedience occurs through "the conscious and deliberate re-creation of property through appropriative and expressive acts that consciously risk violating the law that governs intellectual or tangible property."[56] Building on Katyal's work,[57] this chapter examines how the operation of the derivative rights doctrine can adversely impact even otherwise-protected acts of semiotic disobedience by deeming protected works sacred and inviolable, subject only to reinterpretation as the masters themselves deem compatible with their artistic, economic, or ideological interests.[58] We begin by illustrating how capacious conceptions of derivative rights can operate to stifle challenges to both public and private power in a manner that threatens both progress in the arts and acts of semiotic disobedience.

FLAGS, DRAFT CARDS, AND LICENSE PLATES: DERIVATIVE RIGHTS AND GOVERNMENT PROTEST

Our intellectual property regime exempts some government works from copyright protection. Specifically, the federal government has made the decision that the public weal favors dedicating the work of government servants to the public itself. As such, section 105 of the Copyright Act dedicates the entire creative output of the federal government to the public domain.[59] But, contrary to popular perception, not everything the government creates is owned by the public. Out of respect for federalism principles and state sovereignty, Congress has not excluded other types of government works from protection and, instead, has left this issue to state and local governments to determine for themselves. As a result, no general rule prevents state or local governments from claiming copyright protection over works they create, so long as they meet the normal originality, authorship, and fixation requirements. Additionally, section 105 makes clear that the federal government can hold and exploit copyright interests in works that are assigned to it.[60] As a result of these features of the Copyright Act, it would be entirely possible for government entities to claim copyright protection in works imbued with symbolic meaning such as flags.[61] For instance, assuming the apocryphal tale that Betsy Ross created Old Glory is true, she could have assigned her copyright to the Feds, who could then enforce it for the duration of its term. Meanwhile, each new version of the flag could potentially receive a new copyright.[62] The latest iteration of the American flag, which features fifty stars for the fifty states, only came into being with the admission of Hawai'i to the Union in 1959. As such, the current American flag could theoretically enjoy copyright protection for several more decades. More broadly, there is nothing preventing states or municipalities from protecting their flags, seals, or almost any other creative work under copyright law; after all, section 105's dedication of works to the public domain only applies to those authored by the United States government.[63]

This state of affairs, combined with the broad conception of derivative rights, can lead to some surprising and potentially dangerous consequences. For example, consider the dramatic impact that federal or state government enforcement of copyrights in flags might have on the right to engage in acts of semiotic disobedience. Pursuant to section 106(5) of the Copyright Act, the holder of the copyright to the flag could enjoy the exclusive right to control, among other things, its public display.[64] To fly the flag, one would need the express permission of the government. Disfavored displays of the flag or uses on clothing could trigger cease and desist letters that, unheeded, could lead to suits for injunctions and damages. The mere reproduction of the flag in association with unpopular causes might result in sizeable liability.[65] In sum, friends of the government would enjoy the right to raise the flag and honor our country at their whim while foes doing the same would risk significant legal consequences. The ability to align oneself or one's organization with patriotic values would be determined by the rights holders to Old Glory, the Lone Star flag, or Ka Hae Hawai'i. Thus, the exertion of copyright over flags would lead to a means of controlling access to what are perhaps our most important national and state symbols.

Even if one gets past the public display issue by arguing fair use[66] or waiver by virtue of the government having designated a particular design as the national or state flag, the problematic relationship between intellectual property and patriotic symbols does not end. Under section 106(2) of the Copyright Act, copyright holders alone enjoy the privilege of creating derivative versions of their works.[67] As such, not only do the famous artistic interpretations of the American flag by Jasper Johns and others risk liability and interdiction, but something more unusual might occur: flag burning could even be banned.

Efforts to outlaw flag burning by direct statute have famously failed on constitutional grounds. In 1989, the Supreme Court deemed a Texas statute criminalizing the act unconstitutional on First Amendment grounds.[68] A similar federal statute was struck in 1990.[69] However, courts have shown little compunction about enforcing intellectual property laws, especially copyright, in the face of potential First Amendment problems. After all, as the Supreme Court has asserted, while you may have a right to *your own* free speech, you do not necessarily have a right to make or use the speech (i.e., the copyrighted works) *of others*.[70] And one could argue that the act of mutilation that occurs with the burning of a flag is akin to producing an unauthorized derivative work. The argument has had traction in related contexts. For example, appellate courts have found that the mutilation of a copyrighted work[71] or reframing it in a new context[72] can amount to a violation of 17 U.S.C. § 106(2)'s proscription against the creation of unauthorized derivative works. Moreover, the text of the Copyright Act suggests that alterations and destructions of a work can amount to unlawful derivatives.[73] Given this and other intellectual property jurisprudence,[74] it is not unfathomable that a court might deem debasement of a protected work such as a flag infringing and dismiss any free-speech implications by arguing that copyright law, as a neutral law of general application, does not target speech for content, and that, if one wants to make a point about America, one is free to do so in another way that does not involve the mutilation of the flag.

And it is not just the constitutional right to burn a flag that copyright law threatens. In *Spence* v. *Washington* (1974), for example, the Supreme Court struck a Washington State law that barred the placing of any "word, figure, mark, picture, design, drawing or advertisement" of the flag or the public display of such an altered flag.[75] Under the provision, Washington had prosecuted a college student for flying the American flag upside down, with a peace sign over it, from the window of his apartment as a protest against the invasion of Cambodia and the killings at Kent State University. Since, among other things, the physical integrity of the flag was not at issue and "in a technical sense it was not the property of any government," the Court reasoned that there was no cognizable state interest at issue and, therefore, the student's expressive rights prevailed.[76] But, in a situation where the government could claim a cognizable property interest – say, for example, a copyright – in every printed flag, the logic of *Spence* would not protect the expressive interests of the public. So, for example, the State of Texas could very well copyright the Lone Star Flag (or a new rendition thereof, if the old flag's term has expired) and proceed to regulate its use in the same manner that any rights holder restricts exploitation of its intellectual property. In the end, copyright law can accomplish what direct statutes against flag burning cannot and, in the process, an important avenue of political and social resistance can be effectively suppressed.

Copyright therefore places semiotic control over such works as flags in the hands of rights holders, thereby enabling them to secure and mediate the meaning of important patriotic, humanistic, and cultural symbols through intellectual property law. This, in turn, impacts the right to protest and resist dominant ideologies. In regulating, and even forbidding, certain forms of consumption and customization, copyright law renders political and cultural symbols that come under its scope inviolable, with dangerous consequences for those attempting to challenge mainstream orthodoxies or prevailing mores. After all, government works – content that speaks for and represents the collective state or nation producing them – are precisely the types of creative output most likely to be imbued with powerful semiotic values.

In fact, in recent years, governmental entities have grown increasingly aggressive about enforcing their potential copyright interests, as the State of Georgia illustrated when it sued a nonprofit, Public Resource, for reproducing the Official Code of Georgia Annotated (OCGA) online.[77] While Public Resource sought to enhance public access to, and understanding of, the law by providing the OCGA freely on its website, Georgia asserted copyright protection over the compilation, which sold for $412 in hard copy.[78] Georgia was not alone in this practice; twenty-two other states, two territories, and the District of Columbia also took such a position.[79] But in *Georgia* v. Public.Resource.Org, *Inc.* (2020), the Supreme Court rejected Georgia's infringement claim by a single vote (5–4), ultimately concluding that the OCGA constituted a "government edict," meaning it was effectively authored by the People and could not enjoy copyright protection since "no one can own the law."[80] Notably, however, the Court emphasized the narrowness of its decision, explaining that the government edict doctrine "does not apply to non-lawmaking officials, leaving States free to assert copyright in the vast majority of expressive works they produce."[81] With this invitation from the Supreme Court and the broad availability of protection for works with even the smallest modicum of creativity, protection can vest in not only flag designs but also tax notices, educational pronouncements, or other materials from state and local governments. And, significantly, while some states (such as Colorado) have expressly deeded their official flags to the public domain, others (such as Nebraska) make clear that they have not.[82]

Besides proscribing the desecration of flags, governmental copyrights can also limit other types of protest activity. Consider the way that courts have balanced the public's right to protest the government with the government's interests in protecting its property. In *United States* v. *O'Brien* (1968),[83] the Supreme Court famously addressed whether a conscript's criminal conviction for the burning of his draft card – an act of defiance against the Vietnam War – violated his right to free speech. Even though the law prohibiting the burning of a draft card only facially regulated conduct, the Court recognized that, in the context of a public conflagration, it implicated symbolic speech interests. So, the Supreme Court determined that such laws impacting expressive conduct would receive heightened (intermediate) scrutiny. Ultimately, the Court found that the government's substantial interest in orderly administration of the draft, which would be threatened with the intentional destruction of registration certificates, justified the ban on draft-card destruction, despite the resulting limitation on O'Brien's expressive rights. Importantly, however, the Court took pains to note that its decision to uphold the law rested on the sufficient alternative avenues of communication O'Brien still enjoyed to express his sentiments about the War and the draft.[84] As Akhil Amar has consequently argued, the card-burning ban survived constitutional scrutiny precisely because it was narrowly tailored to meet "genuine concerns" about forgery and because it "did not touch wholly expressive burnings of unofficial draft card replicas[, such that] it would have been no crime to make a lifesize or postsize copy, a replica – a symbol of the draft card and burn *the symbol* as a purely ideological protest."[85] But consider how this calculus changes when the draft card becomes subject to copyright protection. In such an instance, the mere act of creating a replica of the card (an authorized reproduction of a protected work) and the burning of the replica (an unauthorized derivative) become potential copyright infringements, even though the destructive act would now be purely symbolic and would not impact the orderly administration of the draft. Copyright law can therefore render elusive the safety valve for expressive rights and protest activity envisioned by *O'Brien*.

Copyright's derivative rights doctrine has the ability to undo other constitutional protections for acts of semiotic disobedience involving the alteration of governmental symbols for protest purposes. In *Wooley* v. *Maynard* (1977),[86] for example, the Supreme Court reversed the criminal tampering conviction of George and Maxine Maynard, a married couple who had covered up New Hampshire's "Live Free or Die" motto on their motor vehicle plates on the grounds that the message violated their "moral, religious and political beliefs."[87] As the Court held, the State's legitimate interest in encouraging an "appreciate of history, state pride, and individualism" did not outweigh the couple's "First Amendment right to avoid becoming the courier for [the State's ideological] message."[88] But, if we reframe the dispute from a copyright perspective, and the State brings an infringement, rather than criminal tampering, claim, the license plate can enjoy a special inviolability. With a modification to the license plate potentially creating an unlawful derivative work,[89] the Maynards's act of resistance goes from constitutionally protected to liability inducing.

FROM BULL TO BULLY: DERIVATIVE RIGHTS AND THE SEMIOTICS OF WALL STREET

Derivative rights do not only limit the range of acceptable protest activities against the government; they can also suppress resistance against prevailing corporate practices and ideologies. Indeed, a high-profile controversy involving public art in

Manhattan illustrates how the derivative rights doctrine can even exert control over the vernacular landscape while suppressing acts of semiotic subversion.

In the spring of 2017, the placement of a new statue in the heart of Manhattan's Financial District provoked a firestorm of controversy. The work, named *The Fearless Girl* and cast in bronze, depicted a young Latina standing proud and confident, with her ponytail and dress swishing in the wind and her arms against her hips, a look of calm defiance on her face as she gazed assuredly ahead. Even by itself, the statue was provocative. But, placed in context, it became something extraordinary.

As it turns out, *The Fearless Girl* was never intended as a stand-alone project; rather, it was meant to be placed in front of *Charging Bull*, Arturo Di Modica's iconic sculpture of a ferocious whipping bull, which has famously occupied the northern corner of Bowling Green since 1989.[90] *Fearless Girl* therefore directly took on *Charging Bull* and challenged its unabashedly masculine celebration of American capitalism by calling attention to the under-representation of women (especially those of color) on Wall Street. The statue resonated with the millions who visited the Financial District and it instantly became one of the most successful public art installations in recent memory, particularly because it arrived at the height of #MeToo and articulated, in powerful artistic terms, core sentiments of the movement. But since *The Fearless Girl*'s very existence was dependent on, and related to, *Charging Bull*, it also precipitated an intellectual property imbroglio – one that ultimately resulted in its removal. Copyright law told *The Fearless Girl* that she might constitute an unauthorized derivative work, both without copyright protection (*i.e.*, no cognizable authorship) and subject to destruction. Thus, the legal and ontological standoff between Wall Street's *Charging Bull* and *The Fearless Girl* illustrates how the derivative rights doctrine, with its potentially broad applications, can privilege patriarchal narratives and enjoin, as unlawful derivatives, works of resistance to them.

In 1987, Arturo Di Modica endeavored to make an artistic statement that would lift the pall cast over his adopted hometown of New York in the wake of the stock market crash.[91] So he spent two years and dedicated $320,000 of his own money[92] to cast a 3.5-ton, 16-foot-long bronze statue of a bull, nostrils flared, tail whipped, in graceful but ferocious balance. When he completed his project, he presented it as a Yuletide gift to the city by unceremoniously dropping the statue at the busy intersection of Wall and Broad Streets under cover of night on December 15, 1989.[93]

Since Di Modica never bothered to permit the project and the statue badly obstructed traffic, his gesture did not initially receive the welcome he had expected. Not surprisingly, therefore, the New York Police Department and New York Stock Exchange removed the Bull the very next day after it arrived.[94] But Di Modica's stunt garnered headlines, and, more importantly, his work spoke to the public. As a result, the Bull returned to public view two weeks later when the Parks Commissioner elected to place the statue in Bowling Green, where it remains to this day.[95]

For almost three decades, the Bull enjoyed that prized position in the center of the Financial District all to itself. But its monopoly ended on March 7, 2017, when the Bull received a pint-sized visitor.[96] Measuring just four feet, two inches in height, *The Fearless Girl* was the brainchild of State Street Global Advisors (SSgA).[97] As part of a (now very successful)[98] marketing ploy, SSgA commissioned artist Kristen Visbal to create the statue to serve as a commercial tie-in with the firm's celebration of International Women's Day, which featured the launch of SSgA's SHE index fund as part of a campaign to increase female representation on corporate boards.[99]

The commercial motivation for *The Fearless Girl* was undeniable. The plaque beneath the actual Girl read, "[k]now the power of women in leadership. SHE makes a difference," in a direct reference to State Street's new index fund.[100] But these facts did not mean that the statue was a commercial work, particularly for First Amendment purposes, which the Supreme Court has defined as something that *solely* effectuates a commercial purpose.[101] Indeed, *The Fearless Girl* transcended its commercial origins and struck a powerful chord with the public. US House Representative Carolyn Maloney captured the response to the work when she noted that "[t]his statue has touched hearts across the world with its symbolism of the resiliency of women."[102] Although she was originally permitted for just one week, *The Fearless Girl* had her run before the Bull extended.[103]

The Fearless Girl's success did not please everyone, however. Arturo Di Modica, for one, expressed particular consternation, arguing that the statue's positioning in the immediate eye-line of his growling, menacing beast fundamentally altered his work and subverted his artistic vision. While the Bull was once a "symbol of prosperity and for strength"[104] and an awakener of the "animal spirits"[105] of the market, with *The Fearless Girl* in its sights, it appeared to be a pusillanimous oppressor, threatening a diminutive girl. In short, the Bull had become a *bully* (Figure 3.5).

To counter this unwelcome recasting of his work's semiotics, Di Modica took a multi-faceted approach in the fight against *The Fearless Girl* and appealed to the public, politicians, and the law. He whipped up public support by holding a press conference to raise awareness over his grievance and garner support for his cause.[106] He worked political channels by filing a complaint with the Mayor of New York.[107] Finally, he pursued the legal angle by threatening to initiate a lawsuit against the makers of *The Fearless Girl* for violating his copyrights and attendant right of integrity in and to *Charging Bull*.[108] In the process of all this activity, he provoked broader questions about the legal rights of creators to control and patrol the integrity of their artistic visions. But while Di Modica's cause may have been unfairly characterized by some and the attack on his artistic integrity did deserve some sympathy, there were troubling consequences to enforcing copyright along the lines of his legal vision. This is particularly true when one examines Di Modica's position through a critical perspective that considers how the *Bull*, and his attendant copyright, literally embodies the male gaze discussed in Chapter 1

FIGURE 3.5 *Fearless Girl* stares down *Charging Bull* by Anthony Quintano © 2017, licensed via Creative Commons CC BY 2.0 DEED, https://creativecommons.org/licenses/by/2.0/

and how the *Girl* – no matter what her crass commercial origins – represents a work of resistance to traditional patriarchal narratives.

Di Modica's use of copyright law as a means to obliterate *The Fearless Girl* from the Bull's line of sight constituted an effort to give the *Bull* (and, implicitly, its author) the authority to literally control his gaze and determine what can and cannot lie within his scrutiny. And, as Di Modica's legal position suggests, the Bull would give no quarter to a proud and confident young girl in his immediate view. Di Modica's authority to govern the *Bull*'s gaze – to sacralize his creative output in a context of his choice – was a direct function of the rights to which he claimed entitlement by virtue of his authorship: copyright and the neighboring right of integrity.[109] Authorship therefore lay at the heart of the battle to control the *Bull*'s (male) gaze.

Given the etymological roots of the word "authorship," its link to the concept of authority should not be surprising. Sharing the same etymological root, the terms "authority" and "author" derive from the Latin word "auctor," which refers to an originator or promoter. As such, the search for authorship is a quest to determine the originator of a work or, quite literally, the person who possesses authority over it. In one sense, therefore, the idea of authorship speaks to the traditional search for a mastermind *at the time of creation*. But the idea also extends beyond the time of creation and speaks to the issue of continuing power – namely, the ability to control permissible uses and castings of the work *post-creation*. Thus, as Jamie Boyle has argued, authorship is a concept through which the "power to rule the interpretation of the text"[110] is exercised. Boyle's view of authorship draws from the work of Michel Foucault, who grounded authorship in the idea of thrift, a heuristic tool meant to limit the range of meanings that text can possess. To Foucault, authorship serves as "a certain functional principle by which, in our culture, one limits, excludes, and chooses; in short, by which one impedes the free circulation, the free manipulation, the free composition, decomposition, and recomposition of fiction."[111] In other words, authorship functions as a vehicle through which authority to control narratives and semiotics passes. In that spirit, therefore, the location of authorship and its appurtenant rights in one individual can result in demeaning and devaluing the authorial contributions of others. As David Lange has noted, "[w]e value authorship, or so we say insistently in the main theories of the field. And yet it appears, again and again, that we merely value some authors, and then at the expense of others."[112] The *Charging Bull* and *The Fearless Girl* provide a poignant example of this phenomenon: the broader we conceive *Charging Bull*'s authorship, the more we diminish that of *The Fearless Girl*.

Consider, specifically, how extant copyright principles could enable Di Modica to control his vision, snuff out *The Fearless Girl*, and give primacy to his particular narrative about Wall Street and New York. First, since *The Fearless Girl* ineluctably (and by admission of its creator)[113] existed in tandem with, and was dependent on, *Charging Bull*, one might view the former as an unauthorized derivative of the latter, something only copyright holders have the exclusive right to prepare.[114] On cursory examination, it might seem unusual to claim that *The Fearless Girl* is an unauthorized derivative of *Charging Bull*. After all, unlike traditional derivative works (such as a sequel to a movie, a toy based on a video game character, or translation of a novel), the former does not appear to directly usurp any protectable elements, whether literal or not, from the latter. Moreover, *The Fearless Girl*'s physical existence is separate from that of *Charging Bull* – unlike, say, works that build upon pre-existing works.

But section 101 of the Copyright Act defines derivative works quite broadly, as any "work *based upon one or more preexisting works*, such as a translation, musical arrangement, dramatization, fictionalization, motion picture version, sound recording, art reproduction, abridgment, condensation, or any other form in which a work may be recast, transformed, or adapted."[115] Thus, a derivative work need not reproduce any of the constituent parts of an original work.[116] In fact, one could argue that placing such a limitation on the definition of a derivate work would render the exclusive right to derivatives in section 106(2) superfluous and redundant to the exclusive right of reproduction contained in section 106(1).[117] Di Modica's interpretation of derivative might stretch the concept, but the concept has been pliable over the past century. After all, once upon a time, both translations and abridgments were not considered impermissible derivative works but, instead, new works of authorship that reflected significant originality and creativity by the translator and abridger.[118] Thus, regardless of one's position on the ultimate issue of legal liability, there was at least a colorable argument that *The Fearless Girl* was "based upon" *Charging Bull*, per statutory definition. As Di Modica's lawyers put it, "[t]he statue of the young girl becomes the 'Fearless Girl' only because of the *Charging Bull*: the work is incomplete without Mr. Di Modica's *Charging Bull*, and as such it constitutes a derivative of the *Charging Bull*."[119]

The ontological consequences of being deemed a derivative work are draconian, as they legally transform *The Fearless Girl* into a violation of someone else's intellectual property rights (i.e., as an unauthorized reworking of someone else's copyrighted statue) and deprive the work of its own agency (i.e., as an original work of authorship imbued with the attendant rights attached thereto). As an infringement, *The Fearless Girl* would arguably receive no copyright protection of its own[120] and could even face potential destruction.[121] In short, if *The Fearless Girl* constitutes a derivative work, she ceases to have her own legal existence and loses any autonomy she might otherwise possess. Instead, copyright law will make her the property of the Bull, a mere subject of his (male) gaze.

In addition, *The Fearless Girl* arguably gives rise to a claim under the Visual Artist Rights Act (VARA),[122] which has imported limited moral-rights protection into American law by giving certain visual artists the right of integrity and attribution to their works.[123] Di Modica could claim that the placement of the *Girl* in opposition to the *Bull* on Bowling Green constitutes an actionable "intentional distortion, mutilation, or other modification of [the] work which would be prejudicial to [Di Modica's] honor or reputation."[124] After all, by intentionally engaging the *Bull* in a standoff, the *Girl* effectively distorts and mutilates the *Bull*'s meaning. As one critic put it, "intended as a symbol of strength by the artist, the bull takes on a menacing air in relation to the girl."[125] The *Girl* therefore fundamentally recasts the *Bull* from majestic to minacious, noble to nefarious, and magnific to misogynistic. Since Di Modica's artistic standing is inextricably linked with that of his most famous work, the resulting injury to his reputation seems colorable, at the very least.

Di Modica was absolutely right: *The Fearless Girl* fundamentally recast the meaning of his work, and it did so to spectacular effect, in a manner that may well have injured *Charging Bull*'s reputation and, with it, his own. But that is no reason to ban the Girl from the Bull's gaze. In fact, that was precisely the genius of Visbal's work: it tapped into the zeitgeist with surgical precision. With perhaps the unlikeliest of heroes, *The Fearless Girl* poignantly challenged the primacy of the *Bull* and business-as-usual on Wall Street and called on society to redouble its effort to fight persistent gender inequities. Our laws should encourage, not suppress, such poignant artistic expression. But by doing otherwise, we betray important First Amendment values by controlling the semiotics of American capitalism and silencing the views of subordinated communities resisting dominant epistemologies.

To be fair, Di Modica's cause was not without its sympathetic elements. His pain was real and appeared to stem from a genuine concern for his artistic vision, not a repulsion to *The Girl*'s message.[126] But as understandable as Di Modica's position might have been, that did not mean it should be given a legal voice. As Amy Adler has cogently reasoned, "[t]he bull sculpture captured something of that moment [in 1989]. The 'Fearless Girl' is capturing something of our moment.... The possibility of changed meaning is ... painful for an artist, but something we should celebrate as a public policy matter."[127] Art should not remain static, and a rights holder should not be able to wield the long arm of the law to censor the expressive activities of other creative minds who come in the decades and centuries after them.[128]

Indeed, if one gives credence to Di Modica's legal argument, any work that responds to a pre-existing one could be deemed unlawful if created without authorization. So Lynyrd Skynyrd's *Sweet Home Alabama* might well constitute an unauthorized derivative version, and therefore infringement, of Neil Young's *Southern Man*;[129] Haruki Murakami's novel *1Q84*,[130] an unauthorized derivative and infringement of George Orwell's *1984*;[131] and Liz Phair's *Exile in Guyville*,[132] an unauthorized derivative and infringement of Rolling Stones's iconic album *Exile on Main St.*[133] But such dialogues between artworks are a vital process of cultural evolution, and, not surprisingly, these three influential examples touch on key societal fracture lines of race, gender, and ideology. Young and Lynyrd Skynyrd debated the racial politics and cultural heritage of the South during the peak of the civil rights movement. Phair's "feminist landmark" riffed on the Stones ("the ultimate guy band") with her song-by-song response to *Exile on Main St.* to push back against the male domination of the music industry by serving as a "defiant and sexual and unapologetic and vulnerable ... kind of girl-next door[,] casually swinging a sledgehammer at rock 'n' roll as we knew it singing about sex, love and power in a direct, unmediated way that free women before her."[134] And Murakami expanded on themes of Orwell's totalitarian dystopia by exploring the growth of the surveillance state and cultism and the potential resistance to it that comes from art and self-expression. If we were to cast these secondary works as infringing, we would not only deprive the public of important contributions to the annals of music and literature but also stifle pivotal moments of resistance to, and recodings of, ideological narratives.

In the end, calls to extend the copyright monopoly to responsive works that challenge an "original" author's narrative raise fundamental questions about the ontology of authorship and authority. In the controversy over *Charging Bull* and *The Fearless Girl*, does Di Modica, as author of the *Bull*, have authority over how his work is presented and how the space around his statue is used? Or is *The Fearless Girl* an original (*i.e.*, not derivative) work of authorship in and of itself, imbued with its own legal existence and rights such that she can stand before the *Bull* without fear of legal liability? If Di Modica's *Bull* is entitled to a zone of protection around it, then other works of authorship throughout the City would be entitled to similar bubbles. Such a situation would lace the physical geography of public spaces with a lattice of invisible artistic easements that hinder the natural development of the vernacular landscape, restrain the use of real property, and stifle expressive freedoms. Moreover, recognition of such rights would reconceptualize authorship to not only include the work one has fixed but also any other work that depends on, or exists in tandem with, said work – a pernicious expansion of the derivative works doctrine and the very meaning of authorship.

To illustrate the dangers of Di Modica's legal arguments, consider that, if Di Modica's claim had any merit, the very statue he illegally "gave" to New York as an unwanted Christmas present could have exposed *him* to liability.[135] After all, Di Modica complained that an unpermitted transformation had occurred in the meaning of his work. Yet, as the *Bull*'s genesis makes clear, unpermitted transformation of meaning was the very intention of Di Modica's own work. Profoundly impacted by the downturn in the national mood following the 1987 stock market crash, Di Modica wanted to revitalize New Yorkers' sense of optimism and Wall Street's commercial effervescence. He harnessed the symbolic power of public art to achieve this goal by creating a statue that would impact its surroundings and rewrite the semiotics of the Financial District.

The whole point of Di Modica's *Charging Bull* was to morph the psychophysical landscape of New York – to transform a space characterized by pessimism and weakness into one imbued with optimism and strength. When he dropped his work on Manhattan under the cover of night in 1989, he did not even bother to seek permission from the city that owned the land. Just as significantly, he certainly did not garner approval from the many other rights holders of pre-existing works of authorship – the architecture of the surrounding buildings, the insignias of the extant commercial brands occupying nearby spaces, the design of Bowling Green[136] – dotting the same landscape that the *Bull* had invaded. It makes no sense to deprive *Fearless Girl* of the same expressive right to transform this space – from one characterized by unbridled masculinity and domination into one imbued with a spirit of feminism and resistance.

Despite the challenges Di Modica might have faced in establishing legal liability,[137] however, between his infringement and VARA claims, he had a potential case.[138] And therein lies the rub. Empowered by copyright law, the bull stared down and threatened, with viable legal action, anyone who dared stand in his direct line of sight – including a little girl. In the end, therefore, Di Modica got his way. *The Fearless Girl* no longer stands in Bowling Green, courageously defying *Charging Bull*. In December 2018 – at the very height, ironically, of the #MeToo movement – she was unceremoniously relocated to Broad Street, where, somewhat anticlimactically, she now stares down the New York Stock Exchange instead.

FAIR USE AND DERIVATIVE WORKS

While the *Fearless Girl* controversy was resolved short of litigation, when putative rights holders end up asserting their derivative rights in court, they do face limits. In theory, copyright could resolve some of the concerns raised about an expansive derivative rights doctrine with judicious use of legal checks to the doctrine, the most significant of which is fair use. Indeed, despite constituting derivatives, works such as 2 Live Crew's take on Roy Orbison's *Pretty Women*,[139] South Park's use of Samwell's *What What (In the Butt)*,[140] or Paramount's movie-poster riff on Annie Leibovitz's famous photograph of a pregnant Demi Moore for *Vanity Fair*[141] have been deemed noninfringing fair uses. But fair use is notoriously unreliable, as contradictory rulings abound even on remarkably similar fact patterns.[142] Moreover, determinations only come after parties have spent hundreds of thousands of dollars, if not more, in attorneys' fees and costs to reach a merits-based decision.[143] All the while, it is an uphill battle since, as an affirmative defense, the user always bears the burden of proof.[144] And, of course, losses can be extremely costly, given the potential penalties, including statutory damages and fees, when a fair use defense is rejected.[145] Even beyond these shortcomings, its operation has all too often been infected with problematic limitations and reliance on aesthetic judgments that ultimately privilege cultural elites and sacred texts.

Goldsmith v. Warhol *and the Tension between Derivative Works and Fair Use*

One particular paradox exemplifies the difficulty facing arbiters tasked with drawing the fine line between infringing derivatives and those excused as fair use: the concept of transformation. On one hand, Section 106(2) of the Copyright Act secures for copyright holders the exclusive right to "prepare derivative works based upon the copyrighted work,"[146] where a derivative is deemed to be any "work based upon one or more preexisting works, such as a translation, musical arrangement, dramatization, fictionalization, motion picture version, sound recording, art reproduction, abridgment, condensation, or any other form in which a work may be recast, *transformed*, or adapted."[147] Thus, the very statutory definition of what constitutes a derivative work seems to reserve – to the copyright holder – the exclusive right to "transform" an original work. On the other hand, the fair use doctrine, codified in § 107 of the Act, says something else entirely. Indeed, courts have read the first factor – "the purpose and character of the use"[148] – to consider whether a particular use is transformative in nature.[149] The more transformative the use, the more likely a court is to absolve a defendant from infringement liability. As the Supreme Court has explained, "[T]he goal of copyright, to promote science and the arts, is generally furthered by the creation of transformative works. Such works thus lie at the heart of the fair use doctrine's guarantee of breathing space within the confines of copyright…."[150] Thus, while copyright's derivative-rights doctrine seems to grant the exclusive right to engage in transformative use of a work to that work's copyright holder, the fair-use doctrine seems to suggest that transformative uses of works are precisely the types of works that copyright law should immunize from infringement liability. In short, copyright law appears to be giving us mixed messages.

The Supreme Court's most recent foray into fair use – its decision in *Warhol v. Goldsmith* (2023)[151] – tried to sort out this doublespeak but, in the process, only raised more questions and concerns. As we detailed in our discussion of the case in Chapter 1, in the suit, the Andy Warhol Foundation sought declaratory relief through a finding of fair use to shield itself from infringement claims raised by photographer Lynn Goldsmith, who had snapped an image of recording artist Prince that Andy Warhol had used as the starting point for his bold silkscreen renderings of Prince in the early 1980s (Figure 3.6a and b). The Court ultimately held that Warhol's work constituted a derivative work unexcused by the fair use doctrine. In clarifying how Warhol's alleged transformation of Goldsmith's original photograph played into both the derivative-rights and fair-use analysis, the majority decision admitted that, inconveniently, both doctrines rested on transformation.[152] But the Court tried to distinguish between transformations that produce derivative works and transformations that give rise to a cognizable fair use by opining that the threshold transformation necessary to create a derivative work was relatively low, while the threshold transformation necessary to excuse a work as

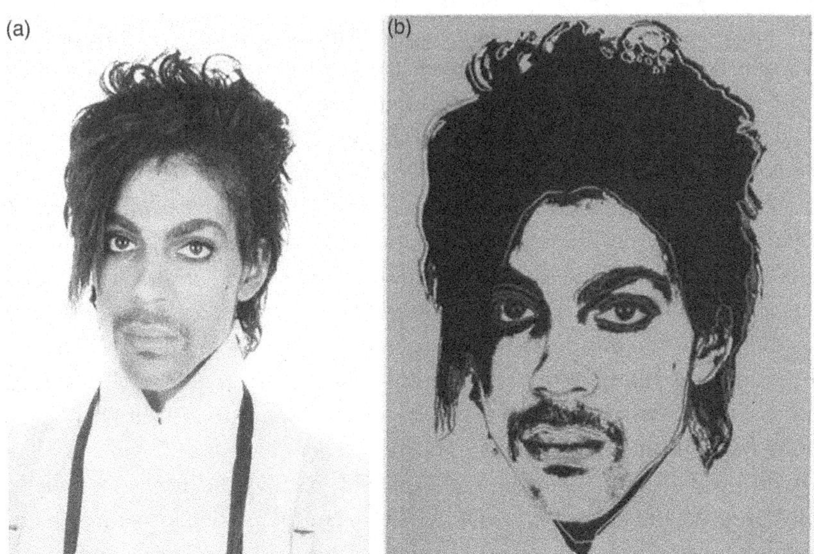

FIGURE 3.6 Comparison of (a) *Prince* (1981) by Lynn Goldsmith with (b) *Orange Prince* (1984) by Andy Warhol, as reported in *Andy Warhol Foundation for the Visual Arts, Inc. v. Goldsmith*, 598 U.S. 508 (2023)

fair use was relatively high[153] and, specifically, required the purpose and character of the secondary work to be sufficiently distinct from the original work.[154] Warhol's work was undoubtedly a derivative work because it literally represented a transformation of Goldsmith's work.[155] But, in the view of the Court, it was insufficiently transformative for the purposes of the fair use defense because it had served the same purpose and had the same character as the original Goldsmith work, as they were both "portraits of Prince used to depict Prince in magazine stories about Prince."[156] The Court then cautioned that too broad a reading of transformative use in application of the fair-use test could effectively "swallow" the derivative works right by forgiving all transformative uses from liability.[157]

The Court was absolutely correct, to a degree: the transformation requirement for a derivative work must necessarily differ from that for fair use, or else the latter doctrine would wholly subsume the derivative right. However, the common use of transformation as a factor in both the fair use and derivative works doctrines did not mandate the direction of the Court's decision. While the Court used this overlap to justify carefully hemming fair-use rights, it could have just as easily drawn on the observation as a basis to reject too broad a view of derivative rights. For example, the Court might have concluded that respect for fair use – and its instrumental role in promoting the ultimate goal of progress and protecting First Amendment rights by limiting the breadth of infringement – necessitated circumscription of the scope of derivative rights instead.

Meanwhile, demanding that truly transformative works must have a different purpose and character from the original work effectively double counts the fourth factor of the fair-use test (mark harm) while also artificially limiting what might constitute a cognizable transformation in the fair-use calculus. On this first point, it is worth remembering that the fourth fair-use factor scrutinizes the harm that the use would do to both the potential and actual market for the original work. In making such a determination, courts inevitably ascertain the degree to which the secondary work (the potential fair use) can serve as a market substitute for the original work. If transformation in the first factor is divined by examining whether the two works serve the same commercial purpose (i.e., are market substitutes), the Court has effectively fused the first and fourth factors together. As the fiery dissent by Justice Kagan sarcastically put it, "You might think that when Congress lists two different factors for consideration, it is because the two factors are, well, different. But the majority transplants factor 4 into factor 1."[158] In response, the *Goldsmith* majority simply waived away this concern with its wholly unsatisfactory observation that the relationship between the two factors "is not absolute."[159]

On this second point, the majority inexplicably narrows the first factor's reference to the "purpose and character of the use" to mean the particular nature of a commercial use: whether it was for the same or a different commercial purpose as the original. In the process, the majority eschews requiring a more fulsome inquiry into the character of a use, including its artistic, communicative, educational, critical, or scientific purposes – a query that would seem more consistent with the preamble of section 107, which expressly references the types of activities ("criticism, comment, news reporting, teaching[,] ... scholarship or research"[160]) illustrative of fair use. The dissent calls this reductionist treatment of the first factor to task, noting that "the majority maintains that those contributions, even if significant, just would not matter. All of Warhol's artistry and social commentary is negated by one thing: Warhol licensed his portrait to a magazine, and Goldsmith sometimes licensed her photos to magazines too."[161] And, in the end, the fact that the particular Warhol image at issue served the same commercial purpose as Goldsmith's image – at least in part – doomed Warhol's fair use claim and will presumably do the same to accused infringers seeking future solace in the defense.

Dangerous Undertakings: Aesthetic Judgments in the Fair-Use Calculus

Against the backdrop of *Goldsmith*'s curtailed notion of fair use that now constitutes binding precedent, it is also worth noting the degree to which the fair-use enterprise has often been infected with troubling aesthetic judgments, sometimes laden with class-based, racist, or sexist biases. At a rhetorical level, courts have historically maintained a steadfast commitment to aesthetic neutrality in their copyright jurisprudence. Consider Justice Oliver Wendell Holmes's enduring admonition from over a century ago. Writing for the majority in *Bleistein* v. *Donaldson Lithographing Co.* (1903), Holmes famously rejected claims by both the lower courts and defendants that the plaintiff's works in an infringement case did not qualify for copyright protection.[162] Cautioning judges to expurgate aesthetic judgments from the courtroom, Holmes found no basis to deny the benefits of copyright to an advertisement featuring renderings of circus performers, despite its prosaic commerciality.[163] As Holmes held, the perceived aesthetic value of a work could not and should not determine its copyrightability.[164] In theory, therefore, commercial copy should receive the same protection as high art. In his most classic formulation, Holmes reasoned that "[i]t would be a dangerous undertaking for persons trained only to the law to constitute themselves final judges of the worth of pictorial illustrations, outside of the narrowest and most obvious limits."[165]

At a certain level, however, interpretation of copyright law necessarily implicates aesthetic considerations, so not all such judgments are unwelcome. As Robert Gorman argues, the Constitution's Copyright Clause – which appears to limit copyright protection to the extent that it promotes "the Progress of Science and useful Arts"[166] – virtually demands such "aesthetic determinations."[167] Thus, in construing conceptual severability for the purposes of distinguishing between works of applied art (which receive copyright protection) and works of industrial design (which do not), courts inevitably make aesthetic judgments about what constitutes art and what defines the proper relationship between form and function as needed to secure legal protection. But as David Fagundes notes, Holmes' admonition did not mean that jurists should altogether avoid "analyzing the content of works of authorship" in order to resolve key issues of copyright law.[168] Rather, the warning is related to the assessment of the worth or merit of a work,[169] and these types of problematic aesthetic judgments appear in many forms. In the narrowest sense, they reflect a judge's feelings about a work's beauty, as embodied in its inherent elements – color, tonality, shape, melody, rhythm, and composition, for example. But aesthetic judgments also come in other guises, including judicial determinations motivated by or based on a work's perceived acceptance or social value.

As we shall see, courts will too frequently draw on a work's or artist's commercial success or cultural resonance as a proxy to ascertain legal worth and, subsequently, the deserved level of protection. The influence of such aesthetic judgments in our copyright jurisprudence therefore inextricably affects the type of works we, as a society, receive from our artists. As Alfred Yen points out, economically motivated artists might "prefer creating works that meet the aesthetic preference of judges because other works would either not get the benefits of copyright protection or wind up being suppressed."[170] Even more fundamentally, however, aesthetic judgments can serve to both maintain and preserve existing power structures. After all, aesthetic judgments are imbued with cultural norms. The seemingly neutral laws of copyright, therefore, have the potential to create a hierarchy of culture that can preserve entrenched interests or solidify particular (often elite) viewpoints, thereby creating a tiered system of protection that, all too often, suppresses narratives of resistance.

With a narrow reading of fair use, a court can protect a work from remix, reinterpretation, and unauthorized mutilation. In short, such a view can preserve a work's aura, inviolability, and canonic status and maximize economic control of its value for its rights holder. With a broader reading of fair use, a court can open the floodgates for the work's use and abuse. Indeed, if the time has come for a work to be metaphorically rejected from the modern canon, there is perhaps no more defining moment than when that work loses its strong copyright protection in court through a fair-use finding. A careful exegesis of copyright jurisprudence reveals that aesthetic decisions, driven by implicit cultural considerations, can dramatically affect the fair use calculus. Embedded cultural norms and assumptions therefore drive copyright law's development, often with adverse consequences for both progress in the arts and for social justice. Two examples – one accepting a fair-use defense, the other rejecting it – illustrate this process in action with respect to the representation of indigenous bodies, depictions of the racial and class history of the United States, and heteronormative orthodoxies and show how fair-use determinations can dangerously become inquisitions into which cultural works are – to quote a celebrated parable about the seductive sway of aesthetics – the "fairest of them all."

The Prince and the Pauper

The Second Circuit's decision in *Cariou* v. *Prince* (2013)[171] illustrates a finding of fair use driven by the problematic and selective invocation of aesthetic considerations

FIGURE 3.7 Comparison of photographs from (a) *Yes Rasta* (2000) by Patrick Cariou with (b) *Graduation* (2008) by Richard Prince, as reported in *Cariou* v. *Prince*, 714 F.3d 694 (2d Cir. 2013)

that enabled Richard Prince, the toast of the cognoscenti and a high-flyer in the art world, to escape liability from infringement claims brought by a relatively unknown (and therefore less powerful) photographer over the depiction of indigenous bodies. In its opinion, the appellate court reversed a judgment finding that thirty works by appropriationist artist Richard Prince infringed images shot by Patrick Cariou, a French ethnographic photographer whose stark black-and-white portraits had captured Rastafarians living at the edges of society in a naturalistic and reverential manner.[172] Prince had taken numerous parts of Cariou's Rastafarian photographs, altered them in various ways (including by painting "lozenges" over the faces of the subjects), and combined them with other appropriated art to form pastiche compositions (Figure 3.7a and b).[173] The Second Circuit ruled that at least twenty-five of Prince's thirty allegedly infringing works were transformative as a matter of law and, therefore, immunized from liability under the fair use doctrine.[174] Though the Second Circuit putatively framed its analysis around the application of the four fair-use factors enumerated in section 107 of the Copyright Act, extraneous aesthetic considerations permeated the court's reasoning.[175] In the end, therefore, the resulting opinion appeared dominated more by obeisance to cultural hierarchy (as reified by elite sensibilities) than by fealty to precedent or neutral application of the fair-use test.[176]

Oppositional casting – of Prince as the rightfully celebrated *enfant terrible* of the contemporary art world and of Cariou as a merely slavish and obscure chronicler of the Rastafarians – frames the central narrative undergirding the court's decision. The court begins by detailing Prince's success along two axes – economic and cultural.[177] His works, we are told, sell for millions of dollars.[178] Meanwhile, he has exhibited at the world's most prestigious museums and in such internationally renowned galleries as the Gagosian.[179] These references are not merely sundry facts peppering the opinion, an observation made plain by the court's bizarre decision to regale the reader with a lengthy list of representatives from the celebrity and art worlds who attended the opening of Prince's exhibit:

> musicians Jay-Z and Beyoncé Knowles, artists Damien Hirst and Jeff Koons [to whom the Second Circuit had recently granted a high-profile fair-use victory[180]], professional football player Tom Brady, model Gisele Bundchen, *Vanity Fair* editor Graydon Carter, *Vogue* editor Anna Wintour, authors Jonathan Franzen and Candace Bushnell, and actors Robert DeNiro, Angelina Jolie, and Brad Pitt.[181]

Even more strangely, the court repeatedly fetishizes Prince's size – that of his pocketbook, of his cultural capital, and even of his literal works.[182] The decision is riddled with language emphasizing the enormity of Prince's composition through stature-conscious phrases telling us, for example, that "Prince's collages ... measure between ten and nearly a hundred times the size of the photographs."[183] As artist and attorney Sergio Muñoz Sarmiento has quipped, the court's fascination with size "would have one think we were reading a narration of what transpires in a boy's high-school gym."[184] With this discussion, the court implicitly legitimizes the critical accolades and monetary rewards Prince has enjoyed. The court then explicitly heralds Prince's work with effervescent language to highlight the magnitude of his apparently unique artistic vision.[185] We are told that, by employing "new aesthetics with creative and communicative results,"[186] Prince has created works that are "jarring," "provocative," and "expressive."[187]

Meanwhile, the decision takes pains to convey Cariou's inferior status in the cultural landscape by denigrating the creative worth of his vision and his success (or lack thereof, at least in mainstream circles). This binary casting – with Prince as a transformative visionary and Cariou as a pedestrian tradesman – ultimately drives the Second Circuit's decision to reverse the lower court's judgment of infringement. Specifically, the majority opinion presents Cariou as merely a competent photographer who happens to "depict[] the natural beauty of Rastafarians and their surrounding environs" – language that paints the plaintiff as more of a factual observer than an inspired *auteur*. Throughout the opinion, the court highlights just how little the plaintiff has achieved in the marketplace. Thus, the court informs us that Cariou's book, which featured the allegedly infringed Rastafarian photographs and was released in 2000, "is currently out of print" and that Cariou only earned $8,000 in royalties from the work as 60% of the sales of the book "sold below the suggested retail price."[188] Not only does the court fail to appreciate that these statistics are entirely common in the world of limited edition art monographs and certainly no indication of failure (far from it – they may actually indicate substantial success),[189] but such details are totally irrelevant to the question facing the court. After all, the Second Circuit has only the issue of liability, and not damages, before it, and the monies earned by Cariou for his photographs have no real bearing on the fair use analysis. However, they implicitly undercut any notion that Cariou's works should enjoy the inviolability assured to works at the apex of copyright's protection regime.

To the extent that Cariou's commercial interests could conceivably come into play in the fourth fair-use factor – the harm to the potential market for the value of Cariou's work – the analysis follows a fundamentally different logic than that embraced in related circuit precedent.[190] Specifically, just a few years earlier, the Second Circuit had protected J. D. Salinger's right to enjoin Fredrik Colting from publishing, under the pseudonym John David California, an unauthorized sequel to *Catcher in the Rye* entitled *60 Years Later*. In rejecting California's fair use defense, the court found that the mark harm factor weighed in favor of Salinger even though he was a notorious recluse who had not published any work in half a century and had vehemently disavowed any interest in doing so.[191] As the *Salinger* court noted, a plaintiff enjoys a right to market potential sequels to, or derivatives of, his work and to decide when, how, and even if he or she might enter the licensing market.[192] By surprising contrast, in *Prince*, the Second Circuit gives little weight to such interests for Cariou. Instead, the majority opinion emphasizes Cariou's meager success and notes that, "[e]xcept for a handful of private sales to personal acquaintances, he has never sold or licensed the individual photographs."[193] To make matters even worse, the court brushes aside the fact that Cariou had attempted to have his own works exhibited in a rival gallery. That gallery ended up losing interest in a potential exhibition of Cariou's when the same images ended up featured at the Gagosian – through Prince's appropriationist work. In a sharp departure from the reasoning of *Salinger*, the court asserts that "[t]here is nothing in the record to suggest that Cariou would ever develop or license secondary uses of his work in the vein of Prince's artworks. Nor does anything in the record suggest that Prince's artworks had any impact on the marketing of the photographs."[194] Both statements, however, were equally true of J. D. Salinger in his dispute with John David California; yet these facts gave the court no pause in issuing an injunction against the publication of *60 Years After*.

Interestingly, although the court has no trouble engaging in aesthetic judgments writ large, it refrains from making aesthetic judgments that might be relevant to those interested in showing respect for the indigenous individuals depicted in the art. Despite suffering from a touch of neocolonial romanticism, Cariou's works at least show a reverence for their subjects – reflecting the photographer's mission to shine a light on those living at the fringes of society around the globe and to express their ultimate humanity. Though black and white, Cariou's images are steeped with a soulfulness that reflects the ten years he lived among them. As one critic puts it, "The photographic practice of Patrick Cariou is imbued with a deep sense of empathy and a desire to understand and celebrate the human experience."[195] By contrast, in Prince's work, one could view the indigenous bodies as mere vehicles for Prince's transgressions and play or, under a more cynical reading, even the butt of his joke.[196] Either way, the court did not assess this aspect of the respective works' approaches to the representation of indigenous bodies. This is not to say that such aesthetic considerations should have entered the fair use calculus, but it is revealing which aesthetic factors merit consideration and which ones do not, a fact that further highlights the selective metrics used by the court.

In the end, the Second Circuit does not deem Prince's artistic efforts actionable because it is unfathomable that such celebrated works could be unlawful. To wit, even though Prince himself had expressly stated in his deposition that he "do[es] n't really have a message" and was not "trying to create anything with a new meaning or a new message" (thereby raising a credible argument that he had waived any transformative-use defense),[197] the court pronounces Prince's works "transformative" as a matter of law, thereby lending judicial confirmation to what the cognoscenti had already declared as true.[198] As a result, the Second Circuit has no problem denying Cariou the sacralization that courts have offered to the works of J. D. Salinger (and so many others) over the years, largely as a consequence of its relative aesthetic judgments about the litigants' art. As the court euphemistically concludes, "Prince's work appeals to an *entirely different sort* of collector than Cariou's."[199] This off-handed but revealing comment powerfully unmasks the class-laden aesthetic judgments driving the court's fair-use finding.

Though the *Cariou* decision has received some criticism – a more recent Second Circuit decision tactfully referred to it as a "high-water mark of our court's recognition of transformative works" while distinguishing it,[200] and the Supreme Court's decision in *Warhol* v. *Goldsmith* (2023) calls its authority in doubt[201] – it technically remains citable precedent, and, moreover, subsequent courts have not attacked its unmeasured aesthetic judgments. Meanwhile, the world no longer enjoys the benefit of Cariou's creative vision and his powerful depictions of marginalized communities. Cariou quit photography in 2006 – only a few years after he published his Rastafarian images.[202]

Undoing the Mythology of the Lost Cause

In *Suntrust* v. *Houghton Mifflin* (2001),[203] the estate of Margaret Mitchell sued to enjoin publication of the novel *The Wind Done Gone* on the grounds that it constituted an unauthorized derivative work based on *Gone with the Wind*. Written by Alice Randall, the first African-American woman to write a number-one country song, *The Wind Done Gone* sought to recast the *Gone with the Wind* story and world from the point of view of African-Americans rather than white aristocrats. Thus, in stark contrast to the original *Gone with the Wind*, Randall's story features Ashley Wilkes expressly identified as gay, direct discussion of interracial sexual relationships, and vivid depictions of the travails of daily life for the victims of the South's rigid and racist social hierarchy.[204] In short, Randall's novel dramatically recoded the Lost Cause narrative of the original work and, in the process, brought Mitchell's whitewashed vision of the South to its knees by forcing a reconsideration of its entire narrative and, hence, ideological enterprise.

Although it was ultimately reversed on appeal, a district court initially enjoined publication of *The Wind Done Gone*, effectively banning the book for a time. In so doing, the court accepted the Mitchell estate's contention of infringement work and rejected Randall's fair-use defense[205] by concluding that *The Wind Done Gone* was a sequel and not a parody, and therefore not the type of transformative use granted fair-use protection.[206] A careful exegesis of the decision, however, reveals the extent to which aesthetic judgments drove the rationale.

Right from the outset, the opinion submits to *Gone with the Wind*'s perceived epistemological heft, emphasizing the novel's place in the cultural canon and its commercial significance – both noting its "widespread acclaim" and its impressive sales in the "tens of millions."[207] These facts are, of course, largely irrelevant to any aesthetically neutral analysis of infringement and fair use. But they set the tone for the court's opinion, which reflects a strong deference to the work's favored aesthetic status – its presumed import and cultural and economic value.[208]

The existing body of fair use precedent all but mandates that parodies receive immunity from infringement liability. As a result, a key portion of the decision comes when the court rejects the idea that *The Wind Done Gone* might constitute some kind of parody and, instead, characterizes the work as a sequel or other form of unauthorized derivative work.[209] Such a polemic introduces a false dichotomy – that sequels and parodies are mutually exclusive concepts when, in fact, they are often intertwined. As a parody, the work is presumed to be transformative and, consequently, entitled to fair use protection for its contribution to progress in the arts.[210] As a sequel, the work is seen as nothing more than an effort to free ride on the authorial conceptions of another. But, of course, a work can be both a parody and a sequel. For example, Mel Brooks's classic *Spaceballs* is, in some senses, both an unauthorized sequel to, and parody of, *Star Wars*. Nevertheless, the court brushes aside this duality. Even while acknowledging that the book has numerous parodic elements, the court nevertheless divines that "the book's *overall purpose* is to create a sequel to the older work and provide Ms. Randall's social commentary on the antebellum South."[211] In pushing the dialectic that casts parody (which gets high fair use protection) in opposition to sequel (which don't), the court uses aesthetic judgment to effectively protect the status of *Gone with the Wind* as an inviolable work.

At the same time, the court further conflates the two prongs of the first factor – commercialism and transformation – as part of its broader narrative that portrays Randall's work as a crude ploy to free-ride on the commercial magnetism of its inspiration: "the purpose of putting the key characters of *Gone with the Wind* in new settings is to entertain and sell books to an active and ready-made market for the next *Gone with the Wind* sequel."[212] To the court, Randall is nothing more than a leech sucking economic value away from Mitchell's genius. But, at some level, the same charge could be leveled at all parodies (which, nevertheless, have historically received strong protection from liability). After all, they all rely upon the original and its status as a recognized work to a certain audience.

As it turns out, a careful parsing of the court's decision reveals that its conclusion stems from aesthetic judgments about the inviolability of *Gone with the Wind*. As the court tautologically posits, "If the defendant is permitted to publish *The Wind Done Gone*, an unauthorized derivative work, then anyone could tell the love story of *Gone with the Wind* from another point of view and/or create sequels or prequels populated by Ms. Mitchell's copyrighted characters without compensation to the Mitchell Trusts."[213] With these words, the court presupposes that the latter result simply cannot occur (despite the existence of the fair use doctrine that plainly creates no such hard-and-fast rule). Put another way, the court assumes, and thereby ensures, that the work must remain inviolate. As a sacred text, *Gone with the Wind* should be protected from unauthorized individuals telling the story from a different point of view.

Consecration is at the heart of the court's concern because a world where the sacred text has been defiled is unimaginable: "[B]y killing two core characters from Gone with the Wind and marrying off another, *The Wind Done Gone* has the immediate effect of damaging or even precluding the Mitchell Trusts' ability to continue to tell the love story of Scarlett and Rhett."[214] Read literally, the court's admonition fails to distinguish between real life – where an individual's death typically precludes the possibility of resurrection – and fiction – where no such limitations exist (particularly for an "unauthorized" vehicle such as *Gone with the Wind*). The statement not only reflects a startling failure of imagination by the court – doubtlessly provoked by the inability to envision the bastardization of the consecrated work – but also does not hold weight empirically. For example, the Star Trek franchise has continued to thrive in telling the stories of Captain Kirk, Mr. Spock, and the USS Enterprise, despite the fact that both Kirk[215] and Spock[216] were killed at various points during the authorized movies. Moreover, audiences can readily discern between authorized and unauthorized sequels of a franchise, and, if they cannot, that is something that the federal Lanham Act could help police through its prohibition of unfair competition and false advertising. Indeed, the universe of fan fiction – which typically appeals to the most fervent connoisseurs of a franchise – is often occupied with works featuring storylines and character developments that are often inconsistent with one another. Despite these apparent contradictions with the authorized canon (and even to other fan fiction), these derivatives are no less enjoyable to their readers.

Of course, the Scarlett and Rhett characters do not die just because Randall says they do. But what the court really fears is that *The Wind Done Gone* will sound not merely the literal death knell for the characters but also for *Gone with the Wind*'s untouchability. Stripped of unadulterated idealization, the work and its characters can no longer survive in the exact form they once possessed. Thus, it is not whether the work is parody or sequel that truly appears to drive the court's decision; it is the destruction of the work's romanticism – a romanticism that, notably, is grounded in a distinctly whitewashed vision of the antebellum South that painfully ignores the harsh realities of life for that society's underclass. Thus, the court's reading of copyright law, driven by aesthetic judgments, has an impact on the discourse about what is perhaps the most famous and popular vision of Southern life during the years of slavery. With the district court's opinion, copyright law is used to preserve a hegemonic vision of the South that has historically prevailed in the American consciousness.

Indeed, it is particularly noteworthy that the Mitchell Estate was particularly horrified at the idea that the world of *Gone with the Wind* might be adulterated with depictions of interracial relationships or homosexuality.[217] During the case, it came to light that the Mitchell Estate had told a potential writer for the *authorized* sequel for *Gone with the Wind*, "You're not going to like this, but the estate will require you to sign a pledge that says you will under no circumstances write anything about miscegenation or homosexuality."[218] Thus, the only way in which the story of *Gone with the Wind* could be told while acknowledging the reality of miscegenation and homosexuality was in *unauthorized* form. Ultimately, then, the district court's decision to beatify the original text and protect it from transmutation effectively controlled the heteronormative narrative of Mitchell and denied Randall the ability to transform "Ashley Wilkes into a homosexual" and to "depict[] … interracial sex, and … multiple mulatto characters."[219]

All told, the battle over the scope of the *Gone with the Wind* copyright in the *Suntrust* case represented a direct struggle over the right and ability to present an alternate vision of Old Dixie, using the familiar terrain of the romanticized antebellum South to bring long-suppressed issues of race, class, and even sexual orientation to the forefront of the story. Choices about what constitutes fair use determine which parts of our cultural output remain sacred and which do not. In rejecting Randall's fair use defense, the district court banned *The Wind Done Gone* from publication. In the process, the derivative rights doctrine and the court's aesthetic judgments shut down (at least for a while) a seminal challenge to a problematic prevailing mythology – one that has played a key role in restraining the protection of civil rights – that works such as *Gone with the Wind* have helped perpetuate.

UNCOVERING A DIFFERENT APPROACH TO DERIVATIVE RIGHTS

As the foregoing discussion indicates, judicial decisions on the permissibility of recasting or reformulating protected works tend to be binary: secondary uses are either deemed impermissible derivative works (in which case the users are liable for infringement, subject to damages and a potential injunction) or fair use (in which case the users can exploit the work without liability and the original rights holders receive no economic participation in this activity). Such an extreme dichotomy raises a reasonable question: Could there be a better way? After all, the protection of derivative rights is not always a bad idea and, even when use of a work is allowed without permission of a rights holder, some economic participation in the secondary use by the underlying rights holder could be both desirable and fair. So, as we think about the extant issues with the current regime, it may be worth considering a third option. And, to that end, the world of music provides us some valuable precedent. Specifically, through the implementation of a successful compulsory licensing regime, the recording industry has dealt with a particular type of derivative work – the cover song – in a manner that has promoted progress in the arts, allowed both reverential tributes and subversive recodings of extant cultural symbols, and provided for compensation to the authors of the original work.

Copyright law usually leaves it ambiguous as to what types of derivatives give rise to liability and which ones are excused as fair use. It's generally a case-by-case determination. However, in one curious area, derivative works are deemed per se allowable, subject to payment of a fixed statutory fee known as a compulsory mechanical license as codified in section 115 of the Copyright Act. This particular exemption has existed since 1909, and its origins relate to a long-defunct technology – the player piano – and a particular compromise that occurred years before the global dissemination of recorded music (Figure 3.8).[220] But the exemption remains alive today and allows anyone to record a "cover" version of a published, nondramatic musical composition and distribute copies of it without the permission of the original composer/copyright holder.[221]

Admittedly, the cover song right is restricted – one must cover the entire song, not just a part of it, and must largely maintain the lyrics, though adjustments to the music style and performative aspects of the vocals are allowed. As a result, 2 Live Crew could not rely on section 115 to clear their version of *Pretty Woman*, which quickly departed, both thematically and lyrically, from the original musical composition. Instead, the band had to fight all the way to the Supreme Court to vindicate its right to parody under the fair-use doctrine in *Campbell* v. *Acuff-Rose Music Inc.* (1994).[222] But while full transformative use of musical compositions cannot be made under the statute, cover artists are free to tinker with the composition in order to adapt it to a particular musical genre: "a compulsory license includes the privilege of making a musical arrangement of the work to the extent necessary to conform it to the style or manner of interpretation of the performance involved."[223]

Notwithstanding the limitations of section 115's compulsory mechanical license, the cover song exemption has spawned significant innovation and transformation in music. For example, consider the musical compositions *All Along the Watchtower* and *Mr. Tambourine Man*, two entries in the great American songbook and essential contributions to the folk-rock canon. Without the existence of the compulsory mechanical license, we may have never heard either song. The reason is simple: both works were composed and originally recorded

FIGURE 3.8 1921 advertisement for Q.R.S. player piano rolls

by Bob Dylan. And, though Dylan is a remarkable songwriter and musician, his recordings simply did not do the songs justice and were quickly forgotten. Instead, it would fall on Jimi Hendrix and The Byrds to render the works into transcendent form by deploying section 115 and rerecording the songs with their own unique perspective and performance. Everyone shared in the success of these covers. While Hendrix's version of *All Along the Watchtower* and The Byrd's rendition of *Mr. Tambourine Man* helped launch both acts into rock's pantheon, these recordings also secured Dylan's place in music history.

Besides creating a benefit for both the original and covering artists, the compulsory license has also helped bring new works to the public, thereby promoting progress in the arts, while also enabling subversive recastings of iconic songs. Thus, without any authorization, Johnny Cash gave the world a hauntingly frail acoustic version of Nine Inch Nails's more muscular and menacing *Hurt*. In the process, he recoded the song from a tortured expression of rage to a poignant, mortality-infused lament. Without Axl Rose's approval, Luna could record a dreamy, lo-fi cover of Guns N' Roses's *Sweet Child O' Mine*. The resulting cover stripped away the bluster of the original to expose its wistful romantic yearning. When Dynamite Hack recorded an acoustic folk–rock rendition of NWA member

Eazy-E's *Boyz-N-The-Hood*, it did not merely bemuse the public with an irony-laden take on one of gangsta rap's most iconic tunes. Rather, replete with a lily-White video featuring the country club set running amok in a three-dimensional World of Ralph Lauren, the band somehow managed to illustrate both the enormous chasm and odd similarities between the treacherous urban conditions depicted in the original song and the privileged WASP lifestyle portrayed in the latter. In all three of these instances, the public received new forms of expression that happened to be built on pre-existing works (and for which the original artists were compensated – albeit at a statutory rate). Additionally, the artists who had the opportunity to perform and record the covers gained the freedom to reinterpret, and therefore, reformulate the semiotics of the cultural canon to explore new meanings and messages.

As the history of modern music has demonstrated, the public and artists have thrived as a result of the availability of the compulsory mechanical license.[224] Indeed, despite its usual support of strong copyright protection, the recording industry has steadfastly promoted the scheme's maintenance. In hearings before the House Committee on the Judiciary in 1967, for example, the industry argued that "performers need unhampered access to musical material on nondiscriminatory terms.... [T]he 1909 statute adopted the compulsory license as a deliberate anti-monopoly condition on the grant of [copyright].... They argue that the result has been an outpouring of recorded music, with the public being given lower prices, improved quality, and a greater choice."[225] At a minimum, then, it is worth asking whether the same logic might apply to motion pictures, literary works, and other copyrightable subject matter because, notably, there is no such right to do a cover book, cover movie, or cover art. The availability of such a right could not only advance the creative logic of copyright – to maximize progress in the arts – but also undo the anti-egalitarian aspects of the derivative rights doctrine that frustrate social resistance to prevailing ideologies by sacralizing cultural and political symbols, protecting them from alteration or remixing and prohibiting their recoding.

At first blush, the broader social stakes involved in allowing or denying the reinterpretation, transformation, or recasting of the average song, novel, artwork, or motion picture may not appear high. After all, the ability to derivatize a hackneyed top-40 pop song, a romance novel, or a movie offering from the Marvel Comic Universe may hardly seem like the stuff of social justice. But the very same doctrines that protect pedestrian works from unwanted adaptation can also prevent semiotic disruption of influential works with enduring cultural, political, and social resonance. So, as we have seen in this chapter, the derivative-rights and fair-use doctrines can regulate the metes and bounds of discourse on geopolitics, race, religion, slavery, Lost Cause narratives, national heritage and identity, animal rights, indigeneity, colonialism, gender roles, capitalism, and corporate governance. The fight over the proper scope of the copyright monopoly is therefore part of the struggle against prevailing ideologies and the symbols that prop them up. A derivative-rights doctrine that is insufficiently checked not only betrays the core purpose of the copyright regime – progress in the arts – but also powerfully undermines the ability of society (and, particularly, marginalized groups) to resist dominant orthodoxies and entrenched powers. Ultimately, these interactions between the derivative-rights and fair-use doctrines do not merely decide how we intend to promote progress in the arts. Rather, they help to separate malleable texts from those we deem sacred; they determine the creators whom we leave unprotected and those whom we reward; and they dictate those who will live under the narrative and those who will, in the end, control it.

4

©ensored

How Copyright's First Amendment Exemption Enables the Powerful to Silence the Powerless

In which we discuss: soap opera secrets, shock jock meltdowns, dancing babies, the soundtrack of arrests, suicide notes, Abu Ghraib, murder confessions, and litigation over first sexual experiences

CELEBRITY SECRETS AND LITIGATION MISCHIEF

Latin celebrities Noelia Lorenzo Monge and Jorge Reynoso had a problem on their hands. Secretly wed in a Las Vegas ceremony in 2007, they had kept their nuptials hidden from the world and had always insisted they were single. But when a tabloid rag obtained wedding photographs from the couple's former bodyguard, Monge and Reynoso's furtive union was exposed. Upon cursory consideration, there was little the couple could do, legally speaking, about these smoking-gun documents that proved that Monge and Reynoso had been lying both to their fans and the public at large. After all, the First Amendment typically provides vigorous protection to news reporting, especially when it is entirely truthful and concerns a matter of public interest. But Monge and Reynoso would not take the outing of their marriage quietly. So they did with copyright law what they could not otherwise do any other way: they made *Maya Magazines*, the owner of the tabloid, pay.

First, Monge and Reynoso purchased the copyright to the photographs. Then, they sued *Maya* for copyright infringement for its unauthorized use of the photographs – not to vindicate any real value in the copyrighted work but as a means of suppressing and punishing truthful speech. The gambit worked when a federal appeals court rejected *Maya*'s fair-use defense and deemed it liable for infringement. According to the court's opinion, *Maya* had engaged in the unauthorized exploitation of unpublished creative works for the highly commercial purpose of tabloid journalism. This purportedly improper usurpation of first publication rights to the photographs deprived the rights holders of the decision to license (or not license) those works as they wished and resulted in infringement liability.

Though Monge and Reynoso savored the victory, it came at a significant and unappreciated cost to the First Amendment. By fetishizing property interests in copyrighted works at the expense of the public right of access to factual information, the decision effectively provided future litigants with a clear road map to circumvent the First Amendment and disingenuously exploit copyright law to punish and suppress legitimate free speech on matters of public interest. And lest one think that the *Maya* decision only governs seemingly frivolous celebrity scandals, the precedent could just as easily be used to attach liability to the next publisher of the *Pentagon Papers* or other unpublished materials containing eminently newsworthy secrets. As Andrew Baum has cautioned, future cases might prevent the press from reproducing emails confirming an affair denied by a general and his book-writing mistress (e.g., General Petraeus and Paula Broadwell) or revealing photographs evidencing a secret same-sex relationship of a gay-bashing congressman.

Indeed, the copyright-as-censorship threat is not just hypothetical. Consider, for example, how effectively conservative talk show host Michael Savage weaponized copyright law a few years ago to prevent criticism of hate speech. In the incident, Savage brought infringement claims against the Council on American–Islamic Relations (CAIR), an advocacy group whose mission is to promote understanding of Islam and to protect the civil liberties of Muslim-Americans.[1] CAIR had excerpted approximately four minutes of a two-hour Savage broadcast without his authorization for a commentary piece meant to call attention to Savage's Islamophobic invective.[2] During that 2007 broadcast, Savage had called the Koran "a book of hate" and deemed Muslims "throwbacks" whom we should deport "without due process."[3] Savage then told Muslims to "[t]ake your religion and shove it up your behind. I'm sick of you," and he exhorted his fans to "[s]peak it out at the supermarket! Tell them what you think of Islam. Tell them what you think of Muslims. Tell them what you think of these things."[4]

Savage's hateful comments drew widespread criticism and, to draw further attention to his controversial statements, CAIR appended excerpts of the broadcasts to one of its own internet articles about Savage's rant.[5] Entitled *National Radio Host Goes on Anti-Muslim Tirade*, the article critiqued Savage's vitriol and encouraged "radio listeners of all faiths to contact companies that advertise on Michael Savage's nationally syndicated radio program to express their concerns about the host's recent anti-Muslim tirade."[6] In short, the use of Savage's broadcast appeared to be a quintessential form of commentary and criticism, immunized from liability both under the strictures of copyright law's fair-use doctrine and the First Amendment.[7] Savage, however, felt that CAIR had violated his exclusive dominion over his intellectual property by reproducing and distributing it without his permission; he therefore sued the organization for copyright infringement in a California federal district court.[8]

To its credit, the court quickly dispensed with the suit by granting a motion for judgment on the pleadings on the grounds that the fair-use doctrine protected CAIR's actions as a matter of law.[9] However, CAIR was left absorbing the costs of defending a meritless suit because the court declined to award CAIR fees,[10] even though it admitted that "[p]laintiff's Copyright Act claim was 'never strong and was litigated anemically.'"[11] The court affirmed this opinion upon a motion for reconsideration.[12]

But the story did not end there. By denying CAIR's motion for fees, the court had failed to deter overreaching claims. So it should have come as no surprise that, shortly thereafter, when confronted with further criticism, Savage once again elected to respond with similarly tenuous claims of copyright infringement over the same piece of intellectual property to quiet his critics.[13] This time Savage targeted Brave New Films, which had incorporated one minute of Savage's comments – only a quarter of CAIR's use, and just a fraction of Savage's two-hour broadcast – as part of a media production it had prepared on his Islamophobic views and had posted on YouTube.[14] Despite the court's ruling of fair use over the exact same footage in the CAIR case, Savage's company – Original Films – claimed that Brave New Films had infringed its rights.[15] The company filed a takedown notice with YouTube.[16] YouTube removed the video just after Brave New Films had taken out a full-page advertisement in the *New York Times* with a link to the video that was meant to generate awareness about the issue.[17] Viewers of the advertisement were left clicking on a dead link. The blow to Brave New Films was significant; the takedown (which YouTube effectuated to protect itself from liability for reasons we will explain later in this chapter) thoroughly neutered the power of its concentrated (and expensive) outreach campaign. Although Brave New Films ultimately sued so that it could have its use of the video restored, the damage had already been done. Savage's disingenuous and abusive use of copyright law silenced his foes at precisely the right moment.[18]

COPYRIGHT'S CENSORSHIP PROBLEM

When those in power dislike free speech, epithets typically follow. Defamation. Hoax. Innuendo. Lie. In recent years, this inauspicious list has gained two new entrants. The first – Fake News – needs no introduction. Some politicians have made a cause célèbre of the concept and called for a fundamental re-examination of our defamation laws to address the problem. The potential dilution of important liability protections for the media poses a grave threat to First Amendment rights. But those rights have already endured a powerful blow from the curious and surprising second addition to the list: copyright infringement.

At first blush, copyright law seems far afield from matters of journalistic freedom and censorship. But that is precisely what ends up making it such a potent tool for political suppression. Courts have systematically immunized copyright claims from meaningful First Amendment checks. As a result, the privileged (and legally represented) have increasingly seized upon this key blind spot in constitutional jurisprudence by recharacterizing unfavorable acts of speech as copyright infringements. In the process, they have harnessed a formidable weapon to circumvent the First Amendment and suppress speech that is hostile to their interests. Played out in the federal court system, this form of lawfare has effectively transformed our intellectual property laws into a potent tool of censorship. While the Fake News debate undoubtedly has the power to wreak havoc on the press's First Amendment freedoms, with all too little fanfare or outcry, copyright law already has.

Monge v. *Maya Magazines* and the Michael Savage controversy are no outliers. The cynical use of copyright law as a means of empowering censorship has grown alarmingly commonplace in recent years as groups on all sides of the culture wars have drawn upon this unexpected tool to silence their opponents. Examples of the disingenuous use of copyright law abound. Creationists have repeatedly used infringement claims to force the takedown of critical materials put online by evolutionists.[19] Reproductive-rights activists have brought infringement litigation to enjoin speech by pro-life forces.[20] Military personnel have ginned up copyright claims to suppress photographs documenting human rights abuses.[21]

In short, copyright law has become the weapon *par excellence* of the twenty-first-century censor. Fueled by a desire to prevent one's perceived foes from making certain types of speech, an individual has no better friend than copyright law. Copyright violations are ubiquitous – with smartphones in our pockets and networked computers at our desks, we all infringe copyright law multiple times a day and leave digital fingerprints to document our infringing activities. If a putative rights holder bothers to investigate, liability can be massive – up to $150,000 per willful act of copyright infringement. Copyright suits are difficult to fend off – the average suit costs hundreds of thousands of dollars to defend. And, perhaps most saliently to the sophisticated censor, the federal courts have almost systematically immunized infringement suits from explicit First Amendment defenses. As the Supreme Court blithely asserted in *Eldred* v. *Ashcroft* (2003), "[C]opyright's built-in free speech safeguards are generally adequate to address" any conflict with the First Amendment.[22]

BANNING BOOKS AND COPYRIGHT'S FIRST AMENDMENT IMMUNITY

The Supreme Court's dismissal of the tension between copyright and expressive rights is, at best, naïve and particularly unusual given the judiciary's otherwise staunch commitment to the protection of free speech. After all, our laws ordinarily *protect*, rather than punish, free expression and news reporting. In the past century, courts have carefully developed strong First Amendment checks to prevent parties from imposing tort liability such as defamation,[23] false light,[24] invasion of privacy,[25] and intentional infliction of emotional distress[26] against ideological adversaries exerting their expressive rights. Our fealty to the First Amendment is normally so unflagging that we will even shield the most repulsive and dangerous forms of speech from legal assault. In *National Socialist Party* v. *Skokie* (1977), for example, the Supreme Court declined to stop neo-Nazis from marching through the streets of an Illinois town and spreading their message of hate among a sizable population of Holocaust survivors, despite the significant threat of violence.[27] In *R.A.V. V. City of St. Paul* (1992), the Court struck an ordinance outlawing cross-burning, despite its terroristic aim at the rights of minorities.[28] And, in *New York Times* v. *United States* (1971), the High Court would not enjoin newspapers from publishing excerpts of the *Pentagon Papers* – sensitive, classified government documents regarding the Vietnam War acquired through the commission of a felony – despite the potentially grave national security concerns and threat to the lives of American troops.[29] But when the specter of copyright infringement rears its ugly head, even the banning of books becomes an option. Now, would-be censors have converted losing tort claims into viable copyright infringement claims that punish their foes for legitimate speech-related activity. These censorious efforts troublingly utilize the apparatus of the state (via a state-granted monopoly) to silence and suppress disfavored speech.

In historical times, copyright infringement would necessarily have constituted pirated copies of someone else's work – a scenario that does not seem to implicate serious First Amendment concerns since any defense by the infringer would involve the dubious right to make speech that is, by all rights, entirely someone else's. In the past, after all, copyright law only protected against literal one-to-one reproductions.[30] But the scope of copyright law has expanded dramatically, especially over the past century.[31] Among other things, it now covers both literal and nonliteral takings and, perhaps most importantly, grants copyright holders the exclusive right to create any derivative – a concept that, as we saw in the previous chapter, has been defined expansively.[32] As a result, works that contain much of one's own speech and original content can constitute infringements, subject to both injunctive relief and damages if these works are deemed an unauthorized derivative – that is, a work that draws upon underlying, pre-existing content that belongs to someone else.[33] Infringements, therefore, can encompass a musical composition with an original melody and original lyrics that happens to lift a bass hook from an old James Brown number;[34] a movie with a unique setting and storyline that features a character from *Star Trek*;[35] or a fanciful reverse postmodern bildungsroman where Holden Caulfield, now a 76-year-old on the run from a nursing home, confronts his creator, J. D. Salinger.[36]

Consider the outcome of this last case. Shortly before his passing in 2010, infamous recluse Salinger came out of hiding, at least legally speaking, to seek an injunction restraining publication of the novel *60 Years Later*, an unauthorized send-up of *The Catcher in the Rye*, purportedly authored by one John David California (the pseudonym of Fredrik Colting).[37] Salinger argued that the work constituted a blatant infringement of his copyright.[38] In *60 Years Later*, the author certainly used the Holden Caulfield character from *Catcher in the Rye*, but its literal borrowing was otherwise largely limited to the use of certain (common and nonprotectable) catchphrases or idioms related to the Caulfield character.[39] Despite the defendant's claims of fair use and First Amendment protection, the federal district court ruled in Salinger's favor and issued an injunction to enjoin publication and distribution of *60 Years Later* after finding that Salinger was likely to prevail on the merits of the case.[40] On appeal, the Second Circuit affirmed the holding.[41] In the process, both the district court and Second Circuit showed little compunction about issuing what amounted to a prior restraint against speech – a step that would be strongly discouraged in virtually any other context.

The result of *Salinger* is typical. A quarter-century ago, Mark Lemley and Eugene Volokh published their seminal analysis of copyright exceptionalism, *Freedom of Speech and Injunctions in Intellectual Property Cases*.[42] As Lemley and Volokh argued, courts have historically disfavored any prior restraint of speech[43] and, in a wide array of cases ranging from libel to obscenity claims, have regularly denied applications for preliminary injunctions to suppress even the clearest violations of the law.[44] All the while, however, courts have shown little hesitation in granting preliminary injunctions in cases of copyright infringement, even when the injunction amounts to a clear prior restraint of speech.[45] Thus, courts are deeply reluctant to enjoin hateful rallies that may stir the most painful emotions and incite violence;[46] they hesitate to stop the dissemination of vile untruths that may irreparably injure someone's reputation;[47] and they may not prevent the publication of classified military documents whose release may cost American lives.[48] Yet, they have no problem issuing a court order that, if violated, would result in imprisonment for the simple act of printing a work of complete fiction, such as *60 Years Later*, that, in their view, likely infringes someone's copyright. Lemley and Volokh, among others, have questioned this trend and argue that, even though copyright is characterized as a form of property, courts should not continue to overlook the important expressive interests at play in the use of copyrighted materials.[49]

Although we commonly view the practice of book banning as long dead and the product of a misguided and bygone era, the list of books officially banned in the USA includes not only *60 Years Later* but also such works as *The Lexicon* (an encyclopedia of all things *Harry Potter*) and *The Cat NOT in the Hat!* (a satirical examination of the O. J. Simpson trial based on Dr. Seuss's *The Cat in the Hat*). Overseas, where *60 Years Later* remains available, some copies proudly proclaim "Banned in the U.S.A."

Banned works such as *60 Years Later*, *The Lexicon*, and *The Cat NOT in the Hat!* pose no threat to national security, contain nothing salacious or ribald, and do not defame anyone, living or dead. And, if these books were being banned by a third-world dictatorship, we would be calling for economic sanctions against the country, writing letters of protest through Amnesty International, and characterizing its incarcerated publisher as a prisoner of conscience. Yet you can't find these books in any American bookstore, as courts would have little compunction about hauling their distributors to hoosegow. If courts are willing to ban books in the name of copyright law, they won't hesitate to silence other types of speech deemed infringing.

At this juncture, an important caveat bears mentioning. This discussion is not suggesting that we should unilaterally condemn attempts to enjoin the publication of works such as *60 Years Later, The Lexicon,* or *The Cat NOT in the Hat!* that draw upon pre-existing fictive worlds stemming from an original author's imagination. In these instances, it is fair to note that these derivatives could not exist without the creative expression of the underlying work. There could be no *60 Years Later, The Lexicon,* or *The Cat NOT in the Hat!* without the work of J. D. Salinger, J. K. Rowling, or Dr. Seuss. Additionally, the motivation typically animating these types of infringement cases is the plaintiff's economic interest in preserving an established market for the licensing of its copyrighted works – something that may serve the ultimate goal of the copyright regime to incentivize progress in the arts. In other words, these cases are not censorious per se, as they are not driven by an active interest in suppressing basic facts or commentary on matters of public concern.

But the results of these cases – which affirm copyright's exemption from separate First Amendment scrutiny and the ability of courts to enjoin speech that is deemed an infringement – have encouraged a much more dangerous type of lawsuit, where plaintiffs such as Noelia Lorenzo Monge and Michael Savage cynically invoke copyright law to silence opponents' viewpoints – often on important cultural and political issues – and to suppress information they would rather hide from public scrutiny. It is these lawsuits that are the subject of the concerns expressed in this chapter. In such cases, putative rights holders have no real licensing market that they are trying to protect. Rather, the goal of such suits is to prevent the dissemination of unfavorable information or commentary. By exploiting the general immunization that copyright claims enjoy from First Amendment scrutiny, these lawsuits succeed all too often, thereby diminishing the vitality of public discourse and subverting free speech rights.

In particular, marginalized communities have borne the brunt of these legal machinations, as this new form of censorship has disproportionally stifled the expressive rights of minority groups and the poor by allowing those in power to muffle resistance. Of course, the legal system has always disadvantaged members of the underclass, who suffer inferior access to counsel and have fewer resources to fund a fight under a legal regime where, ordinarily, parties bear their own fees even when they prevail. But there is something particularly pernicious about the use of copyright law to circumvent free speech rights. Specifically, our legal system has historically guarded against violations of First Amendment rights (rather than, say, breaches of contract) with special vigor. For example, despite the normal "American" rule that parties bear their own fees, statutory fee-shifting has provided at both the state level (through powerful anti-SLAPP [Strategic Lawsuits Against Public Participation] statutes allowing for early resolution and automatic awards of fees for those who have their rights to speech or petition interfered with through litigation on state or common law causes of action) and the federal level (through vehicles such as section 1988, which allows for fees shifting in successful civil rights litigation). Additionally, the Supreme Court has imposed heightened proof requirements and additional elements on certain causes of action that implicate First Amendment rights, such as defamation, false light, and intentional infliction of emotional distress claims related to public figures, which are now subject to the actual malice requirement.

But because copyright is viewed as vindication of a private right and immunized from First Amendment scrutiny, copyright claims are not subject to these procedural and substantive protections safeguarding free speech rights. On top of that, due to the terms of the Digital Millennium Copyright Act (DMCA), which was passed in 1998, copyright enforcement does not only occur through litigation. As the dispute between Michael Savage and CAIR illustrates, in the online environment, internet service providers (ISPs) acting pursuant to the safe harbor provisions of the DMCA increasingly mediate infringement issues. Under the terms of the safe harbor, ISPs that house user-generated content, such as YouTube, Facebook, Instagram, or X, can enjoy immunization from infringement liability for the activities of their users, but only if (among other things) they promptly take down materials upon a claim of infringement by a putative rights holder. ISPs have little incentive to question these takedown demands even though data from Lumen, a longtime transparency database tracking the use of DMCA takedowns for academic study, indicates that a substantial percentage are defective – because the sender does not actually hold a copyright interest in the allegedly infringed work, because the sender fails to provide the information required for a proper takedown notification under section 512(c)(3), because the allegedly infringed work is not subject to copyright protection, because the complained-of use constitutes fair use, or because of any number of other reasons.[50] As a result, ISPs will generally take down the materials rather than considering whether there is a strong substantive legal basis to deem the materials infringing or investigating whether the sender actually possesses appropriate rights to the allegedly infringed materials.[51] The consequence of the DMCA takedown regime is that, without any formal adjudication of infringement, materials accused of being infringing will often be scrubbed online. This powerful extra-legal injunctive power can therefore effectuate the silencing of disfavored speech (wrapped up in the form of a purported infringement) with frightening alacrity and force, particularly as more speech activity inevitably occurs online. With the omnipresence of technical infringements of copyright and strategic deployment of both litigation and DMCA takedowns, entrenched powers have therefore successfully weaponized copyright law as a potent tool of censorship – to the detriment of both the copyright regime and democratic and egalitarian interests.

COPYRIGHT AND CENSORSHIP: THE GROWING THREAT

On both sides of the political aisle, plaintiffs are increasingly turning to copyright as an end run around the First Amendment. As a result, copyright law has also made an unusual and unexpected appearance at the front lines of the so-called culture war[s][52] in recent years. For example, in the debate over gay marriage, activists at each end of the spectrum have exploited copyright law to censor the perspectives of their political foes. In 2009, Stand for Marriage Maine (SFMM), a group supporting a ballot measure to overturn Maine's legalization of same-sex marriage, put together a campaign advertisement shortly before the November 3 vote on the issue. In the spot, SFMM used a twenty-second excerpt from a National Public Radio (NPR) story to advance SFMM's view that the legalization of same-sex marriage could result in children being taught about gay sex in schools.[53] To the disappointment of some of its own political allies,[54] NPR successfully brought a DMCA claim to have the spot removed from YouTube and other Internet sites, effectively eliminating the ability of the spot to gain views on the eve of the election.[55]

NPR's actions mimicked those of some organizations against same-sex marriage, who have made similarly disingenuous appeals to copyright law. In 2009, the National Organization for Marriage (NOM), a nonprofit dedicated to the fight against legalization of same-sex marriage in the United States, launched a $1.5 million advertising campaign entitled *Gathering Storm* in key battleground states.[56] When audition footage from *Gathering Storm* leaked, MSNBC's Rachel Maddow played excerpts on her talk show to criticize the underlying assumptions and merits of the campaign.[57] NOM promptly claimed that Maddow had infringed its copyrights to the footage and successfully served takedown notices to YouTube to remove any "infringing" clips of Maddow's show.[58]

All the while, NOM faced copyright issues of its own. Celebrity-news blogger Perez Hilton, who has been on the receiving end of numerous copyright infringement suits himself,[59] filed DMCA takedown notices to have copies of the actual *Gathering Storm* advertisements removed from YouTube because they drew on three seconds of footage from his personal video blog.[60] NOM had used the footage – in which Hilton attacked Miss California Carrie Prejean for her response to his question about same-sex marriage at the 2009 Miss USA Competition – to argue that same-sex marriage proponents were silencing traditional-marriage advocates on illegitimate grounds.[61]

From controversial issues ranging from same-sex marriage and abortion to evolution and creationism, this pattern of copyright abuse has repeated itself on both sides of the political aisle. In *Northland Family Planning Clinic, Inc.* v. *Center for Bio-Ethical Reform* (2012), for example, an abortion provider sued pro-life activists for copyright infringement for making a video that impermissibly used excerpts of the clinic's own informational videos interspersed with graphic images of bloody fetuses, citations to scripture, and jarring music.[62] Meanwhile, creationists have tried to stifle evolutionist critiques of their activities with similarly cynical claims. In 2007, when a group of atheists operating as the Rational Response Squad (RRS) used seminar materials from Creation Science Evangelism (CSE) to prepare video criticisms of the CSE's teachings on creationism, CSE cried foul through claims of copyright infringement and successfully pushed YouTube to remove all of RSS's videos making use of the seminar materials from the platform and to ban its account.[63] Instead of engaging in robust free speech to convince the public of the merits of their respective views, organizations at the front lines of leading cultural and political issues have waged a proxy war against each other through the prism of copyright law by raising infringement claims as a means to silence their opponents.

In such situations, defendants can admittedly seek salvation in a fair use defense. But the success of such an affirmative defense is not remotely assured. Moreover, there is no viable Rule 11 basis[64] to challenge these types of claims; although they may represent a cynical means to route around the First Amendment limitations that would ordinarily preclude any noncopyright basis to shut down the activities of political opponents, the unauthorized reproduction, distribution, or public display or performance of someone else's copyrighted work clearly meets the prima facie elements for infringement liability. And if plaintiffs wish to hold out for an exorbitant sum of money to vindicate their copyright interests, the law (at least in some circuits) actively encourages their right to do so: plaintiffs can ignore reasonable offers of judgment under Rule 68 in some circuits, which only shift costs but not fees in copyright matters.[65] Finally, to avoid an adverse fees judgment in the event of a fair use finding, the plaintiffs can always place the copyrights to the photographs in a judgment-proof LLC with no other assets.[66] In short, myriad substantive and procedural aspects of copyright law enable entrenched forces to achieve the removal of adverse online content that would otherwise be protected under the First Amendment were it not for the leverage they enjoy under infringement claims.

COPYRIGHT AND THE TENSION BETWEEN INTELLECTUAL PROPERTY PROTECTION AND THE FIRST AMENDMENT

Thus far, we have only talked about the ability of putative rights holders to use copyright law as a vehicle of censorship. The issues raised here are not unique to copyright law and, in fact, extend potentially to all aspects of our intellectual property regime. For example, the property interests that rights holders have in logos and brands (i.e., trademark law) and in names, voices, and likenesses (i.e., right-of-publicity law) regularly clash with expressive interests. As Professor Eric Goldman has bemoaned, putative rights holders have increasingly misused intellectual property interests in trademark and publicity rights to squelch disfavored speech. Referring to publicity rights, Goldman has observed that its "doctrinal boundaries are so amorphous/shapeless that plaintiffs often feel they've got a good case when … the defendant makes an unwanted reference to a person."[67] Goldman also points to the "larger trend of plaintiffs misusing IP laws to scrub online content,"[68] including through the cynical invocation of trademark law.

Thus, censorship issues can arise in all of our intellectual property regimes, where speech activities are potentially converted into property infringements. However, the cynical circumvention of First Amendment protections is especially pronounced, troubling, and pressing in copyright jurisprudence for several reasons.

First, the First Amendment defenses available in copyright law are far less generous than those developed in both right-of-publicity and trademark jurisprudence.[69] Right-of-publicity statutes typically contain absolute exemptions for certain types of activities, such as noncommercial use or news reporting. Moreover, states such as California have adopted very broad transformative-use defenses to right-of-publicity claims.[70] Similarly, trademark law has developed the *Rogers* v. *Grimaldi*[71] test, which strongly protects the unauthorized use of trademarks in artistic work. Defendants in trademark cases also enjoy various forms of fair use that courts have generally read broadly.[72] By sharp contrast, courts have interpreted copyright's fair-use doctrine far more narrowly. In the process, they "have frequently converted the defense into an inquiry on necessity – an analytical gambit that has attached liability to a broad range of expressive, nonparodic, and transformative activities."[73] Indeed, there is perhaps no more explicit proof of the dramatic difference between juridical approaches to First Amendment defenses in copyright law versus trademark and right-of-publicity law than how courts have treated conjunctive intellectual property claims brought over the exact same nucleus of facts. On numerous such occasions, courts have immunized defendants from trademark and right-of-publicity claims on First Amendment grounds but have allowed joined copyright claims based on the same activities to trump expressive concerns.[74]

Second, a prima facie claim for copyright infringement is much easier to make out than a trademark or right-of-publicity claim. A potential defendant need merely reproduce, publicly display, distribute, or create a derivate version of someone else's work to commit an act of copyright infringement – regardless of whether the use is commercial/for-profit or wholly noncommercial.[75] Trademark infringement, by contrast, requires a likelihood of consumer confusion.[76] Right-of-publicity violations typically necessitate some sort of *commercial* misappropriation.[77] So, it is far more common for any given individual or group to run afoul of copyright law than trademark or right-of-publicity law.

Third, the damages regime in copyright law is dramatically more favorable to plaintiffs than the corresponding remedies provided in trademark and right-of-publicity law. In trademark law, monetary recovery is typically limited to actual damages or a disgorgement of profits.[78] Importantly, there are also no statutory, or presumed, damages available unless one engages in counterfeiting.[79] Right-of-publicity remedies vary by state, but even where statutory damages are available, they are comparatively small. California's right-of-publicity statute, for example, provides just $750 in statutory damages per violation.[80] By sharp contrast, plaintiffs in copyright cases can qualify for statutory damages of up to $150,000 per willful act of infringement.[81]

Finally, and perhaps most importantly, copyright violations are ubiquitous and, with the existence of digital fingerprints, far more traceable than ever before.[82] To be fair, the disingenuous invocation of copyright law to achieve an alternate means to silence one's foes is not an entirely novel tactic. Even pre-internet plaintiffs occasionally drew upon the gambit. For example, some four decades ago, Larry Flynt, the founder of *Hustler* magazine, filed such a suit against the Reverend Jerry Falwell for reproducing copies of a *Hustler* parody advertisement about Falwell in fundraising literature sent to members of his Moral Majority. Flynt sued largely in retaliation for Falwell's prior legal action against him; in a case that famously ended up before the Supreme Court, the Reverend had brought claims against *Hustler* for intentional infliction of emotional distress for running that very same advertisement, which suggested that Falwell's first sexual experience was with his mother.[83] Not surprisingly, Falwell lost his claims against Flynt,[84] and Flynt lost his claims against Falwell.[85] The respective reasons both parties failed to receive legal relief reveal something important about copyright jurisprudence. Falwell's intentional infliction claim famously failed on express First Amendment grounds.[86] By contrast, Flynt's copyright claim against Falwell failed on fair-use grounds, an affirmative defense for which Falwell bore the burden of proof.[87]

Flynt's infringement claims against Falwell became realizable (though not ultimately victorious) because Falwell literally had a printing press at his disposal, so he could reproduce thousands of copies of the *Hustler* advertisement to include in his fundraising literature. Possessing the ability to duplicate and distribute copyrighted works on a mass scale was relatively unusual a generation ago; it was something only businesses or wealthy individuals could do. Today, however, almost anyone can engage in such conduct with ease: most of us have, by way of smartphones, scanners, and computers connected to the Internet, the tools of massive digital reproduction and distribution at our fingertips. As such, we all come into contact with, and unwittingly violate, copyright law (i.e., by meeting the elements of a prima facie case of infringement) dozens of times a day.[88] With the existence of digital fingerprints and technologies such as reverse image searches and the Internet Archive's Wayback Machine,[89] our acts of infringement are easily traceable and potentially preserved for all time, should someone seek to make us a target of infringement litigation. As a result, we are all vulnerable to such "gotcha" suits if we have a sufficiently aggrieved party looking to censor our expressive activities. And, notably, the consequences of such suits are far more severe now than they were in 1985, when Flynt sued Falwell. Back then, statutory damages amounted to a maximum of $10,000 per act of infringement or $50,000 per willful act of infringement.[90] Today, they are triple that rate – $30,000 per act of infringement or $150,000 per act of willful infringement.[91]

Thus, while there are legitimate concerns about the ability of rights holders to exploit other intellectual property regimes to suppress First Amendment rights, the problem is particularly pressing in the realm of copyright. The ubiquity of infringement, the relative ease of making out a prima facie case, the narrow nature of the available defenses, and the stiff penalties available for infringement have all combined to make copyright an especially luring regime for would-be censors. The development of hearty First Amendment checks to such claims as invasion of privacy, defamation, and imminent incitements of lawlessness over the past century has (rightfully) precluded aggrieved parties from pursuing traditional tort causes of action against their ideological adversaries for their speech-related activities. Now, however, would-be censors have converted their losing tort claims into viable copyright infringement claims for those same activities.

FIGHTING ALLEGATIONS OF RACISM, TORTURE, BRUTALITY, AND CORRUPTION WITH COPYRIGHT LAW

It is hard to imagine that the Framers of the Constitution envisioned that political wars in the twenty-first century would be fought in proxy battles through the prism of copyright law rather than reliance on robust free speech to convince the public of the merits of one's views. But with the broad immunization of copyright law from First Amendment scrutiny, powerful and sophisticated players in the marketplace of ideas have increasingly resorted to infringement claims as a cynical ploy to censor the speech of those who challenge them.

This trend has not been without pushback, as courts have not been entirely oblivious to the challenges posed by such censorious suits. Some federal courts have responded with tenacity, attempting to deal with the issue of censorious copyright litigation through the use of procedural machinations, including early adjudication through motions to dismiss under Rule 12 of the Federal Rules of Civil Procedure, to mitigate the adverse impact of such disputes on litigants and the public interest.[92] In other instances, they have not only rebuked such claims but also awarded fees to prevailing defendants as a means of deterring such disingenuous uses of copyright litigation in the future. But, all too often, courts have ultimately fallen short. Limitations on the deployment of Rule 12, the factual nature of the (affirmative) fair-use defense, inconsistent application of fee standards, and the availability of extra-judicial relief under the DMCA's takedown regime have all combined to render extant judicial responses ineffective, creating a true censorship crisis. The resulting situation means that defendants with even the most ironclad fair-use defenses still must face backbreaking expenses in litigation – including exposure to discovery – in order to successfully vindicate their rights. And even when defendants spend hundreds of thousands of dollars to fight back and end up prevailing on the merits, courts have shown great reluctance to award fees against losing plaintiffs. Cognizant of the remote chance of having to pay defendants for the ill-advised attempts to enforce their intellectual property rights, putative rights holders have grown increasingly uncompromising in their demands. The courts have issued enough binding and troubling precedent to make censorious cases viable. And, finally, part of the problem is out of the hands of the courts: the extra-judicial relief provided to copyright holders under the DMCA has made censorious uses of copyright law, without reliance on courts, all too easy.

To begin with, when censorious copyright cases have reached a decision on the merits, the federal courts have frequently denied infringement claims and found fair use. Courts have rejected, on summary judgment, a widow's attempt to raise copyright infringement claims when a documentary about her husband did not turn out as favorably as she had hoped.[93] They have rebuked, on summary judgment, a husband's disingenuous attempt to raise copyright infringement claims based on his wife's production of unsavory materials about him in a contentious divorce and custody proceeding.[94] They have denied, on summary judgment, an abortion provider's claims of copyright infringement against a pro-life group for the latter's unauthorized lacing of the former's informational videos with bloody fetuses, citations to scripture, and jarring music.[95] And, most famously, they repudiated, on summary judgment, Larry Flynt's attempts to drum up an infringement claim against his arch-nemesis, the Reverend Jerry Falwell, for Falwell's specious intentional infliction suit against Flynt and Falwell's unauthorized use of an excerpt from *Hustler* magazine in his fundraising materials.[96]

In a small minority of cases, courts have even allowed consideration of the merits of copyright claims at even earlier stages of litigation, including in Rule 12 motions.[97] Holdings embracing such a tactic have enabled the victims of censorious copyright litigation to escape suits prediscovery, before the expenditure of extensive attorneys' fees. Perhaps the most significant such decision is *Brownmark Films, LLC* v. *Comedy Partners*.[98] In *Brownmark*, the Seventh Circuit held, for the first time, that courts within its jurisdiction can dispose of copyright infringement claims based on a fair-use defense at the Rule 12 stage.[99] Among other things, the court emphasized the need, especially post-*Iqbal*,[100] to protect defendants who are the victims of unmeritorious cases from the burdens and costs of discovery and trial.[101] As a result, the court quickly dispensed with a suit brought against the makers of *South Park* for their unauthorized use of the timeless video for the sophisticated and elegant ditty *What (In the Butt)* with their (similarly sophisticated and elegant) parodic "paean to anal sex."[102]

On occasion, federal courts have also taken the additional step of awarding fees to the defendants to deter the filing of such improper infringement suits. In *Bond* v. *Blum*, for example, William Bond drummed up a copyright infringement claim in order to prevent damaging information from coming to light in a custody proceeding.[103] Specifically, Bond had authored an (unpublished) autobiographical manuscript detailing how he beat his father to death with a hammer when he was seventeen.[104] His ex-wife managed to obtain a copy of the manuscript and produced it as an exhibit in custody proceedings to demonstrate that her former husband would not provide an environment suitable for children.[105] Bond then sued his ex-wife and her law firm for copyright infringement, tenuously yet tenaciously arguing that they had engaged in the unauthorized reproduction of his copyrighted manuscript.[106] The trial court found the defendants' use of the manuscript squarely protected by the fair-use doctrine and awarded fees to the defendants on the grounds that the infringement case was "not a close one."[107] As the trial court held, the suit "was frivolous" and "motivated by a desire to suppress the underlying facts of" the plaintiff's work – not to protect the creative expression embodied in the manuscript.[108] The Fourth Circuit affirmed the decision.[109]

Similarly, a court granted attorneys' fees to the defendant in *Hofheinz* v. *AMC Productions* based on the litigation's censorious motivation – the plaintiff's dislike of how the defendants had portrayed her late husband in a documentary.[110] In the case, the widow of renowned filmmaker James Nicholson, the co-founder of American International Pictures, unilaterally retracted what appeared to be a valid grant of permission for the use of movie clips, posters, and photographs in a documentary about her late husband when she did not approve of the movie's final cut.[111] She then sued for infringement.[112] The court awarded fees to the defendants on the grounds that the plaintiff brought the case for improper purposes.[113] Specifically, the timing of her retraction strongly suggested an ulterior motive to ensure that the documentary showcased "her late husband in a more favorable light."[114] The court found the claim objectively unreasonable and frivolous, thereby warranting an award of fees to the defendants.[115]

However, for every *Bond* v. *Blum* or *Hofheinz* v. *AMC*, there are countless cases where courts do not grant fees to prevailing defendants,[116] or because of the sheer cost and uncertainty of litigation, the cases never reach a decision on the merits in the first place. And, despite the *Brownmark* precedent, courts have largely limited early adjudication of copyright cases to instances involving the issue of substantial similarity, not fair use.[117] When courts have addressed fair-use claims, they have typically balked at employing such gate-keeping functions, even post-*Iqbal*, on the grounds that fair use is an affirmative defense (rather than a prima facie element of an infringement claim) and a mixed question of law and fact.[118] Most courts have consequently declined to follow *Brownmark*'s lead.

Consider two examples, both of which – with their use of trumped-up photograph-infringement claims as a vehicle to silence criticism – evoke the abortion hypothetical presented earlier. In *Katz* v. *Chevaldina* – a case whose facts smack of classic copyright-as-censorship – the district court rejected a defendant's attempt to argue fair use at the Rule 12 stage.[119] Irina Chevaldina wrote several blogs that criticized the business activities of Raanan Katz, a noted Florida "real estate developer and minority owner of the Miami Heat."[120] When Chevaldina published several caustic pieces charging Katz with both immorality and illegality in his business dealings, she used a photograph to identify him for her audience.[121] Katz sued, claiming that he owned the copyright to the photograph and that Chevaldina had infringed it.[122] The court refused to address the fair-use issue at the Rule 12 stage and expressly declined to follow *Brownmark*, claiming that, among other things, fair use was a mixed question of fact and law not appropriate for resolution prediscovery.[123] As the court concluded, it is a "general rule that fair-use defenses are not ripe for determination before the summary judgment stage."[124] Katz's suit therefore marched on, despite the fact that it was a transparent attempt to impose liability against Chevaldina for her speech-related activities on a matter of legitimate public concern, a view buttressed when a unanimous Eleventh Circuit panel decided Chevaldina's fair-use defense resoundingly in her favor almost two years later.[125]

In an even more politically charged and disquieting example, four Navy SEALs sued the Associated Press and a reporter when, in the wake of the high-profile scandal at Abu Ghraib, they ran a story that alleged the SEALs had abused Iraqi prisoners.[126] Among other things, the story's photos showed the SEALs "sitting on, lying atop, or stepping on detainees, some of whom are hooded," and depicted "military personnel pointing a firearm at a prisoner's bloody head at point blank range."[127] The SEALs claimed that the publication of the photographs constituted an invasion of their privacy (their faces were shown in some of the photographs) and an infringement of their copyright interests.[128] Based largely on newsworthiness grounds, the *Four Navy SEALs* court did not hesitate to dismiss the privacy-related claims on the motion to dismiss.[129] However, the court declined to dismiss the infringement claim, deeming the issue "inappropriate for determination in a 12(b)(6) motion, since fair use is an affirmative defense to an infringement claim."[130]

The differing results on the privacy and copyright claims in the *Four Navy SEALs* suit are of particular note. Since the privacy claims were grounded in state law, they were properly subject to the special motion to strike under California's Anti-Strategic Lawsuits Against Public Participation (anti-SLAPP) statute, which allows prediscovery challenges to any lawsuit "based upon an act in furtherance of the right to free speech."[131] For such suits, defendants can force a plaintiff to present admissible evidence showing a probability of prevailing on the merits of the claim.[132] Failure to do so results in significant consequences: the suit is dismissed, and a defendant is automatically granted its attorneys' fees.[133] Thus, under the anti-SLAPP statute, the court was indisputably able to consider the merits of the privacy claims at the very outset of the case, and the plaintiffs faced swift repercussions for bringing a censorious claim without merit. When the plaintiffs failed to show a probability of success on the merits, the court not only dismissed the privacy claims but also granted the defendants their fees.[134] By contrast, as a federal cause of action, copyright claims enjoy immunity from special motions to strike under the anti-SLAPP statute. The infringement claims therefore survived, despite their similarly suspect nature. Meanwhile, numerous other courts have declined to adjudicate fair-use issues at the Rule 12 stage.[135] As Eric Goldman has concluded, "[s]uccessful fair use defenses on a motion to dismiss are exceptionally rare."[136] Thus, the inapplicability of the anti-SLAPP statute to copyright claims and the courts' general refusal to consider a fair-use defense – no matter how solid – at the prediscovery stage have combined to make copyright claims particularly valuable weapons for litigious censors.

As such, even when there is an unusually strong fair-use defense to an allegation of infringement, a defendant will often face protracted litigation and substantial costs, no matter how meritorious its position. In many instances, an underfunded defendant must kowtow to a plaintiff's infringement claims, even if the former is ultimately in the legal right. Of course, such an objection could be lodged against litigation of any sort, as well-heeled plaintiffs can often leverage the costs and uncertainty of litigation to wrest concessions from smaller defendants that they would not otherwise receive if the parties enjoyed similar resources. But it is particularly so in copyright law, where, unlike state-law claims that might be subjected to an early motion to dismiss or motion to strike (per an anti-SLAPP statute, as in *Four Navy SEALs*), there is no such early adjudication mechanism and interpretations of Rule 68 and the ability of losing plaintiffs to avoid fees liability can make plaintiffs uncompromising in their demands.

Importantly, the courts are not alone in facing blame for the extant situation, and it is not just in litigation where the copyright-as-censorship problem arises. The abuse of overbroad legal claims (especially those backed by censorious motives) is particularly pernicious in copyright law because of the powerful extra-judicial relief provided to copyright holders under the DMCA – which requires ISPs to promptly remove access to materials on their networks (or face liability themselves) when a rights holder serves them with a takedown notice claiming infringement. In the digital age, much use of copyrighted content takes place online, particularly on social media sites featuring user-generated content. These uses are governed by the DMCA's safe harbor provisions, which provide ISPs with a strong incentive to reactively remove user-generated content that is the subject of any copyright claim in order to preserve their conditional immunity from infringement liability.[137] While senders of DMCA takedown notifications may be obligated to consider fair use in their assessment of whether the material is infringing (though they are not strongly incentivized to do so), ISPs are under no such obligation. Indeed, in a move that incentivizes ISPs to strongly err on the side of taking down allegedly infringing materials rather than leaving them up, ISPs are specifically immunized from liability for the good faith removal of materials, "regardless of whether the material or activity is ultimately determined to be infringing."[138] It is consequently no surprise that, upon receipt of a proper DMCA takedown notice, ISPs will regularly take the materials down and keep them down, absent counter-notification (and, then, only if the plaintiff does not pursue litigation; if litigation is pursued, the ISP is under no obligation to restore access to the material and, in fact, is strongly incentivized to do the opposite).[139] Failure to take down infringing materials upon proper notification could result in an ISP losing its valuable immunity from infringement liability[140] – a potentially disastrous consequence. So, without even relying on litigation, a rights holder can frequently have speech that makes unauthorized use of their copyrighted materials (even if it likely constitutes fair use) effectively removed from the online world.

Thus, even when courts get the ultimate result right and acknowledge an infringement claim's lack of merit, a plaintiff can achieve the success they are seeking – the silencing of their opponents' views – through the DMCA takedown procedure. Consider the Michael Savage example given earlier where, by issuing takedown notifications, Savage managed to have his opponents' outreach work against him effectively wiped from the internet for a critical period – the time of his opponents' advertising blitz. Specifically, Savage forced the removal of critical videos on YouTube just after his opponents had provided links to them in an expensive *New York Times* media buy.[141]

Putative copyright holders regularly abuse the DMCA to force the takedown of online materials that criticize them. In perhaps the most unusual example, an ex-wife used a purported copyright interest she obtained from her late husband to prevent online distribution of his suicide note. The move was particularly ironic and troubling since, when Chris Mackney took his own life on December 23, 2013, he was in the midst of an acrimonious and lengthy custody battle with his ex-wife, Dina. He left behind a lengthy suicide note denouncing her, her family, and her lawyers. During the last months of his life, Chris had maintained a blog detailing his difficult custody battle with Dina and his suicide note immediately generated attention online, where it was reproduced by numerous websites advocating for greater rights for fathers in family courts. Dina clearly did not appreciate her name being dragged through the mud, but the First Amendment precluded action – except under copyright law. Thus, through DMCA takedown notifications, she prevented online distribution of his suicide note – a note that placed responsibility for his untimely passing squarely on her.[142]

In particular, politically oriented abuses of the DMCA to suppress speech tend to abound. AIDS denialists behind a documentary entitled *House of Numbers* – which argues that AIDS is not an actual illness but a conspiracy to sell antiviral medication – have used DMCA takedowns to actively remove videos that feature clips from *House of Numbers* to discredit the denialists' claims.[143] Former Ecuadorian President Rafael Correa used DMCA takedown notifications to US-based ISPs to suppress speech critical of his regime by claiming copyright ownership of parts of video footage being distributed online to substantiate charges of corruption against him.[144] The English Defence League (EDL), a rightwing extremist religious group based in the United Kingdom, has used the DMCA to take down critical commentary about it from a website monitoring hate group activities because the site featured a sixteen-word quotation from one of the EDL's members without permission.[145]

Unfortunately, the abuse is not just limited to powerful interests abroad. Indeed, American law enforcement officers have begun to take advantage of the DMCA for censorious purposes. In recent years, savvy police officers – doubtlessly informed by legal counsel – have begun to employ an unusual practice: playing music when they spot citizens recording them. The choice has nothing to do with the preference of officers to conduct their patrolling activities to the accompaniment of sonorous top 40 tunes. Rather, it is a cynical ploy to exploit copyright laws and its systematic immunization from First Amendment scrutiny.

Of course, citizens have a legal right to record the activities of police officers operating on the public streets and, with the widespread availability of cellphones with cameras, the creation and distribution of such recordings, especially on social media, have helped provide the public with greater transparency over police (mis) conduct. For example, if it had not been for an ordinary teenage bystander, Darnella Frazier, who happened to be on the streets of Minneapolis on May 25, 2020, when she courageously pointed her camera toward Derek Chauvin, the world would have never witnessed his brutal execution of George Floyd. Her recording not only played an instrumental role in holding Chauvin to account for his actions with his murder conviction, but it also provoked worldwide outrage and galvanized support for the Black Lives Matter movement and the call for greater attention to issues of social justice and police brutality.

While many members of the public have applauded such citizen recordings, not all law enforcement officers are as sanguine about the practice. Police accountability activists have noticed that, post-Floyd, some officers are now intentionally playing music by artists such as Taylor Swift and the Beatles (who diligently enforce their rights online) when they notice someone recording them. The reason is simple: if the recording ends up online, it would be subject to swift takedown because it contains copyrighted music which has not been cleared with a synchronization license.

Generally speaking, this explanation for why officers play music has remained jealously guarded, but at least one officer – Sergeant D. Shelby of the Alameda County Sheriff's Department – has copped to the ruse.[146] Upon noticing that members of the Anti-Police-Terror Project were recording him on a public street, he began to blare a track, *Blank Space*, by Taylor Swift. He was no Swiftie. Instead, as he bluntly admitted: "I'm playing my music so that you can't post on YouTube."[147] While a department spokesman later claimed that Sergeant Shelby's comments were "not something we condone or approve,"[148] the potential practice is alarming. As Officer Shelby indicated, he was fully aware that YouTube and other social media sites proactively remove videos featuring music from major artists (whether they might be fair use or not). By folding music into citizen recordings, law enforcement can successfully repress the dissemination of such videos. If Derek Chauvin's fellow officers had cynically undertaken such an action, they would have doubtlessly tried to stifle the distribution of that consequential recording. Copyright law could have rendered the dissemination of that video infringing, thereby potentially preventing one of the most pivotal social movements in recent years – one that spurred massive activism to support redress for the tragic devaluation of black lives – from ever occurring.

Admittedly, the DMCA does provide that users of copyrighted content with strong fair-use claims can force the ISP's hands by filing counter-notifications to require restoration of the allegedly infringing materials online.[149] But this counter-notification procedure is not without its own significant problems. First, as evidenced by the Michael Savage example, the DMCA takedown procedure usually results in a significant period of time where access to the allegedly infringing material is removed online – a period that lasts *no less* than the entire term from receipt of the initial takedown notification to ten business days after receipt of a proper counter-notification.[150] If would-be censors time their DMCA takedown notices carefully, they can have materials removed online during a particularly damaging interval (as in the Savage case), regardless of how good a fair-use claim there might be for the use of those materials. Second, if a DMCA takedown claimant is unwavering in its position and files suit in federal court after receipt of the counter-notification, the ISP is under no obligation to restore access to the materials at all.[151] Thus, when dealing with plaintiffs hell-bent on asserting their rights – in court even, if need be – counter-notifications can be ineffective as a means to undo the removal of materials online.

Finally, when cases go to litigation and arrive at a decision on the merits, the federal courts do not always get them right. As a result, there is some dangerous and controlling precedent that has only empowered censorious uses of copyright law. The *Monge* v. *Maya Magazines, Inc.* decision discussed at the outset of this chapter provides a vivid illustration.[152] A district court originally found *Maya*'s activities protected under the fair-use doctrine. After all, the photographs at issue played a key, if not instrumental, role in the article in which they were featured as the images themselves directly refuted Monge and Reynoso's repeated denials of being married and formed the crux of the news story.[153] Nevertheless, the Ninth Circuit reversed the holding and, in the process, empowered the use of copyright law as a potent tool of censorship. Parties seeking to suppress speech on matters of public import can circumvent First Amendment concerns by achieving their censorious ends via infringement claims. As Judge Milan Smith presciently cautioned in his dissent in the case,

> Under the majority's analysis, public figures could invoke copyright protection to prevent the media's disclosure of any embarrassing or incriminating works by claiming that such images were intended only for private use. The implications of this analysis undermine the free press and eviscerate the principles upon which copyright was founded. Although newsworthiness alone is insufficient to invoke fair use, public figures should not be able to hide behind the cloak of copyright to prevent the news media from exposing their fallacies.[154]

The *Monge* case provides significant legal ballast to the disingenuous use of copyright as a tool of censorship and accentuates the urgent need to develop new tools to fight the threat posed by censorious copyright litigation to public debate, expressive rights, and freedom of speech.

ADDRESSING THE CENSORSHIP PROBLEM

Reform efforts would ideally introduce a consistent and uniform mechanism for addressing the copyright-as-censorship problem. And, the mechanism would give victims of such claims the ability to escape litigation at an early juncture and would also deter plaintiffs from bringing such claims in the future. But to formulate any fix to the censorship problem identified in this chapter, one must first accurately define the problem. In short, any reform effort should not strike too broadly in a way that inadvertently impacts the ability of copyright holders to protect their warranted property interests. Thus, any remedial efforts must effectively distinguish between cynical uses of copyright law to effectuate censorship and legitimate (albeit, sometimes unsuccessful) uses of copyright law to vindicate justifiable rights. Such a distinction is not easy to make, of course, and it may be tempting to resort to such unsatisfying aphorisms as "I know it when I see it."[155] But, a careful comparison of cases on both sides of the censorious/noncensorious ledger yields some key diagnostic factors. With these guidelines in mind, we then examine three separate proposals to combat the copyright-as-censorship problem.

Distinguishing between Censorious Uses of Copyright Law and Legitimate Enforcement Efforts: A Dancing Toddler and Harry Potter

Almost all copyright claims have the ability to adversely impact the freedom of speech. But, the censorious use of copyright is distinct from the general impediments to users' expressive rights that are inherent to most copyright litigation. And to attack the former problem, we must recognize how to distinguish it from the latter.

Consider the infringement claims at issue in the widely discussed *Lenz* v. *Universal* case.[156] The dispute began with Stephanie Lenz's YouTube post of a twenty-nine-second video of her children excitedly dancing to Prince's 1980s classic *Let's Go Crazy*. While thousands of YouTube users found the video adorable, Universal (the copyright holder to the *Let's Go Crazy* sound recording) and Prince (the recording artist) did not.[157] Universal, with Prince's support, deemed the clip infringing and served a takedown notice under the DMCA to have it removed from the site.[158] But Lenz strongly disagreed, claiming the use was an indisputable instance of fair use. She not only served a DMCA counter-notification but also filed suit against Universal in federal court for willfully misrepresenting to YouTube that her actions constituted infringement.[159]

Universal's uncompromising desire to force the removal of a seemingly sweet[160] recording of children taken by their mother gained widespread media attention and condemnation as a quintessential example of copyright overreach by rights holders.[161] But, while Universal's actions may have been bad form, ill-advised, or unremittingly avaricious, they were not censorship. Although Universal's actions may be problematic and cause us to question current copyright law on other grounds, that subject is beyond the scope of this chapter and the specific censorship issue it identifies and addresses.

To be sure, Universal's exertion of rights conflicted with Stephanie Lenz's expressive rights. Universal's infringement claim directly interfered with Lenz's ability to show her children's unbridled love for *Let's Go Crazy*. But no matter what one might think of Universal's actions, it is fair to say that they were not primarily motivated by a desire to suppress Lenz's speech. Rather, the point of Universal's infringement claim was to maximize profits and control the use of a work to which it possessed a copyright. Universal's desire, at the end of the day, was to wrest license fees (sync licenses) for any such uses of its song in derivative videos. Universal's work has actual market value and Universal regularly and aggressively exploits its market value. It has no political agenda except to make money and exercise control. And, Universal did not appear to object to the particular content or the context of the use. Indeed, the message of the use was totally irrelevant to Universal's choice to halt the use.[162]

Or, to take another example, consider *Warner Bros.* v. *RDR Books* (2008), the suit that the studio with the rights to the *Harry Potter* franchise brought against the makers of an unauthorized *Harry Potter* encyclopedia.[163] Warner litigates not because they disapprove of the particular take that the encyclopedia has on the *Harry Potter* universe. Rather, it sues to protect the economic market for *Harry Potter* and Warner's exclusive right to produce its own definitive treatise on the *Harry Potter* world. Warner's actions undoubtedly inflict a cost on the defendant's expressive rights – the author of the *Harry Potter* encyclopedia will not be able to share his particular take on the *Harry Potter* universe with the world. But, Warner's motivation has nothing to do with the suppression of the defendant's speech or his particular message per se.

In both the Universal and Warner Brothers examples, economics ultimately drive the action, not a desire to suppress the unauthorized user's particular message. By contrast, censorious copyright suits are chiefly motivated by the rights holder's thirst to silence the content of the unauthorized user's speech. Thus, a pro-choice group will sue a pro-life group in order to suppress the latter's criticism of the former's informational videos;[164] a prominent radio talk show host will sue a civil-rights group to prevent criticism and dissemination of his hate speech;[165] and a disgruntled widow will sue a filmmaker for infringement of certain materials featured in a documentary when that documentary depicts her deceased husband in a light less flattering than she had hoped.[166] In all of these cases, the plaintiffs do not seek to exploit a legitimate market for their work. Pro-choice groups would not license their informational videos to pro-life groups for criticism; inflammatory radio talk show hosts would not license their programs for use by civil rights watchdogs; and individuals do not license materials to documentarians making unfavorable documentaries about deceased loved ones. Rather, the uses to which the defendants put the works were diametrically opposed to the purpose for which the works were created. As such, their unauthorized use did not interfere with a legitimate licensing market that the creator could have intended to exploit. The absence of a legitimate economic motivation to preserve a rightful market for rights holders is a hallmark (though not a sufficient condition) of copyright-as-censorship cases.

Distinguishing Dignitary Concerns from Censorship: Separating Fiction from Fact

That said, it is worth noting that not all copyright suits lacking an economic driver are censorious in nature. Consider suits seeking to vindicate dignity or privacy interests. When he sues the publisher and author of an unauthorized sequel to *Catcher in the Rye*, J. D. Salinger may want to preserve the right to have his works not made public or his interest in protecting his works from unwanted exposure or derivation. When it sues an author and publisher for a critical recasting of *Gone with the Wind*, the Margaret Mitchell estate may want to protect the novel from unwanted derivations that undermine the integrity of the work. Or, when they sue Republican politicians for misappropriating their songs, Jackson Browne[167] and Don Henley[168] may not wish for their creative output to become associated with causes that might undermine the perceived meaning of their works. In each of these instances, rights holders are acting, at least partially, on noneconomic dignity or privacy interests that courts have deemed legitimate. Of course, there may be censorious motives at play behind such litigation. After all, the Mitchell estate was particularly uncomfortable with *The Wind Done Gone* – not just because it was an unauthorized recasting of *Gone with the Wind*, but precisely because of its content.[169] Among other things, *The Wind Done Gone* made Ashley Wilkes gay and mocked *Gone with the Wind* for its antiquated perspectives on race.[170] And one can only imagine that Browne and Henley might have been far more comfortable with a liberal, rather than conservative, politician making (unauthorized) use of their songs. In each instance, therefore, a desire to suppress the defendants' particular expression may have served as an animating factor in the decision to file suit. But it was not the primary motivator.

Just as importantly, all the works at issue in these cases were highly creative in nature. Thus, efforts to limit the rights of defendants to make use of these works would not result in a denial of the defendants' right to express basic facts or to comment on matters of public concern. Salinger may, in some sense, be "censoring" creative expressions about his book and character when he litigates his derivative-works right; and recognizing Salinger's ability to do so may make for a poor public-policy judgment, especially when the goal of the copyright regime is to encourage progress in the arts. But, Salinger was not suppressing facts. Monge, by contrast, was censoring something vital to the reporting of basic facts on a news item. The SEALs sought to suppress visual evidence of their alleged acts of torture. And, William Bond sought to cover up facts about his history of patricide that may speak to his fitness as a parent in a custody proceeding.

Of course, one could argue that Monge, the SEALs, and Bond all possessed dignity interests that deserve recognition – privacy interests in personal photographs or unpublished manuscripts that reveal deeply intimate details about one's life. However, the works at issue in those cases were not just creative in nature but also highly factual. Since attempts to limit use of these works necessarily implicate the rights of users to express basic facts and comment on matters of public concern, society can, and should, have greater rights to make unauthorized use of factual works than creative ones – a principle already enshrined in the second factor of the fair-use balancing test.[171] The photos in *Monge*, for example, provided incomparable evidence of a matter of public concern – the purported marriage that Monge had denied.[172] William Bond's autobiography provided incomparable insight into his state of mind when he killed his father – a seemingly relevant fact in the custody proceedings involving his children.[173] And, there is no better way to convey to your audience just how offensive a parody advertisement[174] or hate-filled rant[175] might be than to provide a copy of the advertisement or rant along with critical commentary so as to convey the content and nature of the advertisement or rant.

In censorious suits, a plaintiff's primary motivation is a desire to suppress the defendants' particular message or the context of their use. However, motivation can be difficult to independently determine. But as we have seen, two traits typically characterize censorious copyright suits and can indicate the bad faith at play. First, in censorious suits, the plaintiff usually lacks a legitimate economic motivation to preserve a rightful market for the licensing of its copyrighted works.[176] Second, in censorious suits, use of the work at issue strongly advances the expression of basic facts or commentary on matters of public concern. With these indicia of censorious resorts to copyright law in mind, reform efforts should therefore focus on remedying both the abuse of DMCA takedown notifications for suppressive purposes and the disingenuous use of copyright litigation to punish one's ideological adversaries for their speech on matters of public import. To that end, three potential mechanisms for advancing these goals could make sense: (1) the enactment of federal legislation, modeled after state anti-SLAPP (Strategic Lawsuits Against Public Participation) statutes, to deter censorious copyright litigation; (2) the revitalization of an existing cause of action available under the DMCA to deter censorious use of the takedown regime; and (3) the adoption of a "*New York Times* v. *Sullivan*"-style First Amendment check on a narrow but pernicious class of infringement claims – the censorious ones. While the first two options require legislative action, the third only requires judicial invention.

REFORM OPTIONS

A Federal Anti-SLAPP Statute

As we have seen, courts have not been oblivious to the growing use of copyright litigation for censorious purposes and, in some instances, they have developed mechanisms for the early adjudication (and dismissal) of such suits. But the use of such mechanisms has not been entirely satisfactory. First, resort to early motions to dismiss (under Rule 12(b)(6) of the Federal Rules of Civil Procedure) to achieve adjudication of cases out of the gate may be well intentioned but appears to betray the strictures of the Federal Rules. Technically speaking, courts are not supposed to consider facts or materials extraneous to a complaint at the Rule 12 stage.[177] And, historically, fair use has been viewed as a mixed question of law and fact.[178] Courts have regularly questioned whether they have the right to make a fair-use determination through a Rule 12 motion. For example, when John McCain's campaign raised a fair-use defense on a motion to dismiss Jackson Browne's claims for infringement for the unauthorized use of the song *Running on Empty* in a campaign advertisement related to US energy policy, the court balked.[179] As the court noted, "in light of a court's narrow inquiry at this stage and limited access to all potentially relevant and material facts needed to undertake the analysis, courts rarely analyze fair use on a 12(b)(6) motion."[180]

In addition, fair use is an affirmative defense and a mixed question of law and fact. While it may be tempting to decide the issue on a Rule 12 motion, there are challenges in doing so, as a defendant bears the burden on any affirmative defense.[181] Since courts are not supposed to consider facts outside of a complaint on a Rule 12 motion, absent injudicious concessions by the plaintiff, courts are often left with too many factual uncertainties to grant fair use as a matter of law before the opportunity for discovery. When courts have agreed to consider fair-use defenses on a motion to dismiss, they have typically only done so as a result of poor pleading by the plaintiff – whereby factual admissions in the complaint actually made the fair-use defense for the defendant.[182] Thus, the ability of Rule 12 motions to dispense with meritless infringement claims is limited and, though appealing, more expansive use of them would potentially run afoul of the procedural dictates of and constraints on Rule 12.

Second, in practice, courts have been far more inclined to consider substantial similarity rather than fair use at the Rule 12 stage. Such a tactic may make sense when one considers fidelity to the strictures of Rule 12 – namely, if the court has access to the allegedly infringed and the allegedly infringing work, it can make a comparison and determine, as a matter of law, whether there is no plausible claim for infringement without running afoul of Rule 12 limitations. But the availability of Rule 12 relief on substantial-similarity issues does little to alleviate the copyright-as-censorship problem since, as we have seen, most such cases involve fair-use defenses.

Third, while some courts have allowed early adjudication of fair-use issues,[183] most have not. This becomes particularly problematic when a roll of the dice (for example, to which judge a particular case is assigned) determines a court's willingness to bend the strictures of Rule 12 to make a prediscovery decision on a fair-use defense. It also encourages forum shopping. Ideally, similarly situated copyright defendants should equally enjoy an early substantive review of a viable fair-use defense.

Finally, even where courts do engage in early adjudication of cases and the defendant's fair-use claim resoundingly carries the day, courts have been reluctant to issue fee awards against plaintiffs. Such solicitude to censorious copyright plaintiffs only encourages more such litigation in the future.[184] It also fails to make the victims of meritless and censorious infringement litigation whole.

With these observations in mind, reform efforts would ideally introduce a consistent and uniform procedural mechanism for addressing the copyright-as-censorship problem. And the procedure would give victims of such claims the ability to escape litigation at an early juncture and would also deter plaintiffs from bringing such claims in the future. One solution for a consistent methodology for early evaluation of censorious copyright litigation might come in the form of anti-SLAPP statutes that many states have implemented. But because anti-SLAPP statutes exist, as of now, only at the state level, they necessarily do not apply to federal causes of action such as copyright infringement. California's anti-SLAPP iteration, for instance, allows defendants to bring an early motion to strike any cause of action arising from any "conduct in furtherance of the exercise of the constitutional right of petition or the constitutional right of free speech in connection with a public issue or an issue of public interest."[185] For SLAPP-able causes of action brought under California law, a plaintiff must make an immediate showing of a probability of prevailing on the merits. Failure to do so results in dismissal of the claim, with prejudice, and an automatic award of fees to the defendant.[186] Thus, the anti-SLAPP protocol allows victims of meritless litigation to dispose of suits early and, with its automatic grant of fees to prevailing defendants, makes plaintiffs think twice about bringing such litigation in the first place.

Consider how such an anti-SLAPP procedure might apply to the emblematic copyright-as-censorship cases we have discussed. California's anti-SLAPP law defines matters of public issue or interest broadly,[187] literally encompassing "*any issue in which the public is interested*," including matters wholly between private parties and even tabloid fodder.[188] Because copyright-as-censorship cases characteristically involve activities that advance the expression of basic facts or commenting on matters of public concern, the suits would undoubtedly qualify for anti-SLAPP treatment under a federal provision worded similarly to California's. Moreover, the availability of federal anti-SLAPP relief for copyright claims could be limited to cases based on the hallmarks of censorious infringement litigation we described earlier: those where (1) the plaintiff lacks a legitimate economic motivation to preserve an established market for the licensing of its copyrighted works and (2) the defendant's use of the work at issue advances the expression of basic facts or comments on matters of public concern. As such, the existence of anti-SLAPP relief would ideally not dissuade or diminish legitimate attempts by rights holders to vindicate appropriate interests under the Copyright Act.

With a federal anti-SLAPP statute in place, the censorial infringement litigation we have identified would face far greater judicial scrutiny. For example, the claims in *Four Navy SEALs* (allegations of torture against members of the armed services); *Katz* (allegations of corruption against a prominent real estate developer); *Savage* (a hate-filled rant by a prominent radio talk show host and political commentator); and *Monge* (the marital status of a major Latin celebrity) would have all required an early showing by the plaintiff of a probability of success on the merits. And, in most of these instances, the availability of anti-SLAPP relief would have enabled defendants to escape the burdens of the litigation meant to dissuade their speech on matters of public import. In addition, the automatic award of fees provided to a defendant under the anti-SLAPP statute, would have strongly deterred future plaintiffs from such abusive resorts to copyright law.

To be fair, the existence of a federal anti-SLAPP statute for copyright claims is not a complete panacea, and it would not have provided relief in every case of censorial lawfare we have examined. In *Monge*, for example, the court ultimately ruled against the fair-use defense. As such, the court would have denied defense efforts to strike the suit pursuant to any anti-SLAPP statute. But, anti-SLAPP relief would have altered the result in the other cases. In *Four Navy SEALs*, the court could have disposed of the copyright claims just as it had done with the privacy claims under California's anti-SLAPP statute. The Associated Press and its reporter would not have continued to face the threat and expense of litigation on a disingenuous copyright claim aimed to punish the defendants' exposé of torture allegations against the plaintiffs. In *Katz*, a blogger would not be forced to defend herself against a real estate mogul's disingenuous infringement claims, which simply served as a means to censor her reports on allegations of corruption and illegal conduct in the mogul's business dealings. Finally, in *Savage*, the automatic assessment of fees would have at least served as a powerful deterrent against the radio talk show host's subsequent (successful) action to suppress criticism of him for his incendiary views.

DMCA Reform

Regrettably, adoption of a federal anti-SLAPP statute will not address the copyright-as-censorship issue entirely, especially when so much of the action occurs prior to the filing of litigation. As we have seen, putative rights holders have exploited the DMCA's takedown procedure to scrub unfavorable materials online, even under the weakest of infringement claims. Thus, any solution to the copyright-as-censorship problem must address abuse of the DMCA takedown regime. Section 512(f) of the DMCA already provides a potential mechanism to punish such misconduct, but it needs revitalization.

The DMCA provides a powerful means for genuine rights holders to force ISPs to remove infringing content placed online at the direction of users.[189] But Congress recognized that such a weighty tool could lead to abuse, and it appeared to balance this mechanism by providing meaningful relief against complaining parties who overreach in their takedown demands for the removal of allegedly infringing materials online. Specifically, under Section 512(f), the DMCA creates a civil cause of action against those who "knowingly materially misrepresent … that material or activity is infringing"[190] in an online takedown notification. Typically, a person challenging a takedown notification will argue that the copyright owner made such a knowing and material misrepresentation by swearing to have "a good faith belief that use of the material in the manner complained of is not authorized by the copyright owner, its agent, or the law" as required under Section 512(c)(3)(A)(v)'s requirement for proper takedown notices.[191] However, as it turns out, success on a Section 512(f) action is improbable because of how courts have interpreted the mental state required to show that the party filing a DMCA takedown made a knowing material misrepresentation. In the process, therefore, the courts have neutralized this valuable check on DMCA-takedown abuse that Congress had initially written into the Copyright Act.

For example, the leading case on the scienter requirement in Section 512(f), *Rossi* v. *MPAA*, held that the "good faith belief" requirement was entirely subjective, not objective.[192] "A copyright owner cannot be liable simply because an unknowing mistake is made," the court found, "even if the copyright owner acted unreasonably in making the mistake."[193] Instead, the court required "a demonstration of some actual knowledge of misrepresentation" before imposing liability on a party serving a DMCA takedown.[194] Admittedly, in Stephanie Lenz's ongoing battle with Universal, the Ninth Circuit held that content owners must account for fair use when attesting, in their DMCA takedown notifications, that the alleged infringers' activities were not "authorized … by law" under 17 U.S.C. § 512(c)(3)(A)(v).[195] However, the ruling ultimately represented a pyrrhic victory for online users of copyrighted content. The Ninth Circuit still reaffirmed *Rossi*'s subjectivity standard and found that Stephanie Lenz could not show that defendants subjectively believed there was a high probability that her actions constituted fair use.[196] As the Court explained, so long as "a copyright holder forms a subjective *good faith* belief the allegedly infringing material does not constitute fair use, we are in no position to dispute the copyright holder's belief even if we would have reached the opposite conclusion."[197]

Such a reading of "good faith belief" makes for troubling policy. A party issuing a takedown notice can escape Section 512(f) liability by possessing a subjective, good faith belief that the activity about which it complains constitutes infringement.[198] This standard is particularly problematic given that some industries, institutions, and individuals have earnestly argued that virtually all uses of copyrighted works require licenses.[199] As a result of these (inaccurate) beliefs, a veritable Kool-Aid defense arises: if a copyright holder "drinks the Kool-Aid" and genuinely subscribes to these views (and therefore lacks subjective bad faith in sending out an overreaching takedown notification), it cannot suffer liability under Section 512(f), no matter how objectively unreasonable its belief.

As one court noted, the subjective bad-faith requirement makes it all but impossible to prevail on a Section 512(f) claim: "Although there may be cases in which such considerations will arise, there are likely to be few in which a copyright owner's determination that a particular use is not fair use will meet the requisite standard of subjective bad faith required to prevail in an action for misrepresentation under 17 U.S.C. § 512(f)."[200] Modification of Section 512(f)'s bad-faith standard to reflect an objective, rather than subjective, standard for liability that encompasses consideration of fair-use defenses would revitalize Section 512(f) and provide a more potent remedy to guard against censorious and abusive uses of DMCA takedowns. Making statutory damages available for Section 512(f) violations could also help balance the playing field between senders and recipients of takedown notifications and assist in deterring censorious exploitation of the takedown regime. If infringers face statutory damages for violations of copyright, it is only fair that putative rights holders hell-bent on exploiting the copyright regime for censorious purposes face similar damages for their actions.

A New York Times *v.* Sullivan *for Censorious Uses of Copyright*

Both the implementation of a federal anti-SLAPP procedure and a change in Section 512(f)'s scienter standard would likely require legislative action. In addition, although these solutions might improve the problem of copyright lawfare, they will not eliminate it altogether. However, reform that addresses copyright's censorship problem need not only come from Congress. Courts could adopt their own measures to do so and one particular solution could go a long way toward guarding against the weaponization of copyright for censorship purposes: the adoption of an explicit free-speech check on copyright enforcement. Admittedly, efforts to convince courts to introduce a First Amendment constraint on infringement claims have largely failed.[201] But courts' reluctance to place an express First Amendment limit on *all* copyright enforcement may be one significant reason for that failure. Notably, courts have had no problem with imposing carefully circumscribed First Amendment limitations on tort liability in a variety of scenarios. In *New York Times* v. *Sullivan*, the Supreme Court famously held that defamation claims brought by public officials should be subject to a critical First Amendment check: a showing that the defendant acted with actual malice by either intentionally disregarding the truth or acting with reckless indifference toward it.[202] As the Court reasoned, allowing public officials to prevail on defamation claims based on mere negligence alone would cast too great a shadow on the First Amendment by chilling reporting on political matters.[203] The Supreme Court has subsequently extended the holding of *New York Times* to all manner of defamation,[204] false light,[205] intentional infliction of emotional distress,[206] and invasion of privacy[207] cases involving public figures or matters of public concern.

These legal innovations had a common goal: preventing the power of the state (through the courts) from being wielded by private individuals (through the imposition of legal liability) to effectively suppress speech on matters of public concern. However, the courts left a gaping exception: copyright law. Agile and cynical litigants – particularly those with the financial resources to deploy counsel on these matters – have exploited this loophole. In the process, they have given rise to the specter of severe liability for speech related to matters of public concern – precisely the type of liability from which the Supreme Court sought to protect defendants with *New York Times* v. *Sullivan* and its progeny.

Copyright's moment for an explicit First Amendment check has come. The adoption of a *New York Times* v. *Sullivan*-like check on censorious copyright claims – ones that pertain to matters of public concern where the plaintiff seeks to vindicate interests outside of the established market for the licensing of its copyrighted works – could serve as an important step toward combatting censorious infringement litigation. For these types of cases, courts could entertain an early motion to dismiss and provide an award of fees to prevailing defendants. Even in the intellectual property context, courts have independently created First Amendment defenses in specific circumstances. Federal courts have, despite the existence of statutory defenses including fair use, checked trademark liability on First Amendment grounds with the adoption of the *Rogers* v. *Grimaldi* artistic-relevance test.[208] And California courts have, despite the existence of statutory defenses, checked right-of-publicity claims on First Amendment grounds with the adoption of the *Comedy III* transformative-use test.[209] Specifically, courts might be more amenable to applying First Amendment checks on copyright enforcement in a limited spectrum of cases – namely, those that fit the copyright-as-censorship mold. To that end, and based on our earlier discussion on distinguishing legitimate (albeit potentially non-availing) copyright enforcement efforts from those of a censorious nature, courts could deem a defendant's actions protected under the First Amendment and immunized from copyright liability as a matter of law where (1) the plaintiff lacks a legitimate economic motivation to preserve an established market for the licensing of its copyrighted works and (2) the defendant's use of the work at issue advances the expression of basic facts or comments on matters of public concern.

The disingenuous exploitation of copyright law to silence one's critics and suppress publication of unfavorable stories and information has become an all-too-regular occurrence. Through the course of this chapter, we have examined numerous instances in which the cynical invocation of infringement claims has stifled legitimate discourse on issues of racism, religious discrimination, reproductive rights, gay rights, corruption, torture, and police brutality. Rather than merely regulating the marketplace for creative content in a manner that best promotes progress in the arts, copyright law has unwittingly become a leading vehicle through which putative rights holders can impede free speech on issues related to social justice.

The adoption of a reinvigorated section 512(f) claim for abuse of the DMCA takedown system, a federal anti-SLAPP statute, or a *New York Times* v. *Sullivan*-inspired check on infringement liability would serve as important steps toward combatting such censorious infringement enforcement and litigation. Without such reform, the regular weaponization of copyright law as a particularly unsavory form of censorship will continue unabated, privileging the powerful over the weak to disproportionately silence the voices of those from traditionally marginalized groups, including racial minorities, women, the LGBTQ+ communities, and the poor.

Conclusion

An Unhurried View of Copyright in the Age of AI

THE COMING AI WARS: OPPORTUNITIES AND CHALLENGES

As the foregoing chapters have evidenced, the secret life of copyright is riddled with seemingly innocuous public policy decisions that have metastasized, in the long term, into persistent sources of inequality and marginalization along racial, gender, and socioeconomic lines. So, for example, a decision to vest copyrights in the individuals who fix works in a tangible medium has not only failed to recognize the creative contributions of those in front of the camera but also resulted in the propertization of the white male gaze. A desire to avert the fracturing of rights by imposing a mutual-intent requirement for joint authorship has disproportionally deprived female, non-white, and poorer creatives of full participation in the creative economy. A well-intentioned ruling to prevent holders of expired copyrights from extending their monopolies through the cynical invocation of trademark law has all but assured that crediting practices reward clout over creativity, thereby damaging the efficacy of the creative marketplace and disadvantaging those with the least negotiating leverage. An extension of copyright protection to incorporate the universe of spin-off works from an original has ended up suppressing acts of semiotic disruption, propping up entrenched powers, and limiting resistance to prevailing ideological narratives on issues of race, gender, religion, geopolitics, identity, colonialism, capitalism, and corporatism. The immunization of copyright law from First Amendment scrutiny, meant to facilitate the recognition of property rights in one's creative speech, has resulted in the disingenuous weaponization of copyright law as a tool of censorship, helping the powerful to silence their critics with alarming force.

The consistent theme of these cautionary developments is simple: we ignore the social-justice implications of copyright law at our peril. So, at this particular historical moment, when we are just beginning to grapple with the public policy implications of a powerful new technology – generative artificial intelligence (AI) – consideration of the egalitarian consequences of changes to the law of creativity is particularly warranted. Admittedly, there are many unknowns about the evolution of AI, its deployment, and the numerous controversies that it will inevitably spark in copyright law. Nevertheless, no examination of intellectual property and inequality would be complete without at least assessing some of the foreseeable copyright concerns stemming from nascent AI technologies. Indeed, even in its infancy, the AI era has already begun to challenge some of the key doctrines we have discussed through the course of this book, including the concepts of authorship, derivative rights, and fair use.

The growing use of generative AI will force us to address myriad novel issues at the forefront of copyright law. Congress and the courts will have to resolve whether AI-assisted works can constitute works of authorship and, if so, in whom the copyrights to such works might vest; the extent to which unlicensed pre-existing content can serve as training materials for the generation of AI output; the ways in which AI output might run afoul of the property interests of existing copyright holders; and the circumstances, if any, in which AI can make unauthorized use of the likenesses, voices, and identities of real individuals. The outcomes of these debates will determine whose bodies (through images) and minds (through creative output) might become uncompensated fodder for remix in the "creativity machine" of generative AI and whose bodies and minds will remain sacrosanct and inviolable; who will earn royalties, who can demand permission, and who will receive forgiveness; and, in the end, who will have access to, and control of, the building blocks of our culture.

For example, over the past few years, platforms specializing in all manner of creative endeavor, including image generation (Dall-E 2), coding (GitHub Copilot), video creation (Synthesia), creative writing (ChatGPT), music making (Udio), and academic writing (Scribe), have made their public debuts. These systems not only train their models on pre-existing copyrighted content, often used without permission of rights holders, but can also deliver output that arguably constitutes a derivative version of said content, such as a new "Beatles" song, a new "Tarantino" screenplay, or a new "Basquiat" painting. Unsurprisingly, therefore, rights holders from the worlds of journalism, music, art, photography, fiction, and comedy – both individuals and entities representative of the full gamut of subject matter – quickly responded to the launch of these platforms with concern and a tidal wave of infringement litigation. In 2023 alone, the *New York Times* sued Microsoft and OpenAI;[1] a group of visual artists, led by cartoonist and illustrator Sarah Andersen, sued Midjourney, Stability AI, and Deviant Art;[2] photography archive Getty Images sued Stability A.I.;[3] a group of music publishers, including Concord Music Group, Universal Music Publishing Group, and ABKCO, sued Anthropic;[4] and two different groups of authors, led by Sarah Silverman and Michael Chabon, respectively, sued OpenAI and Meta.[5] As these suits wend through the court system, jurists will, for the first time, have to wrestle with the application of our extant copyright laws in the brave new world of generative AI, giving us an opportunity to re-examine the state of our regime.

But before pronouncing on the need for wholesale reform of copyright law to address the challenges posed by AI, it is worth considering the wry wisdom of Professor Benjamin Kaplan. Harvard Law School's inaugural copyright specialist and the author of the very first copyright casebook, Kaplan ribbed our myopic tendency to characterize the defining technological developments of our era as wholly unprecedented shocks to the system. "As a veteran listener at many lectures by copyright specialists over the past decade," he once posited, "I know it is almost obligatory for a speaker to begin by invoking the communications revolution of our time, [and] then to pronounce upon the inadequacies of the present copyright act."[6] Kaplan did not utter these words upon the arrival of ChatGPT, the advent of the internet era, the dawn of home video recording technology, or even at the beginning of the cable revolution. Rather, he expressed his sentiments more than a half-century ago – in 1966 – in his seminal tome, *An Unhurried View of Copyright*.

Kaplan's warning continues to resonate today, urging caution against any rush to assert that today's technological changes and challenges are wholly unprecedented. They are not. Copyright law has proven itself nimble through the centuries and it will adapt. But how it adapts has profound consequences – not just for the future of creativity but also for the cause of equality. The last major revision to copyright law passed almost a half-century ago, in 1976 – at a time long before the world wide web, networked mobile phones, digital streaming, celestial jukeboxes, social media, big data, and generative AI even existed. The surge in public interest in copyright and the explosion of legal questions (and accompanying lawsuits) related to AI will give us a generational opportunity to re-evaluate and fine-tune many long-extant doctrines.

RECONSIDERING AUTHORSHIP IN THE AGE OF AI

Consider, for example, the debate over whether the output of generative AI systems that respond to human prompts can enjoy copyright protection. The question forces confrontation of long-gestating concerns about copyright's authorship doctrine that we discussed in Chapter 1. Thus, in the droll words of technology pundit Benedict Evans, we are facing "a completely new problem that we've been arguing about for 500 years."[7]

Currently, the Copyright Office has taken the position that mere prompting of a generative AI system does not represent sufficient human authorship to support copyrightability of the resulting output. In the government's view, the generative AI models are exercising traditional elements of authorship by taking creative control and determining how prompts are interpreted and applied with the introduction of expressive elements. And because authorship cannot vest in nonhumans (i.e., the generative AI model itself), such output is without copyright protection and, therefore, in the public domain.[8] Notably, however, the Copyright Office continues to study the issue and has indicated that its position on the matter may evolve.[9] Meanwhile, challenges to the Copyright Office's present view are advancing through the court system and may result in a change in the law.[10]

As we saw in Chapter 1, while the Copyright Office is correct that courts have consistently rejected the idea of nonhuman authorship,[11] its position appears to be in some tension with prior jurisprudence involving human authorship with the assistance of a machine intermediary. Specifically, the current debate over the copyrightability of generative AI output shares commonalities with the contretemps over another new technology a century and a half ago: the capturing of images on photosensitive film. At the time, courts wrestled with the question of whether photography was merely a scientific process capturing nature as it existed – mere facts that were unprotectible – or an art form reflecting protectible human creativity and authorship (through a technological instrument). The *Sarony* decision resolved the question by adopting the latter view because of the unmistakable creative acts undertaken by photographers in, among other things, framing the shot, positioning the subject, and selecting an angle, lighting, and focus.[12] To the Supreme Court, the necessary role of a machine (the camera) in mediating human input and visual output did not negate the creativity behind the numerous individual decisions necessary to trigger the aperture and generate an image. This logic is further reflected in modern practice, where sound recordings created by musicians utilizing digital audio workstations such as ProTools receive copyright protection despite the fact that they reflect human input conducted through a machine interface.

The issue of AI copyrightability is far from facile and, assessed in its full complexity, will force us to examine all potential sources of creative input that might give rise to authorial interests in AI output – not just the human prompter at the helm of the machine when it spits out a new work. For example, there are the many authors whose pre-existing content has trained the large language models (LLMs) upon which each generative AI system relies and the contributions of these writers, directors, artists, photographers, musicians, and others may be sufficient, in some cases, to support a claim of authorship in output. To the extent that AI content features subject performances, they may have a basis to demand authorial recognition (particularly since they will be unlikely to have contractually waived claims to copyright in their performances with the users of AI). And, of course, if the machine itself is the creator and we begin to recognize nonhuman authorship under the Copyright Act, we may end up determining that some rights should vest in the company that owns the machine, as a quasi-work-made-for-hire (whereby the machine is effectively in the employ of the company). In short, there is no shortage of different outcomes that could result and questions about ownership of AI output necessarily demand reconsideration of the potential interests that subjects and other contributors should enjoy in works of authorship.

THE PUBLIC POLICY DIMENSIONS OF AI COPYRIGHT

Putting authorial considerations aside, some observers have further wondered whether it would even constitute good public policy to encourage the creation of generative AI-assisted works with the grant of copyright protection, particularly given worries about the potential threat AI poses to human creativity. Despite some heated rhetoric on this issue, history provides some basis to temper excessively dire predictions. For example, although widely feared at the time, the advent of photography did not end art, though it did change it. Starting in the late nineteenth century, the erstwhile premium put on literal recreation of the world gave way to an increasing interest in figurative and abstract methodologies. The resulting new art world gave us such innovative movements as impressionism, dadaism, surrealism, fauvism, expressionism, and conceptualism. The shift in creative approaches to painting and illustration not only changed the way we view art but also how we envision the artist. To someone in the seventeenth century, a woman clicking a button (*i.e.*, a photographer) may not seem like an artist. To someone in the nineteenth century, a man placing a urinal in an art gallery (*i.e.*, Marcel Duchamp), splashing buckets of paint randomly on a canvas (*i.e.*, Jackson Pollock), or throwing three orange balls in the air thirty-six different times to see if he can capture them in a straight line (*i.e.*, John Baldessari) might not appear to be an artist. And to someone in the twentieth century, an individual typing a prompt into a computer might not make an artist. The malleable way in which art has responded to technological change is not limited to painting's reaction to photography. As Farhad Manjoo reminds us, "Technologies that made art easier to produce have rarely ended up stifling human creativity. Electronic synthesizers didn't eliminate the need for people who play musical instruments. Auto-Tune didn't make singing on pitch obsolete. Photography didn't kill painting, and its digitization didn't obviate the need for professional photographers."[13]

There are also ethical dimensions to the public policy debate over AI copyright to consider as well. For example, in early 2024, a furor erupted over the use of AI to finalize *Unfinished Painting* (1989), a deliberately incomplete and striking work by the late Keith Haring, one of the most celebrated contemporary illustrators in the art world. In the original work, Haring's anthropomorphic and hieroglyphic-style renderings, in an effervescent purple, black, and white, fill out only the top left of the canvas. The remaining canvas remains willfully and starkly blank, save a few streaks of paint dripping down to the bottom. As the title and composition make clear, the work serves as a poignant reminder of the unfinished stories of millions (including Haring) who lost their lives during the AIDS epidemic.[14] The unauthorized "completion" of the work obviously raises copyright issues, including whether the resulting output constitutes an unauthorized derivative of the original painting and whether its creation might receive protection under the fair-use

FIGURE C.1 Comparison of (a) *Unfinished Painting* (1989) by Keith Haring with an (b) AI version "completing" it (2024)

doctrine. But it also provokes ethical concerns about the dignitary harm to Haring's artistic vision and his legacy and, not unlike the *Charging Bull/Fearless Girl* controversy discussed in Chapter 3, about the proper metes and bounds of an original author's control over a work's meaning and presentation. Indeed, in a sign of the still-limited sophistication of AI systems, the completed portion of *Unfinished Painting* generated by AI resoundingly failed to pick up on the anthropomorphic undercurrent to Haring's hieroglyphics and, as a result, while the new section may have seemed consistent and appropriate to AI, it does not to any discerning human eye (Figure C.1a and b).

Meanwhile, the growing number of artificially generated "deepfake" photos and videos has generated widespread unease about the unauthorized use of human voices, images, or likenesses in the output of generative AI. Numerous states have already passed legislation barring deepfakes in certain contexts (such as in sexually explicit materials or election-related communications)[15] and even Congress is looking to regulate, if not outright ban, the practice.[16] Thus, the advent of AI does not merely require the sorting of economic interests of rights holders but also important privacy and dignitary interests, such as the right to prevent the mutilation or alteration of one's work or to control one's likeness from unwitting inclusion in a salacious video.

DERIVATIVE RIGHTS, ATTRIBUTION, AND AI

More broadly, adjudication of rights holder litigation against AI companies over the unauthorized use of training materials in the development of LLMs requires a careful balancing act. On one hand, one can imagine there are scenarios where AI output may represent an unlawful derivative of an existing piece of content (such as a *Star Wars* sequel making extensive use of *Star Wars* characters and storylines) and, therefore, constitutes an infringement. On the other hand, one can imagine myriad scenarios where AI output is not infringing because we do not want to make the mere act of reading and processing copyrighted content – without more – give rise to infringement liability. After all, in such a situation, we would risk making the very functioning of the human brain – which constantly ingests pre-existing materials only to spit out new content based on the processing of that data – an infringement.[17] The cognitive capacities we possess as humans represent the ultimate generative intelligence and they irretrievably build on, and respond to, the amalgamation of our content learning. Requiring monetization for any reference point, no matter the scope of the use and whether there is literal appropriation of protectible elements thereof, could vastly expand the copyright monopoly and create a stifling new type of Orwellian "thought crime" – infringement by mental reference – that even the author of *1984* did not foresee. Tolling cognitive activity would have profoundly anti-egalitarian and dystopian consequences and the importance of averting the slippery slope toward such a scenario represents a critical consideration for the crafting of AI law.

Meanwhile, the protests of rights holders who have witnessed their creative work ingested without permission for training LLMs have given rise to a wave of new "ethical" AI systems. Among other things, these systems adopt "ethical sourcing" practices – they learn from only licensed materials and, in the process, effectively provide a form of weak crediting by effectively disclosing the content datasets upon which their models are based.[18] Besides their appeal to those concerned about the moral dimensions of using unlicensed training materials, such platforms also attract users seeking to mitigate liability risk. But issues related to attribution promise to cloud the development of generative AI, including the debate over whether materials generated with the assistance of AI must disclose that fact to consumers (effectively giving a 'credit' to AI) and questions about how to attribute generative AI output and what, if any, crediting norms or requirements will emerge. The wholesale lack of a law of crediting is particularly salient in the AI environment where, absent required disclosures, it may be impossible to trace the origins of generated content.

In part, the sorting of crediting issues will depend on the result of pending litigation that may determine when the unauthorized use of pre-existing content as training materials constitutes infringement. As we have noted, such stalwarts as *The New York Times* and Getty Images have joined forces with all-star authors and creators such as George R.R. Martin, Sarah Silverman, and Michael Chabon to fire the initial shots in this battle by targeting legal claims against the major players in generative AI. How these cases are adjudicated (or, more likely, ultimately settled) will frame the future copyright ecosystem for LLMs. But it is important to note that AI is training on huge swaths of data – in theory, the entire digitized content of humanity. As a result, it is not simply the big players who should have a seat at the table in these discussions. Instead, we must consider how this brave new world of usage and licensing rights will impact creators who are not at the top of the food chain but are, nevertheless, providing AI machinery with the ability to learn from the entire gamut of human innovation and ingenuity. In other words, undercelebrated works, especially obscure content long overlooked but richly deserving of a better fate or reputation, will provide important value to LLMs.

STATUTORY FORMALITIES, COPYRIGHT'S CREATIVE CASTE SYSTEM, AND AI

The wide swath of human creativity from unheralded sources that will help improve LLMs can provide an impetus for reconsideration of one of the most inequitable and pernicious doctrines in copyright law: the timely registration requirement.[19] Although our country prides itself on its strong intellectual property regime, American copyright law has a dirty little secret: we are less protective of the average author than almost any other developed country in the world. This odd result is the direct consequence of the timely registration requirement – a procedural formality that, with little public scrutiny, creates an asymmetrical regime of protection that enables sophisticated, monied rights holders to financially devastate anyone who uses their works without authorization while leaving individuals at the social and economic margins often unable to receive legal relief for even the most willful infringement of their creative output. In short, our copyright regime has created a world of creative haves and creative have-nots that undermines legal protection for artistry and exacerbates inequality by systematically disadvantaging the creative output of the underclass.

Unlike any of its intellectual property allies, the United States demands timely registration of a copyright in order for a rights holder to be eligible to receive statutory damages and attorneys' fees – the two most valuable forms of monetary relief available under the Copyright Act.[20] With timely registration – which requires registration of the copyright of any published work with the United States Copyright Office either prior to the commencement of an infringement or within 3 months of first publication[21] – a rights holder can dangle the legal Sword of Damocles – draconian statutory damages of up to $150,000 per willful act of infringement[22] and recovery of attorneys' fees[23] – over the heads of accused infringers, threatening to hand defendants their heads on a platter with more fervor than Salomé's dance (to licensed music, of course). Without timely registration, a rights holder can, at best, recover just actual damages (usually the theoretical fair market value of a license if the parties had negotiated prior to the infringement), regardless of how willful the infringer's conduct is. In these circumstances, if a rights holder discovers an infringement and then registers her copyright, she is not timely and cannot ever recover the fees necessary to pursue the infringement claim and cannot hold an infringer liable for any amount more than the infringer would have had to pay if they had done the right thing and obtained a license to begin with. Not surprisingly, sophisticated creators – corporations or well-heeled individuals with a cadre of lawyers protecting their interests – timely register their works. Meanwhile, uncounseled creators – those who lack access to legal resources and capital – usually do not. And, of course, uncounseled creators disproportionally come from poor or marginalized backgrounds. So while sophisticated creators enjoy powerful remedies when enforcing their copyrights, uncounseled creators often find themselves in a position where pursuit of an infringement claim will cost more than even the most favorable recovery scenario, leaving them with little practical means to protect their rights when push comes to shove.

Although the law purports to grant copyright protection to any work of authorship with minimal creativity fixed in a tangible medium, whether made by Manet or the Man on the Street, that is simply not the case. All works and creators are not treated alike, and the formalities of the registration requirement establish a hierarchy of more-protected and less-protected works, the untouchable and the readily malleable. With the ostensibly neutral formality of registration, our law creates a veritable copyright caste system featuring two distinct classes of works: content created by sophisticated creators (which enjoys virtual inviolability) and output from uncounseled creators (which receives minimal protection). The resulting gestalt enables dominant social forces to usurp freely (both metaphorically and literally) the creative content of the masses for their own use while simultaneously enjoying the ability to prevent any unauthorized use of their privileged creative content.

Within the confines of this regime, it has been the underclass that typically ends up with minimal protection: an obscure blues musician whose riffs and melodies are appropriated by a major music label's next big thing; a graffiti artist from the urban corridors whose renderings eventually make their way into corporate advertising campaigns and Hollywood movies; an unheralded rural landscape painter whose evocative depictions of nature are used without authorization or payment by a major retailer to set the mood for their western-themed sales catalog; and a struggling dance choreographer, whose uniquely sequenced moves land in the new music video for a leading pop star. In the absence of timely registration, none of these individuals qualify for the recovery of statutory damages or attorneys' fees if they should sue and prevail in a claim of copyright infringement. Since there are also no punitive damages available in copyright law, would-be infringers have little to no disincentive to make unauthorized and uncompensated use of creative works not timely registered. In the end, therefore, these uncounseled copyright holders will find themselves possessing what one court has aptly characterized as "a right without a remedy."[24] All the while, bankrupting penalties face those who would touch the copyrighted works of the modern music industry, the major Hollywood studios, and the publishing world without permission, even when these are built on the unprotected works of others. In my life as a practicing attorney, I have regularly met with creators lacking prior counsel, copyright training, or the benefit of a law degree, and had to deliver the difficult news that, although they have caught someone red-handed exploiting their content unabashedly without permission and for commercial purposes, there is little they can do about it legally because they do not have a timely registered copyright.

The elevation of such a formality into a decisive litmus test for which works can be infringed with impunity and which works cannot be exploited without severe consequences is both lacking in sound basis and deeply troubling for its anti-egalitarian consequences. Copyright's bipartite caste system for the protection of creative works replicates, and even exacerbates, existing socioeconomic hierarchies. Such an outcome is particularly problematic given the instrumental role of intellectual property protection in both the generation of wealth and the exercise of rights in the post-industrial world. The emergence of generative AI offers an opportunity for reconsideration of this problematic system. Specifically, if the creative work of the world is now being scraped to train the LLMs that power generative AI and these models are then spitting out works that are derivative of both the works of sophisticated and uncounseled creators, most of whom never imagined that their work would be exploited in such a manner, our two-tiered system of infringement remedies becomes even more of an affront to egalitarian interests than it already is. We must take pains to avoid the development of a regime where the (already handsomely compensated) major rights holders receive economic participation in the generative AI ecosystem while largely forgotten artists, who provide the backbone of the next generation of (quasi-)human creativity, remain uncompensated.

NEW TECHNOLOGIES AND CREATIVE DOUBLE-STANDARDS

The age of AI also provides other opportunities to evaluate, with greater care than in the past, the impact of the evolving norms and laws regulating AI on issues of distributive justice. As we have seen in the course of this book, when responding to technological changes in prior decades, the law has sometimes betrayed the utilitarian goals of the copyright regime while also doing harm to egalitarian interests. Without adopting the more holistic approach toward copyright doctrine advocated in this book, we risk that danger again with AI. Consider, for example, how the law responded to one of the most significant developments in the field of music during the early digital era: sampling. As Anjali Vats has argued, the law of digital sampling – a technological innovation of the late 1970s that courts only began addressing in the music infringement jurisprudence of the early 1990s – has effectively drawn color lines that cause differing creative rights to be doled out on the basis of racial identity.[25]

Subject to the caveat that we are dealing with a small sample size from which it is difficult to make sweeping generalizations, Vats's argument is a powerful reminder of how the application of seemingly neutral copyright doctrines can quickly take on a pernicious racial valence. Specifically, the way in which courts have characterized defendants and their creative labors in these sampling cases has, all too often, reflected unconscious biases and explicit appeals to demeaning tropes. In these instances, judges have ultimately deemed White uses of sampling to be innovative exploration and decried Black invocations of the practice as theft,[26] thereby adding a new chapter to an already troubling history of privileging White creative activity over that of African Americans. The modern law of sampling has therefore suppressed musical innovation and aggravated social disparities at the same time.

For example, African-American artists such as Biz Markie and N.W.A. have both faced resounding rebukes for their sampling activities. In *Grand Upright Music, Ltd.* v. *Warner Bros. Records Inc.* (1991),[27] rapper Biz Markie faced allegations of infringement for his unauthorized use of several bars from a piano riff on Gilbert O'Sullivan's track *Alone Again (Naturally)*. The peculiarly lacerating and volcanic response of the court to the suit is hard to overstate. Notably, *Grand Upright* represented the first reported decision to consider the permissibility of digital sampling. But rather than demonstrating any solicitude or temperance toward the defendant in light of the unsettled state of the law on this issue of first impression, the Southern District of New York howled with rage. The court opened its decision by literally invoking the Bible. In heavy-handed rhetoric, the court quoted the Seventh Commandment's edict that "thou shalt not steal"[28] to immediately condemn the Markie's actions. In the process, the court not only established an unjustified and false equivalence between property rights in chattel and intellectual property but also unapologetically painted the defendant in a criminal light – despite the civil nature of the proceeding. The court then deemed Markie's infringement brazenly commercial, willful in nature, and the product of a "callous disregard for the law"[29] – a particularly unusual conclusion considering the law on the issue remained uncertain.

As Vats notes, the opinion was redolent with tired and bigoted "racial scripts of Black men as unimaginative, disingenuous, malicious, and dishonest criminals,"[30] as the court appeared hell-bent on treating "Black appropriation … as prurient instead of creative from the outset."[31] Indeed, the uncharitable framing of Biz Markie's sampling activities stands in remarkable contrast to the forbearance granted by courts to such (White) appropriationist artists such as Richard Prince and Jeff Koons in recent years.[32] Unsatisfied with merely throwing the proverbial book at Biz Markie with back-breaking civil liability, the court concluded its decision with a call for the potential imposition of even "sterner measures"[33] (ones not even requested by the plaintiff) against the rapper. Specifically, the trial judge referred Biz Markie to the District Attorney's office for potential *criminal* prosecution. Criminal copyright actions are exceedingly rare and usually only occur against massive commercial pirating operations. So it is no exaggeration to suggest that the court's move, which literally threatened to make a crime of hip-hop, constituted a wildly disproportionate and unusual response, particularly since it related to a (widespread) practice that had been previously untested in the courts.

Meanwhile, in *Bridgeport Music, Inc.* v. *Dimension Films* (2005),[34] the Sixth Circuit rejected a *de-minimis*-use defense when legendary hip-hop artists N.W.A. faced infringement claims for lifting a three-note guitar solo from an old Funkadelic jam for their song *100 Miles and Runnin'*. Instead, the court issued a strict rule dictating that anyone wishing to digitally sample a sound recording must secure permission from the sound recording's copyright holder or face infringement liability. As the court bluntly put it: "Get a license or do not sample."[35] Though the court purported to take no position on the potential application of the fair-use defense to sampling activity, its bright-line edict suggested otherwise.

These decisions would seemingly make the practice of unauthorized sampling verboten. But, to the contrary, in at least two prominent, precedent-setting decisions involving White artists, federal appeals courts resurrected the moribund *de-minimis*-use doctrine and selectively invoked it to excuse unlicensed sampling. In the first such case, *Newton* v. *Diamond* (2003),[36] the Ninth Circuit declined to impose liability on the Beastie Boys for their unlicensed use of a note sequence from (African-American) jazz flautist James M. Newton Jr.'s composition *Choir*. In the second case, *VMG Salsoul, LLC* v. *Ciccone* (2016),[37] the Ninth Circuit forgave Madonna for her unlicensed use of a horn hit (the primarily African-American) Salsoul Orchestra's *Ooh I Love It (Love Break)*. In both instances, the courts waived away the indisputable act of appropriation as merely trifling and, therefore, not actionable – a far cry from the way the *Grand Upright* and *Bridgeport* decisions treated sampling by Black artists. While the relatively small qualitative and quantitative use of the samples in the *Newton* and *VMC Salsoul* cases could have warranted the results alone, the holdings nevertheless stand in stark contrast to the absolutist rhetoric and Draconian judgments announced in *Grand Upright* and *Bridgeport*.

With its dialogic nature, sampling made it possible for recording artists to interface with, and build upon, the past in a radically new way, thereby fostering an explosion of auditory creativity. But the law's mixed reaction to the practice – saddled with the specter of troubling racial dimensions – provides an example to avoid as we begin to develop a legal framework for AI "sampling" – the latest mixing-and-matching tool made possible by technological advancement.

AN UNHURRIED VIEW OF SOCIAL JUSTICE AND COPYRIGHT

For as long as copyright law has existed, new technologies have sprung forth, testing extant doctrines, raising new questions, and provoking debate about the regime's response. But the discourse surrounding these issues has, all too often, failed to grasp the potential egalitarian consequences of copyright policy. For too long, copyright has had an unappreciated social justice problem, obscured by its purported application of neutral principles designed solely to reward creative enterprise and advance progress in the arts. As the myriad cases we have examined through the course of this book indicate, the law governing the vesting, scope, and enforcement of copyright interests has often flouted these goals, with adverse consequences for dignitary interests, the distribution of economic and social power, and racial and gender equality.

Movements such as Black Lives Matter and #MeToo took a critical step in raising public awareness about the far-reaching legacies of systemic discrimination and the ongoing cultural, economic, and legal injustices facing women, people of color, and the poor. But, as these once vital causes begin to face a regrettable tide of public fatigue and, worse yet, backlash, it is important to press them forward in a concrete way by tackling the specific structural impediments to greater equality.

In the grand scheme of things, copyright law may represent only a microscopic part of the issue. But it is a microcosm of the problem. And since our intellectual property laws play an instrumental role in mediating participation and privilege in the age of AI, the right kind of copyright reform can make a meaningful difference – by both advancing egalitarian concerns and better serving the interests of creativity.

Notes

INTRODUCTION

1. *See* Ben Beaumont-Thomas, *2014: When Songwriters Burned the Chorus and Built the Bridge*, THE GUARDIAN (Dec. 22, 2014), https://www.theguardian.com/music/musicblog/2014/dec/22/2014-when-songwriters-burned-the-chorus-and-built-the-bridge (quoting Gordy).
2. U.S. Const., Art. I, § 8, cl. 8.
3. JOHN FISKE, UNDERSTANDING POPULAR CULTURE 19 (2d ed. 2010) (1989).
4. PIERRE BOURDIEU & JEAN-CLAUDE PASSERON, REPRODUCTION IN EDUCATION, SOCIETY, AND CULTURE (Richard Nice trans., Sage Publ'g 2d ed. 1990) (1970).
5. *Id.* at 56 (referring to a diploma as a "juridically sanctioned validation of the results of inculcation").
6. *See, e.g.*, JEN WEBB ET AL., UNDERSTANDING BOURDIEU (2002) (presenting a primer on Bourdieu targeting students of sociology and cultural studies).
7. *See, e.g.*, PIERRE BOURDIEU, DISTINCTION: A SOCIAL CRITIQUE OF THE JUDGMENT OF TASTE (Richard Nice trans., 1984) (analyzing the social meaning imbued in even the most trivial exertions of taste and the role of taste in the construction of identity and class differentiation); BOURDIEU & PASSERON, *supra* note 4, at 56 (analyzing the role of the formal educational system in inculcating values and symbols that perpetuate class differences).
8. This is not to suggest that intellectual property laws inevitably maintain and perpetuate existing social structures. Depending on how they are crafted, they can also facilitate resistance and counter-hegemonic practices.
9. Although the 2023 *Barbie* movie showed remarkable willingness by Mattel to poke fun at its famous creation, the company has not always had a self-effacing sense of humor. Historically, Mattel has aggressively used intellectual property litigation to prevent unauthorized artistic reinterpretations of Barbie. *See, e.g.*, *Mattel, Inc.* v. *Walking Mountain Prods.*, 353 F.3d 792, 816 (9th Cir. 2003) (rejecting Mattel's claims of copyright, trademark, and trade dress infringement against artist Thomas Forsythe for his photographs portraying a sexualized, naked Barbie in absurd positions with vintage household appliances); *Mattel, Inc.* v. *MCA Records, Inc.*, 296 F.3d 894, 906–907 (9th Cir. 2002) (rejecting Mattel's claims that Aqua's pop hit *Barbie Girl*, which lampooned the famous doll, infringed and diluted the "Barbie" trademark).
10. LAWRENCE LESSIG, FREE CULTURE: THE NATURE AND FUTURE OF CREATIVITY 53–64 (2006).

11. By and large, works by foreign authors did not enjoy copyright protection in the United States until 1891. *See* Seth M. Goldstein, Hitchcock's "Rear Window" and International Copyright Law: An Examination of Stewart v. Abend & Its Effect on International Copyright Renewal and Exploitation, 14 CARDOZO J. INT'L & COMP. L. 247, 258 (2006).
12. 17 U.S.C. § 111(c)(1) (granting cable systems a compulsory statutory license to retransmit broadcast signals); Niels B. Schaumann, Copyright Protection in the Cable Television Industry: Satellite Retransmission and the Passive Carrier Exemption, 51 FORDHAM L. REV. 637, 637–40 (1983). Without this exception, cable television would have had a much harder time gaining its foothold in the American living room. Imagine how cable would have fared without unauthorized retransmission of network signals: Cable companies could have offered consumers a panoply of untested alternatives – a 24/7 news channel, a station that played only music videos all day long, a network devoted to B-movies – but it would have come without regular networks. And, of course, the cable stations would have been hard-pressed to obtain licenses for retransmission from the major networks as they had no interest in fueling their own demise by making the transition to cable all the more palatable. The networks wanted cable to come at a cost: you either received the networks or you received the cable stations, not both. However, when cable provides the cable stations plus crystal-clear feeds of network channels, the temptation of subscribing to cable becomes all the greater, if not irresistible.
13. SCOTT EYMAN, LION OF HOLLYWOOD: THE LIFE AND LEGEND OF LOUIS B. MAYER 53 (2005).
14. Peter Edidin, *La-La Land: The Origins*, N.Y. TIMES, August 21, 2005, at C2 (noting that "Los Angeles's distance from New York was also comforting to independent film producers, making it easier for them to avoid being harassed or sued by the Motion Picture Patents Company, a k a the Trust, which Thomas Edison helped create in 1909").
15. In 1908, Edison and nine other patentees formed the Motion Picture Patents Company to pool their intellectual property rights and effectively control nearly all motion picture technology. The MPCC rigorously enforced its patent rights against independent movie producers, bringing infringement claims against any producer not using properly licensed equipment. Alexandra Gil, Breaking the Studios: Antitrust and the Motion Picture Industry, 3 N. Y. U. J. L. & LIBERTY 83, 91–92 (2008).
16. LESSIG, *supra* note 10, at 23–24 (2004).
17. *See, e.g.*, Leslie Espinoza & Angela P. Harris, Afterword: Embracing the Tar-Baby – LatCrit Theory and the Sticky Mess of Race, 85 CALIF. L. REV. 1585, 1598–99 (1997) ("In the 1950s, many white artists became superstars either by re-recording black music for white audiences, like Pat Boone, or by drawing more indirectly on African-American musical traditions, like Elvis Presley. Indeed, the phenomenon called 'rock 'n' roll,' now associated primarily with white artists and white audiences, emerged from the African-American blues tradition.").
18. ANTONIO GRAMSCI, SELECTIONS FROM THE PRISON NOTEBOOKS OF ANTONIO GRAMSCI 12, 161, 170, 416–17 (Quintin Hoare & Geoffrey Nowell Smith eds., 1971). Gramsci's concept of hegemony, grounded in both the consent of the masses and the coercive apparatus of the state, has been used by critical legal studies scholars to analyze legal rights and legal reasoning. *See, e.g.*, Duncan Kennedy, Antonio Gramsci and the Legal System, 6 ALSA F. 32, 32 (1982); Kimberlé Williams Crenshaw, Race, Reform, and Retrenchment: Transformation and Legitimation in Antidiscrimination Law, 101 HARV. L. REV. 1331, 1351–52 (1988) ("Law … embodies and reinforces ideological assumptions about human relations that people accept as natural or even immutable."); Robert Gordon, *New Developments in Legal Theory*, *in* THE POLITICS OF LAW:

A PROGRESSIVE CRITIQUE 281, 286 (David Kairys ed., 1982) ("[T]he most effective kind of domination takes place when both the dominant and dominated classes believe that the existing order, with perhaps some marginal changes, is satisfactory, or at least represents the most that anyone could expect, because things pretty much have to be the way they are." [citing GRAMSCI, *supra*, at 195–96, 246–47]).

19. *See, e.g.*, Duncan Kennedy, The Disenchantment of Logically Formal Legal Rationality, or Max Weber's Sociology in the Genealogy of the Contemporary Mode of Western Legal Thought, 55 HASTINGS L. J. 1031 (2004) (positing the strong affiliation between Weber's sociology of law and the tenets of the critical legal studies movement); Roberto Mangabeira Unger, The Critical Legal Studies Movement, 96 HARV. L. REV. 563, 563 n.1 (1983) (noting the particular influence of the social and historical analyses of Marx and Weber on many critical legal theorists).
20. Foucault's deconstruction of social discourses, legal or otherwise, in relation to discursive power structures has been tremendously influential on critical legal scholarship. *See, e.g.*, Duncan Kennedy, *The Stakes of Law or Hale and Foucault!, in* SEXY DRESSING, ETC. 83 (1993); William P. Alford, On the Limits of "Grand Theory" in Comparative Law, 61 WASH. L. REV. 945, 946 (1986) (noting that "[t]he work of Habermas and Foucault, for example, has attracted a following among American legal scholars, particularly in and around the critical legal studies movement").
21. For further background on the critical legal studies movement, see, for example, CRITICAL LEGAL STUDIES (James Boyle ed., 1992); CRITICAL LEGAL STUDIES (Allan C. Hutchinson ed., 1989); CRITICAL LEGAL STUDIES (Peter Fitzpatrick & Alan Hunt eds., 1987); CRITICAL LEGAL STUDIES: ARTICLES, NOTES, AND BOOK REVIEWS SELECTED FROM THE PAGES OF THE HARVARD REVIEW (1986); Mark Kelman, A GUIDE TO CRITICAL LEGAL STUDIES (1987); Roberto Mangabeira Unger, THE CRITICAL LEGAL STUDIES MOVEMENT (1986); Symposium: Critical Legal Studies, 36 STAN. L. REV. 674 (1984); Mark Tushnet, Critical Legal Studies: A Political History, 100 YALE L. J. 1515 (1991).
22. *See* James Boyle, The Politics of Reason: Critical Legal Theory and Local Social Thought, 133 U. PA. L. REV. 685, 689–90 (1985).
23. *Id.* at 706.
24. *See, e.g.*, Angela Harris, Foreword: The Jurisprudence of Reconstruction, 82 CALIF. L. REV. 741, 743 (1994) ("CRT [Critical Race Theory] is the heir to both CLS [Critical Legal Studies] and traditional civil rights scholarship.").
25. Among other things, critical race theorists have critiqued the traditional critical legal studies movement for not doing enough to focus on systemic issues of race discrimination and nonintentional, but nevertheless significant, forms of racial subordination not easily remedied by legislation such as the Civil Rights Act of 1964. *See* Derrick A. Bell, Who's Afraid of Critical Race Theory?, 1995 U. ILL. L. REV. 893, 899–901 (1995).
26. See, for example, STEVEN BENDER, GREASERS AND GRINGOS: LATINOS, LAW, AND THE AMERICAN IMAGINATION (2003); ROBERT S. CHANG, DISORIENTED: ASIAN AMERICANS, LAW, AND THE NATION-STATE (1999); CRITICAL RACE THEORY: CASES, MATERIALS AND PROBLEMS (Dorothy A. Brown ed., 2003); CRITICAL RACE THEORY: THE CUTTING EDGE (Richard Delgado & Jean Stefancic eds., 2d ed. 2000); CRITICAL RACE THEORY: THE KEY WRITINGS THAT FORMED THE MOVEMENT (Kimberle Crenshaw, Neil Gotanda, Gary Peller & Kendall Thomas eds., 1995); CROSSROADS, DIRECTIONS, AND A NEW CRITICAL RACE THEORY (Francisco Valdes, Jerome McCristal Culp, & Angela P. Harris eds., 2002); RICHARD DELGADO & JEAN STEFANCIC, CRITICAL RACE THEORY: AN INTRODUCTION (2001); RACE AND RACES:

CASES AND RESOURCES FOR A DIVERSE AMERICA (Juan Perea, Richard Delgado, Angela Harris, & Stephanie Wildman eds., 2000); JOHN TEHRANIAN, WHITEWASHED: AMERICA'S INVISIBLE MIDDLE EASTERN MINORITY (2009); THE LATINO/A CONDITION: A CRITICAL READER (Richard Delgado & Jean Stefancic eds., 1998); FRANK H. WU, YELLOW: RACE IN AMERICAN BEYOND BLACK AND WHITE (2002); Keith Aoki, The Scholarship of Reconstruction and the Politics of Backlash, 81 IOWA L. REV. 1467 (1996); Robert S. Chang, Toward an Asian American Legal Scholarship: Critical Race Theory, Post-Structuralism, and Narrative Space, 81 CALIF. L. REV. 1241 (1993); Richard Delgado, Crossroads and Blind Alleys: A Critical Examination of Recent Writings about Race, 82 TEX. L. REV. 121 (2003); Cheryl I. Harris, Critical Race Studies: An Introduction, 49 UCLA L. REV. 1215 (2002); Cheryl I. Harris, Whiteness as Property, 106 HARV. L. REV. 1707 (1993); Tanya Kateri Hernandez, "Multiracial" Discourse: Racial Classifications in an Era of Color-Blind Jurisprudence, 57 MD. L. REV. 97 (1998); Natsu Taylor Saito, Alien and Non-Alien Alike: Citizenship, "Foreignness," and Racial Hierarchy in American Law, 76 OR. L. REV. 261 (1997).

27. Athena D. Mutua, The Rise, Development and Future Directions of Critical Race Theory, 84 DENV. U. L. REV. 329, 336 (2006).
28. *See* Derrick A. Bell, Who's Afraid of Critical Race Theory?, 1995 U. ILL. L. REV. 893, 902 (1995) (citing CHARLES R. LAWRENCE, III, If He Hollers Let Him Go: Regulating Racist Speech on Campus, 1990 DUKE L. J. 431 (1990); Mari J. Matsuda, Public Response to Racist Speech: Considering the Victim's Story, 87 MICH. L. REV. 2320 (1989)).
29. *Id.* at 900.
30. Ann Bartow, Fair Use and the Fairer Sex: Gender, Feminism, and Copyright Law, 14 AM. U. J. GENDER SOC. POL'Y & L. 551, 552, 559–64 (2006) (adding that "[m]any of the professionally prominent, active legal scholars in the intellectual property subject areas, those whose publications obtain high numbers of citations and receive the most numerous and prestigious speaking engagements (citations and conference invitations being important metrics for gauging reputation and prestige), do not explicitly address issues of gender, race, or economic class in their scholarship very frequently.").
31. Jordana R. Goodman, Ms. Attribution: How Authorship Credit Contributes to the Gender Gap, 25 YALE J. LAW & TECH. 309 (2023) (finding, after an empirical study of over 200,000 patent applications and office actions responses from 2016 to 2020, that, even accounting for nongendered partner power differentials, years of practice and other relevant experience, female patent attorneys suffer from a systematic under-crediting in attribution practices as compared to their real contributions to patent-related work).
32. *See, e.g.*, Dan L. Burk, Copyright and Feminism in Digital Media, 14 AM. U. J. GENDER SOC. POL'Y & L. 519, 519 (2006) (addressing the conflict between our existing copyright law and feminist conceptions of hypertext). *See also* Dan L. Burk, Feminism and Dualism in Intellectual Property, 15 AM. U. J. GENDER SOC. POL'Y & L. 183, 185 (2006) (highlighting the role that feminist theory can play in revealing how "the dualism of mind and body that pervades copyright and patent law" can "determine and maintain a pervasive set of power relationships in society").
33. *See, e.g.*, Olufunmilayo B. Arewa, From J.C. Bach to Hip Hop: Musical Borrowing, Copyright and Cultural Context, 84 N. C. L. REV. 547, 550–51 (2006); K. J. Greene, "Copynorms," Black Cultural Production, and the Debate over African-American Reparations, 25 CARDOZO ARTS & ENT. L.J. 1179, 1193 (2008) ("The fleecing of Black artists was the basis of the success of the American music industry...."); K. J. Greene, Copyright, Culture & Black Music: A Legacy of Unequal Protection, 21 HASTINGS COMM. & ENT. L.J. 339, 358–59 (1999); K. J. Greene, *Intellectual Property at the*

Intersection of Race and Gender: Lady Sings the Blues, 16 AM. U. J. GENDER. SOC. POL'Y & L. 365, 371–74 (2008); K. J. Greene, "Copynorms," Black Cultural Production, and the Debate over African-American Reparations, 25 CARDOZO ARTS & ENT. L. J. 1179, 1192 (2008) ("The fleecing of Black artists was the basis of the success of the American music industry"); SIVA VAIDHYANATHAN, COPYRIGHTS AND COPYWRONGS: THE RISE OF INTELLECTUAL PROPERTY AND HOW IT THREATENS CREATIVITY 117–48 (2001) (tracing, among other things, the (mis)appropriation of (predominantly Black) blues by (predominantly White) rock 'n' roll artists over time); ANJALI VATS, THE COLOR OF CREATORSHIP: INTELLECTUAL PROPERTY, RACE AND THE MAKING OF AMERICANS (2020) (assessing the relationship between the political notion of citizenship and the legal concept of creatorship as a sociohistorical matter since the founding of the Republic and, in the process, making the case that intellectual property law has served as an unapologetically (neo)colonial tool of racial capitalism).

34. Llewellyn Joseph Gibbons, Semiotics of the Scandalous and the Immoral and the Disparaging: Section 2(A) Trademark Law after Lawrence v. Texas, 9 MARQ. INTELL. PROP. L. REV. 187, 223 (2005) (documenting and challenging how existing "neutral" trademark rules have been utilized to deny intellectual property protection to "queer marks").
35. *See, e.g.*, Keith Aoki, *Considering Multiple and Overlapping Sovereignties: Liberalism, Libertarianism, National Sovereignty, "Global" Intellectual Property, and the Internet*, 5 IND. J. GLOBAL LEGAL STUD. 443, 461–64 (1998) (discussing how the seemingly neutral harmonization of intellectual property standards has profound North-South implications); Anupam Chander & Madhavi Sunder, The Romance of the Public Domain, 92 CAL. L. REV. 1331, 1354 (2004) (cautioning that the trope of a "romantic public domain" can relegate forms of traditional knowledge to the commons and thereby exacerbate global inequities); STEVEN D. JAMAR & LATEEF MTIMA, CAMBRIDGE HANDBOOK OF INTELLECTUAL PROPERTY AND SOCIAL JUSTICE (2023) (advocating a reformulation of intellectual property regimes so that they address issues of "access, inclusion, and empowerment for marginalized and excluded groups"); Elizabeth L. Rosenblatt, A Theory of IP's Negative Space, 34 COLUM. J.L. & ARTS 317 (2011).
36. *See* Kimberlé W. Crenshaw, Demarginalizing the Intersection of Race and Sex: A Black Feminist Critique of Antidiscrimination Doctrine, Feminist Theory and Antiracist Politics, 1989 U. CHI. LEGAL F. 139 (1989).
37. *See Thomson* v. *Larson*, 147 F.3d 195, 197 (2d. Cir. 1998).
38. Sonya Katyal, Semiotic Disobedience, 83 U. WASH. L. REV. 489 (2006).
39. 17 U.S.C. § 101.
40. 537 U.S. 186, 221 (2023).

1 CAPTURED

1. Matthew S. Schwartz, *Harvard Profits from Photos of Slaves, Lawsuit Claims*, NRP.com (Mar. 21, 2019), https://www.npr.org/2019/03/21/705382289/harvard-profits-from-photos-of-slaves-lawsuit-claims.
2. *Lanier* v. *President and Fellows of Harvard College*, 490 Mass. 37, 72–73 (2022) (Cypher, J., concurring).
3. There is a particularly interesting twist to the story that has been missed in most media accounts, which presume that the works, because of their age, must be in the public domain. Generally, that would be true: Under governing law, works created more than ninety-five years ago have almost all fallen into the public domain, but there are

exceptions, particularly for works that were created long ago but remained unpublished for many years. Specifically, for works that were created before January 1, 1978, but not published until after that (but before January 1, 2003), copyright protection extends, at a minimum, to December 31, 2047, per the operation of 17 U.S.C. § 303(a). In other words, if Harvard were to claim that the daguerreotypes were not first published – as the term is defined under the Copyright Act (an area of great confusion, conflicting holdings and, therefore, substantial wiggle room for creative legal arguments) – until sometime between January 1, 1978, and December 31, 2002, Harvard would arguably still own the copyright to the daguerreotypes until at least 2048. The fact that Harvard was, until recently, wresting licenses for exploitation of the images suggests that the university might take such a position. And, not surprisingly, it appears that Harvard has asserted such a view and backed it up with its rendition of the facts surrounding the photographs, where it is claimed that Aggasiz only showed (not published!) the photographs once and they were tucked away, forgotten, at the Peabody Museum until they were rediscovered in the late 1970s. The narrative conveniently grafts on to a claim for continued protection until at least 2047 per section 303 of the Copyright Act. Harvard actually threatened to sue artist Carrie Mae Weems, who reproduced the images without Harvard's permission in 1995 in her book series *From Here I Saw What Happened and I Cried*. Weems dared Harvard to take legal action, claiming that placing a spotlight on the issue would generate public sympathy in opposition to Harvard's position. Harvard then thought the better of it and, instead, acquired her book series. *See* Parul Sehgal, *The First Photos of Enslaved People Raise Many Questions about the Ethics of Viewing*, N.Y. TIMES (Sept. 29, 2020), https://www.nytimes.com/2020/09/29/books/to-make-their-own-way-in-world-zealy-daguerreotypes.html.

4. *Lanier* v. *President and Fellows of Harvard College*, 2021 WL 8015862, *6 (Sup. Ct. Mass. June 23, 2022).
5. *See* Meghan Keneally, *Erin Andrews Awarded $55 Million in Lawsuit*, ABCNEWS (Mar. 7, 2016, 6:00 PM), http://abcnews.go.com/US/erin-andrews-jury-set-deliberate-75-million-lawsuit/story?id=37460110; *see* Complaint at ¶¶ 8–9, *Andrews* v. *Marriott Int'l, Inc.*, No. 11c4831 (Tenn. Circ. Ct. Dec. 1, 2011).
6. Susan Sontag's seminal contemplation *On Photography*, for example, notes the ways in which photography can objectify individuals into something to be symbolically possessed. SUSAN SONTAG, ON PHOTOGRAPHY 14–15 (1973).
7. *See* Ahiza Garcia, *Why Is the Erin Andrews Nude Video Still Online?*, CNN.COM (Mar. 6, 2016, 8:30 PM), http://money.cnn.com/2016/03/06/media/erin-andrews-video-online-trial [https://perma.cc/VNF5-CFQZ].
8. As CNN noted shortly after the beginning of the Andrews trial, "the video has consistently been one of the top searched items on Google and can still be found on various porn sites." *Id.*
9. *See*, for example, *Bartnicki* v. *Vopper*, 532 U.S. 514, 517, 534 (2001) (holding that the First Amendment protects "speech that discloses the contents of an illegally intercepted communication," albeit so long as the matter involves an issue of "public or general interest").
10. *See* 47 U.S.C. 230(c)(1) ("No provider or use of an interactive computer service shall be treated as the publisher or speaker of any information provided by another information content provider"); *Zeran* v. *Am. Online, Inc.*, 129 F.3d 327, 330 (4th Cir. 1997) (interpreting section 230 as "creat[ing] a federal immunity any cause of action that would make services providers liable for information originating with a third-party

user of the service"); *Doe* v. *Friendfinder Network, Inc.*, 540 F. Supp. 2d 288, 302–303 (D.N.H. 2008) (deeming Section 230 immunity generally applies to state law privacy torts).

11. *See Eldred* v. *Ashcroft*, 537 U.S. 186, 221 (2003); Mark A. Lemley & Eugene Volokh, Freedom of Speech and Injunctions in Intellectual Property Cases, 48 DUKE L. J. 147, 150 (1998) (documenting the courts' lack of hesitation in granting preliminary injunctions in cases of copyright infringement, even when the injunction amounts to a clear prior restraint of speech).
12. To prevail, a plaintiff need only show she owns a valid copyright in a work, defendant had access to her work, and defendant reproduced, publicly displayed, distributed, publicly performed, or created a derivate version of the work. *See A & M Records, Inc.* v. *Napster, Inc.*, 239 F.3d 1004, 1013 (9th Cir. 2001).
13. Assuming timely registration, federal law provides prevailing plaintiffs the right to elect recovery of statutory damages in the amount of $150,000 per willful act of copyright infringement, 17 U.S.C. § 504(c)(2), and, subject to the discretion of the court, the ability to recover reasonable attorney's fees, 17 U.S.C. § 505.
14. *See* 17 U.S.C. § 512(c)(1)(C).
15. That is, to the extent that one existed. One could argue that, as an "illegal" work, Barrett's recording potentially enjoys no copyright protection. *See Villa* v. *Pearson Educ., Inc.*, No. 03-C3717, 2003 WL 22922178, at *2–3 (N.D. Ill. Dec. 9, 2003) (suggesting that illegal graffiti may not be protected under copyright law); *cf. Devils Films, Inc.* v. *Nectar Video*, 29 F. Supp. 2d 174, 175–77 (S.D.N.Y. 1998) (denying a preliminary injunction against the infringement of a pornographic film on the grounds that, inter alia, the films were "obscene" and, therefore, being illegally distributed). In the neighboring field of trademark law, courts have systematically held that illegal trademarks do not enjoy protection. *See CreAgri, Inc.* v. *USANA Health Scis., Inc.*, 474 F.3d 626. 627–28 (9th Cir. 2007) (noting that the Lanham Act requires *lawful* use of a mark in commerce as a predicate for trademark protection).
16. *See Nashville Hotel Video*, Registration No. PA0001790098 (July 28, 2011) (Authorship on Application: Michael David Barrett, Copyright Claimant: Erin Andrews, Transfer: Written Agreement).
17. While peeping "Tinas" certainly exist and men can be subject to the female gaze, this chapter focuses on the more traditional pattern of the man behind the camera and the woman in front of the camera. The gender disparities in the identity of who controls the camera and who is in front of the camera in both the mainstream content creation industries and in the world of amateur pornography, revenge porn, and criminal sexual surveillance warrant such a focus.
18. SONTAG, *supra* note 6, at 14.
19. *Id.* at 14–15.
20. Per Judge Kozinski's original *Garcia* opinion, *Garcia* v. *Google, Inc.* (*Garcia I*), 743 F.3d 1258, 1265 (9th Cir. 2014), the *Andrews* case would seem to be the "rare" instance where there was no waiver through implied license. *See id.* Furthermore, her performance rights would remain with her because there would be no plausible claim that her efforts were made for hire, and there was no contract assigning/transferring such rights away. *See id.* ("[C]opyright interests in the vast majority of films are covered by contract, the work made for hire doctrine or implied licenses."). That said, unlike Cindy Lee Garcia (or Oscar Wilde in *Sarony*), since Andrews was unaware of the camera watching her, she was arguably doing anything but *performing*. Whether human activity conducted without knowledge of its fixation can constitute performance is a topic beyond the scope of this chapter, but certainly one worth considering.

21. Certainly, empowering performer rights could have significant First Amendment consequences with which the courts would have to wrestle, as their recognition and enforcement would impact the creative freedoms of such artists as Arne Svenson. In other circumstances, it could have even broader ramifications. Consider, if you will, if the peeping tom had been Kenneth Starr, going rogue long after the expiry of his Independent Counsel position, and the persons captured on the video had been Monica Lewinsky and President Bill Clinton, reuniting in a private hotel room. Recognizing performer rights in such a scenario might threaten to stifle legitimate news-related uses of the video by media entities, though one imagines that appropriate application of the fair use doctrine could deal with issues regarding unauthorized use of the video.
22. Laura Mulvey, *Visual Pleasure and Narrative Cinema (1975)*, reprinted in FILM THEORY AND CRITICISM: INTRODUCTORY READINGS 833, 837 (Leo Braudy & Marshall Cohen eds., 1999).
23. *See* Thomas F. Ryan, Vision and Spirituality in Post-Katrina New Orleans, 7 SEATTLE J. SOC. JUST. 101, 106 (2008).
24. MULVEY, *supra* note 22, at 837–38.
25. *See*, for example, Yxta Maya Murray, We Just Looked at Them as Ordinary People Like We Were: The Legal Gaze and Women's Bodies, 32 COLUM. J. GENDER & L. 252, 252 (2017) (drawing on the concept of the male gaze to analyze the gender-based dimensions of the legal battles over obscenity, disorderly conduct, and police brutality endured by musicians Wendy O. Williams and Lorien Bourne); Bennett Capers, Rape, Truth, and Hearsay, 40 HARV. J. L. & GENDER 183, 210 (2017) (criticizing rape shield rules as having "created the odd result of courts adopting a 'male gaze' and casting women as sexual objects rather than recognizing them as subjects"); Ann Althouse, The Lying Woman, the Devious Prostitute, and Other Stories from the Evidence Casebook, 88 NW. U. L. REV. 914, 922 (1994) (arguing that the focus in rape trials on the victim's behavior rather than that of the defendant invokes the male gaze, allowing "the violence carried out against [the victim to] recede[] into the background").
26. Margaret Russell, for example, has identified the "dominant gaze," *see* Margaret M. Russell, Race and the Dominant Gaze: Narratives of Law and Inequality in Popular Film, 15 LEGAL STUD. F. 243, 244 (1991), the tendency within popular culture, particularly in visual representations, to "objectify and trivialize the racial identity and experiences of people of color, even when it purports to represent them," David Ray Papke, Peace between the Sexes: Law and Gender in Kramer vs. Kramer, 30 U.S.F. L. REV. 1199, 1204 (1996) (quoting *id.*). Russell's work was influenced by both Mulvey's concept of the male gaze and Frantz Fanon's influential literature on the colonial/white gaze. *See* Russell, *supra*; FRANTZ FANON, BLACK SKIN, WHITE MASKS 90 (2008).
27. 17 U.S.C. § 101.
28. *See Aalmuhammed* v. *Lee*, 202 F.3d 1227, 1231 (9th Cir. 2000) (noting that "the Copyright Act does not define 'author,'" but, oddly enough, that it does define "joint work").
29. U.S. Const. art. 1, § 8, cl. 8 (providing Congress with the authority to, *inter alia*, "secur[e] for limited Times *to Authors* … the exclusive Right to their respective Writings") (emphasis added).
30. 17 U.S.C. § 102.
31. 17 U.S.C. § 201.
32. The legislative record behind the 1976 Copyright Act suggests that Congress intentionally left the neighboring concept of "work of authorship" undefined by design to accommodate potential changes in technology and modalities of expression. *See* H.R. Rep. No. 94-1476, at 51 (1976), *reprinted in* 1976 U.S.C.C.A.N. 5659, 5664 ("The phrase

'original works of authorship' … is purposely left undefined," since, among other things, "[a]uthors are continually finding new ways of expressing themselves, but it is impossible to foresee the forms that these new expressive methods will take"); Diana C. Obradovich, Note, *Garcia* v. *Google: Authorship in Copyright*, 31 Berkeley Tech. L.J. 785, 788 n.26 (2016). However, the same legislative history appears to have little to say about the actual term "author."

33. David Nimmer, Copyright in the Dead Sea Scrolls: Authorship and Originality, 38 Hous. L. Rev. 1, 11 (2001).
34. *Id.* at 57–58 (citing *Author*, Worcester's Dictionary (1860)).
35. *Community for Creative Non-Violence* v. *Reid*, 490 U.S. 730, 737 (1988).
36. 17 U.S.C. § 102.
37. *See* Copyright Act of 1790, 1 Stat. 124 (1790) (only extending copyright protection to books, charts, and maps).
38. Congress extended copyright protection to photographs in 1865, *see* Copyright Act of 1865, ch. 126, 13 Stat. 540 (1865), and paintings and drawings in 1870, *see* Copyright Act of 1870, ch. 230, 16 Stat. 198 § 86 (1870).
39. In 1971, Congress extended federal protection to sound recordings fixed after February 15, 1972. *See* Sound Recordings Act, Pub. L. No. 92-140, 85 Stat. 391 (1971).
40. As John Shulman noted in Congressional testimony many decades ago, the issue of default rules for copyright vesting is often irrelevant to industry as "the contract between the author and the picture company will establish the status, whether [the work] is a work made for hire or whether it is not. We have that all the time…. So many of the things that were spoken about here as being difficult are not really so because if you have a sound law, the rest is handled by contract." *Copyright Law Revision: Hearings on H.R. 4347, H.R. 5680, H.R. 6831, H.R. 6835 before the Subcomm. No. 3 of the H. Comm. on the Judiciary*, 89th Cong. 1717 (1965) (statement of John Schulman), *reprinted in* 7 Omnibus Copyright Revision Legislative History 1717 (George S. Grossman ed., 1976).
41. *Naruto* v. *Slater*, No. 15-cv-04324-WHO, 2016 BL 25049 (N.D. Cal. January 28, 2016).
42. *Garcia* v. *Google, Inc.* (*Garcia I*), 743 F.3d 1258 (9th Cir. 2014), *amended and superseded by* 766 F.3d 929 (9th Cir. 2014), *rev'd by* 786 F.3d 733 (9th Cir. 2015) (en banc).
43. *Bollea* v. *Gawker Media, LLC*, 913 F. Supp. 2d 1325 (M.D. Fla. 2012).
44. 111 U.S. 53, 60 (1884).
45. Copyright Act of 1865, ch. 126, 13 Stat. 540 (Act of March 3, 1865).
46. U.S. Const., Art. I., § 8, Cl. 8.
47. Or, as Christine Haight Farley has put it, the Court had to ask: "Was it a scientific process involving the mere transmission of light, or did the resulting product reflect the genius of a Romantic author?" Christine Haight Farley, The Lingering Effects of Copyright's Response to the Invention of Photography, 65 U. Pitt. L. Rev. 385, 409 (2004).
48. *Id.* at 386 (noting that "it is a well-known case in copyright law frequently cited for propositions about the originality standard").
49. *Id.* at 433.
50. *Id.* at 434.
51. *Id.* at 433.
52. *Sarony*, 111 U.S. at 54.
53. *Id.* at 57–58.
54. As various commentators have noted, the idea of the "master mind" is a key concept in the romantic view of authorship, which conceptualizes authors as solitary geniuses

whose mythic individual efforts result in the creation of original works *ex nihilo*. *See* JAMES BOYLE, SHAMANS, SOFTWARE AND SPLEENS: LAW AND THE CONSTRUCTION OF THE INFORMATION SOCIETY 51–60 (1997); James Boyle, The Search for an Author: Shakespeare and the Framers, 37 AM. U. L. REV. 625, 629 (1988); Peter Jaszi, Toward a Theory of Copyright: The Metamorphoses of "Authorship," 1991 DUKE L. J. 455, 455–63 (1991).

55. Oren Bracha, The Ideology of Authorship Revisited: Authors, Markets, and Liberal Values in Early America, 118 YALE L. J. 186, 187 (2008).
56. *Id* (noting that this romantic conception of authorship "lies at the normative heart of our vision of copyright."). For example, the concept is central to the reigning joint authorship standard, which makes the possibility of joint authorship exceedingly difficult to achieve. This reluctance to recognize co-authorship appears to betray the realities of the artistic process and the multiplicity of important, original, and creative contributions in the development of works protected under the Copyright Act.
57. *Cmty. for Creative Non-Violence* v. *Reid,* 490 U.S. 730, 737 (1989).
58. *See id.*
59. The DMCA safe harbor was not at issue since Garcia sought an injunction and the DMCA safe harbor does not apply to equitable relief. *See* 17 U.S.C. § 512(a)–(d), (j) (2011) (limiting the DMCA safe harbor to monetary relief).
60. *Garcia* v. *Google, Inc.* (*Garcia II*), 786 F.3d 733, 737 (9th Cir. 2015).
61. *Id.*
62. *Garcia I*, 743 F.3d at 1268 ("Garcia has shown that removing the film from YouTube will help disassociate her from the film's anti-Islamic message and that such disassociation will keep her from suffering future threats and physical harm.").
63. *Garcia I*, 743 F.3d at 1258.
64. *Garcia II*, 786 F.3d at 749 (Kozinski, J., dissenting).
65. *See* Order Denying Appellee's Second Emergency Stay Motion, *Garcia* v. *Google, Inc.*, No. 12-57302 (9th Cir. Feb. 28, 2014) ("This order does not preclude the posting or display of any version of 'Innocence of Muslims' that does not include Cindy Lee Garcia's performance.").
66. *See* Eric Goldman, *Internet Law Professors File Amicus Brief in "Innocence of Muslims" Case – Garcia* v. *Google,* TECH. & MARKETING L. BLOG (Apr. 16, 2014), http://blog.ericgoldman.org/archives/2014/04/internet-law-professors-file-amicus-brief-in-innocence-of-muslims-case-garcia-v-google.htm.
67. James Grimmelman (@grimmelm), Twitter (Feb. 26, 2014, 2:01 PM), https://twitter.com/grimmelm/status/438796071113097216.
68. Mike Masnick, *Horrific Appeals Court Ruling Says Actress Has Copyright Interest in "Innocence of Muslims," Orders YouTube to Delete Every Copy*, TECHDIRT (Feb. 26, 2014), https://www.techdirt.com/articles/20140226/12103626359/horrific-appeals-court-ruling-says-actress-has-copyright-interest-innocence-muslims-orders-youtube-to-delete-every-copy.shtml.
69. *See Garcia* v. *Google:* 12-57302, U.S. Cts. for the 9th Circuit, http://www.ca9.uscourts.gov/content/view.php?pk_id=0000000725 (last updated July 6, 2015, 12:40 PM).
70. *Garcia* v. *Google, Inc.* (*Garcia II*), 786 F.3d 733, 737 (9th Cir. 2015).
71. *Garcia* v. *Google, Inc.* (*Garcia I*), 743 F.3d 1258, 1265 (9th Cir. 2014). Kozinski dismissed these concerns by noting the prevalent use of contracts in industry and by encouraging a wide reading of implied licenses so as to preclude any such balkanization of rights in the vast majority of cases. *See id.*

72. *Garcia II*, 786 F.3d at 753 (Kozinski, J., dissenting).
73. In rejecting Garcia's copyright claim, the *en banc* panel in *Garcia* v. *Google* posited that "she never fixed her acting performance in a tangible medium"; that is, the performance was fixed by someone other than her – writer-director Mark Basseley Youssef and his crew. *Garcia* v. *Google, Inc.* (*Garcia II*), 786 F.3d 733, 737, 743 (9th Cir. 2015). As the court concluded, "however one might characterize Garcia's performance, she played no role in fixation." *Id.* at 744.
74. The fixation requirement, which purportedly derives from the Constitution's reference to "writings" as the subject matter of federal copyright protection, U.S. Const. art. I, § 8, cl. 8, dictates that a copyright cannot vest in an expression of an idea that does not have a tangible embodiment. *See* 17 U.S.C. § 102(a). Thus, a speech, dance performance, parade, or sporting event has no copyright protection unless it is fixed in a tangible medium. While there are debates as to whether fixation is constitutionally required, *see, e.g.*, Megan Carpenter & Steven Hetcher, Function over Form: Bringing the Fixation Requirement into the Modern Era, 82 Fordham L. Rev. 2221, 2236 (2014) (noting that, although "numerous courts and commentators have seen fixation as a constitutional requirement … fixation de jure did not exist prior to the 1976 Act [and] the U.S. copyright system functioned without the fixation requirement for nearly the first two centuries of its existence."), it is an express part of the 1976 Copyright Act, and it is said to serve a variety of purposes, including advancing evidentiary interests, *see, e.g.*, Russ VerSteeg, Jurimetric Copyright: Future Shock for the Visual Arts, 13 Cardozo Arts & Ent. L.J. 125, 132 (1994) (noting fixation's critical role in ensuring that "a copyright claimant will be able to provide a court documentary evidence of the copyrightable subject matter"); Gregory S. Donat, Fixing Fixation: A Copyright with Teeth for Improvisational Performers, 97 Colum. L. Rev. 1363, 1400 (1997) (noting that without the fixation requirement, "copyright law would forever be mired in disputes over the definition and boundaries of the works claiming copyright protection."), that, among other things, help define the "metes and bounds" of a copyrighted work. *See* Carpenter & Hetcher, *supra*, at 2240 ("fixation helps to define the metes and bounds of a copyright work."). But it is worth noting that, by virtue of ensuring that written documentation of a work's creation exists, the fixation requirement fulfills its evidentiary interests regardless of whether it is the author who does the actual fixing or not.
75. This purported condition of protection has never been expressly dictated by the Constitution or the Copyright Act. Admittedly, the Constitution does suggest that authors receive copyright in "their" writings. U.S. Const. art. I, § 8, cl. 8. Depending on the interpretation of "their," one could make a plausible argument that the fixation does, in fact, need to be done by the author, but it appears that no court has expressly grappled with that issue. Indeed, the relevant section of the U.S. Code that embodies the fixation requirement, section 102(a), merely dictates that a work of authorship must be fixed to earn copyright protection; notably, ***it does not say by whom***. *See* 17 U.S.C. § 102(a) (extending the subject matter of federal copyright protection to "original works of authorship fixed in any tangible medium of expression, now known or later developed, from which they can be perceived, reproduced, or otherwise communicated"). Meanwhile, section 101 defines "fixed" to include embodiment in a tangible medium either "by or under the authority of the author." 17 U.S.C. § 101. The *Garcia* court waived away the "under authority" portion of the statute by stating that "Garcia claims she never agreed to the film's ultimate rendition or how she was portrayed in *Innocence of Muslims*, so she can hardly argue that the film or her cameo in it was fixed 'by or under [her] authority." *Garcia* v. *Google, Inc.* (*Garcia II*), 786 F.3d 733, 744 (9th Cir. 2015). But such a position confuses the film's "ultimate rendition" with its actual fixation, which first occurred with

its recording on the set. The latter was arguably done under Ms. Garcia's authority, as she gave a performance knowing full well that she was going to be recorded on film. Of course, this does raise the issue as to whether there should be a difference in copyright ability between performances where the performer is aware that he or she is being recorded (as in *Garcia*) or not (e.g., a surreptitiously recorded sex tape).

76. U.S. CONST., Art. I., § 8, Cl. 8 (mandating that copyright protection "promote progress in ... the useful arts").
77. Section 102 of the Copyright Act, which governs authorship, makes no statement about authorship-as-fixation. Instead, it simply states that "[c]opyright protection subsists ... in original works of authorship fixed in any tangible medium of expression." 17 U.S.C. § 102. If anything, section 102 goes out of its way to avoid saying *in whom* copyright subsists. Authorship-as-fixation might be one way to read the authorship requirement, but it certainly is not the only way. Moreover, since the requirement for vesting copyright in an author presumably stems from the Constitution, *see* U.S. CONST. art. I, § 8, cl. 8, the issue is ultimately one of constitutional, rather than statutory, interpretation.
78. *See Cmty. for Creative Non-Violence* v. *Reid*, 490 U.S. 730, 737 (1989).
79. *See Garcia II*, 786 F.3d at 749 (Kozinski, J., dissenting).
80. *See Lindsay* v. *The Wrecked and Abandoned Vessel R.M.S. Titanic, No. 97 Civ. 9248(HB)*, 1999 WL 816163, at *5 (S.D.N.Y. Oct. 13, 1999) ("where a plaintiff alleges that he exercised such a high degree of control over a film operation – including the type and amount of light used, the specific camera angles to be employed, and other detail-intensive artistic elements of a film – such that the final product duplicates his conceptions and visions of what the film should look like, the plaintiff may be said to be an 'author' within the meaning of the Copyright Act"). Notably, however, the *Lindsay* court did caution that the nonfixers must have a close relationship with the fixation. *Id.*
81. *See supra* note 75.
82. Daniel Kreps, *U2 Debut Another New Song on European Tour*, Rolling Stone (Aug. 23, 2010), http://www.rollingstone.com/music/news/u2-debut-another-new-song-on-european-tour-20100823 (quoting Bono as saying "No one has heard this before – not even us.").
83. U2gigs.com, *U2 Helsinki 2010-08-21 Every Breaking Wave (New Song)*, YouTube (Aug. 21, 2010), https://www.youtube.com/watch?v=q9C-z-dljsY (capturing the Aug. 21, 2010 performance).
84. *See Feist Publications, Inc.* v. *Rural Telephone Service Co.*, 499 U.S. 340, 346 (1991).
85. This issue has arisen in the analogous context of bands re-recording their greatest hits in order to circumvent bad record deals and re-channel to themselves revenues from exploitation of their most famous sound recordings, a gambit made most famous in recent years by Taylor Swift. But the practice has a long history. For example, in 2007, veteran Southern California punk rockers Social Distortion put out an album of greatest hits. Six of the twelve tracks on the album were not original recordings but, instead, re-recordings of their most famous songs. *See Social Distortion – Greatest Hits Discography*, Discogs, https://www.discogs.com/Social-Distortion-Greatest-Hits/release/2564606 (last visited July 8, 2017). By re-recording the songs, Social Distortion presumably avoided having to get a license from their old record label (who owned the copyright to the sound recordings) to release those songs. Instead, the band could simply rely on the fact that they did not require permission of the record label since they owned the rights to the underlying musical compositions and could create new recordings of those as they saw fit. After all, 17 U.S.C. § 114(b) provides that "[t]he exclusive rights of the owner of copyright in a sounding recording under clauses (1) and (2) of section 106 do not extend to the making or duplication of another sound recording that consists entirely of an independent fixation

of other sounds, even though such sounds imitate or simulate those in the copyrighted sound recording." Moreover, in a worst-case scenario, Social Distortion could even rest on the compulsory mechanical license and argue that their re-recordings were merely cover versions of the originals (even though the colloquial understanding of the term implies a completely different artist doing a version of someone else's songs) if they follow the appropriate procedures under 17 U.S.C. § 115 and related regulations. Of course, the project of re-recording one's greatest hits is quite different from doing a live album or an acoustic album, where the ultimate recordings will (and are meant to) sound fundamentally different. In the case of re-recording, the artist typically attempts to make the sound recording sound exactly the same, often going through grueling measures to achieve such an effect. *See, e.g.*, Glenn Tilbrook, *How Squeeze Seized the Keys to Their Back Catalogue*, The Guardian (Oct. 25, 2010, 5:17 AM), https://www.theguardian.com/music/musicblog/2010/oct/25/squeeze-back-catalogue-up-junction (noting the painstaking, three-year process that the members of the band Squeeze undertook to re-record their hits so that they would sound the same as the original recordings).

86. For example, John Fogerty was infamously sued for infringing himself. Although a jury ultimately rejected the claim, the case survived summary judgment and went through extensive appeals (including a Supreme Court opinion) and Fogerty ultimately had to bear his own fees in defending the allegations. *See Fogerty* v. *Fantasy, Inc.*, 510 U.S. 517 (1994).

87. *See* 17 U.S.C. § 106(2) (granting copyright holders the exclusive rights to prepare derivatives based on their work).

88. Works that constitute infringements themselves are not entitled to copyright protection. *See* 17 U.S.C. § 103 ("[P]rotection for a work employing preexisting material in which copyright subsists does not extend to any part of the work in which such material has been used unlawfully."); 1–3 Melville B. Nimmer, Nimmer on Copyright, § 3.06 (1978). Thus, works that constitute unauthorized derivatives do not receive copyright protection, no matter how original or meritorious they might be. *See Pickett* v. *Prince*, 207 F.3d 402, 406–407 (7th Cir. 2000) (denying copyright protection to any portion of an unauthorized derivative work) (Posner, J.); *Eden Toys, Inc.* v. *Florelee Undergarment Co., Inc.*, 697 F.2d 27, 34 n.6 (2d Cir. 1982); *Gracen* v. *Bradford Exch.*, 698 F.2d 300, 303 (7th Cir. 1983); *Sobhani* v. *@Radical.Media, Inc.*, 257 F. Supp. 2d 1234, 1238 (C.D. Cal. 2003) ("Accordingly, if a work is derived from a previous work, and the new work thereby infringes a copyright in the previous work, then the new work is an unauthorized (and infringing) derivative work."); *Anderson* v. *Stallone*, No. 87-0592 WDKGX, 1989 WL206431, at *10 (C.D. Cal. 1989) ("[N]o part of an infringing derivative work should be granted copyright protection."). The legislative history behind the 1976 Copyright Act firmly supports this position. As the House of Representatives noted, "the bill prevents an infringer from benefiting, through copyright protection, from committing an unlawful act." H.R. Rep. No. 94-1476, at 57 (1976), *as reprinted in* 1976 U.S.S.C.A.N. 5659, 5671. Thus, an authorized bootleg recording of a music composition constitutes an unauthorized derivative version of that musical composition and, as a result, likely has no copyright.

89. *See, e.g., Dowling* v. *United States*, 473 U.S. 207, 214–16 (1985) (noting that convicted bootlegger did not challenge copyright infringement judgment against her, which relied on a theory of infringement of musical compositions for the creation of the sound recording).

90. Contract law might get in the way, depending on the nature of the terms and conditions of admittance to the concert, but enforcement is questionable and the remedies are quite different (and substantially worse) than for copyright infringement.

91. Rebecca Tushnet, Performance Anxiety: Copyright Embodied and Disembodied, 60 J. COPY. SOC'Y 209, 211 (2013).
92. There is a question as to whether such performances can be registered so as to qualify for the recovery of statutory damages and attorneys' fees, so plaintiffs moving for relief under this provision of the Copyright Act might, in practice, be limited to recovery of actual damages alone.
93. Although some scholars have questioned the constitutionality of section 1101, courts have generally upheld its validity by suggesting that the commerce clause (rather than the copyright clause) permitted its passage. *See* Craig W. Dallon, The Anti-Bootlegging Provisions: Congressional Power and Constitutional Limitations, 13 VAND. J. ENT. & TECH. 255, 257 (2011) (noting "a sharp division among copyright scholars" on the issue, but concluding that "the [court] decisions to date [on the issue] evince a growing consensus upholding these provisions.").
94. *See* 17 U.S.C. § 1101 (extending the protections of the anti-bootlegging provision only to "live musical performances").
95. Andrew Ross Sorkin, *Peter Thiel, Tech Billionaire, Reveals Secret War with Gawker*, N.Y. TIMES (May 25, 2016) http://www.nytimes.com/2016/05/26/business/dealbook/peter-thiel-tech-billionaire-reveals-secret-war-with-gawker.html?_r=0.
96. The strategy failed. Bollea's application for a preliminary injunction on the copyright claims was rejected by a federal court. *See Bollea* v. *Gawker Media, LLC*, 913 F. Supp. 2d 1325, 1331 (M.D. Fla. 2012). Bollea's subsequent application for a preliminary injunction on the privacy invasion claims in a separate state court proceeding was initially granted but then overturned as a prior restraint in violation of the First Amendment by Florida's Second District Court of Appeals. *See Gawker Media, LLC* v. *Bollea*, 129 So. 3d 1196 (Fla. Dist. Ct. App. 2014).
97. *Bollea*, 913 F. Supp. 2d at 1327 ("Plaintiff commenced this action by filing a five-count complaint against Defendants asserting claims for (1) invasion of privacy by intrusion upon seclusion, (2) publication of private facts, (3) violation of the Florida common law right of publicity, (4) intentional infliction of emotional distress, and (5) negligent infliction of emotional distress. Following the hearing on the original Motion for Preliminary Injunction, Plaintiff filed a First Amended Complaint adding a new claim for copyright infringement.").
98. 17 U.S.C. § 501(b) (limiting standing for infringement claims to "the legal or beneficial owner of an exclusive right under a copyright"); *McCormick* v. *Amir Const. Inc.*, 279 Fed. Appx. 470, 471 (9th Cir. 2008) ("Section 501(b) [of the Copyright Act] grants standing to sue under the Copyright Act only to one owning a copyright") (citing *Silvers* v. *Sony Pictures Entm't, Inc.*, 402 F.3d 881, 885 (9th Cir. 2005)).
99. The copyright registration for the video, *see The Unauthorized Video*, Copyright Registration Number Pa0003639502 (Nov 3, 2012), lists Bubba the Love Sponge as its author and brings the registration in the name of Terry Gene Bollea by virtue of a transfer (via written agreement). As Hogan's attorney, Charles Harder, explained, "Bubba owned and operated the recording machinery, therefore when we settled with him, Bubba transferred to Hulk all of the rights of the tape." Eriq Gardner, *How to Keep a Celebrity Sex Tape Off the Internet*, The Hollywood Reporter: Esq. (May 22, 2013, 8:00 AM), http://www.hollywoodreporter.com/thr-esq/celebrity-sex-tape-how-keep-526546.
100. The only language in the decision remotely related to the issue of standing and ownership was the court's notation that "Plaintiff now contends that he recently obtained and registered a copyright for the Video." *Bollea*, 913 F. Supp. 2d at 1327.

101. The question of copyright in surveillance footage does not appear to have ever been addressed, though it was raised in a case involving a casino suing for infringement of their surveillance footage, where the defendant argued that the video lacked sufficient creativity for copyright protection. *See* Defendant's Motion for Summary Judgment at *4–6, *Southwest Casino and Hotel Corp.* v. *Flyingman*, No. CIV-07-0949 (W.D. Okla. Aug. 28, 2008). As David Vaver argued, "whether scenes taken by an automatic surveillance camera are authored by anyone is doubtful: the person responsible for positioning the camera is no Atom Egoyan. Such authorless films may have no copyright at all." David Vaver, Intellectual Property Law: Copyright, Patents, Trademarks 54–55 (1997).
102. *Burrows-Giles Lithographic Co.* v. *Sarony*, 111 U.S. 53 (1884).
103. Of course, if Hogan and Clem's creative contributions as performers gave rise to a copyright interest, they would likely constitute joint authors of the work. But such a position would lead to problems for Hogan. Besides the uphill battle in making a performance copyright claim, Hogan would certainly have been reluctant to take such a position if the consequence would be the vesting of joint author in Heather Clem as well. A joint author possesses the right to unilaterally license rights to the work, so, in that event, Gawker could have debunked any infringement claim that Hogan might have brought by simply obtaining a license from Heather Clem.
104. *See* Adrian Horton, *Exploiting the Exploited: The Problem with* Pam & Tommy, The Guardian (Feb. 15, 2022), available at https://www.theguardian.com/tv-and-radio/2022/feb/15/pam-and-tommy-hulu-series-pamela-anderson-consent.
105. The Next Friends claimed that Naruto (a male macaque) was the macaque featured in the selfies. *See Naruto* v. *Slater*, 2015 WL 5576925, at ¶1, Case No. 15-cv-04324 (N.D. Cal. Filed Sept. 21, 2015). But Blurb's Motion to Dismiss challenges this claim and states that the macaque in the selfies was a different macaque – one that was female. *See* Defendant Blurb, Inc.'s Notice of Motion and Motion to Dismiss the Complaint for Copyright Infringement, 2015 WL 9392536, at *3-4 (N.D. Cal. Nov. 6, 2015). For the purposes of this Chapter, we will assume that it was, in fact, Naruto in the photographs.
106. As he stated in his Complaint, had the selfies "been made by a human using Slater's unattended camera, that human would be declared the photographs' author and copyright owner." *Naruto*, 2015 WL 5576925, at ¶5.
107. *See* Compendium of Copyright Office Practices § 313.2 (3d ed.) ("[t]o qualify as a work of 'authorship' a work must be created by a human being. Works that do not satisfy this requirement are not copyrightable") (citations omitted).
108. *Naruto* v. *Slater*, Order Granting Motions to Dismiss, 2016 WL 362231 (N.D. Cal. Jan. 28, 2016).
109. *See Naturo* v. *Slater*, 888 F.3d 418 (9th Cir. 2016).
110. *Id.* at 11 ("My experience of these monkeys suggested that they were not just highly intelligent but were also aware of themselves.... It was only a matter of time before one pressed the shutter resulting in a photo of herself. She stared at herself with a new found appreciation, and made funny faces – in silence – just as we do when looking in a mirror.").
111. *See* Brief of Defendant-Appellees David John Slater and Wildlife Personalities, Ltd., at *3-4, No. 16-15469 (9th Cir. Aug. 25, 2016) ("Slater, an award-winning nature photographer, set up what became the Monkey Selfie in the course of several grueling days in an Indonesian jungle. Developing a keen understanding of their subjects is a critical skill for any professional photographer, and that was vital here for Slater as he slowly built a trustful, friendly relationship with a group of crested macaque monkeys."). As Slater himself explained, "It was my artistry and idea to leave [the macaques] to play

with the camera and it all in my eyesight. I knew the monkeys were very likely to do this and I predicted it. I knew there was a chance of a photo being taken." Hayden Smith, *Can Monkey Who Took Grinning Self-Portrait Claim Copyright?* METRO (July 14, 2014), available at http://metro.co.uk/2011/07/14/can-monkey-who-took-grinning-self-portrait-claim-copyright-77773/ (quoting Slater).

112. *Id.*
113. *Sarony*, 111 U.S. at 53. Ironically, although *Sarony* gave rise to modern authorship-as-fixation jurisprudence, the decision itself put no value on who actually clicked the camera shutter. In fact, in that case, the individual who snapped the shot was Benjamin Richard, not Napoleon Sarony – the putative "photographer" in whom the Court vested authorship.
114. *As the Number of Paparazzi* v. *Celebrity Copyright Cases Grows, How Big of a Problem Is This Really*, THE FASHION LAW (July 15, 2019), available at https://www.thefashionlaw.com/as-the-number-of-paparazzi-v-celebrity-copyright-cases-continues-to-grow-how-big-of-a-problem-is-this-really.
115. *See O'Neil* v. *Ratajkowski*, Case No. 1:19-cv-09769 (S.D.N.Y. Oct. 23, 2019).
116. This is the statutory maximum allowed for a single willful act of infringement under the Copyright Act. *See* 17 U.S.C. § 504(c)(2).
117. In fact, Ratajkowski did not change her approach to social media posting, as she was once again sued, in 2021, for infringing two other paparazzi shots in which she starred. *See Mateo* v. *Ratajkowski*, Case No. 2:21-cv-05684 (C.D. Cal. July 14, 2021).
118. Emily Ratajkowski, *Buying Myself Back: When Does a Model Own Her Own Image?*, THE CUT (Sep. 15, 2020), available at https://www.thecut.com/article/emily-ratajkowski-owning-my-image-essay.html.
119. *Id.*
120. *See Splash News & Picture Agency, LLC* v. *Moschino, S.P.A., Jeremy Scott, and Belcalis Marlenis Almanzar* p/k/a Cardi B, Case No. 2:19-cv-09220 (C.D. Cal. Oct. 26, 2019).
121. 137 S. Ct. 1002, 1014 (2017).
122. *See* Answer and Counterclaim, Dkt. #16, Case No. 2:19-cv-09220 (C.D. Cal. January 6, 2020).
123. *See supra*, note 88.
124. *See* Stipulation to Dismiss Case, Dkt #27, Case No. 2:19-cv-09220 (C.D. Cal. Mar. 27, 2020).
125. *Cariou* v. *Prince*, 714 F.3d 694 (2013).
126. *See id.*
127. Josh Russell, *Proof Is in the Pixels for Appropriation Artist Richard Prince*, COURTHOUSE NEWS SERVICE (July 28, 2020), available at https://www.courthousenews.com/proof-is-in-the-pixels-for-appropriation-artist-richard-prince/.
128. *Id.* (quoting McNatt's attorney, Caitlin Fitzpatrick).
129. Lizzie Plaugic, *The Story of Richard Prince and His $100,000 Instagram Art*, THE VERGE (May 30, 2015), available at https://www.theverge.com/2015/5/30/8691257/richard-prince-instagram-photos-copyright-law-fair-use.
130. *See, e.g.*, *Graham* v. *Prince*, Case No. 1:15-cv-10160 (S.D.N.Y. Dec. 30, 2015); *McNatt* v. *Prince*, Case No. 1:16-cv-08896 (S.D.N.Y. Nov. 16, 2016).
131. Ryan Patrick Hooper & LaToya Cross, *Meet Zoe Ligon, the Sex Educator Calling Out MOCAD's Controversial "New Portraits" Exhibit*, WDET (Nov. 6, 2019), https://wdet.org/posts/2019/11/06/88857-meet-zoe-ligon-the-sex-educator-calling-out-mocads-controversial-new-portraits-exhibit/.
132. *Id.* (quoting Zoe Ligon as explaining that, "part of the reason I take 'sexy selfies' is because I am reclaiming my own sexual image.").

133. Naomi Rea, *Appropriation Art or Revenge Porn? The Subject of a Richard Prince Instagram Portrait Slams the Artist's Use of Her Image*, ArtNet (Nov. 5, 2019), available at https://news.artnet.com/art-world/richard-prince-appropriation-instagram-1696413.
134. *Id.* (quoting Zoe Ligon).
135. As Borowy-Reeder posited, the exhibit provoked such inquiries as, "Is social media empowering people or co-opting artistic production? Where do our expectations and perceptions around privacy and consent lead us when using social media? What are you consenting to when posting? Is all photograph exploitative?" *Id.* (quoting Ellen Borowy-Reeder).
136. Emily Ratajkowski, *Buying Myself Back: When Does a Model Own Her Own Image?*, The Cut (Sep. 15, 2020), available at https://www.thecut.com/article/emily-ratajkowski-owning-my-image-essay.html.
137. *Id.*
138. Michael Ordoña, *This Picture of Emily Ratajkowski Is Free to Look at. But Its NFT Sold for* $140,000, L.A. Times (May 17, 2021), available at https://www.latimes.com/entertainment-arts/story/2021-05-17/emily-ratajkowski-nft-sells-for-140000. While Ratajkowski owns the Prince *New Portrait* print in which she starred, her purchase would not have typically included the copyright to that work. That copyright would remain with the artist – Richard Prince. And, ironically, if Prince were to get aggressive, he could plausibly claim that the unauthorized NFT, which reproduced his work without permission, was an act of infringement. But such a step might be myopic, as the legality of Prince's own actions in creating the *New Portraits* themselves is very much in question. As such, it would take a galling level of chutzpah (and poor judgment) for Prince to threaten legal action against Ratajkowski, a fact that she probably banked on when she elected to proceed with the NFT.
139. While Ratajkowski may not have hundreds of millions of dollars, she enjoys both some wealth and tremendous social media influence – a form of cultural cachet that she can convert into power and money in a manner that has enabled her to buy herself back (albeit not without significant sacrifices and financial stress).
140. Rosanna McLaughlin, *Emily Ratajkowski's 'The Cut' Essay and Why We Can't Buy Our Way Out of Today's Toxic Image Economy*, Frieze.com (Sep. 28, 2020), available at https://www.frieze.com/article/some-thoughts-emily-ratajkowskis-cut-essay.
141. *Id.* (quoting Huxtable Tweet).
142. Mulvey, *supra* note 22, at 837.
143. The display of the female body, as depicted or captured by a man, for a primarily male audience, has long been a hallmark feature of Western visual culture. *See* Terry Barrett, Approaches to Postmodern Art-Making, 28 FATE Rev. 1, 9 (2007).
144. *New Yorkers Threaten to Sue Artist Who Secretly Photographed Them in Their OWN Apartments and Is Selling Prints for* $7500, Daily Mail (May 16, 2013), available at http://www.dailymail.co.uk/news/article-2325757/New-Yorkers-threaten-sue-artist-secretly-photographed-OWN-apartments-selling-prints-7-500-dollars.html.
145. *See, e.g.*, Catherine Wagley, *Arne Svenson: The Neighbors*, Photograph (Feb. 1, 2013), available at https://photographmag.com/articles/arne-svenson-the-neighbors/ (referring to the collection of photographs as "lyrical. They look the way a Milan Kundera novel sounds – removed and hazy, melancholically preoccupied with small moments.").
146. *See* Daily Mail, *supra* note 144 (quoting promotional materials from Arne Svenson's website).
147. *Id.*
148. *Id.*

149. *See Foster* v. *Svenson*, 7 N.Y.S.3d 96, 98–99 (N.Y. App. Div. 2015) (noting that "[d]espite defendant's professed effort to obscure his subjects' identity, plaintiffs' children were identifiable in these photographs, one of which showed their son in his diaper and their daughter in a swimsuit; the other showed plaintiff mother holding her daughter").
150. Laura C. Mallonee, *Artist Who Furtively Photographed His Neighbors Wins in Court, Again*, HYPERALLERGIC (Apr. 21, 2015), http://hyperallergic.com/200601/artist-who-furtively-photographed-his-neighbors-wins-in-court-again [https://perma.cc/HJ4P-ZNZT].
151. *Id.*
152. *See Foster*, 7 N.Y.S.3d at 98–99.
153. *Id.* at 99.
154. Although, increasingly, they do, as the *Andrews* case, discussed *infra*, illustrates. *See* Complaint at ¶¶ 8–9, *Andrews* v. *Marriott Int'l, Inc.*, No. 11c4831 (Tenn. Circ. Ct. Dec. 1, 2011).
155. *See Foster* v. *Svenson*, No. 55, 2013 WL 3989038 at *6 (N.Y. Sup. Ct. Aug. 5, 2013).
156. *See Foster*, 7 N.Y.S.3d at 98. Although it ruled in his favor, the New York appellate court characterized Svenson's actions as "disturbing," "intrusive," and "troubling" and called upon the New York legislature to consider new laws to protect individuals from these sorts of "heightened threats to privacy posed by new and ever more invasive technologies." *Id.* at 105–106.
157. *Id.* at 103–104 ("Defendant's used [sic] of the photos falls within the ambit of constitutionally protected conduct in the form of a work of art.... Since the images themselves constitute the work of art, and art work is protected by the First Amendment, any advertising undertaken in connection with the promotion of the art work was permitted.").
158. *Id.* at 98 (quoting promotional materials on Arne Svenson's website).
159. *See Eldred* v. *Ashcroft*, 537 U.S. 186, 221 (2003) ("[C]opyright's built-in free speech safeguards are generally adequate to address [any conflict with free speech rights].").
160. The unpublished nature of the work strongly mitigates against any fair use right at all. *See Harper & Row, Publishers, Inc.* v. *Nation Enters.*, 471 U.S. 539, 564 (1985) (holding that there is a heavy presumption against fair use of unpublished works as the "scope of fair use is narrower with respect to unpublished works"); *Salinger* v. *Random House, Inc.*, 811 F.2d 90, 97 (2d Cir. 1987) (finding that unpublished works "normally enjoy complete protection against copying" in rejecting a fair use defense and enjoining the publication of a biography of J.D. Salinger that quoted and paragraphed unpublished letters by the reclusive author).
161. Of course, this assumes that the "work" was unpublished, raising philosophical questions as to whether raising the curtains covering a home's glass windows constitutes a "publication" of one's performative work while in the house. *See* 17 U.S.C. § 101 (defining publication as "the distribution of copies or phonorecords of a work to the public by sale or other transfer of ownership, or by rental, lease, or lending" and "offering to distribute copies or phonorecords to a group of persons for purposes of further distribution, public performance, or public display").
162. The phenomenon of revenge porn first received international attention with the website *IsAnyoneUp*, where users would post naked images and videos and also link to the subject's social media profiles, thereby revealing their real names, addresses, and other identifying information. *See* Bob Garfield, *Revenge Porn's Latest Frontier*, WNYC (Dec. 2, 2011), http://www.wnyc.org/story/173718-revenge-porns-latest-frontier/#transcript [https://perma.cc/RXX4-28XQ].

163. *See State 'Revenge Porn' Legislation*, NAT'L CONF. ST. LEGISLATURES (Dec. 3, 2014), https://web.archive.org/web/20141211110621/; http://www.ncsl.org/research/telecommunications-and-information-technology/state-revenge-porn-legislation.aspx [https://perma.cc/KV69-WJRR].
164. *See* CYBER CIVIL RIGHTS INITIATIVE, CCRI'S 2013 NONCONSENSUAL PORNOGRAPHY (NCP) RESEARCH RESULTS 1 (2013), https://www.cybercivilrights.org/wp-content/uploads/2016/11/NCP-2013-Study-Research-Results-1.pdf [https://perma.cc/L5FT-ALC9]. A recent study by the Data & Society Research Institute pegged the gender disparity as slightly less severe (finding that women were twice as likely as men to have someone threaten to expose nude photos of them online), but nevertheless found that a whopping 1 in 10 women under the age of 30 "have experienced threats of nonconsensual image sharing." DATA & SOCIETY RESEARCH INSTITUTE, NONCONSENUAL IMAGE SHARING: ONE IN 25 AMERICANS HAS BEEN A VICTIM OF "REVENGE PORN" 6 (2016), https://datasociety.net/pubs/oh/Nonconsensual_Image_Sharing_2016.pdf [https://perma.cc/XYL8-5WHK].
165. *See* John A. Humbach, The Constitution and Revenge Porn, 35 PACE L. REV. 215, 216 n.6 (2014) (noting that, although both men and women can be victims of revenge porn, gender-slanted phenomena such as slut-shaming can cause revenge porn to have a more pernicious impact on the lives of women) (quoting Emily Poole, Hey Girls, Do You Know? Slut-Shaming on the Internet Needs to Stop, 48 U.S.F. L. REV. 221, 222, 232–33 (2013) ("When it comes to sexual expression, females are denied the freedoms enjoyed by men" and "[t]he emotional harms caused by slut-shaming [including revenge porn] can follow a woman around for years, damage her self-perception, and possibly cause her either to dismiss her own sexuality or be labeled as easy.").
166. *See* Danielle Keats Citron & Mary Anne Franks, Criminalizing Revenge Porn, 49 WAKE FOREST L. REV. 345, 349 (2014) ("Current civil law remedies, including copyright remedies, are an ineffective deterrent to revenge porn. If they were [effective], we would likely not be witnessing the rise in reports of victimization as well as the proliferation in revenge porn websites.").
167. *See* Humbach, *supra* note 165, at 217 (asserting that present revenge porn laws "seem to fly directly in the face of the free speech and press guarantees of the First Amendment … [by constituting] unconstitutional content discrimination, viewpoint discrimination and speaker discrimination, not to mention prior restraint"). *But see* Citron & Franks, *supra* note 166, at 385 (arguing that targeted laws combating revenge porn would not violate the First Amendment because, inter alia, "[t]he nonconsensual disclosure of someone's sexually explicit images does little to advance expressive autonomy and self-governance and does much to undermine private self-expression"). California's recent anti-revenge-porn legislation, passed as SB 255 & SB 1255, has not yet undergone full constitutional scrutiny by a court. *See* Cal. Pen. Code § 647(j)(4).
168. Lawyers representing revenge porn victims recognize that the powerful legal and extrajudicial remedies afforded by copyright law make establishing ownership rights to the recordings in question the most potent means for achieving meaningful relief for their clients. For example, Elisa D'Amico, an attorney who cofounded the pro bono Cyber Civil Rights Legal Project, which provides legal assistance to victims of revenge porn, has flagged the importance of "obtaining the copyright to videos and photos that have been posted online without consent" as a means to get them removed from the internet. *See* Garcia, *supra* note 7.
169. *See* 17 U.S.C. § 512(c)(3)(A)(i) (requiring that a DMCA takedown notification come from someone acting on the authority of "the owner of an exclusive right that is allegedly infringed").

170. *See* 17 U.S.C. § 501(b) ("The legal or beneficial owner of an exclusive right under a copyright is entitled … to institute an action for any infringement of that particular right committed while he or she is the owner of it."); *McCormick* v. *Amir Constr. Inc.*, 279 Fed. App'x. 470, 471 (9th Cir. 2008) ("Section 501(b) [of the Copyright Act] grants standing to sue under the Copyright Act only to one owning a copyright [or an exclusive right thereto].") (citing *Silvers* v. *Sony Pictures Entm't, Inc.*, 402 F.3d 881, 885 (9th Cir. 2005)).
171. *See Michaels* v. *Internet Entm't Grp., Inc.*, 5 F. Supp. 2d 823, 828–29 (C.D. Cal. 1998).
172. *See id.* at 830–31. Anderson Lee intervened in the case and separately registered the copyright to the video, claiming that she was, at a minimum, a joint author. *See Private Home Tape*, Registration Nos. Pau002256130 (March 3, 1998) and Pau002313975 (July 20, 1998) (supplement to Pau002256130) (listing Michaels and Anderson Lee as "authors of a work made for hire"). Initially, Michaels registered the work as the sole author. *See Private Home Tape*, Registration No. Pau002215508 (Jan. 22, 1998).
173. Durst Declaration in Support of Ex Parte Application for Temporary Restraining Order, *Durst* v. *Gawker Media LLC*, No. CV05-1575 (C.D. Cal. Mar. 2, 2005).
174. *See* Stipulation and Order re Permanent Injunction at 3–4, *Durst* v. *Gawker Media LLC*, No. CV05-1575 (C.D. Cal. Mar. 2, 2005); Chris Harris, *Fred Durst Strikes Back After Sex Tape Leak*, MTV NEWS (Mar. 7, 2005), http://www.mtv.com/news/1497823/fred-durst-strikes-back-after-sex-tape-leak [https://perma.cc/E2CH-NKFS].
175. Even here, significant speaking roles in front of the camera continue to disproportionately go to men. Between 2014 and 2015, women represented 42 percent of all speaking characters on broadcast television programs. MARTHA M. LAUZEN, BOXED IN: PORTRAYALS OF FEMALE CHARACTERS AND EMPLOYMENT OF BEHIND-THE-SCENES WOMEN IN 2014-15 PRIME-TIME TELEVISION 2 (2015), http://womenintvfilm.sdsu.edu/files/2014-15_Boxed_In_Report.pdf [https://perma.cc/9JDY-G2R8]. Yet women only "comprised 22% of [all] protagonists featured in the top 100 domestic grossing films in 2015." MARTHA M. LAUZEN, IT'S A MAN'S (CELLULOID) WORLD: PORTRAYALS OF FEMALE CHARACTERS IN THE TOP 100 FILMS OF 2015 1 (2016) http://womenintvfilm.sdsu.edu/files/2015_Its_a_Mans_Celluloid_World_Report.pdf [https://perma.cc/6WPD-TTF4]. Furthermore, certain types of women (e.g., older women, women from minority racial groups) are disproportionately absent from the screen. *See id.*
176. MARTHA M. LAUZEN, THE CELLULOID CEILING: EMPLOYMENT OF BEHIND-THE-SCENES OF WOMEN ON TOP CROSSING U.S. FILMS IN 2023 3 (2023), https://womenintvfilm.sdsu.edu/wp-content/uploads/2024/01/2023-Celluloid-Ceiling-Report.pdf.
177. *Id.* at 2
178. Jeffrey Toobin, *Girls Behaving Badly*, NEW YORKER (May 30, 2005).
179. *Id.*
180. *See* ROBERT BRAUNEIS & DOTAN OLIAR, Copyright's Race, Gender and Age: A First Quantitative Look at Registrations 24 (2016).
181. *See id.* at 26.
182. *See* FRANTZ FANON, Black Skin, White Masks 90 (2008).
183. This reference to "body" includes the physical body as well as voices and other performances rendered through the body.
184. K. J. Greene, Copyright, Culture & Black Music: A Legacy of Unequal Protection, 21 HASTINGS COMM. & ENT. L. J. 339, 356–57 (1998).

185. *See* SIVA VAIDHYANATHAN, Copyrights and Copywrongs: The Rise of Intellectual Property and How It Threatens Creativity 117–48 (2001) (tracing the appropriation of blues music by rock 'n' roll artists over time); K. J. Greene, Intellectual Property at the Intersection of Race and Gender: Lady Sings the Blues, 16 AM. U. J. GENDER, SOC. POL'Y & L. 365, 371–74 (2008); K. J. Greene, "Copynorms," Black Cultural Production, and the Debate over African-American Reparations, 25 CARDOZO ARTS & ENT. L. J. 1179, 1193 (2008) ("The fleecing of Black artists was the basis of the success of the American music industry....").
186. *See* Greene, *Copyright, Culture & Black Music, supra* note 184, at 378 ("Perhaps the most taxing structural element of the copyright regime vis-a-vis Black artists has been the requirement of reducing works to a tangible form.").
187. *See* Gregory S. Donat, Fixing Fixation: A Copyright with Teeth for Improvisational Performers, 97 COLUM. L. REV. 1363, 1405 (1997) (arguing that copyright law "continues to cling needlessly to the fixation requirement, and does so to the detriment of whole classes of artists [including improvisational performers such as jazz musicians] and to the benefit of no one but the bootlegger").
188. *See, e.g.*, Greene, *Copyright, Culture & Black Music, supra* note 184, at 368 (arguing that, regrettably, the defining characteristic of black cultural production in the United States has been "its one-way direction – white performers obtaining economic and artistic benefits at the expense of minority innovators").
189. *Id.* at 377.
190. Emily Behzadi, Desettling Fixation, 102 N.C. L. REV. 865 (2024).
191. Greene, *Copyright, Culture & Black Music, supra* note 184, at 358–59.
192. *Id.* at 343.
193. *The Andy Warhol Foundation for the Visual Arts, Inc.* v. *Goldsmith*, No. 1:17-cv-02532 (S.D. N.Y. April 7, 2017).
194. *The Andy Warhol Foundation for the Visual Arts, Inc.* v. *Goldsmith*, 382 F. Supp. 3d 312 (S.D.N.Y. 2019).
195. *The Andy Warhol Foundation for the Visual Arts, Inc.* v. *Goldsmith*, 992 F.3d 99 (2d. Cir. 2021).
196. *The Andy Warhol Foundation for the Visual Arts, Inc.* v. *Goldsmith*, 598 U.S. 508 (2023).
197. Such case law includes *Cariou* v. *Prince*, 714 F.3d 694 (2013) and *Blanch* v. *Koons*, 396 F. Supp. 2d 476, 478 (S.D.N.Y. 2005), *aff'd*, 467 F.3d 244, 259 (2d Cir. 2006).
198. Of course, critics may view this as a dangerous slippery slope of the *Goldsmith* decision.
199. *Comedy III Productions, Inc.* v. *Gary Saderup, Inc.*, 25 Cal. 4th 387, 406 (2001).
200. *Id.*
201. Rosanna McLaughlin, *Emily Ratajkowski's 'The Cut' Essay and Why We Can't Buy Our Way Out of Today's Toxic Image Economy*, FRIEZE (Sep. 28, 2020), available at https://www.frieze.com/article/some-thoughts-emily-ratajkowskis-cut-essay.
202. The right of publicity might represent a countervailing force in this context, though it did not develop in earnest until the latter half of the twentieth century and it only limits the rights of a copyright holder in certain contexts, such as express commercial uses. *See* Mark Bartholomew, A Right Is Born: Celebrity, Property, and Postmodern Lawmaking, 44 CONN. L. REV. 301, 309–15 (2011) (charting the emergence and growing legal strength of the right of publicity, particularly from the 1950s onward). An interesting story could perhaps be told about the right of publicity's emergence as a counter to the male gaze that, perhaps not coincidentally, emerged at the same time that pushback against the male gaze first began during the rise of modern feminism.

2 TICK TICK ... BOOM!

1. *See Thomson* v. *Larson*, 147 F.3d 195, 197 (2d. Cir. 1998).
2. *Id.* 197–98.
3. *Id.* at 198.
4. *Id.*
5. *Id.*
6. *Id.* at 202.
7. *Id.* at 205.
8. *Id.*
9. For example, Jessica Litman argues:

   > All authorship is fertilized by the work of prior authors, and the echoes of old work in new work extend beyond ideas and concepts to a wealth of expressive details. Indeed, authorship *is* the transformation and recombination of expression into new molds, the recasting and revision of details into different shapes. What others have expressed, and the ways they have expressed it, are the essential building blocks of any creative medium. If an author is successful at what she does, then something she creates will alter the landscape a little. We may not know who she is, or how what she created has varied, if only slightly, the way things seem to look, but those who follow her will necessarily tread on a ground distorted by her vision. The use of the work of other authors in one's own work inheres in the authorship process.

   Jessica Litman, Copyright as Myth, 53 U. PITT. L. REV. 235, 243–44 (1991).
10. *See, e.g.*, Anne Barron, Copyright Law and the Claims of Art, 4 INTELL. PROP. Q. 368, 368 (2002) ("It has become commonplace of critical legal scholarship that copyright's primary social function is to give form to a 'Romantic' aesthetic; that the key doctrinal features of copyright law – especially the concept of authorship – have been crucially shaped by this aesthetic; and that the law of copyright is centrally oriented toward promoting forms of cultural production that comply with the core values of the Romantic movement."); Shubha Ghosh, Enlightening Identity and Copyright, 49 BUFF. L. REV. 1315, 1317 (2001) (noting that "[c]opyright law is premised on the assumption of the 'romantic author' – the lone genius that creates valuable expression"); Peter Jaszi, On the Author Effect: Contemporary Copyright and Collective Creativity, *in* THE CONSTRUCTION OF AUTHORSHIP: TEXTUAL APPROPRIATION IN LAW AND LITERATURE 29, 35 (Martha Woodmansee & Peter Jaszi eds., 1994) (positing that "[t]he instance of 'moral rights' is but one example of how the Romantic conception of 'authorship' is displaying a literally unprecedented measure of ideological autonomy in legal context").
11. *Nottage* v. *Jackson* [1883] 11 Q.B.D. 627 at 635 (Eng.).
12. *See Burrow-Giles Lithographic Co.* v. *Sarony*, 111 U.S. 53, 60 (1884) ("The question here presented is one of first impression under our Constitution, but an instructive case of the same class is that of *Nottage v. Jackson*....").
13. *Nottage* v. *Jackson* [1883] 11 Q.B.D. 627 at 627, 633 (Eng.).
14. *Id.* at 628.
15. *Id.*
16. *See generally id.*
17. *See id.* at 629–30.
18. *Id.* at 638. Interestingly, the *Nottage* decision served to invalidate the concept of works-made-for-hire under UK copyright law for many years. *See, e.g.*, Peter Jaszi, Toward a Theory of Copyright: The Metamorphoses of "Authorship," 1991 DUKE L. J. 455, 486–87

(1991) (noting how romantic Anglo-American notions of authorship, as epitomized by *Nottage*, cut against the recognition of a work-for-hire doctrine). This aspect of the *Nottage* holding was certainly not adopted in the United States, where works made for hire were, at a minimum, implicitly recognized by the Supreme Court in *Bleistein*. *See Bleistein* v. *Donaldson Lithographing Co.*, 188 U.S. 239, 248 (1903); *see also* I. T. Hardy, An Economic Understanding of Copyright Law's Work-Made-for-Hire Doctrine, 12 COLUM.-VLA J. L. & ARTS 181, 181 & n.1 (1987) (noting that the work-made-for-hire doctrine was first codified in the United States with the Copyright Act of 1909, *id.* at 181, but that the *Bleistein* decision gave the doctrine its first Supreme Court recognition, *id.* at 181 n.1).

19. *Nottage* v. *Jackson* [1883] 11 Q.B.D. 627 at 635 (Eng.) (Cotton LJ) ("In my opinion, 'author' involves originating, making, producing, as the inventive or master mind, the thing which is to be protected, whether it be a drawing, or a painting, or a photograph.").
20. *Nottage*, 11 Q.B.D. at 637 (Bowen LJ).
21. *Nottage*, 11 Q.B.D. at 632 (Brett MR).
22. Interestingly, Bowen rejected the idea that the authorship could vest in a single *corporate* body as a work-made-for-hire. *See Nottage*, 11 Q.B.D. at 638 (Bowen LJ).
23. *Id.* at 637–38. Bowen wrote, "[t]he person who drew this section evidently thought that in ninety-nine cases out of a hundred there would be only one author. The idea of there being two authors seems never to have presented itself to him; which shows that he took rather the notion I have formed in common with the rest of the Court as to the definition of the term…." *Id.* at 637. Brett also struggled with the contention that two individuals could be deemed authors: "Can two people be the authors of a photograph? It is difficult to say, but, if they are, for whose life is it to last?" he asked. *Nottage*, 11 Q.B.D. at 631 (Brett MR).
24. *Burrow-Giles Lithographic Co.* v. *Sarony*, 111 U.S. 53, 57–58 (1884) (emphasis added).
25. Oren Bracha, The Ideology of Authorship Revisited: Authors, Markets, and Liberal Values in Early American Copyright, 118 YALE L. J. 186, 188 (2008). *See also* Martha Woodmansee, The Genius and the Copyright: Economic and Legal Conditions of the Emergence of the "Author," 17 EIGHTEENTH-CENTURY STUD. 425, 427–30 (1984) (detailing the foundations of the romantic notion of the author as a genius creating ex nihilo on copyright law).
26. Bracha, *supra* note 25, at 188.
27. J. M. Costa & E. Heuvelink, Introduction: The Tomato Crop and Industry, *in* TOMATOES 1, 2 (Ep Heuvelink ed., 2005).
28. The tomato was often confused with the deadly nightshade. *Id.*
29. Jefferson was a pioneer in the growing of tomatoes. *See, e.g.*, Andrew F. Smith, The Tomato in America: Early History, Culture, and Cookery 28 (1994).
30. According to Silvano Serventi and Françoise Sabban, the "first concrete information concerning pasta products in Italy dates from the thirteenth or fourteenth century." SILVANO SERVENTI & FRANÇOISE SABBAN, Pasta: The Story of a Universal Food 10 (Antony Shugaar trans., Columbia University Press 2002) (2000).
31. As Harold McGee notes: "It's a story often told, and often refuted, that the medieval traveler Marco Polo found noodles in China and introduced them to Italy." Harold McGee, On Food and Cooking: The Science and Lore of the Kitchen 571 (Scribner 2004) (1984).
32. *See* Theopolis Fair, Asia and Latin America in the Context of World History, *in* ASIA IN WESTERN AND WORLD HISTORY 782, 787 (Ainslie T. Embree & Carol Gluck eds., 1997) (noting that "[b]efore 1492 black pepper was widely used, but native Americans used a totally unrelated plant of many colors, shapes and intensities…. The cooks of the subcontinent adopted these American peppers and cayennes and incorporated them into their dishes.").

33. K. Pushkaran, Genetic Diversity of Bananas in South India with Specific Reference to Kerala, *in* BANANAS AND FOOD SECURITY 199, 200 (Claudine Picq et al., eds., 1998).
34. *See* MICHAEL T. MURRAY, JOSEPH PIZZORNO & LARA PIZZORNO, The Encyclopedia of Healing Foods 224 (2005).
35. RICHARD M. JUANG, Africa and the Americas: Culture, Politics, and History 74 (2008) (noting that corn is native to the Americas and was introduced to Africa around 1500).
36. Roland Barthes, The Death of the Author, *in* Image, Music, Text 142, 146 (1977).
37. Christian G. Stallberg, Towards a New Paradigm in Justifying Copyright: An Universalistic-Transcendental Approach, 18 FORDHAM INTELL. PROP. MEDIA & ENT. L. J. 333, 337 (2007–2008).
38. Google Books and the related Hathi Trust digitization project faced steep opposition from major publishers. Ultimately, the federal courts decided that the digitization of the world's books – without authorization of rights holders – generally constituted fair use and could continue largely unabated. *See Authors Guild, Inc.* v. *HathiTrust*, 755 F.3d 87 (2d Cir. 2014); *Authors Guild, Inc.* v. *Google, Inc.*, 804 F.3d 202 (2d 2015).
39. In its most well-known form, *The Serenity Prayer* reads: "God grant me the serenity to accept / the things I cannot change/courage to change the things I can, / and wisdom to know the difference." Fred R. Shapiro, *Who Wrote the Serenity Prayer?*, YALE ALUMNI MAGAZINE, July–Aug. 2008, at 34, 36, available at http://www.yalealumnimagazine.com/issues/2008_07/serenity.html.
40. *Id.* at 35.
41. *Id.* at 35, 37–38. Interestingly, the prior versions of the *Prayer* unearthed by Shapiro were by women, most of whom were involved in volunteer or educational activity. Elisabeth Sifton, *It Takes a Master to Make a Masterpiece*, YALE ALUMNI MAG., July–Aug. 2008, at 40, *available at* http://www.yalealumnimagazine.com/articles/3416 [http://perma.cc/L6LN-GKFK].
42. Shapiro, *supra* note 39, at 39. Elisabeth Sifton, Niebuhr's daughter, has adamantly denied Shapiro's allegations. In an intervention entitled *It Takes a Master to Make a Masterpiece*, she argues, among other things, that the prayer must have come from a gifted practitioner from a particular theological context who could have only been her father. Sifton, *supra* note 41, at 40–41. Notably, the title of her article immediately plays into our most romantic notions of authorship, which seek to reduce creation to a lone genius rather than to the iterative and accretive contributions of many.
43. *See* WILLIAM V. PIETSCH, The Serenity Prayer Book (1992).
44. In 2009, Duke researcher Stephen Goranson found a citation to Niebuhr as the *Prayer*'s author contained in a Christian student newsletter published in 1937. Laurie Goodstein, *Serenity Prayer Skeptic Now Credits Niebuhr*, N.Y. TIMES, Nov. 28, 2009, at A11. Shapiro responded that "[t]he new evidence does not prove that Reinhold Niebuhr wrote [*The Serenity Prayer*], but it does significantly improve the likelihood that he was the originator," and that he would list the *Serenity Prayer* under Niebuhr's name in the next edition of *The Yale Book of Quotations*. *Id.*
45. This assumes he conformed to the strictures of the 1909 Copyright Act governing at the time and filed the necessary renewal to keep the copyright in effect.
46. 17 U.S.C. § 110(3) (immunizing from infringement liability any "performance of a nondramatic literary or musical work or of a dramatico-musical work of a religious nature, or display of a work, in the course of services at a place of worship or other religious assembly.").
47. *See* B. HAMILTON, Twelve Step Sponsorship: How It Works 125 (1996).
48. *See* Thomas F. Cotter, Gutenberg's Legacy: Copyright, Censorship, and Religious Pluralism, 91 CALIF. L. REV. 323, 335 n.47 (2003) ("In the United States, religious works

have constituted a significant portion of the works registered by copyright owners from the creation of federal copyright system in 1790.").

49. *See, e.g.*, *Worldwide Church of God* v. *Phila. Church of God, Inc.*, 227 F.3d 1110 (9th Cir. 2000) (reversing a district court's finding of fair use and holding that the reproduction and dissemination of a religious text entitled *Mystery of the Ages*, the copyright to which was held by the Worldwide Church of God, constituted copyright infringement by a splinter group using the text in the course of worship); *Religious Tech. Ctr.* v. *Henson*, No. 97-16160, 1999 WL 362837 (9th Cir. June 4, 1999) (affirming liability of defendant for copyright infringement of the Church of Scientology's work entitled *NOTs 34*); *Urantia Found* v. *Maaherra*, 895 F. Supp 1329 (D. Ariz. 1995) (rejecting defendant's First Amendment defense to plaintiff's claims of copyright infringement in religious works).
50. Kirby Ferguson, *Everything Is a Remix* Part 4: *System Failure*, EVERYTHING IS A REMIX (Feb. 16, 2012), http://everythingisaremix.info/blog/everything-is-a-remix-part-4 [http://perma.cc/K2TX-669J].
51. *Id.*
52. *See, e.g.*, *Aalmuhammed* v. *Lee*, 202 F.3d 1227, 1231 (9th Cir. 2000); *Childress* v. *Taylor*, 945 F.2d 500, 507 (2d Cir. 1991). *See also* Mary LaFrance, Authorship, Dominance, and the Captive Collaborator: Preserving the Rights of Joint Authors, 50 EMORY L. J. 193, 200 (2001) (arguing that courts have privileged intention over creative effort in formulating the joint authorship doctrine).
53. *See, e.g.*, *Fisher* v. *Brooker* [2009] UKHL 41, [80–81] (granting former Procol Harum organist Matthew Fisher a 40 percent interest in the copyright to *A Whiter Shade of Pale* based on his composition of organ parts for the song).
54. *See* Copyright Act 1956, 4 & 5 Eliz. 2, c. 74, § 11(3) (U.K.) (defining a "work of joint authorship" as "a work produced by the collaboration of two or more authors in which the contribution of each author is not separate from the contribution of the other author or authors"). *See also* *Beckingham* v. *Hodgens* [2002] EWCA 143, [49] (Eng.) (expressly rejecting the view that the United Kingdom's Copyright Act of 1956 "requires, as one of the elements of joint authorship, the existence of a common intention as to joint authorship").
55. *See* David M. Liston, Songwriter, Side Musician, or Sucker?: The Challenge of Distinguishing Composers from Contributors Under U.S. Copyright Law and the Lessons of a Famous British Case, 65 RUTGERS L. REV. 891, 911 (2013) ("It must be emphasized that United Kingdom copyright law … does not require mutual intent on the part of the alleged coauthors in order to find a work of joint authorship.").
56. *See* 17 U.S.C. § 101.
57. *See, e.g.*, Shyamkrishna Balganesh, Unplanned Coauthorship, 100 Va. L. Rev. 1683, 1699–700 (2014) ("While intention certainly entailed a scrutiny of the parties' state of mind – either subjective or objective – the legislative history was silent on the question of what the intention needed to be directed at to meet the definition's requirement. Was it sufficient if the parties evinced an intention to collaborate in the production of the work? Or did they need to additionally carry an intention to become coauthors as a legal matter, by producing a work of joint authorship and recognizing its consequences? Not surprisingly, courts have struggled to answer these questions – despite their continuing emphasis on the idea of intention.").
58. *Id.* In addition, intent could be read in either subjective or objective terms. On this issue, courts split. The Ninth Circuit has adopted a purely objective intent standard, *see* *Aalmuhammed* v. *Lee*, 202 F.3d 1227, 1234 (9th Cir. 2000) ("[P]utative coauthors make objective manifestations of a shared intent to be coauthors, as by denoting the authorship

of *The Pirates of Penzance* as 'Gilbert and Sullivan.' … [W]ere the mutual intent to be determined by subjective intent, it could become an instrument of fraud….”). However, the Second Circuit has adopted a more mixed standard that gives heavy consideration to subjective intent, *see Childress* v. *Taylor*, 945 F.2d 500, 507–508 (2d Cir. 1991) (holding that all participants must view themselves as joint authors); *Thomson* v. *Larson*, 147 F.3d 195, 201 (2d Cir. 1998) (“[C]o-authorship intent does not turn solely on the parties' own words or professed state of mind.”), as has the Seventh Circuit, *see Erickson* v. *Trinity Theatre, Inc.*, 13 F.3d 1061, 1068–69 (7th Cir. 1994). Some observers have argued that both the legislative history of the 1976 Copyright Act and the “common design” jurisprudence that preceded it suggest that courts should be properly using an objective, rather than subjective, standard when evaluating joint authorship claims. *See, e.g.*, Therese M. Brady, Manifest Intent and Copyrightability: The Destiny of Joint Authorship, 17 FORDHAM URB. L. J. 257, 257–58 (1989) (noting that, among other things, “predicating these property rights on state of mind, when actions manifest the opposite, deprives authors of constitutional rights”).

59. *See, e.g.*, JAMES BOYLE, Shamans, Software and Spleens: Law and the Construction of the Information Society 51–60 (1997). As various commentators have noted, the idea of the “master mind” is a key concept in the romantic conception of authorship. *See* James Boyle, The Search for an Author: Shakespeare and the Framers, 37 AM. U. L. REV. 625, 629 (1988); Peter Jaszi, *supra* note 18, at 455–63.
60. Roberta Rosenthal Kwall, Author-Stories: Narrative's Implications for Moral Rights and Copyright's Joint Authorship Doctrine, 75 S. CAL. L. REV. 1, 44–45 (2001).
61. *Aalmuhammed*, 202 F.3d at 1232.
62. *Id.*
63. *Childress* v. *Taylor*, 945 F.2d 500, 508–509 (2d Cir. 1991).
64. *Id.* at 504. In part, such a tack might be influenced by the presumed alternative: that recognition of joint authorship would necessarily grant the nondominant author a 50 percent share in the work, including all profits generated therefrom. *See, e.g.*, *Thomson* v. *Larson*, 147 F.3d 195, 201 (2d Cir. 1998) (“[S]ince coauthors are afforded equal rights in the co-authored work, the 'equal sharing of rights should be reserved for relationships in which all participants fully intend to be joint author.'”) (citing *Childress*, 945 F.2d at 509). As Mary LaFrance notes, many courts incorrectly presume that co-authorship creates a duty to split profits evenly among co-authors. *See* LaFrance, *supra* note 52, at 194; *see also* 1–6 NIMMER ON COPYRIGHT § 6.08 (2016) (“In the absence of agreement to the contrary, the traditional approach has been that all joint authors share equally in the ownership of the joint author … even when it is clear that their respective contributions to the joint work are not equal.”). But such a result is not at all dictated by law. A 50-50 split is a presumption, at best; courts are, in fact, free to allocate co-authorship shares along different lines if it comports with the parties' intention or better reflects the “relative proportion [of] their individual [creative] contributions” to the final work. *See* 1–6 NIMMER ON COPYRIGHT § 6.08 (2016); *see also* 17 U.S.C. § 201(a) (dictating no particular allocation of shares for co-authors).
65. LaFrance, *supra* note 52, at 223–24.
66. After all, dominant authors can easily contract away such a problem ex ante (and, potentially, even ex post) by using their leverage to have weaker parties sign work-made-for-hire agreements and/or assignments of any conceivable copyright interest they might possess. *See Copyright Law Revision: Hearings on H.R. 4347, H.R. 5680, H.R. 6831, H.R. 6835 Before Subcomm. No. 3 of the Comm. on the Judiciary, 89th Cong. 1717 (1965) (statement of John Schulman), reprinted in 7 OMNIBUS COPYRIGHT REVISION HISTORY 1717 (George S. Grossman ed., 2001) [hereinafter “Schulman Statement”].*

67. *See* Brief for Professors Shyam Balganeshkrishna et al. as Amici Curiae in Support of Neither Party at 13, *Garcia* v. *Google, Inc.*, 786 F.3d 733 (2015) (No. 12-57302) ("The master-mind concept narrows the range of joint authors down to one or a few individuals for administrative convenience or to avoid unjustified windfalls, not out of fidelity to legislative intent.").
68. Jaszi, *supra* note 18, at 459.
69. *See id.* at 456.
70. *See id.*
71. LaFrance, *supra* note 52, at 224. The Ninth Circuit has acknowledged this problem and clarified that the intent requirement should be read objectively, rather than subjectively. *See Aalmuhammed* v. *Lee*, 202 F.3d 1227, 1234 (9th Cir. 2000) ("We say objective manifestations because, were the mutual intent to be determined by subjective intent, it could become an instrument of fraud, were one coauthor to hide from the other an intention to take sole credit for the work.").
72. *See* Schulman Statement, *supra* note 66.
73. The law already grants broad powers to those with superior bargaining power; there appears to be no need to concoct a joint-authorship test that doubles the impact of such power disparities, especially when those with greater leverage fail to secure appropriate rights when they have a chance. *See* Schulman Statement, *supra* note 66.
74. *Aalmuhammed*, 202 F.3d at 1234 (noting that "putative coauthors make objective manifestations of a shared intent to be coauthors, as by denoting the authorship of *The Pirates of Penzance* as 'Gilbert and Sullivan'").
75. *Childress* v. *Taylor*, 945 F.2d 500, 508 (2d Cir. 1991); *Thomson*, 147 F.3d at 203. With the *Aalmuhammed* decision, the Ninth Circuit expressly elevated "control" as the most important determining factor in a joint authorship determination. *Aalmuhammed*, 202 F.3d at 1234. Yet, as Shyamkrishna Balganesh, Justin Hughes, Peter Menell, and David Nimmer have argued, "[t]he fact that some members of the creative enterprise have more power or control than others does not categorically exclude less powerful creative collaborators from joint authorship." *See* Brief of Amici Curiae Professors Shyamkrishna Balganesh et al., *supra* note 67, at 17.
76. *See, e.g.*, Kwall, *supra* note 60, at 52 n.238 (quoting Lynn Thomson, *The Rewards of Collaboration, Parabasis*, J.A.S.K. THEATER PROJECTS, at 12 (Spring 1997) (Thomson, in describing her litigation experience over her claims to joint authorship of *Rent*, writes that "[t]he primary experience of the lawsuit, especially in the Second Circuit and with the strangeness of the *Childress* decision, was that the law – or perhaps, the interpretation and application of the law – was remote from the truth of what happened to me, remote from the truth of how, in fact, art is actually made at the end of the century. What happens 'in the room' and what is protected in the law are so unconnected.")).
77. Kwall, *supra* note 60, at 55.
78. As Kwall contends, women and foreign-born individuals are particularly disadvantaged under such situations. *Id.* at 54 n.249 ("[T]o the extent nondominant authors are women or foreign born individuals, the bargaining power may be further eroded.").
79. Kwall, *supra* note 60, at 44–45.
80. *Id.* at 52 n.238 (quoting Lynn Thomson, *The Rewards of Collaboration, Parabasis*, J.A.S.K. THEATER PROJECTS, at 12 (Spring 1997).
81. Ann Bartow, Fair Use and the Fairer Sex: Gender, Feminism, and Copyright Law, 14 AM. U. J. GENDER SOC. POL'Y & L. 551, 552 (2006).
82. *See id.* at 552 n.1.
83. Bartow, *supra* note 81, at 578.

84. VIRGINIA WOOLF, A Room of One's Own 51 (1929).
85. There is good reason to think that such differences may be culturally produced, rather than inherent, particularly in societies that reward collaborative activities by women while prizing male autonomy and independence. *See infra*, notes 81–84.
86. Anna Abraham, Gender and Creativity: An Overview of Psychological and Neuroscientific Literature, 10 BRAIN IMAGING AND BEHAV. 609, 614 (2016).
87. Mark A. Runco et al., Gender and Creativity, *in* HANDBOOK OF GENDER RESEARCH IN PSYCHOLOGY, VOLUME 1: GENDER RESEARCH IN GENERAL AND EXPERIMENTAL PSYCHOLOGY 344, 351 (Joan C. Chrisler & Donald R. McCreary eds., 2015).
88. *See* Sandra W. Russ, Gender Differences in Primary Process Thinking and Creativity, *in* THE PSYCHODYNAMICS OF GENDER AND GENDER ROLE 70–73 (Robert F. Bornstein & Joseph M. Masling eds., 2002).
89. *See* Julia B. Bear & Anita Williams Woolley, The Role of Gender in Team Collaboration and Performance, 36 INTERDISCIPLINARY SCIENCE REVIEWS 146, 148 (2011).
90. Kwall, *supra* note 60, at 54 (quoting Lynn Thomson, … *And an Artist Is an Artist Is an Artist*, AM. THEATRE, Sept. 1998, at 8).
91. Bartow, *supra* note 81, at 578.
92. Kwall, *supra* note 60, at 54 (quoting Lynn Thomson, … *And an Artist Is an Artist Is an Artist*, AM. THEATRE, Sept. 1998, at 8).
93. *See* Kwall, *supra* note 60, at 54 (quoting Lynn Thomson, *To My Colleagues*, LITERARY MANAGERS & DRAMATURGS AM. REV., Aug. 6, 1997, at 4 (quoting the trial judge in *Thomson* v. *Larson* as saying that "[i]t seems equally clear that we wouldn't be here if [Jonathan Larson] were alive because [Lynn Thomson's] name might well be credited on the title page and an economic arrangement arguably more equitable would have been reached")).
94. Nzingha Hooker, Something More Than Intent: Redefining Joint Authorship to Include America's Native Communities, 41 AIPLA Q.J. 771, 795 (2013).
95. LAUREN R. LENHART, NORMATIVE NOTIONS OF AUTHORSHIP AND PARTICIPATION IN THE ISOCIETY (2009), https://www.ideals.illinois.edu/bitstream/handle/2142/15228/Notions_of_Authorship1.pdf [https://perma.cc/8AM8-8B8Z]. As an Australian court considering protection for Aboriginal art noted, "[t]he right to create paintings and other artworks depicting creation and dreaming stories, and to use pre-existing designs and well recognised totems of the clan, resides in the traditional owners (or custodians) of the stories or images. Usually that right will not be with only one person, but with a group of people…." *Milpurrurru* v. *Indofurn Pty. Ltd.* (1994) 54 F.C.R. 240, 245 (Austl.).
96. *See, e.g.*, SAM RICKETSON, The Berne Convention for the Protection of Literary and Artistic Works: 1886–1986 313 (1987) (noting that it is unlikely that copyright protection extends under the Berne regime to works of folklore that are authored by the community); Christine Haight Farley, Protecting Folklore of Indigenous Peoples: Is Intellectual Property the Answer?, 30 CONN. L. REV. 1, 30–31 (1997) (noting that among other challenges to the protection of folklore under the United States Copyright Act and the copyright laws of other nations is the fact that "most artwork is actually executed by a group. The making of art in the indigenous community is not the lonely, secluded, individual process idealized in the west, but instead a group process in which many people participate at various levels…. This custom poses a problem for copyright law since copyright law vests the rights in the one who executes the work."); Michael Newcity, Protecting the Traditional Knowledge and Cultural Expressions of Russia's "Numerically-Small" Indigenous Peoples: What Has Been Done, What Remains to Be Done, 15 TEX. WESLEYAN L. REV. 357, 397 (2009) ("The justification for the exclusion of folklore from

the list of works eligible for protection is simply that, though they would satisfy other criteria – e.g., creativity – these works are not created by a single author or group of coauthors, but are created by an entire ethnic group on the basis of its myths, legends, and beliefs."); *see generally* MICHAEL F. BROWN, WHO OWNS NATIVE CULTURE? (2003) (exploring the difficulties faced by indigenous communities in defending their cultural creations).

97. It is worth noting that Cindy Lee Garcia "unequivocally disclaim[ed] joint authorship of the film" as part of her litigation against Google. *Garcia* v. *Google, Inc.*, 786 F.3d 733, 742 (9th Cir. 2015) (en banc). Garcia likely elected this position for strategic reasons as joint authorship would not have achieved her chief goal: enjoining exploitation of the work by her putative co-author. *See Ashton-Tate Corp.* v. *Ross*, 916 F.2d 516, 522 (9th Cir. 1990) (noting that copyright law allows each co-author to exploit a work so long as he/she accounts for profits to other co-authors). However, even if her goal had been noninjunctive, any joint authorship claim she would have advanced would have been dead on arrival: it was indisputable that the "dominant" author – the director of the work – had no intent to be a co-author with her.
98. *See, e.g., id.*
99. Rebecca Tushnet, Naming Rights: Attribution and Law, 2007 Utah L. Rev. 789, 791 (2007).
100. Jane C. Ginsburg, The Most Moral of Rights: The Right to Be Recognized as the Author of One's Work, 8 Geo. Mason J. Int'l Com. L. 44, 45 (2016).
101. 17 U.S.C. § 106; *see also* John Tehranian, Parchment, Pixels, and Personsood: User Rights and the IP (Identity Politics) of IP (Intellectual Property), 82 U. Colo. L. Rev. 1, 38–39 (2011).
102. Jorge Luis Borges, The Library of Babel, *in* Collected Fictions 112, 112–18 (Andrew Hurley trans., Viking Penguin 1998).
103. PAUL GOLDSTEIN, Copyright's Highway: From Gutenberg to the Celestial Jukebox 28 (Stanford University Press 2003) (1994) (promoting Goldstein's concept of the "celestial jukebox," where digital technologies will enable the efficient and seamless distribution of all manner of entertainment products and informational works to consumers around the world with the touch of a button); Paul Goldstein, Copyright in the New Information Age, 40 Cath. U. L. Rev. 829, 829–30 (1991) (referring, for the first time, to Goldstein's prescient concept of the "celestial jukebox," borrowed from an unknown poet, where, "[s]ooner than you expect, systems may evolve that can store a digital version of every motion picture and sound recording ever created, enabling individuals around the world to summon up these works on command, through satellite or some yet unforeseen communications vehicle"); *see also* COMM. ON THE JUDICIARY, DIGITAL PERFORMANCE RIGHT IN SOUND RECORDINGS ACT OF 1995, H.R. REP. NO. 104-274 at 5–9, 12–13 (1st Sess. 1995) (referencing the concept of the "celestial jukebox" whereby "interactive services … enable a member of the public to receive, on request, a digital transmission of the particular recording that [that] person wants to hear").
104. Mike Glyer, *Eric Flint (1947–2022)*, FILE 770 (July 17, 2022), https://file770.com/eric-flint-1947-2022 [https://perma.cc/V6RR-BWSU] (quoting Eric Flint).
105. Besides illuminating the inadequacies of our present authorial regime, these two incidents also reveal that this Article's author may be prone to exhibiting disturbing signs of both pettiness and delusionality. I implore you to excuse these character flaws (often attributed to "artistic" mentalities) and consider the arguments presented in this Article on their merits and without the weight of the author's considerable baggage.
106. While entirely possible, for purposes of sanity and the preservation of self-worth, I shall ignore this prospect.

107. Laura A. Heymann, The Trademark/Copyright Divide, 60 SMU L. Rev. 55, 95 (2007).
108. *Id.* at 96.
109. *See* Christopher Jon Sprigman, Christopher Buccafusco & Zachary Burns, What's a Name Worth?: Experimental Tests of the Value of Attribution in Intellectual Property, 93 B. U. L. Rev. 1389, 1391 n.1 (2013) (detailing the studies in recent years establishing the general sense of attribution's value to creatives).
110. 17 U.S.C. § 201(a) (vesting, as a default rule, copyright in the author of a work).
111. *Id.* § 106 (detailing the exclusive rights enjoyed by copyright holders).
112. *Id.* § 302(a) (granting a term of protection of the lifetime of an author plus seventy years to any work created by an individual and not as a work made for hire).
113. *See, e.g.*, Lawrence Lessig, Free Culture: The Nature and Future of Creativity 8 (2004) (using the term "permission culture" to refer to the way in which heavy enforcement of intellectual property rights has impaired the ability of the public to create and share culture).
114. *See* Eric E. Johnson, The Economics and Sociality of Sharing Intellectual Property Rights, 94 B. U. L. Rev. 1935, 1980 (2014) (noting the existence of 172 million pages with Creative Commons licenses by fall 2008).
115. *Id.* at 1980–81. As Jessica Silbey also notes, "To cultivate reputation, interviewees describe widely and freely sharing their work despite IP protection that controls access to maximize rent. IP's blunt protections disserve the multifaceted and contextually specific nature of reputational interests." Jessica Silbey, The Eureka Myth: Creators, Innovators, and Everyday Intellectual Property 151 (2015).
116. *See* Anupam Chander & Madhavi Sunder, The Romance of the Public Domain, 92 Calif. L. Rev. 1331, 1361 (2004) (finding that just 2 percent of Creative Commons works do not require proper attribution as a condition of use); Glenn Otis Brown, *Announcing (and Explaining) Our New 2.0 Licenses*, Creative Commons (May 25, 2004), http://creativecommons.org/weblog/entry/4216 [https://perma.cc/E39L-WKRM] (noting that 97–98 percent of Creative Commons contributors chose to preserve their right to attribution). More recent data on Creative Commons licenses suggests that these numbers have remained relatively consistent over time. A 2014 report found that, while 76 percent of Creative Commons contributors allow uncompensated adaptations of their work and 58 percent allow commercial use of their works, just 4 percent waive attribution. *See State of the Commons*, Creative Commons (2014), https://web.archive.org/web/20151104081140/; https://stateof.creativecommons.org/report [https://perma.cc/7QLK-K3M8]. Thus, while all Creative Commons licenses allow some kind of use that might otherwise be infringing, 96 percent condition any use on attribution. *See id.*
117. *See* Johnson, *supra* note 114, at 1937 ("Sharing is ubiquitous in our world, yet it is something of a wallflower in the scholarly literature.").
118. *See id. at* 1937–39.
119. *Id.* at 1938; *see also* Greg Lastowka, Digital Attribution: Copyright and the Right to Credit, 87 B. U. L. Rev. 41, 59 (2007) (arguing that "prestige, not money drives open-source production" and that "standard Free and Open-Source Software (F/OSS) licenses are characterized by a trade of standard copyright protections for authorial attribution").
120. Sprigman et al., *supra* note 109, at 1408–11. Indeed, subjects were willing to drop their payment demand by some 35 percent (from $202.26 to $132.28), on average, when attribution was provided. *See id.*
121. *See id.* at 1415 (finding that "professional and advanced amateur photographers value attribution far more than do … casual snapshooters").

122. *Id.* at 1417.
123. Silbey's ethnographic study is based on "fifty face-to-face interviews that [she] conducted with a wide range of scientists, engineers, musicians and artists, their business associates, and intellectual property lawyers over the course of four years … [as] part of an effort to learn more about the intersection of intellectual property law on the one hand, and creative and innovative work on the other." SILBEY, *supra* note 115, at 4.
124. *See id.* at 149, 166–69 (2015) (detailing, among other things, how her interviewees would commonly refer to their creative or innovative output in familial terms (as offspring), as priceless, or as a key part of their identity).
125. *Id.* at 166.
126. Roman Mars, *The Real Book*, 99% Invisible Podcast (Apr. 6, 2021), https://99percentinvisible.org/episode/the-real-book/transcript.
127. *Id.*
128. Catherine L. Fisk, Credit Where It's Due: The Law and Norms of Attribution, 95 GEO. L. J. 49 (2006).
129. *Id* at 50, 52.
130. *See* Stephanie Plamondon Bair, Rational Faith: The Utility of Fairness in Copyright, 97 B. U. L. REV. 1487, 1519 (2017).
131. *See* Onne Janssen, Job Demands, Perceptions of Effort-Reward Fairness and Innovative Work Behaviour, 73 J. OCCUPATIONAL & ORGANIZATIONAL PSYCH. 287, 295 (2000).
132. TERESA AMABILE & STEVEN KRAMER, THE PROGRESS PRINCIPLE: USING SMALL WINS TO IGNITE JOY, ENGAGEMENT, AND CREATIVITY AT WORK 245 (2011).
133. For example, in her taxonomy of attribution, Fisk identifies four functions served by crediting: (1) a nonmonetary incentive to spur further creativity; (2) a mechanism by which to lay blame for failure; (3) a branding purpose that facilitates consumption decisions; and (4) a humanizing function for creative output. *See* Fisk, *supra* note 128. Three of these four functions – discipline, branding, and humanization – focus on the value that attribution provides to nonauthors.
134. *Id.* at 50.
135. To put it in reverse terms, crediting also promotes a "discipline" function – a mechanism by which to "allocate blame." *Id.* at 61.
136. Laura A. Heymann, The Birth of the Authornym: Authorship, Pseudonymity, and Trademark Law, 80 NOTRE DAME L. REV. 1377, 1373 n.1 (2005) (quoting *Qualitex Co.* v. *Jacobson Prods. Co.*, 514 U.S. 159, 163–64 (1995)).
137. *Id.* at 1446.
138. *Id.* at 1448–49.
139. *See* Plamondon Bair, *supra* note 130, at 1507 ("Given the widespread belief that fairness plays a role in intellectual property law, we may add efficiency to our system by openly acknowledging this role.").
140. Fisk, *supra* note 128, at 65.
141. Some might criticize this practice as blatant masquerading, akin to massive agricultural conglomerates using family farmers to put a sympathetic face on their efforts to lobby Congress for government subsidies. On the other hand, in some instances, the protections sought by entertainment companies can inure to the benefit of individual artists as well.
142. *See* Peter Kafka, *The Music Industry Signs Up Taylor Swift and U2 in Its Fight against YouTube*, VOX (June 20, 2016, 5:45 AM), https://www.vox.com/2016/6/20/11974514/taylor-swift-youtube-dmca-music-letter [https://perma.cc/2HGK-FCKE]. The letter also sought to increase public awareness of the role of the Digital Millennium Copyright

Act (DMCA) (and, in particular, its safe harbor) in the current situation and to lay the foundation for congressional reform by noting that the DMCA "was written and passed in an era that is technologically out-of-date compared to the era in which we live. It has allowed major tech companies to grow and generate huge profits by creating ease of use for consumers to carry out almost every recorded song in history in their pocket via a smartphone, while songwriters' and artists' earnings continue to diminish." Anthony Ha, *Taylor Swift and Other Big Names Join the Music Industry's Campaign against YouTube*, TechCrunch (June 20, 2016, 2:33 PM), https://techcrunch.com/2016/06/20/taylor-swift-dmca-letter [https://perma.cc/JSU6-9NUG] (quoting the letter).

143. *See* Patrick Goldstein, *Hollywood Deals with Piracy, A Wary Eye on CDs*, L.A. Times (Sept. 9, 2003, 12:00 AM), https://www.latimes.com/archives/la-xpm-2003-sep-09-et-gold9-story.html [https://perma.cc/6L3K-9GSR] (detailing the anti-piracy campaign by the Motion Picture Association and noting the role of David Goldstein, a set painter, in the spots).
144. Silbey, *supra* note 115, at 146.
145. 17 U.S.C. § 106A(a)(1)(A)–(B).
146. *Id.* § 412 (providing that "[i]n any action under this title, ***other than an action brought for a violation of the rights of the author under*** section 106A(a) … no award of statutory damages or of attorney's fees … shall be made" if the infringement occurred before registration, unless registration occurred within three months after first publication of the work) (emphasis added).
147. *Id.* § 106A. "Visual arts" are defined in 17 U.S.C. § 101.
148. *Id.* § 101.
149. *Id.* § 101 ("A work of visual art does not include … any … motion picture or other audiovisual work.").
150. *Id.*
151. *Id.* ("A work of visual art does not include … any work made for hire.").
152. *Id.*
153. *Id.* § 1202(c)(2)–(3) (defining CMI as including "[t]he name of, and other identifying information about, the author of a work" and "[t]he name of, and other identifying information about, the copyright owner of the work, including the information set forth in a notice of copyright" when "conveyed in connection with copies or phonorecords of a work or performances or displays of a work").
154. *Id.* § 1202(a).
155. *Id.* § 1202(b)(1).
156. *Id.* § 1202(a).
157. *Id.* § 1202(b)(1).
158. Secondary liability is another matter. Knowledge is an essential element of any claim for contributory liability. *See A&M Recs., Inc.* v. *Napster, Inc.*, 239 F.3d 1004, 1020 (9th Cir. 2001) (noting that "contributory liability requires that a secondary infringer 'know or have reason to know' of direct infringement" (citations omitted)).
159. It is an axiomatic principle of copyright law that infringement constitutes a strict liability tort. *See, e.g.*, *Jacobs* v. *Memphis Convention & Visitors Bureau*, 710 F. Supp. 2d 663, 678 n.21 (W.D. Tenn. 2010) ("Copyright infringement, however, is at its core a strict liability cause of action, and copyright law imposes liability even in the absence of an intent to infringe the rights of the copyright holder."); *Faulkner* v. *Nat'l Geographic Soc.*, 576 F. Supp. 2d 609, 613 (S.D.N.Y. 2008) ("Copyright infringement is a strict liability wrong in the sense that a plaintiff need not prove wrongful intent or culpability in order to prevail."); *Educ. Testing Serv.* v. *Simon*, 95 F. Supp. 2d 1081, 1087 (C.D. Cal. 1999) (noting

copyright infringement "is a strict liability tort"); *Gener-Villar* v. *Adcom Grp., Inc.*, 509 F. Supp 2d 177, 124 (D.P.R. 2007) ("[T]he Copyright Act is a strict liability regime under which any infringer, whether innocent or intentional, is liable.").

160. Although state of mind never impacts the liability calculus for direct infringement claims, it can impact damages awards. While actual damages are not mitigated in any way by a defense of innocent infringement, statutory damages can be. *See* 17 U.S.C. § 504(c); *Fitzgerald Publ'g Co.* v. *Baylor Publ'g Co.*, 807 F.2d 1110, 1113 (2d Cir. 1986) ("Even an innocent infringer is liable for infringement.... Innocence is only significant to a trial court when it fixes statutory damages, which is a remedy equitable in nature."); *see also* R. Anthony Reese, Innocent Infringement in U.S. Copyright Law: A History, 30 Colum. J.L. & Arts 133, 182–83 (2007) (noting the declining value of the innocent infringement defense through the course of American copyright history).

161. One might argue that section 1202 actually has a triple scienter requirement, as the knowledge component has two independent criteria that must be met: "(1) knowledge of the *existence* of copyright management information and (2) knowledge that the copyright management information *has been removed or altered.*" *Falkner* v. *Gen. Motors LLC*, 393 F. Supp. 3d 927, 939 (C.D. Cal. 2018).

162. 17 U.S.C. § 1202(c).

163. *See, e.g., Textile Secrets Int'l, Inc.* v. *Ya-Ya Brand Inc.*, 524 F. Supp. 2d 1184, 1201 (C.D. Cal. 2007) (finding that section 1202 was not "intended to apply to circumstances that have no relation to the Internet, electronic commerce, automated copyright protections or management systems, public registers, or other technological measures or processes as contemplated in the DMCA as a whole"); *IQ Grp., Ltd.* v. *Wiesner Publ'g, LLC*, 409 F. Supp. 2d 587, 597 (D.N.J. 2006) (finding that section 1202 "should not be construed to cover copyright management performed by people, which is covered by the Copyright Act, as it preceded the DMCA; it should be construed to protect copyright management performed by the technological measures of automated systems"). *But see Murphy* v. *Millennium Radio Grp. LLC*, 650 F.3d 295, 305 (3d Cir. 2011) (rejecting the logic of *IQ Group* and *Textile Secrets* and holding that section 1202 claims are "*not* restricted to the content of 'automated copyright protection or management systems'" and "potentially lie[] whenever [CMI] is falsified or removed, regardless of the form in which that [CMI] is conveyed," whether digital or not).

164. *Merideth* v. *Chi. Trib. Co.*, No. 12 C 7961, 2014 U.S. Dist. LEXIS 2346, at *7–8 (N.D. Ill. Jan. 9, 2014).

165. This is particularly true prediscovery and yet, with the "plausibility" pleading standards of *Iqbal* and *Twombly*, *see Ashcroft* v. *Iqbal*, 556 U.S. 662, 678 (2009); *Bell Atl. Corp.* v. *Twombly*, 550 U.S. 544, 556 (2007), courts will routinely dismiss section 1202 claims at the Rule 12 stage – prior to allowing discovery, *see, e.g., Spinelli* v. *Nat'l Football League*, 903 F.3d 185, 204–205 (2d Cir. 2018) (affirming dismissal of section 1202 removal claim on the grounds that the complaint failed to identify specific instances where the original photograph which the defendant accessed contained CMI and where said CMI was then removed by the defendant).

166. *See, e.g., Schiffer Publ'g, Ltd.*, v. *Chronicle Books*, LLC, No. 03-4962, 2004 U.S. Dist. LEXIS 23052, at *45 (E.D. Pa. Nov. 12, 2004) (holding that a plaintiff's subjective belief that the disputed work was not under copyright protection precluded imposition of liability under section 1202).

167. *See, e.g., William Wade Waller Co.* v. *Nexstar Broad., Inc.*, No. 4-10-CV-00764 GTE, 2011 U.S. Dist. LEXIS 72803, at *12–13 (E.D. Ark. July 6, 2011) (granting summary judgment to the defendants on a section 1202 claim since the intentional cropping of a

copyright notice from an image was insufficient to show that the defendant had acted with intent to "induce, enable, facilitate or conceal infringement").

168. *See, e.g.*, *Chevrestt* v. *Am. Media, Inc.*, 204 F. Supp. 3d 629, 632 (S.D.N.Y. 2016) (granting a defendant's motion to dismiss since "there are no factual allegations supporting an inference that [the defendant]'s CMI alteration or removal was done intentionally"); *Stevens* v. *Corelogic, Inc.*, 194 F. Supp. 3d 1046, 1052–53 (S.D. Cal. 2016) (granting summary judgment to the defendants on the plaintiff's section 1202 claims on the grounds that "[the p]laintiffs present no evidence that [the defendant] intentionally removed CMI" and that "[the p]laintiffs fail to provide any evidence that [the defendant] knew or had reasonable grounds to know that the removal of CMI in the metadata would lead to copyright infringement"); *Kelly* v. *Arriba Soft Corp.*, 77 F. Supp. 2d 1116, 1122 (C.D. Cal. 1999) (granting summary judgment to the defendant on the plaintiff's section 1202 claims on the grounds that, *inter alia*, "[the p]laintiff has not offered any evidence showing [the d]efendant's actions were intentional, rather than merely an unintended side effect").

169. *Cf. Sid Avery & Assocs., Inc.* v. *Pixels.com*, LLC, 479 F. Supp. 3d 859, 870–71 (C.D. Cal. 2020) (finding that allowing contributors to place watermarks containing false CMI on images contained on a network was insufficient to form the basis for section 1202 claim against the network operator since the allowance of such watermarks could be for reasons other than to "induce, enable, facilitate, or conceal infringement").

170. 15 U.S.C. § 1125(a)(1).

171. 2 J. Thomas McCarthy, Trademarks and Unfair Competition § 25.1, at 170 (1973).

172. *Smith* v. *Montoro*, 648 F.2d 602, 606–607 (9th Cir. 1981).

173. *Id.* at 607. The court recognized that was particularly the case in the film industry:

> [B]ig box office names are built, in part, through being prominently featured in popular films and by receiving appropriate recognition in film credits and advertising. Since actors' fees for pictures, and indeed, their ability to get any work at all, is often based on the drawing power their name may be expected to have at the box office, being accurately credited for films in which they have played would seem to be of critical importance in enabling actors to sell their "services," i.e., their performances. *Id.*

174. *See* John T. Cross, Giving Credit Where Credit Is Due: Revisiting the Doctrine of Reverse Passing Off in Trademark Law, 72 Wash. L. Rev. 709, 717–20 (1997) (detailing the explosion of cases allowing reverse passing off claims under section 43(a) of the Lanham Act following the Ninth Circuit's *Montoro* decision and the application of such claims to myriad artistic works, including musical compositions, sound recordings, books, scripts, and, quite bizarrely, dolls).

175. *See generally Dastar Corp.* v. *Twentieth Century Fox Film Corp.*, 539 U.S. 23 (2003).

176. Specifically, Dastar took the original series, edited it down to "slightly more than half" its original length and then "substituted a new opening sequence, credit page, and final closing …; inserted new chapter-title sequences and narrated chapter introductions; moved the 'recap' in the Crusade television series to the beginning and retitled it as a 'preview'; and removed references to and images of the book." *Id.* at 26–27.

177. *Id.* at 26. Released in 1949, the series had a twenty-eight-year copyright term under the 1909 Copyright Act, meaning that failure to timely renew the work by 1977 would result in its ceding to the public domain.

178. That said, Fox did try to claim that the Dastar video set violated the rights to the original Eisenhower book upon which the *Crusade in Europe* television series was based, which

allegedly remained under copyright protection. *See Twentieth Century Fox Film Corp.* v. *Ent. Distrib.*, 34 F. App'x 312, 314 (9th Cir. 2002); *Dastar*, 539 U.S. at 28 n.2.

179. *See, e.g., TrafFix Devices, Inc.* v. *Mktg. Displays, Inc.*, 532 U.S. 23, 26–27 (2001) (drawing on trademark law to raise infringement claims against an imitator of a plaintiff's dual spring mechanism for road signs when the plaintiff's patent in said system had expired).
180. *See Dastar Corp.* v. *Twentieth Century Fox Film Corp.*, 537 U.S. 1099 (2003) (granting certiorari to unpublished Ninth Circuit decision in *Twentieth Century Fox*, 34 F. App'x 312).
181. *Dastar*, 539 U.S. 23 at 38.
182. *Id.* at 34.
183. *See generally Eldred* v. *Ashcroft*, 537 U.S. 186 (2003).
184. Justin Hughes, American Moral Rights and Fixing the Dastar "Gap," 2007 UTAH L. REV. 659, 685 (2007).
185. *Eldred*, 537 U.S. at 208, 218.
186. Notably, the *Dastar* Court was not the first to recognize this problem. Decades earlier, Judge Learned Hand had flagged this issue. *See Capitol Recs., Inc.* v. *Mercury Recs. Corp.*, 221 F.2d 657, 664–68 (2d Cir. 1955) (Hand, J., dissenting). In a prescient 1955 dissent in a suit between Capitol and Mercury Records, *id.*, Hand cautioned against the use of unfair competition law to achieve copyright-like protection that would "grant to an author a perpetual monopoly" over works in a way that would circumvent their eventual and proper dedication to the public domain, *id.* at 666–67; *see also Sinatra* v. *Goodyear Tire & Rubber Co.*, 435 F.2d 711, 718 (9th Cir. 1970) (noting Hand's concern over "allow[ing] unfair competition protection where Congress has not given federal protection … in effect granting state copyright benefits without the federal limitations of time to permit definite public domain use"). Hand's concern was not merely the injury to reasonable investment-backed expectations and commerce but also the broadside such legal machinations represented to public access to creative works and the exercise of attendant First Amendment rights.
187. *Dastar*, 539 U.S. at 31–32.
188. *Id.* at 32.
189. *See* Jane C. Ginsburg, Moral Rights in the U.S.: Still in Need of a Guardian Ad Litem, 30 CARDOZO ARTS & ENT. L. J. 73, 81 (2012) [hereinafter Ginsburg, *Moral Rights*]; Jane C. Ginsburg, The Right to Claim Authorship in U.S. Copyright and Trademarks Law, 41 HOUS. L. REV. 263, 268 n.17 (2004) [hereinafter Ginsburg, *Right to Claim Authorship*] ("Federal district court decisions subsequent to *Dastar* have declined to limit that decision's impact to copyright-expired works."); Graeme W. Austin, The Berne Convention as a Canon of Construction: Moral Rights after Dastar, 61 N. Y. U. ANN. SURV. AM. L. 111, 113 (2005) (noting that, although "the *Dastar* Court seemed particularly solicitous of the public domain," its interpreting progeny has "not, however, confined the ruling to public domain materials" and, in the process, has significantly diminished "[w]hatever protections to the right to claim authorship of one's works that the Lanham Act formerly provided").
190. K. J. Greene, Trademark Law and Racial Subordination: From Marketing of Stereotypes to Norms of Authorship, 58 SYRACUSE L. REV. 431, 442 (2008).
191. *Dastar*, 539 U.S. at 36 (citing 15 U.S.C. § 1125(a)(1)(A)).
192. *Id.* at 35. The opinion put a fine point on the scope of crediting that a broader reading of section 43(a)'s "designation of origin" reference would compel by assessing the type of attribution that might be required to distribute the film *Carmen Jones*. As the Court posited, to avoid liability for reversing passing off under *Montoro* and its progeny, a

distributor might have to give attribution "not just to MGM, but to Oscar Hammerstein II (who wrote the musical on which the film was based), to Georges Bizet (who wrote the opera on which the musical was based), and to Prosper Mérimée (who wrote the novel on which the opera was based)." *Id.*

193. *Id.*
194. *Id.*
195. Mary LaFrance, When You Wish upon *Dastar*: Creative Provenance and the Lanham Act, 23 CARDOZO ARTS & ENT. L. J. 197, 235 (2005).
196. There have been a few outlier decisions that have at least entertained the possibility that *Dastar* did not kill all attempts to vindicate attribution rights. In *Gensler* v. *Strabala*, for example, the Seventh Circuit left possible room for attribution claims based on Gensler's clever recharacterization of its claim as about designation of origin for services, rather than an intangible good. *Gensler* v. *Strabala*, 764 F.3d 735, 736–37 (7th Cir. 2014). But commentators such as Mark McKenna and Lucas Osborn have argued that such a distinction is unavailing, in that it "depends on a mischaracterization of *Dastar*." Mark P. McKenna & Lucas S. Osborn, Trademarks and Digital Goods, 92 NOTRE DAME L. REV. 1425, 1436 (2017); *see also Masck* v. *Sports Illustrated*, No. 13-10226, 2013 U.S. Dist. LEXIS 81677, at *9 (E.D. Mich. June 11, 2013) (refusing to grant a motion to dismiss a misattribution claim on the basis of the *Dastar* because the court was "not ready … to conclude that Plaintiff's photo [was] an intangible item" and not a tangible good, to which the Lanham Act's definition of origin would apply).
197. Rick Mortensen, D.I.Y. After *Dastar*: Protecting Creators' Moral Rights through Creative Lawyering, Individual Contracts and Collectively Bargained Agreements, 8 VAND. J. ENT. & TECH. L. 335, 353 (2006).
198. *See, e.g.*, Ginsburg, *Right to Claim Authorship*, *supra* note 189, at 266 (noting that *Dastar* "drastically limited invocation of the trademarks law to enforce authors' interests in being recognized as the creators of their works" and giving the "(despondent) answer that in the United States neither the copyright nor the trademarks laws establish a right of attribution generally applicable to all creators of all types of works of authorship").
199. 15 U.S.C. § 1125(a)(1)(B).
200. *Dastar*, 539 U.S. at 38.
201. *Time Warner Cable, Inc.* v. *DIRECTV, Inc.*, 497 F.3d 144, 153 (2d Cir. 2007); *Turbon Int'l, Inc.* v. *Hewlett-Packard Co.*, 769 F. Supp. 2d 262, 268 (S.D.N.Y. 2011) (noting that to be actionable under section 43(a)(1)(B), "[t]he misrepresentation must be 'material,' in that it would influence consumers' purchasing decisions").
202. *See, e.g.*, *Williams* v. *UMG Recordings, Inc.*, 281 F. Supp. 2d 1177, 1186 (C.D. Cal. 2003) (rejecting a reverse passing off claim related to failure to attribute on the grounds that "[t]he Ninth Circuit has consistently held that state law unfair competition claims are 'congruent' with Lanham Act claims" and that *Dastar* precludes such a claim under the Lanham Act). In California, although state unfair competition law mirrors federal law in terms of liability, remedies can differ. *See* Cal. Civ. Code § 3294 (providing for the availability of punitive damages for any torts under state law, such as unfair competition, when the defendant acts with oppression, fraud, or malice).
203. By 2007, the Southern District of New York had no compunction about declaring that "[i]t is well-settled that a claim for reverse passing off predicated on the theory that defendant's product replicates plaintiff's expressions contains no extra element and is therefore preempted." *Silverstein* v. *Penguin Putnam, Inc.*, 522 F. Supp. 2d 579, 608 (S.D.N.Y. 2007). To this day, courts have continued to take this viewpoint. *See, e.g.*, *Shepard* v. *Eur. Pressphoto Agency*, 291 F. Supp. 3d 465, 475–76 (S.D.N.Y. 2017) (holding that an

unfair competition claim that the defendants misrepresented the plaintiff's photos as their own was preempted); *Ryoo Dental, Inc.* v. *Han*, No. SACV 12-308-JLS, 2015 U.S. Dist. LEXIS, at *8–9 (C.D. Cal. July 9, 2015) (holding that state law false advertising and unfair competition claims against a defendant for copying a website and passing it off as his own work constitutes a reverse passing off claim that is preempted, per *Dastar*, by federal copyright law); *Aagard* v. *Palomar Builders, Inc.*, 344 F. Supp. 2d 1211, 1218 (E.D. Cal. 2004) (expressly rejecting a claim for "reverse palming off" of certain house design plans under state unfair competition as "preempted by the Copyright Act"); 1 Melville B. Nimmer & David Nimmer, Nimmer on Copyright § 1.15[E][2] (2022) (contending that a reverse passing off claim "is in fact a disguised copyright infringement claim and, hence, preempted"). *See also* Tom W. Bell, Misunderestimating *Dastar*: How the Supreme Court Unwittingly Revolutionized Copyright Preemption, 65 Md. L. Rev. 206, 232 (2006); Michael Landau, Dastar v. Twentieth Century Fox: The Need for Stronger Protection of Attribution Rights in the United States, 61 N.Y.U. Ann. Surv. Am. L. 273, 304–305 (2005). Indeed, even prior to *Dastar*, some courts had taken this position. *See, e.g., Fisher* v. *Dees*, 794 F.2d 432, 440 (9th Cir. 1986) ("Assuming *arguendo* that the false claiming of authorship constitutes a separate tort under California law, such a cause of action is nevertheless preempted by federal law.").

204. *See generally Demas* v. *Levitsky*, 738 N.Y.S.2d 402 (N.Y. App. Div. 2002). Demas also sued Cornell University for failing to protect her from Levitsky's actions.
205. *Id.* at 406–407.
206. *Id.* at 406–407.
207. *Id.* at 407.
208. *Id.*
209. For example, Demas had her breach of fiduciary duty and contract claims dismissed on the grounds that she could not demonstrate the existence of either. *Id.* at 408. Indeed, most circumstances of crediting abuse will not involve the existence of a contract calling for crediting rights (due to power differentials that will likely preclude such a provision, even if there is privity of contract between the two parties) or a fiduciary duty (which is imposed for only special relationships).
210. *See* Sprigman et al., *supra* note 109, at 1402 ("The paucity of formal IP protection for attribution rights in the U.S. does not, however, mean that creators are unable to obtain credit for their efforts; it simply means that creators must use the property rights that U.S. IP law gives them as leverage to *negotiate* for attribution. Instead of being a subject of IP law, attribution in the U.S. becomes a subject of contract law and the operation of social norms that either favor or disfavor attribution within specific creative communities and industries.").
211. *See* David A. Gerber, Copyright Reigns–Supreme: Notes on Dastar Corp. v. Twentieth Century Fox Film Corp., 93 Trademark Rep. 1029, 1033 (2003) ("Academia and Hollywood are perhaps the industries most focused on creative credits. Anti-plagiarism codes (in the former) and collective bargaining agreements containing elaborate credit requirements (in the latter) are common methods by which these industries self-regulate the provision of credit.").
212. *See* Sara Rimer, *When Plagiarism's Shadow Falls on Admired Scholars*, N.Y. Times (Nov. 24, 2004), https://www.nytimes.com/2004/11/24/nyregion/when-plagiarisms-shadow-falls-on-admired-scholars.html.
213. *Id.*
214. Of course, more recently, Harvard President Claudine Gay faced plagiarism accusations (albeit of more dubious merit than those leveled against Ogletree and Tribe) when she

resigned from her position in early 2024. But her decision occurred in a hyper-politicized environment galvanized by her response to campus antisemitism in the wake of the Israel–Hamas war, and, notably, she maintained her tenured faculty position, to which she returned. Gay faced a firestorm of controversy over public remarks she made before Congress, allegations suggesting she had shown insufficient commitment to fighting the scourge of antisemitism on campus, and a widespread campaign by numerous significant donors to the University to withhold their future support if she remained in her position. It is therefore fair to wonder if the plagiarism claims operating alone would have been enough to result in any adverse action against her, particularly when they resulted in no formal censure action by the University. *See* Max Matza, *Claudine Gay Resigns as Harvard University President*, BBC.com (Jan. 2, 2024), https://www.bbc.com/news/world-us-canada-67868280.

215. *See, e.g.*, Robert Davenport, Screen Credit in the Entertainment Industry, 10 Loy. Ent. L. J. 129, 154–55, 159–60 (1990) (detailing the guild-related crediting provisions for writers, directors, and actors).
216. *See infra* notes 221–223 and accompanying text.
217. Fisk, *supra* note 128, at 80 ("Equality and fairness are fairly high in the formal credit process.... [But b]ecause the system costs significant time and effort, the credit system seems to work only for those contributors (directors, producers, writers, and actors) for whom the financial value of credit is large enough to make it economically sensible to invoke the whole cumbersome process.").
218. Founded in 1990, IMDb.com is the Internet Movie Database, which touts itself as "the world's most popular and authoritative source for movie, TV and celebrity content." *What Is IMDb?*, IMDb https://help.imdb.com/article/imdb/general-information/what-is-imdb/G836CY29Z4SGNMK5 [https://perma.cc/VC9T-3KR4]. IMDb is likely the most comprehensive publicly searchable movie information system in the world; its IMDbPro system is used widely by entertainment professionals, and individual IMDb profiles serve as important resumes and business cards in the industry.
219. *See* Davenport, *supra* note 215, at 129 (noting that "[s]creen credit is probably the single most important factor for artists in the entertainment business. This factor determines who is 'hot' and who is not; it is the basis for determining whether artists are offered subsequent assignments and their increase in compensation for those assignments").
220. *See generally* Directed by Allen Smithee (Jeremy Braddock & Stephen Hock eds., 2001).
221. Fisk, *supra* note 128, at 80.
222. *Id.* at 77.
223. Greene, *supra* note 190, at 444.
224. Historian Margaret Rossiter coined this phrase as a reference to the systematic undervaluing and lack of crediting to women in the sciences. *See* Margaret W. Rossiter, The Matthew Matilda Effect in Science, 23 Soc. Stud. Sci. 325, 325–26 (1993).
225. Jessica Gelt, *Relative of Discredited "Big Eyes" Artist Makes a Defense*, L.A. Times (Jan. 2, 2015, 5:30 AM), https://www.latimes.com/entertainment/arts/la-et-cm-keane-nephew-20150102-story. html [https://perma.cc/Z7AY-NLSJ]; *see Keane* v. *Keane*, No. 87-1741, 1990 WL 2874, at *2–4 (9th Cir. Jan. 18, 1990).
226. Mary Pilon, *Monopoly's Inventor: The Progressive Who Didn't Pass "Go,"* N.Y. Times (Feb. 13, 2015), https://www.nytimes.com/2015/02/15/business/behind-monopoly-an-inventor-who-didnt-pass-go.html [https://perma.cc/8TM9-AAXU].
227. William A. Camfield, Marcel Duchamp: Fountain 13 (1989); *How Duchamp Stole the Urinal*, Scot. Rev. of Books (Nov. 4, 2014), https://www.scottishreviewofbooks.org/2014/11/how-duchamp-stole-the-urinal [https://perma.cc/78R6-ZWLV] (citing an Apr. 11, 1917 letter, not made public until 1983, wherein

Duchamp admits that Fountain was the work of "[o]ne of [his] female friends," thereby contradicting public claims he made to sole authorship of the work).

228. Jordana R. Goodman, Ms. Attribution: How Authorship Credit Contributes to the Gender Gap, 25 YALE J. LAW & TECH. 309, 316 (2023).
229. *Id.* at 316.
230. *Id.* at 314.
231. *Id.*
232. *Id.* at 320–26.
233. Fisk, *supra* note 128, at 80.
234. THE BEATLES: GET BACK (Apple Corps Limited & WingNut Films 2021).
235. Richard would later claim that he solo-authored *Tutti Frutti*, a claim that LaBostrie rejected in asserting that she, and not Richard, wrote the song alone. *See* JEFF HANNUSCH, I HEAR YOU KNOCKIN': THE SOUND OF NEW ORLEANS RHYTHM AND BLUES 222 (1985). The actual provenance of the song therefore remains a mystery.
236. Although the facts surrounding who actually wrote the song are in dispute, besides Richard and LaBostrie, the official musical composition contains a songwriting credit for Joe Lubin. *See Songview Search*, BMI, https://repertoire.bmi.com/Search/Search?Main_Search_Text=tutti%20frutti&Main_Search=Title&Sub_Search=Please%20Select&Search_Type=all&View_Count=0&Page_Number=0 [https://perma.cc/5GMA-NGUV].
237. *See* K. J. Greene, Copyright, Culture & Black Music: A Legacy of Unequal Protection, 21 HASTINGS COMM. & ENT. L. J. 339, 376 (1999) (citing JIM DAWSON & STEVE PROPES, WHAT WAS THE FIRST ROCK AND ROLL RECORD? 189 (1992)). Art Rube owned Specialty records, and there is a dispute as to whether Joe Lubin was a pseudonym he would use to earn royalties on songs or whether this was actually songwriter Joe Lubin, who had written songs for the likes of Doris Day, Lainie Kazan, and others. Dawson and Proper argue the former, while others, including the New York Times, have claimed the latter. *See* Associated Press, *Joe Lubin, 84, Co-Writer of 'Tutti Frutti'*, N.Y. TIMES (Oct. 20, 2001), https://www.nytimes.com/2001/10/20/arts/joe-lubin-84-co-writer-of-tutti-frutti.html [https://perma.cc/VT2X-JJ6Q].
238. Roman Mars, *The Real Book*, 99% Invisible Podcast (Apr. 6, 2021), https://99percentinvisible.org/episode/the-real-book/transcript ("What exactly Mills contributed is debated, but it's clear that he used his power to get his name on many of Eillington['s] songs and reap more royalties for himself").
239. TED GIOIA, The Jazz Standards: A Guide to the Repertoire, 387 (2012).
240. *Id.*
241. Greene, *supra* note 237, at 378.
242. Spenser Clark, Hold Up: Digital Sampling, Copyright Infringement, and Artist Credit through the Lens of Beyoncé's Lemonade, 26 J. INTELL. PROP. L. 131, 134–35 (2019) (describing Beyoncé's crediting decisions as having no "rhyme or reason").
243. *Id.*
244. *See id.* at 135; *see also* Brittany Spanos, *Ezra Koenig Explains Writing Credit on Beyonce's 'Lemonade'*, ROLLING STONE (Apr. 25, 2016), https://www.rollingstone.com/music/music-news/ezra-koenig-explains-writing-credit-on-beyonces-lemonade-73547 [https://perma.cc/756Z-B7JA]; Ezra Koenig (@arzE), TWITTER (Apr. 25, 2016, 11:05 AM), https://twitter.com/arzE/status/724660587523805184 [https://perma.cc/E3C4-W7EV].
245. Clark, *supra* note 242, at 135.
246. Fisk, for example, has presented a compelling case for the existence of an independent law of attribution that operates outside of the intellectual property laws dealing

with infringement; *see* Fisk, *supra* note 128, at 106–107 ("[C]redit is valuable and, consequently, collaborators often are tempted opportunistically to claim credit where it is not due. The temptation cannot be fully controlled simply by voluntary agreement."), and she proposes an implied right of attribution in every employment agreement that could be expressly waived depending on the nature of the attributive work, *id.* at 111–12.

3 CONTROLLING THE NARRATIVE

1. Anthony O. Miller, *Court Halted Dime Edition of "Mein Kampf": Cranston Tells How Hitler Sued Him and Won*, L.A. TIMES (Feb. 14, 1998), available at https://www.latimes.com/archives/la-xpm-1988-02-14-mn-42699-story.html.
2. *Id.*
3. Wendi A. Maloney, Mein Kampf *Infringer Aimed to Warn of Hitler Threat*, Copyright Notices 9–10 (May 2015).
4. This argument was ultimately rejected in *Houghton Mifflin Co.* v. *Stackpole Sons*, 104 F.2d 306, 307 (2d Cir. 1939), which was issued on June 9, 1939 – just days before a federal court enjoined Cranston's translation on July 14, 1939.
5. *See Houghton Mifflin Co.* v. *Noram Pub. Co.*, 28 F. Supp. 676 (S.D.N.Y. 1939). Houghton Mifflin had succeeded in enjoining another (critical) translation of *Mein Kampf* released by publisher Stackpole Sons. Although a federal court initially questioned whether *Mein Kampf* enjoyed copyright protection and therefore refused the requested injunction, the United States Court of Appeals for the Second Circuit reversed, finding that *Mein Kampf* remained under protection and that the Stockpole Sons version infringed its copyright. *See Houghton Mifflin Co.* v. *Stackpole Sons*, 104 F.2d 306, 307 (2d Cir. 1939).
6. *Id.* at 79.
7. Anthony O. Miller, *Court Halted Dime Edition of "Mein Kampf": Cranston Tells How Hitler Sued Him and Won*, L.A. TIMES (Feb. 14, 1998), available at https://www.latimes.com/archives/la-xpm-1988-02-14-mn-42699-story.html.
8. 17 U.S.C. § 107.
9. *See* 17 U.S.C. § 101 (defining a derivative work as any "work based upon one or more preexisting works, such as a translation, musical arrangement, dramatization, fictionalization, motion picture version, sound recording, art reproduction, *abridgment*, condensation, or any other form in which a work may be recast, transformed, or adapted.") (emphasis added).
10. *Stowe* v. *Thomas*, 23 F. Cas. 201, 207 (C.C.E.D. Pa. 1853).
11. *Id.* at 206.
12. *Id.*
13. *Id.* at 207.
14. *Id.* at 202 & n.2.
15. *Id.* at 202.
16. *Id.* at 208.
17. *See Story* v. *Holcombe*, 23 F. Cas. 171, 173 (C.C.D. Ohio 1847) (No. 13,497).
18. *Wheaton* v. *Peters*, 33 U.S. 591, 651 (1834).
19. 9 F. Cas. 342, 345 (C.C.D. Mass. 1841) (No. 4901).
20. The 255-page statistic excludes official documents and documents that had appeared in publication prior to Sparks's own use.
21. *Id.* at 349 (quoting *Lewis* v. *Fullarton*, 48 Eng. Rep. 1080, 1081 (K.B. 1839)).
22. The influence of Blackstone on Story's vision of copyright is not at all surprising. Justice Story was Blackstone disciple and, as Hannibal Travis has noted, Story was the author

of "a three volume series of *Commentaries on the Constitution of the United States*, in which he quotes so many passages from Blackstone's *Commentaries* that he may have been liable for infringement under *Folsom* or *Harper & Row*, had not Blackstone's work been in the public domain due to the 1790 Copyright Act's reservation of its protections to U.S. citizens." Hannibal Travis, Pirates of the Information Infrastructure: Blackstonian Copyright and the First Amendment, 15 BERKELEY TECH. L. J. 777, 821 n.223 (2000).

23. *Folsom* v. *Marsh*, 9 F. Cas. 342, 345 (C.C.D. Mass. 1841) (No. 4901).
24. *See* Kathryn Schulz, *"Bambi" Is Even Bleaker Than You Thought*, THE NEW YORKER (Jan. 17, 2022), available at https://www.newyorker.com/magazine/2022/01/24/bambi-is-even-bleaker-than-you-thought.
25. *See* Meghan Cox Gurdon, *"The Original Bambi" Review: Afterlife of a Fawn*, WALL ST. J. (Jan. 14, 2022), available at https://www.wsj.com/articles/the-original-bambi-book-review-afterlife-of-a-fawn-11642175311 (criticizing Chambers's translation for its significant whitewashing of this motif). Jack Zipes, whose own translation was released by Princeton University Press in 2022, expressly accuses Chambers of numerous errors and omissions. *See* Jack Zipes, *Introduction: Born to Be Killed*, *in* THE ORIGINAL "BAMBI": THE STORY OF A LIFE IN THE FOREST ix, xviii (Jack Zipes, trans., 2022). But not everyone believes the Chambers translation to be inferior. *See, e.g.*, Kathryn Schulz, *"Bambi" Is Even Bleaker than You Thought*, THE NEW YORKER (Jan. 17, 2022), available at https://www.newyorker.com/magazine/2022/01/24/bambi-is-even-bleaker-than-you-thought.
26. As Jack Zipes contends, Chambers "had limited understanding of Austrian German and spent little time in Austria. Consequently, his translation is filled with all sorts of errors and fails to capture Salten's unusual Viennese style of writing and anthropomorphism. Moreover, he mistranslates many German idioms, omits phrases, and does not covey Salten's profound personal and philosophical dilemma." *Id.*
27. Meghan Cox Gurdon, *"The Original Bambi" Review: Afterlife of a Fawn*, WALL ST. J. (Jan. 14, 2022), available at https://www.wsj.com/articles/the-original-bambi-book-review-afterlife-of-a-fawn-11642175311.
28. Sabine Strumper-Krobb, "I Particularly Recommend It to Sportsmen." Bambi in America: The Rewriting of Felix Salten's Bambi, 23 AUSTRIAN STUDIES 123–42 (2015).
29. Zipes, *supra* note 25, at xxii.
30. As Kathryn Schulz observes, "authors do not necessarily get the last word on the meaning of their work, and plenty of other people believe that 'Bambi' is no more about animals than 'Animal Farm' is. Instead, they see in it what the Nazis did: a reflection of the anti-Semitism that was on the rise all across Europe when Salten wrote it." *See* Kathryn Schulz, *"Bambi" Is Even Bleaker than You Thought*, THE NEW YORKER (Jan. 17, 2022), available at https://www.newyorker.com/magazine/2022/01/24/bambi-is-even-bleaker-than-you-thought. Particularly salient in this regard are the works of Iris Bruce and Paul Reitter. *See* Iris Bruce, *Which Way Out? Schnitzler's and Salten's Responses to Cultural Zionism*, in A COMPANION TO THE WORKS OF ARTHUR SCHNITZLER (ed. Dagmar C.G. Lorenz, 2003) (proposing a reading of the "Zionist overtones" in Bambi with its evocation of the "experience of exclusion and discrimination"); Paul Reitter, *Bambi's Jewish Roots*, JEWISH REVIEW OF BOOKS (Winter 2014), available at https://jewishreviewofbooks.com/articles/618/bambis-jewish-roots (noting the viability of "interpretations of Salten's animal stories as allegories of the Jewish experience," despite Salten's silence on the issue).
31. *Twin Books Corp.* v. *Walt Disney Co.*, 83 F.3d 1162 (9th Cir. 1996).
32. Meghan Cox Gurdon, *"The Original Bambi" Review: Afterlife of a Fawn*, WALL ST. J. (Jan. 14, 2022), available at https://www.wsj.com/articles/the-original-bambi-book-review-afterlife-of-a-fawn-11642175311.

33. Zipes, *supra* note 25, at xxi–xxii.
34. *See* Copyright Act of 1790, ch. 15, § 1, 1 Stat. 124 (limiting infringement claims to the unauthorized printing, reprinting, publishing, or vending of a copyrighted book, chart, or map).
35. John Tehranian, Et Tu, Fair Use? The Triumph of Natural-Law Copyright, 38 U. C. DAVIS L. REV. 465, 489–91 (2005) (documenting the historical emergence of the derivative-rights doctrine as an outcome of natural-law copyright sensibilities and noting its role in controlling the remix and reinterpretation of creative works).
36. *Daly* v. *Palmer*, 6 F. Cas. 1132 (C.C.S.D.N.Y. 1868).
37. As Paul Goldstein has argued, *Daly* "augur[ed] copyright's break from the confines of "copies," and the eventual statutory expansion of derivative rights." Paul Goldstein, Derivative Rights and Derivative Works in Copyright, 30 J. COPYRIGHT SOC'Y 209, 213 (1983).
38. *Daly*, 6 F. Cas. at 1133.
39. *Id.* at 1138.
40. Goldstein, *supra* note 37, at 213. *See also* Bruce E. Boyden, *Daly* v. *Palmer*, or the Melodramatic Origins of the Ordinary Observer Test, 68 SYRACUSE L. REV. 137, 149, 162 (2018).
41. Copyright Act of 1870, ch. 230, § 86, 16 Stat. 198 (1870) (providing that "authors may reserve the right to dramatize or to translate their own works").
42. Copyright Act of 1909, Pub. L. 60–349, 35 Stat. 1075, 1075. (1909). The Act gave authors the exclusive right to "translate the copyrighted work into other languages or dialects, or make any other version thereof, if it be a literary work; to dramatize it if it be a non-dramatic work; to convert it into a novel or other nondramatic work if it be a drama; to arrange or adapt it if it be a musical work; to complete, execute, and finish it if it be a model or design for a work of art." *See id.* § 1(b).
43. 17 U.S.C. § 106(2).
44. *Id.* § 101 (emphasis added).
45. *See Harry Potter*, WBSHOP.COM, http://www.wbshop.com/category/wbshop_brands/harry+potter.do?nType=2 [http://perma.cc/977J-A7JB].
46. *See, e.g., Campbell* v. *Acuff-Rose Music, Inc.*, 510 U.S. 569, 579 (1994) ("[T]he goal of copyright, to promote science and the arts, is generally furthered by the creation of transformative works.").
47. Kirby Ferguson, *Everything Is a Remix Part 4: System Failure*, EVERYTHING IS A REMIX (Feb. 16, 2012), http://everythingisaremix.info/blog/everything-is-a-remix-part-4 [http://perma.cc/K2TX-669J].
48. *Id.*
49. *See generally* John Tehranian, Parchment, Pixels, & Personhood: User Rights and the IP (Identity Politics) of IP (Intellectual Property), 82 U. COLO. L. REV. 1, 23 (2011).
50. JEAN BAUDRILLARD, THE CONSUMER SOCIETY 25 (1998) (1970); *see also* F. Vigneron & L. W. Johnson, *A Review and a Conceptual Framework of Prestige-Seeking Consumer Behavior*, 1999 ACAD. OF MARKETING SCI. REV. 1, 4, *available at* http://www.amsreview.org/articles/vigneron01-1999.pdf.
51. DON SLATER, CONSUMER CULTURE AND MODERNITY 132 (1997) (arguing that "all consumption is cultural" because "in order to 'have a need' and act on it we must be able to interpret sensations, experiences, and situations and we must be able to make sense of (as well as transform) various objects, actions, resources in relation to these needs" and "when we meaningfully formulate our needs in relation to available resources, we draw on languages, values, rituals, habits, and so on, that are social in nature, even when we individually contest, reject, or reinterpret them").

52. *See generally* THORSTEIN VEBLEN, THE THEORY OF THE LEISURE CLASS: AN ECONOMIC STUDY OF INSTITUTIONS 75 (1928) (1899) (coining the term "conspicuous consumption" to refer to the act of using one's consumption activities to manifest social power).
53. JOHN FISKE, READING THE POPULAR 1 (1989).
54. Sonya Katyal, Semiotic Disobedience, 84 WASH. U. L. REV. 489 (2006).
55. *Id.* at 493.
56. *Id.*
57. *Id.* at 491 (Critiquing the "near-sovereign protection to [the] symbolism [of corporate speech] through the every-expanding vehicle of intellectual property protection.").
58. *Id.* at 562 (arguing that "the law has provided a wide berth of protection for [acts of semiotic disobedience] through its substantial [First Amendment] jurisprudence protecting those who dissent from symbols of national leadership").
59. 17 U.S.C. § 105 (deeming that "[c]opyright protection under this title is not available for any work of the United States Government ....").
60. As section 105 of the Copyright Act provides, the exemption for copyright in federal government works does not "preclude[]" the federal government "from receiving and holding copyrights transferred to it by assignment, bequest, or otherwise." *Id.*
61. Governmental entities can also claim additional, albeit more narrow, protection under trademark laws or laws against false association.
62. Provided the changes or additions possess the requisite originality, a new copyright can be secured for the revised flag. *See, e.g., Waldman Publ'g Corp.* v. *Landoll, Inc.*, 43 F.3d 775, 782 (2d Cir. 1994) (noting that, to qualify for protection as a derivative work and to be separately copyrightable, the derivative must contain "a distinguishable variation that is more than merely trivial" and that "[t]he test of originality is concededly a low threshold"). Of course, the new copyright would only extend to the new elements in the flag.
63. The exclusion in section 105 only applies to "any work of the United States Government." 17 U.S.C. § 105.
64. The government would need to circumvent the provisions of section 109(c), which allow certain automatic display rights for owners of a legitimate copy of a copyright work; but that might be accomplished by characterizing every "sale" of a flag as merely a license, subject to certain terms and conditions. *See* 17 U.S.C. § 109(c).
65. Copyright law, of course, provides plaintiffs who have timely registered their copyrighted works with the option of recovering statutory damages, even in instances where actual damages did not occur or would be impossible to prove, as well as the possibility of injunctive relief. *See* 17 U.S.C. §§ 501(c)(1) & 502(a).
66. Fair use, of course, could shield users from liability from such infringement claims, but its protections are inadequate in practice for a number of reasons. Among other things, fair use is notoriously ambiguous, provides no *ex ante* protection against costly copyright litigation, and constitutes an affirmative defense for which a defendant bears the burden of proof. *See generally*, John Tehranian, Et Tu, Fair Use: The Triumph of Natural-Law Copyright, 38 U.C. DAVIS L. REV. 465 (2005).
67. 17 U.S.C. § 106(2).
68. *Texas* v. *Johnson*, 491 U.S. 397, 418–20 (1989).
69. *United States* v. *Eichman*, 496 U.S. 310, 317 (1990).
70. *Eldred* v. *Ashcroft*, 537 U.S. 186, 221 (2003).
71. In *Munoz* v. *Albuquerque A.R.T. Co.*, for example, the Ninth Circuit affirmed an Alaskan federal district court's decision that the mounting of purchased art works on a tile constituted the creation of a derivative work in violation on the Copyright Act. 38 F.3d 1218 (9th Cir. 1994) (de-published), *aff'g* 829 F. Supp. 309 (D. Alaska 1993); *see also Mirage*

Editions, Inc. v. *Albuquerque A.R.T. Co.*, 856 F.2d 1341 (9th Cir.1988); *but see Lee* v. *A.R.T. Co.*, 125 F.3d 580, 583 (7th Cir. 1997) (rejecting the logic of *Munoz* and *Mirage Editions*).

72. *See, e.g.*, *Gilliam* v. *Am. Broad. Cos.*, 538 F.2d 14, 21 (2d Cir. 1976) (finding that the "unauthorized editing of the underlying work, if proven, would constitute an infringement of the copyright in that work similar to any other use of a work that exceeded the license granted by the proprietor of the copyright").
73. The idea of destruction as a derivative right is implicit in the Copyright Act's specific exclusion of architectural works from this potential consequence of the derivative rights doctrine. *See* 17 U.S.C. § 120(b) ("Notwithstanding the provisions of section 106(2), the owners of a building embodying an architectural work may, without the consent of the author or copyright owner of the architectural work, make or authorize the making of alterations to such building, and destroy or authorize the destruction of such building."). The existence of such terms for architectural works suggests that, for copyrightable subject matter outside of architecture, an alteration, mutilation, or destruction does, in fact, constitute the creation of a derivative work in violation of 17 U.S.C. § 106(2).
74. *See Eldred*, 537 U.S. at 221.
75. *Spence* v. *Washington*, 418 U.S. 405, 407 (1974).
76. *Id.* at 408–409, 415.
77. *Georgia* v. *Public.Resource.Org, Inc.*, 140 S. Ct. 1498 (2020).
78. *Id.* at 1505.
79. *Id.* at 1513 (Thomas, J., dissenting).
80. *Id.* at 1507
81. *Id.* at 1510.
82. *Compare* State of Colorado, Division of Central Services, Department of Personnel & Administration, *State Branding Guidelines – The Elements*, available at https://dcs.colorado.gov/ids/state-branding-guidelines/the-elements (asserting that "[t]he State Flag is public domain. All citizens have the privilege of use in occasions they deem fitting and appropriate.") *with* State of Nebraska, Secretary of State, *Permission to Use State Seal of State Flag*, available at https://sos.nebraska.gov/permission-use-state-seal-or-state-flag (claiming ownership over state flag) vs. ("The Secretary of State is the official keeper of the Great Seal of the State of Nebraska Nebraska Constitution Art. IV, Sec. 24; Neb. Rev. Stat. Sec. 84–501). The secretary determines how it is used and by whom. The state seal is not in the public domain, and it is not available for the public's use.... There are also restrictions of the use of the Nebraska state flag, which uses the seal as its centerpiece. Requests for permission to use the state seal or state flag images must be made in writing to the Secretary of State's Office."). That said, Nebraska has been using the current iteration of its flag since 1925, which means, even if it enjoyed copyright protection, it has now definitely fallen into the public domain. But nothing prevents states from adopting a new flag (just as Utah and Mississippi recently did) every time an old one is about to go into the public domain.
83. *United States* v. *O'Brien*, 391 U.S. 367 (1968).
84. *Id.* at 382; Sonya Katyal, Semiotic Disobedience, 84 WASH. U. L. REV. 489, 559 (2006) ("The Court in *O'Brien* strongly emphasized the importance of incentivizing alternatives to the destruction of government property and recognized the expressive nature of his actions.").
85. Akhil Reed Amar, The Case of the Missing Amendments: *R.A.V.* v. *City of St. Paul*, 106 HARV. L. REV. 124, 138 (1992).
86. 430 U.S. 705 (1977).
87. *Id.* at 707.
88. *Id.* at 717.

89. *See infra*, note 116.
90. Associated Press, *Wall St.'s Bronze Bull Moves 2 Blocks South*, N.Y. TIMES (Dec. 20, 1989), http://www.nytimes.com/1989/12/20/nyregion/wall-st-s-bronze-bull-moves-2-blocks-south.html [https://perma.cc/DWD6-7K2C].
91. Robert D. McFadden, *SoHo Gift to Wall St.: A 3 ½-Ton Bronze Bull*, N.Y. TIMES (Dec. 16, 1989), http://www.nytimes.com/1989/12/16/nyregion/soho-gift-to-wall-st-a-3-1-2-ton-bronze-bull.html [https://[perma.cc/BRL6-PZ47].
92. Bruce Lambert, *Neighborhood Report: Lower Manhattan; A Campaign to Save a Bull*, N.Y. TIMES (Oct. 3, 1993), http://www.nytimes.com/1993/10/03/nyregion/neighborhood-report-lower-manhattan-a-campaign-to-save-a-bull.html [https://perma.cc/SEJ6-8RZL].
93. McFadden, *supra* note 91.
94. *Id.*
95. Lambert, *supra* note 92.
96. *See* Bethany McLean, *The Backstory behind That "Fearless Girl" Statue on Wall Street*, THE ATLANTIC (Mar. 13, 2017) https://www.theatlantic.com/business/archive/2017/03/fearless-girl-wall-street/519393/ [https://perma.cc/N45F-9V7F].
97. *See* Jen Wieczner, *Why the Fearless Girl Statue's Controversial "SHE" Plaque Was Removed*, FORTUNE (Apr. 17, 2017), http://fortune.com/2017/04/17/fearless-girl-statue-nyc-plaque-she-nasdaq/ [https://perma.cc/LWH3-6JKL].
98. In terms of publicity, State Street is certainly getting more attention than it could have hoped for, even if the price tag for its advertising ultimately comes with significant legal fees (and a potential judgment down the road).
99. *See* McLean, *supra* note 96; Wieczner, *supra* note 97.
100. Wieczner, *supra* note 97. Notably, SSgA removed the plaque on April 2, 2017. *See id.* Even though they claim the move had nothing to do with the legal controversy, *see id.*, it is fair to speculate that they may have done so to de-emphasize the commercialism of the work in order to lower the possibility of legal liability.
101. *See Pittsburgh Press Co.* v. *Pittsburgh Comm'n on Human Relations*, 413 U.S. 376, 385 (1973) (defining commercial speech as speech that does "no more than propose a commercial transaction"). *But see Bolger* v. *Youngs Drug Prods. Corp.*, 463 U.S. 60, 64–67 (1983) (rejecting a per se test to determine what constitutes commercial speech).
102. Roisin O'Connor, *"Fearless Girl" Statue Facing Down Charging Bull of Wall Street in New York to Stay Until 2018*, THE INDEPENDENT (Mar. 27, 2017), http://www.independent.co.uk/arts-entertainment/art/news/fearless-girl-charging-bull-wall-street-new-york-boradway-2018-bronze-statue-stand-up-a7651471.html [https://perma.cc/F6ZL-5NML].
103. *Id.*
104. Linda Massarella & Jeremy Olshan, *Wall Street Bull Artist Knows BS When He Sees It*, N.Y. POST (Mar. 20, 2017, 11:26 AM), https://nypost.com/2017/03/20/that-is-not-a-symbol-wall-street-bull-artist-calls-out-fearless-girl-statue/ [https://perma.cc/JJ73-TMKQ] (quoting sculptor Modica).
105. *Id.*
106. Lisa Massarella, *"Charging Bull" Artist Plans Revenge against "Fearless Girl,"* N.Y. POST (Apr. 12, 2017, 2:17 p.m.), https://nypost.com/2017/03/20/that-is-not-a-symbol-wall-street-bull-artist-calls-out-fearless-girl-statue/.
107. *See* Letter from Norman Siegel, Kate Fletcher, Steven Hyman & Oliver Chernin, Attorneys for Arturo Di Modica, to the Honorable Bill de Blasio, Mayor of New York City (Apr. 11, 2017), https://www.scribd.com/document/344998311/Letter-to-Mayor-DeBlasio-on-Charging-Bull-vs-Fearless-Girl [https://perma.cc/KT8U-7U5T].

108. O'Connor, *supra* note 102.
109. Absent a work-made-for-hire arrangement, Modica, as the creator of the Bull, is its copyright holder. Moreover, as the author of the statue, he is potentially entitled to the rights of integrity and attribution secured under the Visual Artist Rights Act, codified in section 106A of the Copyright Act. *See* 17 U.S.C. § 106A.
110. James Boyle, The Search for an Author: Shakespeare and the Framers, 37 AM. U. L. REV. 643, 635 (1988).
111. Michel Foucault, *What Is An Author? in* TEXTUAL STRATEGIES: PERSPECTIVES IN POST-STRUCTURALIST CRITICISM 146, 158–59 (J. Harari ed., 1979).
112. David Lange, At Play in the Fields of the Word: Copyright and the Construction of Authorship in the Post-Literate Millennium, 55 L. & CONTEMP. PROBS. 139, 143 (1992).
113. Sculptor Kristen Visbal readily admits that the statue was made to "go with *Charging Bull*" and, among other things, ensured that *Fearless Girl* had the same patina as *Charging Bull*. *See* Erin Arvedlund, *Wall Street's "Fearless Girl" Speaks, Via Sculptor Kristen Visbal*, PHILA. INQUIRER (May 23, 2017), http://www.philly.com/philly/business/personal_finance/Fearless-Girl-Speak-Sculptor-Kristen-Visbal-to-Raise-Funds-For-Girls-Inc-of-Delaware-Speak-May-18.html [https://perma.cc/P3TG-KCCH].
114. *See* 17 U.S.C. § 106(2).
115. *See* 17 U.S.C. § 101 (emphasis added).
116. *See Mirage Editions, Inc.* v. *Albuquerque* A.R.T. *Co.*, 856 F.2d 1341, 1342–44 (9th Cir. 1988) (finding that placing art prints or book pages featuring art and placing them onto ceramic tiles created an authorized derivative version of the books and therefore constituted copyright infringement, even though there was no copying of the original works). *But see Lee* v. A.R.T. *Co.*, 125 F.3d 580, 581–82 (7th Cir. 1997) (finding that placing of copyrighted postcards on tiles was akin to the framing of a work and did not constitute the creation of an unauthorized derivative work).
117. *See* 17 U.S.C. § 106(1) (granting copyright holders the exclusive right to reproduce their protected works); § 106(2) (granting copyright holders the exclusive right to prepare derivative versions of their protected works).
118. *See, e.g., Stowe* v. *Thomas*, 23 F. Cas. 201, 207 (C.C.E.D. Pa. 1853) (finding that an unauthorized German translation of Uncle Tom's Cabin did not violate Harriet Beecher Stowe's copyright to the book since, *inter alia*, "[t]o make a good translation of a work, often requires more learning, talent and judgment, than was required to write the original"); *Wheaton* v. *Peters*, 33 U.S. 591, 651 (1834) ("An abridgement fairly done, is itself authorship, requires mind; and is not an infringement, no more than another work on the same subject.").
119. Letter, *supra* note 107, at 1 (emphasis added).
120. *See* 17 U.S.C. § 103(a) (protection for a derivative work "employing preexisting material in which copyright subsists does not extend to any part of the work in which such material has been used unlawfully"); 1–3 NIMMER ON COPYRIGHT § 3.06 (noting that works that are infringements themselves are not entitled to copyright protection); *Anderson* v. *Stallone*, No. 87-0592 WDKGX, 1989 WL 206431, at *8 (C.D. Cal. April 26, 1989) (holding that a screenplay featuring unauthorized use of the copyrighted Rocky character was an infringing work that did not enjoy copyright protection, even as to its noninfringing portions).
121. *See* 17 U.S.C. § 503(a)–(b) (allowing for the "impounding" and "destruction or other reasonable disposition" of any infringing work).
122. *See* 17 U.S.C. § 106A.
123. Among other things, VARA does not apply to motion pictures, excludes works-made-for-hire, applies only to original works or limited editions of less than 200, and its integrity

right can only be raised by works of "recognized stature." *See* 17 U.S.C § 101 (defining "work of visual art"); 17 U.S.C. § 106A(a)(3)(B) (limiting to works of recognized stature).

124. 17 U.S.C. § 106A(a)(3)(A).
125. Nicola Brown, *Why "Fearless Girl" Matters for Brands*, SKYWORD (Apr. 7, 2017), https://www.skyword.com/contentstandard/storytelling/why-fearless-girl-matters-for-brands/ [https:/perma.cc/S248-554A].
126. As such, it is not fair to demonize Di Modica as a misogynist. For example, in the wake of the controversy, Mayor Di Blasio blustered that "[m]en who don't like women taking up space are exactly why we need the Fearless Girl." *See* Mark Moore, *De Blasio defends "Fearless Girl" Statue*, N.Y. POST (Apr. 12, 2017), http://nypost.com/2017/04/12/de-blasio-defends-fearless-girl-statue/ [https://perma.cc/4WDJ-629W]. Such comments fail to distinguish the artist from the artwork and unfairly portray Modica and his representatives, who insist that they appreciate the feminist message of *The Fearless Girl* but just wish it did not involve the *Bull*, as standing in the way of women's rights.
127. Ben Rosen, *Can the "Charging Bull" Sculptor Control His Artwork's Meaning?*, CHRISTIAN SCI. MONITOR (Apr. 14, 2017), http://www.csmonitor.com/USA/Society/2017/0414/Can-the-Charging-Bull-sculptor-control-his-artwork-s-meaning [https://perma.cc/9JH3-TAEN].
128. This is particularly true for pieces of art that are meant by their own creator to serve as public art and, as a result, to be consumed by the public as a whole. Artworks placed in public enjoy particular visibility and provide particular advantages to their authors, as they can become career-making events for artists who otherwise struggle to develop their reputations and feathers in the cap for established artists looking to burnish their brand. *See, e.g.*, Rachel Donadio, *Jeff Koons Sent Paris Flowers. Can It Find the Right Vase?*, N.Y. TIMES (June 20, 2017), https://www.nytimes.com/2017/06/20/arts/design/jeff-koons-bouquet-of-tulips-paris.html?_r=0 [https://perma.cc/KU9P-3AU4] (noting that, according to "[s]ome in French cultural circles," Jeff Koons' "donation" of the concept for a sculpture of balloon tulips to Paris to honor the victims of the 2015 terrorist attack at the Bataclan Theater "was practically foisted on the city … [and was] more of a coup for the artist and his private donors than for Paris"). In turn, it is important to recognize that public meanings can change and the artist cannot (and should not be able to) control such transformations.
129. LYNYRD SKYNYRD, *Sweet Home Alabama, on* SECOND HELPING (1974). Among other things, *Sweet Home Alabama* constitutes a direct response to, and recasting of, the image of the South presented in Neil Young's *Southern Man*. As the famous second verse of the latter goes, "Well I heard Mister Young sing about her/Well I heard ole Neil put her down/Well I hope Neil Young will remember/A southern man don't need him around anyhow." *Id.*
130. HARUKI MURAKAMI, 1Q84 (2009). Murakami's dystopian novel is loosely based on an alternative version of the world of 1984.
131. GEORGE ORWELL, 1984 (1949).
132. LIZ PHAIR, EXILE IN GUYVILLE (1993).
133. THE ROLLING STONES, EXILE ON MAIN ST. (1972).
134. Jessica Bennett, *Liz Phair Is Not Your Feminist Spokesmodel*, N.Y. TIMES (May 3, 2018), https://www.nytimes.com/2018/05/03/arts/music/liz-phair-exile-in-guyville-reissue-interview.html.
135. Di Modica did not play by the rules and violated the physical property rights of others when he presented his *Bull* to New York in 1989, making it ironic that he would now be complaining about the violation of his property rights. Vivian M. Warfield, the Director of the New York Arts Commission at the time of Di Modica's gift noted that, although

she liked the *Bull*, she could not help but ask, "What about the artists who play by the rules?" As she observed, such artists "would love to have an extended exhibit in a prime spot free of charge." Lambert, *supra* note 92.

136. The use of the term "works of authorship" is more metaphoric than literal in this sentence, although, technically speaking, works of architecture are protected by copyright, *see* 17 U.S.C. § 102(a)(8) (placing architectural works within the subject matter of copyright protection), as are many commercial logos that have a modicum of creativity, *see, e.g., Bouchat* v. *Baltimore Ravens, Inc.*, 241 F.3d 350, 354–57 (4th Cir. 2000) (noting the protection granted to the Baltimore Raven's former logo). Finally, even the design of a park could conceivably receive copyright protection. *See* 17 U.S.C. § 101 (noting that protection for architectural works extends to "the overall form as well as the arrangement and composition of spaces and elements in the design").

137. Modica's success on a VARA claim was far from assured. First, since Charging Bull was created before 1990, title to the work must not have been transferred from the author prior to 1990 in order to qualify the Bull for VARA protection. *See* 17 U.S.C. § 106A(d)(2). In addition, VARA specifically states that "modification of a work of visual art which is the result of conservation, or of the public presentation, including lighting and placement, of the work is not a destruction, distortion, mutilation, or other modification … unless the modification is caused by gross negligence." 17 U.S.C. § 106A(c)(2). This exemption – which appears to exclude "modification" that results from "public presentation … of the work" from liability in the absence of gross negligence – would create a potential defense for SSgA, though it is unclear what would constitute "gross negligence" in this context. Finally, all VARA claims are subject to a fair use defense. *See* 17 U.S.C. § 107. In particular, the third prong of the fair-use test, which examines "the amount and substantiality of the portion used in relation to the copyrighted work as a whole," 17 U.S.C. § 107(3), could be particularly difficult for Modica to overcome. After all, that factor traditionally focuses on how much of an infringed work is literally taken by the infringer and, in this case, the amount is zero. Unless a court takes a more metaphysical, rather than physical, view of what "use" means, it would appear unprecedented to decline a fair-use defense when no new physical use is made of an allegedly infringed work.

138. Modica's lawyers also raised a thinly-supported Lanham Act violation in their correspondence with Mayor Di Blasio. *See* Letter, *supra* note 107, at 2.

139. *Campbell* v. *Acuff-Rose Music, Inc.*, 510 U.S. 569 (1994).

140. *Brownmark Films, LLC* v. *Comedy Partners*, 682 F.3d 687 (7th Cir. 2012).

141. *Leibovitz* v. *Paramount Pictures Corp.*, 137 F.3d 109 (2d Cir. 1998).

142. *Compare Rogers* v. *Koons*, 960 F.2d 301 (2d Cir. 1992) (finding that modern artist Jeff Koons' appropriation of a postcard image of a couple and some puppies (*Puppies* by Art Rogers) as the basis for a sculptural work satirizing suburban American aesthetic sensibilities did not constitute fair use) *with Blanch* v. *Koons*, 467 F.3d 244 (2d Cir. 2006) (finding that modern artist Jeff Koons' partial use of a photograph entitled *Silk Sandals by Gucci* – a commercial work used in advertising – in his painting *Niagara*, which had been commissioned by Deutsche Bank, constituted fair use because).

143. AIPLA, Report of the Economic Survey, I–202 (2023) (noting that the median cost for litigating a middle-of-the-road copyright infringement suit in 2023 was $525,000 per side).

144. *See, e.g., Associated Press* v. *Meltwater U.S. Holdings, Inc.*, 931 F. Supp. 2d. 537, 550 (S.D.N.Y. 2013) ("Because fair use is an affirmative defense, the burden of proof rests with the party relying on the defense."). Moreover, most of the fair use factors focus on

what is being taken from a rights holder, rather than on what kind of use is being made of the work. As such, the fair use test, as presently constituted, adopts a strong natural-law vision of authorial rights. *See* John Tehranian, Et Tu, Fair Use? The Triumph of Natural-Law Copyright, 38 U.C. DAVIS L. REV. 465, 508 (2005).

145. 17 U.S.C. § 504(c)(2) & 505.
146. 17 U.S.C. § 106(2).
147. *Id.* § 101 (emphasis added).
148. *Id.* § 107.
149. *See, e.g.*, *Campbell* v. *Acuff-Rose Music, Inc.*, 510 U.S. 569, 579 (1994); *Castle Rock Entm't, Inc.* v. *Carol Publ'g Grp., Inc.*, 150 F.3d 132, 142–43 (2d Cir. 1998).
150. *Campbell*, 510 U.S. at 579 ("[T]he more transformative the new work, the less will be the significance of other factors, like commercialism, that may weigh against a finding of fair use.").
151. *Andy Warhol Foundation for the Visual Arts, Inc.* v. *Goldsmith*, 598 U.S. 508 (2023).
152. *Id.* at 529.
153. *Id.* ("the degree of transformation required to make 'transformative' use of an original must be beyond that required to qualify as a derivative").
154. *Id.* at 531–32 ("A use that shares the purpose of a copyrighted work … is more likely to to provide 'the public with a substantial substitute for matter protected by the [copyright owner's] interest in the original work[k] or derivative of it," which undermines the goal of copyright") (citations omitted) (citing *Authors Guild* v. *Google, Inc.*, 804 F.3d 202, 207 (2d Cir. 2015)).
155. *Id.* at 535.
156. *Id.* at 526.
157. *Id.* at 541.
158. *Id.* at 578 (Kagan, J., dissenting).
159. *Id.* at 536 n.12.
160. *Id.* at 578 (Kagan, J., dissenting) (citing 17 U.S.C. §107).
161. *Id.* at 575 (Kagan, J., dissenting).
162. *See Bleistein* v. *Donaldson Lithographing Company*, 188 U.S. 239 (1903).
163. *Id.* at 251.
164. *Id.* at 251–52. As Holmes argued, "That these pictures had their worth and their success is sufficiently shown by the desire to reproduce them without regard to the plaintiffs' rights." *Id.* at 252.
165. *Id.* at 251.
166. U.S. CONST., art. I, § 8, cl. 8.
167. Robert A. Gorman, Copyright Courts and Aesthetic Judgments: Abuse or Necessity? 25 COLUM. J.L. & ARTS 1, 2 (2001) (noting that "it is not at all rare to find courts addressing the question, 'what is art?' And it is quite common to find copyright courts assessing – sometimes covertly, sometimes openly – whether a work has merit, worth or social value.").
168. David Fagundes, *Who Is the Bad Art Judge? Aesthetic Nondiscrimination in Andy Warhol Foundation* v. *Goldsmith*, N.Y.U. L. REV. FORUM (Dec. 28, 2023), https://www.nyulawreview.org/forum/2023/12/who-is-the-bad-art-judge-aesthetic-nondiscrimination-in-andy-warhol-foundation-v-goldsmith/.
169. *See id.*
170. Alfred C. Yen, Copyright Opinions and Aesthetic Theory, 71 S. CAL. L. REV. 247, 248–49 (1998).
171. *Cariou* v. *Prince*, 714 F.3d 694 (2d Cir. 2013).
172. *Id.* at 712.

173. *Id.* at 699–703.
174. The court remanded the analysis over the remaining five works to the district court. *Id.* at 712.
175. *Id.* at 705–11.
176. *Id.*
177. *Id.* 699–704.
178. *Id.* at 709.
179. *Id.* at 609–704.
180. *See Blanch* v. *Koons*, 467 F.3d 244 (2d Cir. 2006).
181. *Cariou*, 714 F.3d at 709.
182. Sergio Muñoz Sarmiento, *Judicial Activism and the Return of Modernism in the Cariou* v. *Prince Decision*, available online at http://hyperallergic.com/69939/judicial-activism-and-the-return-of-modernism-in-the-cariou-v-prince-decision.
183. *Cariou*, 714 F.3d at 700.
184. Sarmiento, *supra* note 182.
185. *Id.* at 707–708.
186. *Id.* at 708.
187. *Id.* at 706.
188. *Id.* at 699.
189. Indeed, data revealed during antitrust litigation involving the major publishing houses suggests that the overwhelming majority of publications (more than 90%) at even the most commercially successful publishers sell fewer than 1000 copies. *See* Elle Griffin, *No One Buys Books* (Apr. 22, 2024), https://www.elysian.press/p/no-one-buys-books.
190. *Compare id.* at 708–709, *with Salinger* v. *Colting*, 641 F. Supp. 2d 250, 267–68 (S.D.N.Y. 2009), *vacated and remanded on other grounds*, 607 F.3d 68, 83 (2d Cir. 2010) ("we conclude, with the District Court, that Defendants are not likely to prevail in their fair use defense").
191. *Salinger*, 641 F. Supp. 2d 250, 268 (quoting *Salinger* v. *Random House, Inc.*, 811 F.2d 90, 99 (2d Cir. 1987)).
192. *Id.*
193. *Cariou*, 714 F.3d at 699.
194. *Id.* at 709.
195. Elena Martinique, *Chronicles of Worlds Largely Unseen – In Conversation with Patrick Cariou*, WIDEWALLS (Apr. 21, 2023), https://www.widewalls.ch/magazine/patrick-cariou-interview.
196. To be fair, one could argue that Prince sought to deconstruct noble savage mythologies.
197. *Cariou*, 714 F.3d at 707.
198. *Id.* at 708 (explaining that, despite the fact that Prince's artworks are commercial, "we do not place much significance on that fact due to the transformative nature of the work.").
199. *Id.* at 709 (emphasis added).
200. *TCA Television Corp.* v. *McCollum*, 839 F.3d 168, 181 (2d Cir. 2016).
201. *Andy Warhol Foundation for Visual Arts, Inc.* v. *Goldsmith*, 11 F.4th 26, 38 (2d. Cir 2021), *aff'd*, 598 U.S. 508 (2023).
202. Victor Moulin, *Patrick Cariou: Vague à L'âme*, POLKA MAGAZINE (Sept. 8, 2022), https://www.polkamagazine.com/patrick-cariou-vague-a-lame/.
203. *Suntrust Bank* v. *Houghton Mifflin Co.*, 136 F. Supp. 2d 1357, 1363 (N.D. Ga. 2001), *vacated*, 252 F.3d 1165 (11th Cir. 2001) and *rev'd*, 268 F.3d 1257 (11th Cir. 2001).
204. *Suntrust*, 268 F.3d at 1270–71.
205. *Suntrust*, 136 F. Supp. 2d at 1386.

206. *Id.* at 1378.
207. *Id.* at 1363.
208. *Id.*
209. *Id.* at 1378.
210. *See Campbell* v. *Acuff-Rose Music, Inc.*, 510 U.S. 569, 575 (1994) (stating that "[f]rom the infancy of copyright protection, some opportunity for fair use of copyrighted material has been thought necessary to fulfill copyright's very purpose, 'To promote the Progress of Science and Useful Arts.'")
211. *Id.* (emphasis added).
212. *Suntrust,* 136 F. Supp. 2d at 1379 ("The court finds that *The Wind Done Gone* is unquestionably a fictional work that has an overarching economic purpose.... [T]he commercial purpose of The Wind Done Gone weighs strongly in favor of the plaintiff on the first factor ... ").
213. *Id.* at 1382.
214. *Id.*
215. William Shatner & David Fisher, Up Till Now 287 (2008) ("Well. Kirk may have been dead in the movies, but there was no reason he had to be dead in the publishing industry. I sold my treatment to Simon & Schuster and Star Trek: The Return became a best-selling novel.").
216. Ross S. Kraemer, William Cassidy & Susan L. Schwartz, Religions of Star Trek 161 (2003).
217. *Suntrust,* 136 F. Supp. 2d at 1364.
218. *Suntrust,* 268 F.3d at 1282.
219. *Id.*
220. In 1908, the Supreme Court determined that perforated rolls of music used with player pianos did not constitute copies subject to the exclusive rights secured under the Copyright Act. *See White-Smith Music Publ'g Co.* v. *Apollo Co.*, 209 U.S. 1, 18 (1908). Because the rolls were only machine-readable (*i.e.*, they could not be read as musical compositions by even those skilled in the arts and were therefore not intelligible to humans – a requirement of the term "copies"), the Court reasoned that "we cannot think that they are copies within the meaning of the copyright act." *Id.* In response to the ruling, Congress passed the Copyright Act of 1909, which held that piano rolls created from underlying musical compositions constituted unauthorized reproductions of those compositions. Copyright Act of 1909, ch. 320, § 1(e), 35 Stat. 1075. But as a compromise, the Act simultaneously granted those who wished to manufacture and distribute mechanical embodiments of musical compositions a compulsory license (known as the compulsory mechanical license) under certain conditions. *Id.* § 25(e).
221. 17 U.S.C. § 115. Instead, cover artists need only provide notice of their intention to record a cover song and then make payment of a fixed per-album fee to the copyright owner. *Id.* § 115(b)–(c).
222. 510 U.S. 569 (1994).
223. *Id.* § 115(a)(2).
224. *See, e.g.*, Kenneth M. Achenbach, Grey Area: How Recent Developments in Digital Music Production Have Necessitated the Reexamination of Compulsory Licensing for Sample-Based Works, 6 N. C. J. L. & Tech. 187, 209–11 (2004) (noting the benefit of the cover song right to the music industry, upstart artists and established ones alike).
225. Copyright Law Revision: Report to Accompany H.R. 2512, House Committee on the Judiciary, 90th Cong., 1st sess., House Document no. 83, at 66 (8 March 1967) (quoted in Lawrence Lessig, Free Culture 58 (2004)).

4 ©ENSORED

1. *Savage* v. *Council on Am.-Islamic Relations, Inc.*, No. C 07-6076 SI, 2008 WL 2951281, at *1 (N.D. Cal. July 25, 2008).
2. *Id.*
3. Plaintiff Brave New Films' Notice of Motion and Motion for Partial Summary Judgment at 1, *Brave New Films 501(C)(4)* v. *Weiner*, No. CV 08-04703 SI, 2009 WL 1622385 (N.D. Cal. June 10, 2009) No. CV 08-04703 SI, 2009 WL 527974.
4. *Id.* at *3.
5. *National Radio Host Goes on Anti-Muslim Tirade*, COUNCIL ON AM. ISLAMIC RELATIONS (Nov. 1, 2007), http://www.cair.com/press-center/press-releases/2768-national-radio-host-goes-on-anti-muslim-tirade.html.
6. *Id.*
7. *See Savage*, 2008 WL 2951281, at *6.
8. *Id.* at *2.
9. *Id.* at *15.
10. *Savage* v. *Council on Am.-Islamic Relations, Inc.*, No. C 07-06076 SI, 2009 WL 188848, at *1 (N.D. Cal. Jan. 26, 2009) (denying CAIR's request for fees).
11. *Id.* (quoting *Savage* v. *Council on Am.-Islamic Relations, Inc.*, No. C 07-06076 SI, 2008 WL 4890892, at *2 (N.D. Cal. Nov. 12, 2008)).
12. *Id.*
13. Joan Brunwasser, *Brave New Films Sues Shock Jock Michael Savage*, OPEDNEWS (Oct. 10, 2008, 4:19 PM), http://www.opednews.com/articles/Brave-New-Films-Sues-Shoc-by-Press-Release-081010-626.html.
14. *Id.*
15. *Id.*
16. *Id.*
17. *See* Plaintiff Brave New Films' Notice of Motion and Motion for Partial Summary Judgment at *7, *Brave New Films 501(C)(4)* v. *Weiner*, No. CV 08-04703 SI, 2009 WL 1622385 (N.D. Cal. June 10, 2009) No. CV 08-04703 SI, 2009 WL 527974. ("As a result of that takedown notice, YouTube removed not only 'Michael Savage Hates Muslims' from Brave New Films' channel, but disabled Brave New Films' entire channel at a critical time in the presidential election cycle, rendering unavailable a large number of videos that expressed important political views, and just as Brave New Films ran a full-page ad in the New York Times.").
18. *See* Stipulation and Order Dismissing Complaint at *2, *Brave New Films 501(C)(4)* v. *Weiner*, No. 308CV04703 2009 WL 3413839 (N.D. Cal. Sept. 11, 2009).
19. Sam Bayard, *Creationist–Atheist Brouhaha over DMCA Takedown Notices*, DIGITAL MEDIA L. PROJECT (Sept. 20, 2007), http://www.dmlp.org/creationist-atheist-brouhaha-over-dmca-takedown-notices.
20. *Northland Family Planning Clinic, Inc.* v. *Ctr. for Bio-Ethical Reform*, 868 F. Supp. 2d 962 (C.D. Cal. 2012).
21. *Four Navy SEALs* v. *Associated Press*, 413 F. Supp. 2d 1136 (S.D. Cal. 2005).
22. 537 U.S. 186, 221 (2003).
23. *See, e.g.*, *N.Y. Times Co.* v. *Sullivan*, 376 U.S. 254 (1964).
24. *See, e.g.*, *Time, Inc.* v. *Hill*, 385 U.S. 374 (1967).
25. *See, e.g.*, *Cox Broad. Corp.* v. *Cohn*, 420 U.S. 469 (1975).
26. *See, e.g.*, *Hustler Magazine, Inc.* v. *Falwell*, 485 U.S. 46 (1988).
27. *See Nat'l Socialist Party of Am.* v. *Vill. of Skokie*, 432 U.S. 43, 43–44 (1977).

28. *See R.A.V.* v. *City of St. Paul* (1992).
29. *See N.Y. Times Co.* v. *United States*, 403 U.S. 713, 714 (1971).
30. *See, e.g.*, *Stowe* v. *Thomas*, 23 F. Cas. 201, 207 (C.C.E.D. Pa. 1853) (No. 13,514) (holding that the unauthorized German translation of Harriet Beecher Stowe's novel, *Uncle Tom's Cabin*, did not constitute infringement because it was transformative and not a mere slavish reproduction).
31. *See* NEIL WEINSTOCK NETANEL, COPYRIGHT'S PARADOX 55 (2008) ("It has been largely since Congress enacted the Copyright Act revision of 1976 that copyright's scope and duration have burst from their moorings, growing with unwonted precipitousness and force."); Oren Bracha, The Ideology of Authorship Revisited: Authors, Markets, and Liberal Values in Early American Copyright, 118 YALE L. J. 186, 230–31 (2008) (noting how, in the years following the Civil War and into the modern era, "the scope of copyright protection and the tests for infringement were expanded well beyond verbatim copying and came to cover increasingly abstract and remote zones of similarity to the protected work").
32. 17 U.S.C. §§ 101, 106(2) (granting copyright owners the exclusive right to prepare derivative works based upon the copyrighted work and defining derivative works expansively to constitute any "work based upon one or more preexisting works, such as a translation, musical arrangement, dramatization, fictionalization, motion picture version, sound recording, art reproduction, abridgment, condensation, or any other form in which a work may be recast, transformed, or adapted"); *see also* Bracha, *supra* note 31, at 231 ("By the dawn of the twentieth century, the accumulation of specific entitlements and the expanding scope of protection would lead to the emergence of a general logic of derivative works in copyright thinking. Under this mode of thinking, copyright would be conceived of as the right to control any aspect of the intellectual work, irrespective of medium, format, or form."); John Tehranian, Whither Copyright? Transformative Use, Free Speech, and an Intermediate Liability Proposal, 2005 BYU L. REV. 1201, 1248 (2005) (arguing that "the broad exclusive right of copyright owners to prepare derivative works has swallowed up the ability of transformative users to escape infringement liability, thereby undermining the key goal of the federal copyright regime").
33. *See Capitol Records, Inc.* v. *Naxos of Am., Inc.*, 372 F.3d 471, 481 (2d Cir. 2004) (noting that "[a]s long as a defendant's work incorporates protectable elements of the plaintiff's work, the plaintiff is entitled to relief" under federal copyright law, regardless of the value of the defendant's contributions to the allegedly infringing work).
34. For example, numerous cases have held that the slightest unauthorized sample can result in a finding of infringement, even if (and regardless of whether) a significant and expressive new musical work is created through use of the sample. *See, e.g.*, *Bridgeport Music, Inc.* v. *Dimension Films*, 383 F.3d 390, 398 (6th Cir. 2004) (holding that any unauthorized sample of a sound recording, no matter how small, constitutes copyright infringement); Grand *Upright Music Ltd.* v. *Warner Bros. Records, Inc.*, 780 F. Supp. 182, 183 (S.D.N.Y. 1991) (quoting *Exodus* 20:15, equating the Seventh Commandment with the law of copyright, admonishing "[t]hou shall not steal," and rejecting a fair-use defense in a music sampling case).
35. *Cf. Anderson* v. *Stallone*, No. 87-0592 WDKGX, 1989 WL 206431, at *7–10 (C.D. Cal. April 25, 1989) (finding that an unauthorized script for a potential sequel to the *Rocky* movies violated the copyright to the characters in the *Rocky* franchise held by Sylvester Stallone).
36. *See generally Salinger* v. *Colting* (*Salinger I*), 641 F. Supp. 2d 250 (S.D.N.Y. 2009) (granting injunction enjoining the sale of *60 Years After* as an unauthorized derivative work

based on *Catcher in the Rye*, regardless of the originality of contributions by the author of *60 Years After*).

37. *Id.* at 253.
38. *See generally id.*
39. *Id.* at 263–67.
40. *Id.* at 269.
41. *See Salinger* v. *Colting* (*Salinger II*), 607 F.3d 68, 83–84 (2d. Cir. 2010) (affirming district court's finding that Salinger was likely to prevail on merits but remanding case for full consideration of factors from *eBay, Inc.* v. *MercExchange, L.L.C.*, 547 U.S. 388 (2006), before injunction could issue).
42. Mark A. Lemley & Eugene Volokh, Freedom of Speech and Injunctions in Intellectual Property Cases, 48 Duke L. J. 147 (1998).
43. *Id.* at 156–57.
44. *See, e.g., Near* v. *Minnesota ex rel.* Olson, 283 U.S. 697 (1931) (deeming prior restraints invalid in all but the most extreme circumstances).
45. *See, e.g., Dr. Seuss Enters., L.P.* v. *Penguin Books USA, Inc.*, 109 F.3d 1394, 1406 (9th Cir. 1997) (enjoining publication of *The Cat NOT in the Hat!*, a satirical examination of the OJ Simpson trial based on Dr. Seuss's *The Cat in the Hat*), *cert. dismissed*, 521 U.S. 1146 (1997); *Warner Bros. Entm't Inc.*, v. *RDR Books*, 575 F. Supp. 2d 513, 554 (S.D.N.Y. 2008) (enjoining publication of *The Lexicon*, an encyclopedia of all things *Harry Potter*); *Twin Peaks Prod., Inc.* v. *Publ'ns Int'l, Ltd.*, 996 F.2d 1366, 1370 (2d Cir. 1993) (finding that defendants' book about television program *Twin Peaks* infringed copyrights in teleplays for series); *Castle Rock Entm't, Inc.* v. *Carol Publ'g Group, Inc.*, 955 F. Supp. 260, 268 (S.D.N.Y. 1997) (holding that *Seinfeld Aptitude Test*, trivia book on all things *Seinfeld*, constituted unauthorized derivative work that infringed Castle Rock's copyright in *Seinfeld* television program).
46. *See, e.g., R.A.V.* v. *City of St. Paul*, 505 U.S. 377, 396 (1992) (invalidating, on First Amendments grounds, a St. Paul ordinance that banned cross burning); *Nat'l Socialist Party of Am.* v. *Vill. of Skokie*, 432 U.S. 43, 44 (1977) (protecting, under the First Amendment, the right of neo-Nazis to march and spread their message of hate at a rally in the town of Skokie, Illinois).
47. *See, e.g., Near*, 283 U.S. at 723 (rejecting, on First Amendment grounds, an attempt to enjoin publication of anti-Semitic and libelous news article).
48. *See, e.g., N.Y. Times Co.* v. *United States*, 403 U.S. 713, 714 (1971) (rejecting, under the First Amendment, a government attempt to enjoin publication of the Pentagon Papers).
49. Lemley & Volokh, *supra* note 42, at 182–85.
50. In their extensive empirical study of a representative sample of 108 million takedown notices collected over a six-month period by the Lumen Database, Jennifer M. Urban, Joe Karaganis and Brianna L. Schofield estimated that approximately 30% of notifications were potentially problematic. Urban et al., Notice and Takedown in Everyday Practice 41 (version 2, 2017), *UC Berkeley Public Law Research Paper No. 2755628*, available at https://papers.ssrn.com/sol3/papers.cfm?abstract_id=2755628.
51. Urban et al. note that "Few OSPs have the staff or expertise to deal with large numbers of boundary cases. Most OSPs reported acting conservatively in order to avoid liability, opting to take down content even when they are uncertain about the strength of the underlying claim. In some cases, OSPs simply take substantive claims at face value and remove everything if notices conform to section 512's basic requirements. Four services among our respondents reported a takedown rate of 100%. OSPs uniformly described their conservatism as a result of necessarily prioritizing avoiding liability over taking risks

that might protect expression. As one described it, 'the process forces you to try to stay out of making judgment calls [and] to take [takedown requests] at face value.'" URBAN et al., NOTICE AND TAKEDOWN IN EVERYDAY PRACTICE 41 (version 2, 2017), *UC Berkeley Public Law Research Paper No.* 2755628, available at https://papers.ssrn.com/sol3/papers.cfm?abstract_id=2755628.

52. *See Lawrence* v. *Texas*, 539 U.S. 558, 602 (2003) (Scalia, J., dissenting).
53. Ben Sheffner, *NPR Makes Copyright Claim over Anti-Same-Sex Marriage Ad; Another Political Fair Use Fight*, COPYRIGHTS & CAMPAIGNS (Oct. 21, 2009, 8:23 PM), http://copyrightsandcampaigns.blogspot.com/2009/10/npr-makes-copyright-claim-over-anti.html.
54. For example, *Queerty*, a leading gay-rights blog, bemoaned that no matter how repulsive SSFM's views were, NPR's tactic was regrettable for its lack of respect for free speech and unfettered political debate. *See Stand for Marriage Maine Is Hateful, But They Should Be Able to Use NRP's Report*, QUEERTY (Oct. 21, 2009), http://www.queerty.com/stand-for-marriage-maine-is-hateful-but-they-should-be-able-to-use-nprs-report-20091021/.
55. Even if someone accused of uploading infringing content on a user-generated content site that receives a DMCA takedown notification fights the notification with a counter-notification under 17 U.S.C. § 512(g), it takes typically 10 to 14 business days for the materials to be restored – well past Election Day. *See* Sheffner, *supra* note 53 ("NPR's takedowns are especially harmful because even if SFMM sends DMCA counternotices, sites generally won't restore the videos until 10–14 business days have elapsed, in order to maintain their safe harbor claim. Thus the videos won't reappear until well after the Nov. 3 election. So NPR's copyright claims, even if meritless, will achieve their intended, speech-silencing effect." [internal citation omitted]). Plus, even after a counter-notification, the filer of the original DMCA takedown notice can file suit and have the materials permanently removed, pending resolution of the civil action.
56. Kate Pickert, *A Storm Over Gay Marriage*, TIME MAG. (Apr. 10, 2009), http://content.time.com/time/nation/article/0,8599,1890523,00.html.
57. Kevin Poulsen, *Anti-Gay-Rights Group Gets MSNBC Clip Pulled from YouTube*, WIRED (Apr. 13, 2009, 2:53 PM), http://www.wired.com/2009/04/anti-gay-rights/.
58. *Id.*
59. *See, e.g.*, *X17, Inc.* v. *Lavandeira*, 563 F. Supp. 2d. 1102 (C.D. Cal. 2007). As Ben Sheffner has argued, "Perez Hilton (né Mario Lavandeira) may be the unlikeliest copyright enforcer on earth. The blogger rose to fame by posting photos of celebrities – without permission from the copyright owners – and defending himself from the inevitable lawsuit by claiming that his crude scribbling of penises, cocaine, and semen on the subjects' faces rendered his conduct fair use." Ben Sheffner, *Perez Hilton, Copyright Copy? Blogger Issues Takedown Notice over Anti-Gay-Marriage Ad*, COPYRIGHTS & CAMPAIGNS (May 1, 2009, 9:18 AM), http://copyrightsandcampaigns.blogspot.com/2009/05/perez-hilton-copyright-cop-blogger.html.
60. Sam Bayard, *Perez Hilton Sends DMCA Takedown Over Anti-Gay-Marriage Ad*, DIGITAL MEDIA L. PROJECT (May 4, 2009), http://www.dmlp.org/blog/2009/perez-hilton-sends-dmca-takedown-over-anti-gay-marriage-ad.
61. Perez Hilton called Prejean a "dumb bitch." *Id.*
62. 868 F. Supp. 2d 962 (C.D. Cal. 2012) (ultimately granting summary judgment to defendants on the basis of fair use). *See also* Rebecca Tushnet, *Abortion Criticism as Fair Use: Parody/Satire Mucks up the Analysis Once Again*, REBECCA TUSHNET'S 43(B)LOG, (June 28, 2012), http://tushnet.blogspot.com/2012/06/abortion-criticism-as-fair-use.html.

63. *See* Bayard, *supra* note 60. Ironically, through its terms and conditions, CSE's own website appeared to have waived any copyright interest to its videos by claiming the videos were "not copyrighted" and encouraging their dissemination. *Id.*
64. Rule 11 of the Federal Rules of Civil Procedures allows courts to sanction attorneys for pursuing frivolous claims or engaging in vexatious tactics.
65. Under Rule 68 of the Federal Rules of Civil Procedure, a defendant can make an offer of judgment to a plaintiff on a claim and, if the plaintiff declines the offer of judgment and the ultimate "judgment that the offeree finally obtains is not more favorable than the unaccepted offer," then "the offeree must pay the costs incurred after the offer was made." FED. R. CIV. P. 68. If the underlying statute giving rise to the cause of action defines fees as a species of costs, the Supreme Court has held that fees shift for Rule 68 purposes. *See Marek* v. *Chesny*, 473 U.S. 1, 10 (1985) (allowing an award of fees under Rule 68 to a nonprevailing party when fees are defined as costs in the underlying statute). In these circumstances, courts award fees to a nonprevailing party when the prevailing party earns at trial less than the offer of judgment. *See id.* Since it states that "the court may also award a reasonable attorney's fee to the prevailing party as part of the costs," Section 505 of the Copyright Act appears to qualify for *Marek* treatment and the shifting of fees under Rule 68. 17 U.S.C. § 505. Yet the various circuit courts are split on this issue. Some courts have shifted awards of fees to nonprevailing defendants when a judgment ultimately obtained by the plaintiff is not more favorable than the unaccepted offer. *See, e.g., Jordan* v. *Time, Inc.*, 111 F.3d 102, 105 (11th Cir. 1997) (holding that a Rule 68 award of costs includes attorneys' fees, even if the defendant is not the prevailing party); *Baker* v. *Urban Outfitters, Inc.*, 431 F. Supp. 2d 351, 361–62 (S.D.N.Y. 2006) (holding that a Rule 68 award of costs includes attorneys' fees, even if the defendant is not the prevailing party). Others have refused. *See, e.g., UMG Recordings, Inc.* v. *Shelter Capital Partners LLC*, 667 F.3d 1022, 1048–51 (9th Cir. 2011); *Harbor Motor Co.* v. *Arnell Chevrolet-Geo, Inc.*, 265 F.3d 638, 645–47 (7th Cir. 2001) (holding that, for a claim of copyright infringement, "only prevailing parties can receive attorney's fees pursuant to Rule 68"). In the latter circuits, plaintiffs are therefore not incentivized to accept reasonable settlement offers out of fear of later facing an adverse fees judgment.
66. Many copyright holders now move their copyrights into special-purpose LLCs whose sole function is litigating infringement claims. These LLCs are frequently undercapitalized. Thus, a defendant may be limited in collecting a judgment for attorneys' fees against one of these LLCs, especially if the copyright's own value is de minimis.
67. Eric Goldman, *Siblings Use Publicity Rights to Try to Block Sister from Blogging about Mom* – In re Reynolds, TECH. & MKTG. L. BLOG (April 27, 2014), http://blog.ericgoldman.org/archives/2014/04/siblings-use-publicity-rights-to-try-to-block-sister-from-blogging-about-mom-in-re-reynolds.htm.
68. *Id.*
69. Mark Bartholomew & John Tehranian, An Intersystemic View of Intellectual Property and Free Speech, 81 GEO. WASH. L. REV. 1, 9–47 (2013).
70. Importantly, the transformative-use test used in California as a defense to any right-of-publicity violation is far broader than copyright's transformative-use consideration, which is embodied as just one part of one factor in the four-part fair-use balancing test. *Compare Comedy III Prods., Inc.* v. *Gary Saderup, Inc.*, 21 P.3d 797, 807, 808 & n.10 (setting out transformative-use test), *with* 17 U.S.C. § 107.
71. *See generally Rogers* v. *Grimaldi*, 875 F.2d 994 (2d Cir. 1989). *But see Jack Daniel's Properties, Inc.* v. *VIP Products LLC*, 599 U.S. 140 (2023) (holding the *Rogers* defense

inapplicable in instances when a defendant uses a plaintiff's trademark as a designation of source for the defendant's own goods or services).

72. Bartholomew & Tehranian, *supra* note 69, at 48–52.
73. *Id.* at 9.
74. *See, e.g.*, *Walt Disney Prods., Inc.* v. *Air Pirates*, 581 F.2d 751, 758–59 (9th Cir. 1978) (affirming grant of summary judgment for plaintiff and rejecting fair-use and First Amendment defenses on copyright claim but denying summary judgment on trademark infringement claim); *Ty, Inc.* v. *Publ'ns Int'l, Ltd.*, No. 99 C 5565, 2000 WL 1499449, at *9, *15 (N.D. Ill. Oct. 6, 2000) (rejecting defendant's fair-use and First Amendment defenses and granting plaintiff's motion for summary judgment on copyright claim while refusing to grant summary judgment on plaintiff's trademark infringement claim), *rev'd*, 292 F.3d 512 (7th Cir. 2002); *Jackson* v. *MPI Home Video*, 694 F. Supp. 483, 492 (N.D. Ill. 1988) (issuing preliminary injunction against defendant for copyright infringement yet refusing to grant such an injunction on publicity rights claim); *see also Eldred* v. *Reno*, 239 F.3d 372, 376 (D.C. Cir. 2001) (stating that copyright law does not raise "the same concern under the First Amendment" of suppressing ideas as trademark law); *Dillinger, LLC* v. *Elec. Arts Inc.*, 795 F. Supp. 2d 829, 836–38 (S.D. Ind. 2011) (granting motion for dismissal of right-of-publicity claim on basis that material was protected under First Amendment, but refusing to dismiss accompanying trademark claim).
75. 17 U.S.C. § 501.
76. 15 U.S.C. § 1114.
77. *See, e.g.*, CAL. CIV. CODE § 3344(a) (limiting California's statutory right-of-publicity claim to knowing use of "another's name, voice, signature, photograph, or likeness, in any manner, *on or in products, merchandise, or goods, or for purposes of advertising or selling, or soliciting purchases of, products, merchandise, goods or services*" (emphasis added)).
78. 15 U.S.C. § 1117.
79. *Id.* § 1117(b).
80. CAL. CIV. CODE § 3344(a).
81. 17 U.S.C. § 504(c)(2).
82. *See* JOHN TEHRANIAN, INFRINGEMENT NATION: COPYRIGHT 2.0 AND YOU, at xvi, 86 (2011).
83. *See Hustler Magazine, Inc.* v. *Falwell*, 485 U.S. 46, 48 (1988).
84. *Id.* at 57.
85. *Hustler Magazine Inc.* v. *Moral Majority Inc.*, 796 F.2d 1148, 1156 (9th Cir. 1986).
86. *Falwell*, 485 U.S. at 48.
87. The First Amendment was not entirely absent from the district court's fair-use decision, which was affirmed by the Ninth Circuit, but, by the court's own admission, it played only a small role in the decision. *See Hustler Magazine, Inc.* v. *Moral Majority, Inc.*, 606 F. Supp. 1526, 1536 (C.D. Cal. 1985) ("Although the First Amendment does not provide a defense to copyright infringement, when an act of copying occurs in the course of a political, social or moral debate, the public interest in free expression is one factor favoring a finding of fair use."), *aff'd*, 796 F.2d 1148 (9th Cir. 1986).
88. TEHRANIAN, *supra* note 82, at 2.
89. INTERNET ARCHIVE: WAYBACK MACHINE, https://archive.org/web/ (indexing and archiving, by its own count, hundreds of billions of web pages, many going back years).
90. *See* 17 U.S.C. § 504(c). In 1976, they were $250 minimum, $5,000 maximum; in 1978, they increased to $10,000 maximum for ordinary infringement or $50,000 maximum for willful infringement. *See* Copyright Act of 1976, Pub. L. No. 94–553, § 504(c), 90 Stat. 2541, 2585. In 1989, they were raised to $20,000 maximum for ordinary infringement or $100,000 maximum for willful infringement. *See* Berne Convention Implementation

Act of 1988, Pub. L. No. 100–568, §10, 102 Stat. 2853, 2860. In 1999, they were raised to $30,000 maximum for ordinary infringement or $150,000 maximum for willful infringement. *See* Digital Theft Deterrence and Copyright Damages Improvement Act of 1999, § 2, Pub. L. No. 106–160, 113 Stat. 1774.

91. 17 U.S.C. § 504(c)(2).
92. FED. R. CIV. P. 12(b)(6) (allowing for a motion to dismiss on the grounds that, as a matter of law, relief cannot be granted on the claim asserted).
93. *Hofheinz* v. *AMC Prods., Inc.*, No. CV-00-5827 (CPS), 2003 WL 25293919, at *1 (E.D.N.Y. Apr. 23, 2003).
94. *Bond* v. *Blum*, 317 F.3d 385, 390 (4th Cir. 2003).
95. *Northland Family Planning Clinic, Inc.* v. *Ctr. for Bio-Ethical Reform*, 868 F. Supp. 2d 962, 966 (C.D. Cal. 2012) (granting summary judgment to defendants on the basis of fair use).
96. *Hustler Magazine Inc.* v. *Moral Majority Inc.*, 606 F. Supp. 1526 (C.D. Cal. 1985), *aff'd*, 796 F.2d 1148 (9th Cir. 1986).
97. *See, e.g.*, *Denison* v. *Larkin*, 64 F. Supp. 3d 1127, 1128 (N.D. Ill. 2014) (granting a motion to dismiss, on fair-use grounds, infringement claims brought by an attorney for the State Bar's unauthorized reproduction of her blog in disciplinary hearings against her); *Savage* v. *Council on Am.-Islamic Relations, Inc.*, No. C 07-6076 SI, 2008 WL 2951281, at *1 (N.D. Cal. July 25, 2008) (granting a motion to dismiss infringement claims by Michael Savage for a civil-rights group's unauthorized use of excerpts from his radio show to call attention to his controversial statements therein).
98. *Brownmark Films, LLC* v. *Comedy Partners*, 682 F.3d 687 (7th Cir. 2012).
99. *Id.* at 691–92.
100. *Ashcroft* v. *Iqbal*, 556 U.S. 662, 679 (2009) (holding that Fed. R. Civ. P. 8 dictates that "only a complaint that states a plausible claim for relief survives a motion to dismiss. Determining whether a complaint states a plausible claim for relief [is] a context-specific task that requires the reviewing court to draw on its judicial experience and common sense" (citation omitted)).
101. *Brownmark*, 682 F.3d at 691 ("We are sympathetic to the goal of curtailing nuisance suits….").
102. *Id.* at 689.
103. *Bond* v. *Blum*, 317 F.3d 385, 390 (4th Cir. 2003).
104. *Id.*
105. *Id.* at 391.
106. *Id.*
107. *Id.* at 398.
108. *Id.* at 397–98.
109. *Id.*
110. *Hofheinz* v. *AMC Prods., Inc.*, No. CV-00-5827 (CPS), 2003 U.S. Dist. LEXIS 16940, at *20–21 (E.D.N.Y. Sept. 1, 2003).
111. *Id.* at *3–5.
112. *Id.* at *5–6.
113. *Id.* at *18–19.
114. *Id.* at *18.
115. *Id.* at *20–21.
116. *See, e.g.*, *Jartech, Inc.* v. *Clancy*, 666 F.2d 403, 407 (9th Cir. 1982) (reversing grant of attorneys' fees to defendants when plaintiffs brought copyright infringement claim for unauthorized use of copies of plaintiffs' pornographic movie as part of a local government's

nuisance abatement action on the grounds that the plaintiffs "have offered explanations for their prosecution of this suit, which, in the opinion of this court, reflect a sincere interest in the settlement of close legal questions" and that the plaintiffs "initiated this suit only after defendants had reproduced and used their registered properties in a manner which was arguably illegal"); *Savage* v. *Council on Am.-Islamic Relations, Inc.*, No. C 07-06076 SI, 2009 WL 188848, at *1 (N.D. Cal. Jan. 26, 2009) (denying prevailing defendant's request for fees).

117. For example, some circuits have determined that, when both the copyrighted work and the allegedly infringing work are before the court and capable of examination and comparison, district courts may entertain a motion to dismiss as a vehicle for resolving the issue of substantial similarity as a matter of law. *See, e.g., Nelson* v. *PRN Prods., Inc.*, 873 F.2d 1141, 1143–44 (8th Cir. 1989) (determining that a district court could properly decide substantial similarity as a matter of law on a motion to dismiss); *Christianson* v. *West Publ'g Co.*, 149 F.2d 202, 203 (9th Cir. 1945) ("There is ample authority for holding that when the copyrighted work and the alleged infringement are both before the court, capable of examination and comparison, non-infringement can be determined on a motion to dismiss."). As such, district courts have increasingly found the issue of substantial similarity subject to adjudication on a motion to dismiss, if the case is appropriate. *See, e.g., Rosenfeld* v. *Twentieth Century Fox Film*, No. CV 07-7040 AHM, 2008 WL 4381575, at *6 (C.D. Cal. Sept. 25, 2008) (citing *Christianson* for the proposition that substantial similarity may be considered on a motion to dismiss); *Thomas* v. *Walt Disney Co.*, No. C-07-4392 CW, 2008 WL 425647, at *2 (N.D. Cal. Feb. 18, 2008) (deciding substantial similarity on a motion to dismiss); *Zella* v. *E.W. Scripps Co.*, 529 F. Supp. 2d 1124, 1130–31 (C.D. Cal. 2007) (citing *Christianson* and determining that substantial similarity may be decided on a motion to dismiss); *Identity Arts* v. *Best Buy Enter. Servs. Inc.*, Nos. C 05-4656 PJH, C 06-1631 PJH, 2007 WL 1149155, at *5 (N.D. Cal. April 18, 2007) (finding no obstacle to addressing substantial similarity on a motion to dismiss under Rule 12(c)); *Gal* v. *Viacom Int'l, Inc.*, 403 F. Supp. 2d 294, 305 (S.D.N.Y. 2005) ("[T]here is ample authority for the proposition that a district court may make that determination [of substantial similarity] on a motion to dismiss for failure to state a claim under Rule 12(b)(6)."); *Cory Van Rijn, Inc.* v. *Cal. Raisin Advisory Bd.*, 697 F. Supp. 1136, 1145 (E.D. Cal. 1987) (granting motion to dismiss based on lack of substantial similarity).

118. *Cf. Harper & Row Publishers, Inc.* v. *Nation Enters*, 471 U.S. 539, 560 (1985) ("Fair use is a mixed question of law and fact.").

119. *Katz* v. *Chevaldina*, 900 F. Supp. 2d 1314, 1315–16. (S.D. Fla. 2012).

120. *Id.* at 1315.

121. *Id.*

122. *Id.*

123. *Id.* at 1315–17.

124. *Id.* at 1316.

125. *Katz* v. *Chevaldina*, No. 14-14525, at *12 (11th Cir. Sept. 17, 2015) (denying Katz's infringement claims and holding that "every reasonable factfinder would conclude the inclusion of the Photo in [Chevaldina's] blog posts constituted fair use").

126. *Four Navy SEALs* v. *Associated Press*, 413 F. Supp. 2d 1136, 1140 (S.D. Cal. 2005).

127. *Id.* at 1141.

128. *Id.* at 1142.

129. *Id.* at 1144.

130. *Id.* at 1148.

131. *Id.* (citing Cal. Civ. Proc. Code § 425.16(b)).
132. Cal. Civ. Proc. Code § 425.16(b).
133. *Id.* § 425.16(c).
134. There is a potential strategic lesson here too for the plaintiffs: they should not have brought the state-law claims for privacy invasion since those are subject to the anti-SLAPP statute; they should have solely relied on copyright law.
135. *See, e.g., Browne* v. *McCain*, 612 F. Supp. 2d 1125, 1130 (C.D. Cal. 2009) (noting that "in light of a court's narrow inquiry at this stage and limited access to all potentially relevant and material facts needed to undertake the analysis, courts rarely analyze fair use on a 12(b)(6) motion").
136. Eric Goldman, *Blogger Wins Fair Use Defense ... On a Motion to Dismiss! – Righthaven* v. *Realty One*, Tech. & Mktg. L. Blog (Oct. 21, 2010), http://blog.ericgoldman.org/archives/2010/10/righthaven_defe.htm.
137. *See* 17 U.S.C. §§ 512(c), (i) (conditioning receipt of the DMCA safe harbor from infringement liability on compliance with, inter alia, the designation of an agent for receipt of takedown notices, removal of infringing material upon receipt of takedown notifications, and termination of the accounts of repeat infringers under appropriate circumstances).
138. 17 U.S.C. § 512(g)(1).
139. *See* 17 U.S.C. § 512(c)(1)(C) (conditioning receipt of the DMCA safe harbor on expeditious removal of "the material that is claimed to be infringing or to be the subject of infringing activity" upon receipt of a DMCA takedown). Of course, ISPs have a strong incentive to draw users to their sites with alluring content, infringing or otherwise. As such, they are often less proactive than rights holders might like in affirmatively removing materials without rights holder notification or preventing the initial uploading of infringing materials in the first place. *See* Annemarie Bridy, Graduated Response and the Turn to Private Ordering in Online Copyright Enforcement, 89 Or. L. Rev. 81, 95 (2010) ("From the provider's point of view, terminating any customer's access is a distasteful prospect because every user's continued access translates into revenue for the provider and users whose access is terminated can usually take their business to a competitor.").
140. *See* 17 U.S.C. § 512(c)(1)(C).
141. *See* Plaintiff Brave New Films' Notice of Motion and Motion for Partial Summary Judgment at 7, *Brave New Films 501(C)(4)* v. *Weiner*, No. CV 08-04703 SI, 2009 WL 1622385 (N.D. Cal. Feb. 27, 2009) No. CV 08-04703 SI, 2009 WL 527974 ("As a result of that takedown notice, YouTube removed not only 'Michael Savage Hates Muslims' from Brave New Films' channel, but disabled Brave New Films' entire channel at a critical time in the presidential election cycle, rendering unavailable a large number of videos that expressed important political views, and just as Brave New Films ran a full-page ad in the New York Times.").
142. Mike Masnick, *Ex-Wife Allegedly Using Copyright to Take Down Husband's Suicide Note*, Techdirt (Apr. 25, 2014, 12:09 PM), https://www.techdirt.com/articles/20140425/11184127030/ex-wife-allegedly-using-copyright-to-take-down-husbands-suicide-note-where-he-blames-their-custody-battle.shtml. As the presumptive heir to Chris's estate, Dina claimed copyright ownership in the suicide letter and promptly began serving DMCA takedown notifications to have the work removed online. For a sample of Dina's takedown notices, see Letter from Rachelle E. Hill, attorney for Dina Mackney, to A Voice for Men, LLC (Apr. 15, 2014), http://www.avoiceformen.com/wp-content/uploads/sites/2/2014/04/Letter-to-AVOICEFORMEN.COM-redacted.pdf. In the process, she not only made headway in having the contents of the note scrubbed from cyberspace, she threatened to undo her husband's final dying wish – that his side of the story be known to the world.

143. Cory Doctorow, *AIDS Deniers Use Bogus Copyright Claims to Censor Critical YouTube Videos*, BoingBoing (Feb. 15, 2014, 3:00 PM), http://boingboing.net/2014/02/15/aids-deniers-use-bogus-copyrig.html.
144. Glen Garvin, Opinion, *Glen Garvin Commentary: Phony Copyright Claims Exploit Holes in U.S. Internet Law*, Columbus Dispatch (Dec. 19, 2013, 5:35 AM), http://www.dispatch.com/content/stories/editorials/2013/12/19/phony-copyright-claims-exploit-holes-in-u-s–internet-law.html.
145. Cory Doctorow, *UK Website Taken Down by Spurious Copyright Complaint Regarding UK Ultra-Right Groups*, BoingBoing (Oct. 10, 2012, 5:52 PM), http://boingboing.net/2012/10/10/uk-website-taken-down-by-spuri.html.
146. Tim Cashing, *Law Enforcement Officer Openly Admits He's Playing Copyright Music to Prevent Citizen's Recording from Being Uploaded to YouTube*, TechDirt (July 6, 2021), available at https://www.techdirt.com/2021/07/06/law-enforcement-officer-openly-admits-hes-playing-copyrighted-music-to-prevent-citizens-recording-being-uploaded-to-youtube/.
147. *Id.*
148. *Id.*
149. *See* 17 U.S.C. § 512(g)(2)–(3).
150. *See id.* § 512(g)(2)(C).
151. *Id.*
152. *Monge* v. *Maya Magazines, Inc.*, 688 F.3d 1164 (9th Cir. 2012).
153. *Id.*
154. *Id.* at 1184.
155. *See Jacobellis* v. *Ohio*, 378 U.S. 184, 197 (1964) (Stewart, J., concurring).
156. *See generally Lenz* v. *Universal Music Corp.*, 572 F. Supp. 2d 1150 (N.D. Cal. 2008).
157. Prince and Universal issued a statement making clear that they intended to scrub the internet of user-generated content making use of Prince's works without authorization as a matter of principle. *Id.* at 1152 (quoting statement to ABC News). Ironically, while Prince took his intellectual property rights quite seriously, he may not have felt the same way about other peoples' real property rights. *See, e.g.*, Stephen M. Silverman, *Prince Sued for Painting House Purple*, People Mag. (Mar. 21, 2006, 2:00 PM), http://www.people.com/people/article/0,1175339,00.html (detailing NBA superstar Carlos Boozer's suit against Prince for painting his house purple without permission).
158. *Lenz*, 572 F. Supp. 2d at 1152.
159. *Id.* at 1152–53.
160. Mainstream audiences apparently did not consider that the child was dancing to a song replete with references to phone sex and "purple bananas."
161. *See, e.g.*, Chris Francescani, *The Home Video Prince Doesn't Want You to See*, ABC News (Oct. 26, 2007), http://abcnews.go.com/TheLaw/home-video-prince/story?id=3777651.
162. *Lenz*, 572 F. Supp. 2d at 1152 (noting Universal and Prince's intention, as a matter of principle, to scrub the internet of all user-generated content making unauthorized use of Prince's songs).
163. *See Warner Bros. Entm't Inc.* v. *RDR Books*, 575 F. Supp. 2d 513, 546–47 (S.D.N.Y. 2008) (holding that, although the encyclopedic guide to *Harry Potter* was transformative, it took "too much original expression" and ultimately infringed Warner's copyright).
164. *See Northland Family Planning Clinic, Inc.* v. *Ctr. For Bio-Ethical Reform*, 868 F. Supp. 2d 962 (C.D. Cal. 2012).
165. *See Savage* v. *Council on Am.-Islamic Relations, Inc.*, No. C 07-6076 SI, 2008 WL 2951281, at *1 (N.D. Cal. July 25, 2008).

166. *See Hofheinz* v. *AMC Prods*., Inc., No. CV-00-5827 (CPS), 2003 U.S. Dist. LEXIS 16940 (E.D.N.Y. Sept. 1, 2003).
167. *See Browne* v. *McCain*, 612 F. Supp. 2d 1125 (C.D, Cal. 2009) (denying motion to dismiss copyright (and trademark) infringement claims for use of his song in television commercial supporting McCain's presidential campaign).
168. *See Henley* v. *DeVore*, 733 F. Supp. 2d 1144 (C.D. Cal. 2010) (rejecting trademark infringement claim but granting summary judgment on copyright infringement claim for unauthorized use of songs in political advertisement for Senate candidate Chuck DeVore).
169. *See Suntrust Bank* v. *Houghton Mifflin Co.*, 268 F.3d 1257, 1259 (2001).
170. *Id.* at 1270.
171. *See* 17 U.S.C. § 107; *Harper & Row Publishers, Inc.* v. *Nation Enters*, 471 U.S. 539, 563 (1985) ("The law generally recognizes a greater need to disseminate factual works than works of fiction or fantasy.").
172. *Monge* v. *Maya Magazines, Inc.*, 688 F.3d 1164, 1169 (9th Cir. 2012).
173. *Bond* v. *Blum*, 317 F.3d 385, 390 (4th Cir. 2003).
174. *See Hustler Magazine, Inc.* v. *Falwell*, 485 U.S. 46, 48 (1988).
175. *Savage* v. *Council on Am.-Islamic Relations, Inc.*, No. C 07-6076 SI, 2008 WL 2951281, at *1 (N.D. Cal. July 25, 2008).
176. As the Supreme Court has held, "use that has no demonstrable effect upon the market for, or the value of, the copyrighted work need not be prohibited in order to protect the author's incentive to create." *See Hustler Magazine, Inc.* v. *Moral Majority, Inc.*, 796 F.2d 1148, 1155 (9th Cir. 1986) (quoting *Sony Corp. of Am.* v. *Universal City Studios, Inc.*, 464 U.S. 417, 450 (1984)).
177. St. *George* v. *Pinellas Cnty*., 285 F.3d 1334, 1337 (11th Cir. 2002).
178. *See, e.g.*, *Harper & Row Publishers, Inc.* v. *Nation Enters*, 471 U.S. 539, 544 (1985).
179. *Browne* v. *McCain*, 612 F. Supp. 2d 1125, 1130 (C.D. Cal. 2009).
180. *Id.*
181. *See, e.g.*, Associated Press v. Meltwater U.S. Holdings, Inc., 931 F. Supp. 2d. 537, 550 (S.D.N.Y. 2013) ("Because fair use is an affirmative defense, the burden of proof rests with the party relying on the defense.").
182. *See, e.g.*, *Denison* v. *Larkin*, 64 F. Supp. 3d 1127, 1132 (N.D. Ill. 2014) ("Additionally, although a plaintiff need not plead facts in the complaint to defeat potential affirmative defenses, where 'the allegations of the complaint itself set forth everything necessary to satisfy [an] affirmative defense,' the plaintiff pleads himself out of court." (quoting *Brooks* v. *Ross*, 578 F.3d 574, 579 (7th Cir. 2009))); *Scott* v. *WorldStarHipHop, Inc.*, No. 10 Civ. 9538(PKC)(RLE), 2011 WL 5082410, at *8 (S.D.N.Y. Oct. 25, 2011) (admitting that, as an affirmative defense, fair use is "not normally an appropriate grounds for dismissing a claim on a Rule 12(b)(6) motion" but that it can be addressed if the defense "appears on the face" of plaintiff's complaint); *see also Levingston* v. *Earle*, No. CV-12-08165-PCT-JAT, 2014 WL 1246369, at *2 (D. Ariz. March 26, 2014) (failing to address the propriety of adjudicating fair use on a motion to dismiss given its status as an affirmative defense).
183. *See, e.g.*, *Burnett* v. *Twentieth Century Fox Film Corp*., 491 F. Supp. 2d. 962, 967 (C.D. Cal. 2007) (considering and granting a motion to dismiss on fair use grounds while assuming that such relief is available on a 12(b)(6) motion on the basis that courts "may conduct a fair use analysis, as a matter of law, where the facts are presumed or admitted").
184. *See, e.g.*, *Savage* v. *Council on Am-Islamic Relations., Inc.*, No. C 07-6076 SI, 2008 WL 2951281, at *1 (N.D. Cal. July 25, 2008).
185. CAL. CIV. PROC. CODE § 425.16(e).
186. *Id.* § 425.16(c).

187. Indeed, California Code of Civil Procedure section 425.16(a) mandates that the anti-SLAPP statute "shall be construed broadly."
188. *Nygard, Inc.* v. *Uusi-Kerttula*, 159 Cal. App. 4th 1027, 1042 (Cal. Ct. App. 2008).
189. *See* 17 U.S.C. § 512(c) (providing for takedown notice procedure for infringing "information residing on systems or networks at direction of users").
190. *Id.* § 512(f)(1).
191. *Id.* § 512(c)(3)(A)(v).
192. *Rossi* v. *Motion Picture Ass'n of Am.*, 391 F.3d 1000, 1004–1005 (9th Cir. 2004). Numerous courts have adopted *Rossi's* subjectivity standard. *See Tuteur* v. *Crosley-Corcoran*, 961 F. Supp. 2d 333, 342–43 (D. Mass. 2013); *Third Educ. Group, Inc.* v. *Phelps*, 675 F. Supp. 2d 916, 927 (E.D. Wis. 2009); *Dudnikov* v. *MGA Entm't, Inc.*, 410 F. Supp. 2d 1010, 1013 (D. Colo. 2005).
193. *Rossi*, 391 F.3d at 1005.
194. *Id.*
195. *Lenz* v. *Universal Music Corp*, No. 13-16106, at *11 (9th Cir. Sept. 14, 2015).
196. *Id.* at *21–22.
197. *Id.* at *17 (emphasis in original).
198. 17 U.S.C. § 512(c)(3)(A)(v). The DMCA requires that the complaining party serving a takedown notice have a "good faith belief that use of the material in the manner complained of is not authorized by the copyright owner, its agent, or the law." *Id.*
199. James Boyle, *Afterword* to KEITH AOKI ET AL., TALES FROM THE PUBLIC DOMAIN: BOUND BY LAW? 67–70 (2006) (critiquing content creation industries' nurturing of a "permissions culture," where every use of a creative work purportedly requires permission and payment to a putative rights holder). Such views are not without some support in relevant precedent. Indeed, cases such as *Bridgeport Music* have only bolstered such absolutist positions. *See Bridgeport Music, Inc.* v. *Dimension Films*, 383 F.3d 390, 398 (6th Cir. 2004) (holding that any unauthorized sample of a sound recording, no matter how small, constitutes copyright infringement and cautioning all would-be users of copyrighted work to "[g]et a license or do not sample").
200. *Lenz* v. *Universal Music Corp.*, 572 F. Supp. 2d 1150, 1155 (N.D. Cal. 2008) (citing *Rossi*, 391 F.3d 1004).
201. *See* Jennifer E. Rothman, Liberating Copyright: Thinking Beyond Free Speech, 95 CORNELL L. REV. 463, 464 (2010) ("Even though there have been ever-increasing calls by intellectual property (IP) scholars for greater First Amendment scrutiny in copyright cases, there has been a virtually unrelenting rejection of First Amendment review in copyright cases.").
202. N.Y. *Times Co.* v. *Sullivan*, 376 U.S. 254, 279 (1964).
203. *Id.* at 300 (Goldberg, J., concurring).
204. *See Gertz* v. *Robert Welch, Inc.*, 418 U.S. 323 (1974) (extending *New York Times Co.* v. *Sullivan* to requiring a showing of actual malice for imposition of punitive damages in defamation claims pertaining to a matter of public concern, even if the plaintiff is a private figure); *Curtis Publ'g Co.* v. *Butts*, 388 U.S. 130 (1967) (extending *New York Times Co.* v. *Sullivan* to requiring a showing of actual malice for liability in defamation claims brought by any public figures).
205. *See Time, Inc.* v. *Hill*, 385 U.S. 374 (1967).
206. *See Hustler Magazine, Inc.* v. *Falwell*, 485 U.S. 46 (1988).
207. *See Cox Broad. Corp.* v. *Cohn*, 420 U.S. 469 (1975).
208. *See generally Rogers* v. *Grimaldi*, 875 F.2d 994 (2nd Cir. 1989). Under *Rogers*, so long as use of a plaintiff's trademark is "artistically relevant" to the defendant's expressive work,

there can be no liability under the Lanham Act unless the defendant's use of the plaintiff's trademark is explicitly misleading – that is, making an *affirmative statement* of the plaintiff's *sponsorship* or endorsement, beyond the mere use of the plaintiff's name or other characteristic. *Id.* at 1000–1001. However, since the Supreme Court's ruling in *Jack Daniel's Properties, Inc.* v. *VIP Products LLC*, 599 U.S. 140 (2023), courts have declined to apply the *Rogers* defense in instances when a defendant uses a plaintiff's trademark as a designation of source for the defendant's own goods or services.

209. *See generally Comedy III Prods., Inc.* v. *Gary Saderup, Inc.*, 21 P.3d 797, 807, 808 & n.10 (Cal. 2001). The *Comedy III* test provides that a defendant's expressive activity can serve independent and absolute defense to a prima facie violation of the right of publicity in California if it is sufficiently transformative, with the relevant inquiry being "whether the celebrity likeness is one of the raw materials from which an original work is synthesized, or whether the depiction or imitation of the celebrity is the very sum and substance of the work in question." *See id.* at 800–801, 809.

CONCLUSION

1. *See The New York Times Co.* v. *Microsoft Corp.*, Case No. 1:23-cv-11195 (S.D.N.Y. filed Dec. 27, 2023).
2. *See Andersen* v. *Stability AI Ltd.*, Case No. 3:23-cv-00201 (N.D. Cal. filed Jan. 13, 2023).
3. *See Getty Images (US), Inc.* v. *Stability AI, Inc.*, Case No. 1:23-cv-00135 (D. Del. filed Feb. 3, 2023).
4. *See Concord Music Group, Inc.* v. *Anthropic PBC*, Case No. 3:23-cv-01092 (M.D. Tenn. filed Oct. 18, 2023).
5. *See Silverman* v. *OpenAI, Inc.*, Case No. 3:23-cv-03416 (N.D. Cal. filed July 7, 2023); *Silverman* v. *Meta Platforms, Inc.*, Case No. 3:23-cv-03417 (N.D. Cal. filed July 7, 2023); *Chabon* v. *OpenAI*, Case No. 3:23-cv-04625 (N.D. Cal. filed Sep. 8, 2023); *Chabon* v. *Meta Platforms, Inc.*, Case No. 3:23-cv-04663 (N.D. Cal. filed Sep. 12, 2023).
6. Benjamin Kaplan, An Unhurried View of Copyright (1966).
7. Benedict Evans, *Generative AI and Intellectual Property*, Ben-Evans.com (Aug. 27, 2023), https://www.ben-evans.com/benedictevans/2023/8/27/generative-ai-ad-intellectual-property.
8. *Copyright Registration Guidance, Works Containing Material Generated by Artificial Intelligence*, 88 Fed. Reg. 16, 190 (Mar. 16, 2023) (to be codified at 37 C.F.R. pt. 202).
9. *See Artificial Intelligence and Copyright, Notice of Inquiry*, 88 Fed. Reg. 59, 942 (Aug. 30, 2023).
10. In 2019, computer scientist Stephen Thaler became the first person to seek registration of an AI-assisted work when he submitted a copyright application for an image, *A Recent Entrance to Paradise*, generated by his AI system dubbed the Creativity Machine. The Copyright Office demurred and, after numerous requests for reconsideration, made a final decision to reject the application. *See* Copyright Review Board, *Second Request for Reconsideration for Refusal to Register* A Recent Entrance to Paradise, Correspondence ID 1-3ZPC6C3; SR # 1-7100387071 (Feb. 14, 2022), https://www.copyright.gov/rulings-filings/review-board/docs/a-recent-entrance-to-paradise.pdf. Thaler filed suit in federal district court to challenge the ruling and, after losing there, *see* Memorandum Opinion, Dkt No. 24, Case No 1:22-cv-01564-BAH (D.D.C. Aug. 18, 2023) (granting the Copyright Office's motion for summary judgment to affirm its decision in rejecting Thaler's application for copyright registration), he appealed to the D.C. Circuit, which affirmed the

application rejection. *See Thaler* v. *Perlmutter*, __ F.4th __, 2025 WL 839178 (D.C. Cir., Mar. 18, 2025)

11. *See, e.g., Naruto* v. *Slater*, 888 F.3d 418 (9th Cir. 2018) (rejecting an attempt to vest copyright protection in Naruto, the macaque, for his famous selfie).
12. *Burrow-Giles Lithographic Co.* v. *Sarony*, 111 U.S. 53, 55 (1884).
13. Farhad Manjoo, *A Creator (Me) Made a Masterpiece with A.I.*, N.Y. Times (Aug. 25, 2023), https://www.nytimes.com/2023/08/25/opinion/ai-art-intellectual-property.html.
14. *AI "Completes" Keith Haring's Unfinished Artwork, Raising Ethical Issues and Copyright Concerns*, Designboom (Jan. 11, 2024), https://www.designboom.com/art/ai-keith-haring-unfinished-panting-ethical-copyright-concerns-01-11-2024/.
15. *See, e.g.*, Cal. Civil Code § 1708.86(b) (creating a cause of action for sexually explicit deepfakes); Cal. Elec. Code § 20010(a) (creating a cause of action for election-related deepfakes).
16. *See, e.g.*, Preventing Deepfakes of Intimate Images Act (proposing a federal cause of action for sexually explicit deepfakes); Nurture Originals, Foster Art, and Keep Entertainment Safe (NO FAKES) Act (proposing a broad federal right of publicity interdicting the use of unauthorized digital replicas of any individual in audiovisual works or sound recordings); No Artificial Intelligence Fake Replicas and Unauthorized Duplications (No AI FRAUD) Act (same).
17. *See, e.g.*, Mike Masnick, *The NY Times Lawsuit against OpenAI Would Open Up the NY Times to All Sorts of Lawsuits Should It Win*, TechDirt, https://www.techdirt.com/2023/12/28/the-ny-times-lawsuit-against-openai-would-open-up-the-ny-times-to-all-sorts-of-lawsuits-should-it-win/ (Dec. 28, 2023). ("Reading/processing data is not a right limited by copyright … If the courts (or legislature) decide otherwise, it would upset pretty much all of the history of copyright and create some significant real world problems… If the NY Times successfully argues that reading a third party article to help its reporters 'learn' about the news before reporting their own version of it is copyright infringement, it might not like how that it turned around by tons of news organizations against the NY Times.").
18. *See* Kate Knibbs, *Here's Proof You Can Train an AI Model without Slurping Copyrighted Content*, Wired (Mar. 20, 2024), https://www.wired.com/story/proof-you-can-train-ai-without-slurping-copyrighted-content/.
19. This discussion of the timely registration requirement is explored in greater depth in my article *The Emperor Has No Copyright: Registration, Cultural Hierarchy, and the Myth of American Copyright Militancy*, 24 Berkeley Technology Law Journal 1397 (2009).
20. *See* 17 U.S.C. § 412(2) ("[N]o award of statutory damages or of attorney's fees … shall be made for … any infringement of copyright commenced after first publication of the work and before the effective date of its registration, unless such registration is made within three months after the first publication of the work.").
21. *Id.*
22. 17 U.S.C. § 504(c)(2).
23. 17 U.S.C. § 505.
24. *Business Trends Analysts, Inc.* v. *Freedonia Group, Inc.*, 887 F.2d 399, 406 (2d Cir. 1989).
25. Anjali Vats, The Color of Creatorship: Intellectual Property, Race, and the Making of Americans, 86–92 (2020).
26. *Id.* at 89–91.
27. *Grand Upright Music, Ltd.* v. *Warner Bros. Records, Inc.* 780 F. Supp. 182 (S.D.N.Y. 1991).

28. *Id.* at 183.
29. *Id.* at 185.
30. VATS, *supra* note 25, at 91.
31. *Id.*
32. *See, e.g., Prince* v. *Cariou*, 714 F.3d 694 (2d Cir. 2013); *Blanch* v. *Koons*, 960 F.2d 301 (2d Cir. 2006).
33. *Grand Upright*, 780 F. Supp. at 185.
34. *Bridgeport Music, Inc.* v. *Dimension Films*, 410 F.3d 792 (6th Cir. 2005).
35. *Id.* at 801.
36. *Newton* v. *Diamond*, 388 F.3d 1189 (9th Cir. 2004).
37. *VMG Salsoul, LLC* v. *Ciccone*, 824 F.3d 871 (9th Cir. 2016).

Printed by Integrated Books International,
United States of America